TOO CRITICAL TO FAIL

Too Critical to Fail

How Canada Manages Threats to Critical Infrastructure

KEVIN QUIGLEY, BEN BISSET,
AND BRYAN MILLS

McGill-Queen's University Press
Montreal & Kingston • London • Chicago

© McGill-Queen's University Press 2017

ISBN 978-0-7735-5160-2 (cloth)
ISBN 978-0-7735-5161-9 (paper)
ISBN 978-0-7735-5259-3 (ePDF)
ISBN 978-0-7735-5260-9 (ePUB)

Legal deposit fourth quarter 2017
Bibliothèque nationale du Québec

Printed in Canada on acid-free paper that is 100% ancient forest free
(100% post-consumer recycled), processed chlorine free

McGill-Queen's University Press acknowledges the support of the Canada
Council for the Arts for our publishing program. We also acknowledge
the financial support of the Government of Canada through the Canada
Book Fund for our publishing activities.

Library and Archives Canada Cataloguing in Publication

Quigley, Kevin, 1971–, author
    Too critical to fail: how Canada manages threats to critical
    infrastructure / Kevin Quigley, Ben Bisset, and Bryan Mills.

    Includes bibliographical references and index.
    Issued in print and electronic formats.
    ISBN 978-0-7735-5160-2 (cloth). – ISBN 978-0-7735-5161-9 (paper). –
    ISBN 978-0-7735-5259-3 (ePDF). – ISBN 978-0-7735-5260-9 (ePUB)

    1. Infrastructure (Economics) – Government policy – Canada.
    2. Infrastructure (Economics) – Security measures – Canada. I. Bisset,
    Ben, 1984–, author II. Mills, Bryan, 1985–, author III. Title.

HC120.C3Q85 2017   363.0971   C2017-904278-5
                                            C2017-904279-3

This book was typeset by Marquis Interscript in 10.5/13 Sabon.

In memory of the forty-seven people who died as a result of the train derailment in Lac-Mégantic on 6 July 2013, and for their families and friends, who continue to grieve

Contents

Tables and Figures

TABLES

FIGURES

Acknowledgments

Research for this book started in 2008 when Kevin Quigley received a Social Sciences and Humanities Research Council (SSHRC) Standard Operating Grant to study the contextual issues that influence the exchange of sensitive information about critical infrastructure (CI). Since that time, our research on CI has been supported by a SSHRC Partnership Development Grant and a SSHRC Insight Grant. We have also received financial support from the Government of Canada's Kanishka Project, the Centre for Security Science, Public Safety Canada, and the Canada School of Public Service's Innovative Public Management Research Fund. Without this support, this work would not have been completed, at least not at this time or to this standard. Research assistants – mostly graduate students – were called upon to review drafts of material and conduct media analyses, literature reviews, and interviews; they also contributed to grant applications and prepared conference presentations. While there are too many to thank, we are grateful for their contributions. The evidence of their hard work can be found in the pages that follow.

We also benefited from exchanges with colleagues at home and abroad. The work in the book has been presented in North America, South America, Europe, Asia, and the Middle East. We have also collaborated extensively on multidisciplinary risk analyses with colleagues at the University of Strathclyde's Business School in the United Kingdom, in particular.

Some of the work in this book has appeared in a slightly different form in previous publications. Chapter 3 appeared in *Canadian Public Administration* (Wiley) as a paper by Kevin Quigley entitled "Man plans, God laughs: Canada's national strategy for protecting critical infrastructure." Sections of chapter 11 appeared in the *Journal of Homeland Security and Emergency Management* (De Gruyter) in a paper co-authored by Kevin Quigley and Bryan Mills entitled "'Set adrift': Fatalism as organizational culture at Canadian seaports."

Some of the previously published work has benefited immensely from the hard work and insight of others. Chapter 8 was co-authored by Kevin Quigley, Calvin Burns, and Kristen Stallard and published in *Government Information Quarterly* (Elsevier) as a paper entitled "'Cyber gurus': A rhetorical analysis of the language of cybersecurity specialists and the implications for security policy and critical infrastructure protection." Chapter 9, co-authored by Kevin Quigley, Colin Macdonald, and John Quigley, appeared in *Canadian Public Administration* (Wiley) as a paper entitled "Pre-existing condition: Taking media coverage into account when preparing for H1N1." The central structure and arguments of the book were presented in a proceedings for a workshop held at Dalhousie University, Halifax, in March 2015. The workshop was designed specifically to solicit feedback on our work and was supported by the Kanishka Project and attended by public servants and academics. We are grateful for everyone's contributions.

Colin Macdonald was an important member of our research team at the Critical Infrastructure Protection Initiative at Dalhousie. He coordinated several activities and contributed directly to the research. Colin continued to give his time generously well after he had left the project for other challenges. Janet Lord has been an indispensable copyeditor who has helped us to clarify our meaning in a variety of papers and several iterations of this manuscript.

At McGill-Queen's University Press, we are thankful for the assistance of the managing editor, Ryan Van Huijstee, our editors, Jacqueline Mason and Kathleen Kearns, and the creative contributions of the design and marketing teams. We are also grateful for the skilful copyediting of Jennifer Thomas as we approached the finish line.

We would also like to acknowledge the sixty-eight interview subjects who gladly gave their time to provide thoughtful and informed views and whose contributions were essential to the outcome.

We owe a debt of gratitude to those close to us in our personal lives. Much of our spare time was sacrificed in completing this research. In a sense, we surreptitiously, if not selfishly, shared the burden with them.

About halfway through this research, on 6 July 2013, we, like many, were overwhelmed by the carnage and devastation caused by the train derailment in Lac-Mégantic, Quebec. After having studied different disasters and crises over the years, we watched closely as the chaos and tragedy unfolded, followed by the industry and government responses. While we witnessed many of the patterns that we had seen before in our research, we recognize too the profound sense of grief that is unique to those who were most affected by the event, and that no public institutions or policies can ever adequately address such loss. We dedicate our work to the memory of the victims and to their families and friends, with a commitment to continue to pursue answers to difficult questions about how we reconcile the dangers and opportunities that modern infrastructure presents. We hope that this book, however modestly, advances this complex discussion.

Abbreviations

BP	British Petroleum
CAER	Community Awareness and Emergency Response
CBRNE	Chemical, Biological, Radiological and Nuclear and Explosives
CEO	Chief Executive Officer
CI	Critical Infrastructure
CIP	Critical Infrastructure Protection
CN	Canadian National
CP	Canadian Pacific
CPA	Canada Port Authority
CRTI	CBRNE Research and Technology Initiative
CSIS	Canadian Security Intelligence Service
CSST	Quebec Commission on Workplace Health and Safety
C-TPAT	Customs-Trade Partnership Against Terrorism
DT	The *Daily Telegraph*
E2	Environmental Emergency
EMA	Emergency Management Act
EMO	Emergency Management Office
FAST	Free and Secure Trade
G&M	The *Globe and Mail*
IGH	Interest Group Hypothesis
IRGC	International Risk Governance Council
ISIS	Islamic State of Iraq and Syria
IT	Information Technology
MIACC	Major Industrial Accidents Council of Canada
MMA	Montreal, Maine & Atlantic Railway Limited
NAP	National Advisory Panel

NAT	Normal Accidents Theory
NDP	New Democratic Party
NFIP	National Flood Insurance Program
NPM	New Public Management
NS&AP	National Strategy and Action Plan for Critical Infrastructure
OECD	Organisation for Economic Co-operation and Development
ORH	Opinion-responsive hypothesis
PCO	Privy Council Office
PHAC	Public Health Agency of Canada
PIP	Partners in Protection
PMI	Protective Measures Index
PRA	Probabilistic Risk Assessment
PSN	Public Sector Networks
RAC	Railway Association of Canada
RAP	Rational Actor Paradigm
RC	Responsible Care
RCMP	Royal Canadian Mounted Police
RMI	Resilience Measurement Index
RRAP	Regional Resiliency Assessment Program
SARS	Severe Acute Respiratory Syndrome
SILE	Security, Intelligence and Law Enforcement
SIR	Suspicious Incident Reporting
SMES	Small and Medium-sized Enterprises
SMS	Safety Management Systems
TED	Technology, Entertainment, Design
TSB	Transportation Safety Board

TOO CRITICAL TO FAIL

1

Introduction

On 13 May 2014, while he worked with his young son on his boat in the backyard, Thomas Harding was surrounded by a SWAT team, sirens wailing, and led away in handcuffs (Hamilton 2014). Later that day he and two colleagues, Jean Demaître and Richard Labrie, were marched into a makeshift courtroom in full view of the press, in a town still in ashes. They were charged with forty-seven counts of criminal negligence causing death (Hamilton 2014).

While the dramatic nature of the arrest may have been a shock to his young son, it must have been more of a surprise to Harding. Everyone knew where Harding lived; he was not considered a flight risk. The events to which the charges pertained had occurred a full ten months earlier. Thomas Walsh, Harding's lawyer, had notified the police that Harding would voluntarily come to the court when asked to appear to face the charges (CBC News 2014).

The temporary courthouse was in Lac-Mégantic, a town most people had never heard of before the early hours of 6 July 2013, when the brakes failed on an unattended freight train carrying 7.7 million litres of petroleum in the form of crude oil (TSB 2014). Harding had been the train's sole conductor on the evening of 5 July. A few hours after he left for the night, this unattended train, owned and operated by Montreal, Maine & Atlantic Railway (MMA), a small company and Harding's employer, rolled 11 km before derailing in the town of 5,000. The resulting fires and explosions killed forty-seven people,[1] forced the evacuation of 2,000 more, and destroyed much of the downtown area. The coroner identified most of the bodies by DNA or dental records (Muise 2014). It was the deadliest rail disaster in Canada since Confederation (Canadian Press 2013).

In its report on the incident, published three months after Mr Harding appeared in court, the Transportation Safety Board (TSB) pointed to numerous failures. It identified eighteen distinct causes and contributing factors, including the fact that the train was left unattended on a main line, the failure to set enough handbrakes, the lack of a backup safety mechanism, poor maintenance on the loco-motive, and several failures of training and oversight (TSB 2014). Twenty-five different companies were accused of sharing respon-sibility for the derailment, and they contributed approximately $450 million for an out-of-court settlement fund for the victims (Haig 2015). To date, six people, including Harding, all MMA staff, have faced criminal charges (Atkins and Stevenson 2015).[2] MMA faced potential fines but the CEO, Edward Burkhardt, has never appeared in court over the matter. The company filed for bankruptcy protection – it did not hold sufficient insurance to cover its losses – and has since been sold (Rakobowchuk 2014; Woods 2013; Marowits 2014).

Despite the TSB (2014, 11) concluding that "the tragedy in Lac-Mégantic was not caused by one single person, action or organiza-tion," the government has so far refused to hold a public inquiry or accept any responsibility, and it is unclear how public officials have been held to account for their role. Three causes identified by the TSB were attributed to the regulator, Transport Canada: inadequate oversight of operational changes, limited follow-up on safety defi-ciencies, and an ineffective safety management audit program. Transport Canada was one of the contributors to the settlement fund but refused to disclose how much it contributed. The minister of transport, Marc Garneau, would simply say, "We don't acknowl-edge that we had any responsibility; however, we did want to make a contribution because of the impact of this terrible tragedy in Lac-Megantic" (Blatchford 2016).

At virtually the same time as flames ripped through Lac-Mégantic, on the other side of the country, a good portion of the Canadian province of Alberta sat underwater. Between 19 June and 12 July 2013, heavy rainfall triggered the worst flooding in Alberta's history, which washed across nearly one-quarter of the province. The regions along the Bow, Elbow, Highwood, Red Deer, Sheep, Little Bow, and South Saskatchewan rivers and their tributaries were the most affected. Five people died as a result of the floods and over 100,000 were forced to leave their homes. Thirty communities declared local states of emergency, the province declared its first-ever state of emergency, nearly 14,500 homes were damaged, and eighty schools and ten health facilities were affected (MNP LLP 2015). Water rose to the tenth row of seats at the Saddledome arena in Calgary. In that city's Stampede Park, stables and barns were under more than 2 m of water. The flood destroyed approximately 1,000 km of roads and washed away hundreds of bridges and culverts, including the Bonnybrook rail bridge, resulting in a train derailment. The debris flood of the Bow and Elbow rivers inundated dozens of city parks and more than 100 km of riverside pathways with water, mud, downed trees, and other debris. Most estimates put the final costs of the flood in excess of $6 billion, which made it the costliest disaster in Canadian history.

The findings of the flood post-mortem conducted by the accounting firm MNP LLP were largely positive. The report concluded that extensive emergency management skills, capability, and legislation exist within the province (MNP LLP 2015, 7). It deemed the Public Safety Governance framework document developed after the 2011 Slave Lake fires to be effective and recommended that it continue to be used and refined. Having this framework document in place before the 2013 floods helped set the conditions for the province's successful response to the floods. The manner in which it was developed, including leveraging best practices from other Canadian and American jurisdictions and extensive stakeholder consultation, was deemed to be a model that other jurisdictions should emulate. Polls suggested people felt very positive about the role of public servants in the flood response, with ninety-five per cent of Albertans describing the work done by emergency responders as "excellent" (eighty-two per cent) or "good" (twelve per cent) (Insights West 2013). The UK newspaper the *Guardian* noted that the mayor of Calgary, Naheed Nenshi, emerged from the crisis with folk hero status, with friendly vandals taping his face onto Superman posters, and other people producing fundraising T-shirts with an illustration of the mayor wearing a scuba mask accompanying the slogan "Keep calm and Nenshi on" (Toro 2014). Of the $6 billion in losses caused by the flood, only $2 billion was covered by insurance; as a result, the Alberta government announced that its Disaster Recovery Program would cover $3.1 billion in uninsurable loss and damage suffered by individuals, small businesses, municipalities, and other groups (MNP LLP 2015). Ultimately, the program funded a number of losses that were beyond the program's original scope.

We might classify both of these events – the Lac-Mégantic derailment and the Alberta floods – as black swan events, which are low-probability/high-consequence disasters with elements of randomness and bad luck (Taleb 2007). Yet the juxtaposition of these two cases raises important questions about the manner in which we prepare for and respond to disasters in our communities. Despite the fact that the Alberta floods cost thirteen times more than the train derailment in Lac-Mégantic, why was there three times more media coverage of the train derailment than of the floods? Given that both events were devastating and costly, what explains the negative assessment of key actors and processes in the media coverage and audits after the Lac-Mégantic derailment but the relatively positive assessment of actors and processes after the Alberta floods? Why in Lac-Mégantic were some held to account in a specific, intense, and public manner while others implicated in the derailment remained largely anonymous and silent? While the post-mortem in Alberta was largely positive and some actors were celebrated, why were town planners not held to account for planning decisions that exposed communities to such devastating natural dangers? The comparison between the Lac-Mégantic derailment and the Alberta floods highlights an important dimension of critical infrastructure (CI) failures: however random they may seem, the disasters that occasionally befall CI occur in a particular political, market, legal, social-psychological, cultural, and popular context, which influences the likelihood and consequence of these events and contributes to the manner in which we interpret, respond to, and apportion blame for them.

WHAT THIS BOOK IS ABOUT

This book is written within the discipline of public administration. It draws on the social science of risk literature to understand better the risk regulation regimes that monitor, interpret, respond to, and try to limit the possibility and consequence of failures in Canada's CI. We will examine contextual pressures that influence these regimes, including market, public opinion, media, interest group, and institutional pressures. The Canadian government has identified ten interconnected CI sectors (Public Safety Canada 2015).

We focus much of the analysis in this book on two of these: (1) the Canadian transportation sector and (2) the chemicals sector.[3] As part of our analysis of the chemicals sector, we will also analyze the water sector, which depends on chemicals, and emergency services, which manage the risks of chemical spills.

We use black swans, such as natural disasters, terrorist attacks, major industrial accidents, pandemics, and cyber threats, as a lens for examining and understanding these risk regulation regimes. In particular, we return throughout the book to several recent and notable black swan events, including the Lac-Mégantic train derailment, the Air India bombing, the Walkerton water contamination, the Elliott Lake mall collapse, Montreal's de la Concorde overpass collapse, the Sunrise Propane explosion in Toronto, and the shootings by Michael Zehaf-Bibeau on Parliament Hill.[4] We also consider events that had the potential to create devastation, such the 2009 H1N1 flu pandemic, the 2007 Canada Revenue Agency software defect, and the Toronto 18 and VIA Rail terror plots. While we focus largely on events in Canada, we also refer to comparable events in the United States, the United Kingdom, and Australia to expand the data pool and gain insights into Canada's response to black swans on the basis of a comparative perspective.

To structure our analysis, we use the meso-level risk regulation regime framework of Hood, Rothstein, and Baldwin (2001). Our use of the framework enables us to develop answers to the questions we raised earlier about the wide discrepancies between how we prepare for, respond to, and think about CI failures. We apply the framework to answer the central research questions of this book: First, how does context influence risk regulation? Secondly, and as a corollary to the first question, how effective are these regulation regimes? An examination of the contextual pressures that influence risk regulation regimes raises important questions about how we manage the assets that enable and protect our civilization. How effective is insurance and the rule of law at influencing risk regulation in CI? Does media coverage of disasters enhance or diminish transparency and accountability? Before such events occur, what role does government have in ensuring the safety and security of Canada's CI? Is the government's responsibility somehow less if the CI is privately owned? When CI fails, who do we hold to account for these failures and how do we hold them to account? Do we learn anything from these failures? If so, how and what do we learn?

Finally, do Canadians have confidence in the governance model that oversees CI, and if so, is this confidence warranted?

WHAT IS CRITICAL INFRASTRUCTURE?

The prefix *infra* derives from Latin and means below or within. *Structure* means the way something is built, arranged, or organized. Traditionally, the word *infrastructure* refers to the physical assets upon which we rely every day, but which we don't always see; infrastructure often exists below or within. You might think of CI as the skeleton of our society; it includes transportation networks, water and food distribution systems, energy and utilities, and telecommunications and banking systems. There is no one definition of CI. Some authors, such as Egan (2007), have attempted to define CI in terms of the consequence of failure, using criticality as a frame of reference. De Bruijne and Van Eeten (2007) limit CI to hard technologies, including the large-scale technical grids vital to the functioning of society.

CI as a concept originated in the computer science and engineering literature, and references to it are much more likely to be found in engineering journals than social science ones. The concept of infrastructure and protecting it against threats is an ancient one. Our modern understanding of CI grew out of vulnerabilities that emerged in the change from "big box" computing in the 1950s and 1960s, in which large machines did all the computing work and existed under the control of the IT department, to highly dispersed technologies, such as desktops and microchips, whose use grew exponentially in the 1980s and 1990s. The emergent networks became more complex and difficult to control. While the new systems increased efficiencies, they also created vulnerabilities in supply chains, manifested during events like the Year 2000 computer bug (Y2K), which prompted much more careful examination of risks in our CI (Quigley 2008).

Today, systems engineers and computer programmers design programs that show the interdependence between critical systems and the consequences that failure in one system will have for interdependent systems. These models are complex and labour intensive to build and maintain.

Governments use broad definitions of CI. The first federal definition of CI adopted in the United States, for example, was put forth by President Clinton in Executive Order 13010 in 1996; it noted that "certain national infrastructures are so vital that their incapacity or destruction would have a debilitating impact on the defense or economic security of the United States." Definitions have changed over time; most definitions now emphasize the impact on people when CI fails. Canada's National Strategy for Critical Infrastructure (Public Safety Canada 2009b) defines CI as "processes, systems, facilities, technologies, networks, assets and services essential to the health, safety, security or economic well-being of Canadians and the effective functioning of government." A review by the Organisation for Economic Co-operation and Development (OECD 2008) of CI definitions argues that most countries use a broad definition of CI and it is largely consistent across countries. Similarly, Public Safety Canada underscored the common view of CI held by Australia, Canada, New Zealand, the United Kingdom, and the United States in its report entitled *Forging a Common Understanding for Critical Infrastructure: Shared Narrative* (Public Safety Canada 2014b).

In fact, CI is not a universal concept; there are a number of interpreted and arbitrary elements to it. To start, the concept can be understood as a form of Western hegemony that attempts to reinforce and stabilize global supply chains that benefit Western and other technologically advanced societies. CI documents are typically underpinned by an assumption about the value of private enterprise and markets; they assume the importance and perhaps inevitability of global supply chains and the sometimes-fragile technologies we adopt, they assume that rare and powerful threats to CI exist, and they assume that a proactive and preventive stance is the best approach to managing these risks. They also frequently assume a key role for the private sector in managing these assets. Most countries – especially in the developing world – do not have formal CI strategies so it is impossible to detect the degree of variation between countries. If they do have formal plans, the extent to which they have been written with a Western audience in mind is not clear.

Even a cursory view of CI documents in the English-speaking West suggests that there is variation in the manner in which governments approach the topic. CI has largely been defined by governments through illustration and categorization (Egan 2007). Canada's National Strategy for Critical Infrastructure (Public Safety Canada 2009b) specifies ten critical sectors, the United States specifies sixteen, Australia eight, and the United Kingdom thirteen (see table 1.1.) The number of sectors even within a country is not necessarily

Table 1.1 Critical infrastructure sectors in four countries

Canada	United States	United Kingdom	Australia
Energy and utilities	Energy	Energy	Energy
Information and communication technology	Information technology	Communications	Communications
Finance	Financial services	Finance	Banking and finance
Health	Health care and public health	Health	Health
Food	Food and agriculture	Food	Food chain
Water	Water and waste water systems	Water	Water services
Transportation	Transportation systems	Transport	Transport
Safety	Defence industrial base	Defence	
Government	Government facilities	Government	
Manufacturing	Critical manufacturing	Space	
	Chemical	Chemicals	
	Nuclear reactors, materials, and waste	Civil nuclear	
	Emergency services	Emergency services	
	Commercial facilities		
	Communications		
	Dams		

Sources: Attorney-General's Department (2017); Centre for the Protection of National Infrastructure (2017); Department of Homeland Security (2013a); Public Safety Canada (2009b).

stable; the US until recently named eighteen sectors and the UK named nine sectors. Australia has also adopted cross-sectoral groups, such as space. The variation across international borders is important not least because it underscores the fact that despite the similarities in these countries in terms of their dependence on modern technological systems and global supply chains, their local practices, policies, and institutional arrangements are different.

There is also variation within each sector. In Canada, for instance, some subsectors are competitive (trucking), while others are monopolistic (bridges); some are heavily regulated (airports) while others have more flexibility (trucking); some are regulated primarily by one order of government (bridges, airports, and seaports), while others are regulated by several (rail and trucking). These differences do not simply influence regulatory complexity; anthropologists warn that these differences generate different organizational cultures, tensions, power relationships, and approaches to management (Hood 1998).

This variation is acknowledged in Canada by the fact that in its national strategy, government leaves considerable flexibility for each sector to develop its own risk profile and practices for CI. Governments are also loath to designate specific organizations, facilities, or firms as CI; participation in CI protection exercises and associations is largely voluntary. Governments also struggle to develop effective metrics by which to judge the success of CI protection initiatives. There are very few detailed plans or reports publicly available. Audits typically show that progress in developing a CI community is slow (see, for example, Auditor General of Canada 2009, 2012b).

This slowness to mobilize and the overall lack of meaningful reporting on CI is ironic given the declared "critical" nature of the infrastructure. Therein lies a further challenge: understanding the concept of *critical*. What is *non*-critical infrastructure? Some sectors are not mentioned on government lists. Justice and education are not identified as CI; public spaces, stadia, and community centres, despite their importance in emergencies, are also not on some national lists. Generally, however, just as governments are loath to name organizations as critical they are equally loath to define organizations as non-critical. One often doesn't realize the extent of interdependence and importance of a system until a failure occurs.

If we loosen the parameters of a rational approach to understanding CI in which risk is understood strictly as the product of a probability and consequence calculation, the question of what is critical becomes even more contested. From a psychologist's standpoint, what is critical is a constructed concept and is subject to cognitive manipulation. Certain infrastructure failures – those that result in the death of a single child, for example – generate highly emotional media coverage and public reactions and disproportionate responses that do not align with rational calculations. Equally, CI failures that do not generate profile or emotional responses, such as credit card fraud or computer glitches in government departments, can be overlooked by all but the most affected.

There are also questions about power and accountability. Despite the rhetoric of the merits of markets and competition that is common in CI strategy documents, a considerable amount of CI is monopolistic in nature; it is highly regulated and its owners and operators are sheltered not only from competition but also from public accounting for progress in critical infrastructure protection (CIP).

All of these elements raise important questions about how Canada manages risks to its critical assets. If CI constitutes services "*essential* to the health, safety, security or economic well-being of Canadians" (emphasis added), shouldn't we be concerned about the technical and social aspects of its care? This book aims to delve more deeply into sectors identified as critical to explore the social context that pressures risk regulation regimes in these sectors, the variation that manifests in different sectors as a result of these pressures, and the consequences of this variation.

BLACK SWANS AS A LENS THROUGH WHICH TO EXAMINE RISK REGULATION REGIMES

Canada's national strategy and action plan (Public Safety Canada 2009b, 2014) note that high-impact, low-frequency events (including black swans) are rare but devastating and require special attention because of the potential for massive loss should they occur. Much of the CI literature includes references to disasters. The literature frequently brings our attention to the fragile and interdependent nature of CI, pointing out that one small, seemingly innocuous failure can have a massive impact. For example, overgrown tree branches in Ohio caused the failure of the Northeast power grid in 2003, which affected over 55 million people, cost over $10 billion, and left some without power for over a week; it was the second largest blackout in history. The focus, in both the popular media and the academic literature, thus lies squarely on low-probability/high-consequence events.

It need not be this way. From a rational standpoint, high-probability/low-consequence events (the opposite of black swans) by definition occur all the time and on balance should be given the same consideration as low-probability/high-consequence events.[5] But they are not. In 2014, for example, Canada recorded 1,834 motor vehicle fatalities (over five people per day) (Transport Canada 2016), and each year over 37,000 Canadians are estimated to die because of tobacco use (over 100 people per day) (Health Canada 2009a). Yet neither statistic receives the same degree of media coverage as natural disasters such as the 2013 Alberta floods or industrial failures such as the Lac-Mégantic derailment. As psychologists note, we tolerate predictable risks over surprises, even if the former take a greater toll in both financial and human terms. People have a strong aversion to disasters, which are also interpreted and amplified in a media culture in ways that smaller accidents or highly dispersed events are not.

The term *black swan* was popularized by Nassim Nicholas Taleb (2007) in a book of the same name, in which he defines a black swan as an event that is deemed unlikely to occur on the basis of historical data, has significant consequences, and, in hindsight, is rationalized to seem natural or inevitable.[6] Taleb's argument is primarily a criticism of applied statistics and its mainstream proponents. His central concern is that statisticians dismiss black swans as mere outliers, when in fact such events tend to have enormous historical importance, shaping subsequent political, economic, and social development. "Although unpredictable large variations are rare," writes Taleb, "they cannot be dismissed as outliers because, cumulatively, their impact is so dramatic" (2007, 236). Rather than seeking out and understanding the sources of randomness and variation, statisticians insist on predictive models based on inaccurate causal assumptions. Taleb suggests that this practice, which he describes as a form of "epistemic arrogance" (2007, 145), is common in most professions.

The black swan argument has been criticized from several perspectives. Brown (2007) suggests that Taleb's book makes basic mathematical errors and fails to cite the numerous statistical techniques that have been developed to grapple with extreme events. Statisticians, for example, separate frequency and consequence and model these independently so rare events are not necessarily dismissed if their consequences are deemed significant. Moreover, it is common practice for statisticians to incorporate expert judgment into their statistical models (see, for example, Norrington et al. [2008]); methods such as Bayesian networks are used to combine expert judgment and event data to assess risks. Westfall and Hilbe (2007) point to a definitional paradox at the heart of the idea of black swans: if probabilistic forecasting is impossible, then one may as well assume a future full of white swans. From a CI perspective, there are valid questions to ask about the extent to which the black swan concept differs from other approaches to understanding risk, such as normal accidents theory.

In our study, we use black swans to highlight important features of CI risk regulation regimes. They draw our attention to the limits of rationality and traditional risk management. By definition, black swans are difficult to predict; only in hindsight are the causes said to be evident. Black swans, when they occur, thus expose previously unknown vulnerabilities within a regime; they are an opportunity to question the assumptions and beliefs that undergird a regime and the risks that routine risk operations do not address. Black swans also lay bare the limitations of these assumptions and beliefs by inviting an examination of the specific ways in which they failed to predict and mitigate failure.

CRITICAL INFRASTRUCTURE IN CONTEXT

Historically, disasters were much more consequential than they are today. While an event like 9/11 is seared in the popular imagination as the quintessential low-probability/high-consequence event, its 3,000 deaths appear well down in the league table of disasters (National Commission on Terrorist Acts 2004), and this is equally true if you add the estimated 1.2 to 2.0 million people who died as a result of the War on Terror that followed (Physicians for Social Responsibility 2015). In 541–42, the Plague of Justinian killed 25 million people (Rosen 2007) – 5,000 a day at its peak (Frith 2012). The Black Death killed more than 50 million in the 1340s (Frith 2012). A third of the world's population is believed to have died prematurely as a result of wars and natural disasters during the Little Ice Age in the seventeenth century (Parker 2013). More than 50 million died as a result of the Spanish flu in 1917–20 (Johnson and Mueller 2002). The 1931 flood in China killed 4 million if the famines that followed are included (O'Connor and Costa 2004). About 1 million people starved to death as a result of the Great Famine in mid-nineteenth century Ireland and a further million left Ireland, resulting in a twenty per cent drop in the population (Boyle and O Gráda 1986). It is estimated that 38 million people died in the First World War (Public Broadcasting Service 2016) and 60 million in the Second World War, or three per cent of the world's population at the time; many of those who died were young (Barger 2008).

In fact, modern society has made considerable progress in managing most risks. This is true of both the developed and the developing world. Life expectancy is up (National Institute on Aging 2011), diets are largely improved (Rosen 1999), smoking rates are down (World Health Organization 2015), and death rates of most cancers are down (Hashim et al. 2016). Advances in health and technology have improved quality of life around the planet (National Institute on Aging 2011).

While some risks recede, others become more pronounced. Societies joined by electronic networks and global supply chains have increased technical complexity. Interdependence itself is not new; global trade – and its associated risks – have existed for millennia (Kline 2014), but the speed at which trade occurs and people move and travel is new. The rise in multinational organizations has made it difficult for governments to hold these organizations to account in a specific jurisdiction. Moreover, black swan events defy the market solutions we have developed, such as insurance, because of the difficulty in obtaining reliable probability and consequence data; global supply chains have drawn in more small and medium-sized enterprises (SMEs) with little excess capacity to manage risks. Importantly, people's expectations have also changed in recent decades. The growth of wealth, the social state, and human rights since the Second World War has generated higher expectations of the State, particularly in the West (Congleton and Bose 2010; Elliott 2011). There has also been a parallel trend, particularly pronounced over the last thirty years, of increasing optimism about the private sector's capacity to deliver services more efficiently than the public sector and in a more tailored fashion to its specific customers (Hood 1991). Finally, our current media culture allows us to access coverage of disasters immediately and at a low cost; the public is simultaneously fascinated and troubled by these events (Moeller 2006). Collectively, these forces have increased public expectation and decreased our tolerance of and capacity to cope with disruption.

Efforts to protect CI, the academic literature points out, can be divided into two categories on the basis of their level of specificity (Hood et al. 2001). At the smaller, or microscopic, level are CIP approaches that target specific hazards, treating them as discrete problems to be solved by applying improved security routines, engineering standards, or management practices. Safeguards to prevent terrorist attacks against nuclear installations, standards to improve rail safety, and earthquake preparedness are examples of activities based on a microscopic perspective of CIP. At the micro level, risk management varies widely from sector to sector and from hazard to hazard.

In the other category are approaches that view CIP through a macroscopic lens. CIP efforts in this category look beyond specific hazards. Instead, they seek to develop frameworks to guide risk management across all CI sectors. The same general processes are applied for every potential hazard. Indeed, the "all hazards approach" to risk management has emerged as a guiding principle of many emergency management agencies. Government programs to promote resilience and risk-based CIP measures similarly fall into the macro category by assuming that general principles can be applied successfully across sectors and risk profiles.

The micro and macro perspectives on risk are crucial for understanding certain aspects of CIP. As analytical tools, however, neither perspective offers a satisfactory explanation for *variation* across CI sectors and events. A cursory consideration of CIP practices reveals that CI owners and operators implement a wide array of different measures, often for similar risks. Why is security at airports so regimented and thorough while security at other transportation infrastructure such seaports, rail, and bridges remains relatively free of such control? You might suggest that people are more concerned about their safety on airplanes. Yet public opinion does not always influence risk regulation: recent pandemics and cybersecurity failures have generated strong reactions from governments despite only modest concerns from the public. Indeed, the style of government intervention also varies. Some critical sectors, such as trucking, have safety and security standards imposed on them while others, such as the chemicals sector, develop their own standards largely free of government intervention.

The reasons for the variation in how we manage risks to CI, we suggest, can be found by studying the context in which CI exists. CI owners and operators are influenced not only by the specific details of perceived risks (microscopic conditions) or by overarching concerns about resilience or adaptability (macroscopic considerations).

They are also influenced by middle, or meso-level, factors such as market structure, public opinion, media coverage, organizational culture, and interest group pressure and sophistication. To borrow from Pal (1997), context matters when it comes to understanding the regulation of CIP risks. Yet context is rarely considered in practice, and it receives little attention in the academic literature.

The idea of a meso-level perspective on risk regulation comes from Hood, Rothstein, and Baldwin's book, *The Government of Risk* (2001). In examining contextual factors, Hood and colleagues rely on the concept of regimes. A regime is a comprehensive idea. It captures all the different ways a society, including government, businesses, and citizens, think about and act on risks. More specifically, a regime includes the "institutional geography, rules, practices, and animating ideas" that shape risk regulation (Hood et al. 2001, 9). Although regimes are complex, they are bounded, meaning they can be compared and contrasted.

This book takes a broad look at Canada's CI and the risks with which it must contend. The transportation sector and the manufacture of chemicals provide considerable scope to explore risk regulation. The transportation sector is highly fragmented and competitive, yet interdependent, and it has moved progressively from public to private ownership. It is quintessentially global and local. It has a high public profile: people use it daily. The chemicals sector, in contrast, has always been largely privately owned but heavily regulated. It is not a popular industry; while chemicals may be pervasive, the sector tries to keep a low profile. It is largely global, with a handful of multinationals dominating it.

We note here the important distinction between the terms *safety* and *security*. They are often used interchangeably and, indeed, at times our interview participants conflated them. Security risks involve human aggressors who are influenced by a variety of environmental and personal factors and may come from within or outside the target institution (Reniers and Pavlova 2013, 8). While their outcomes may be similar, security and safety risks demand different approaches to risk management. "Protecting installations against intentional attacks," write Reniers and Pavlova, "is fundamentally different from protecting against random accidents or acts of nature" (2013, 9; see also Russell and Simpson 2010). Human aggressors, for example, are adaptive agents; they will modify their behaviour in light of security practices that organizations adopt. Generally, safety

plans tend to be more transparent, are informed by more reliable
data, and are regulated more clearly. Safety plans are also more
clearly entrenched in the organizational culture and legal tradition
of many critical sectors.

WHAT WE FOUND

Between 2011 and 2015, we conducted sixty-eight semi-structured
interviews with CI owners and operators and regulators,[7] a media
analysis of forty post-9/11 CI events, an examination of polling
data, and an extensive literature review. (See appendix 1 for a
description of our methods, appendix 2 for a full list of interview
participants, and appendix 3 for a complete list of media events.)

Our analysis of these data leads to several conclusions. Markets,
left to their own devices, rarely prepare for black swan events. In
fact, markets can increase the probability of black swan events
occurring by rewarding risk-taking behaviours; we saw this in the
Lac-Mégantic tragedy, in which regulatory standards and business
practices designed to improve efficiencies and reduce costs contributed to a rail disaster. SMEs, companies like MMA, provide the adaptive capacity that markets value in global supply chains, but they
often don't have adequate risk management staff, expertise, or insurance. Staff often follow routines and executives respond to profit
motives; neither pay much attention to preventing disasters that they
feel are unlikely to occur and can't even imagine. This makes perfect
market sense. Markets reward behaviours and ways of thinking that
don't always contribute to successful CIP.

Governments must address these failures caused by market forces,
but they are ill equipped to do so. Since the 1980s, the dominant
narrative in Canada has been that private industry with a profit
motive is better at managing CI than government. As a result, most
CI has been privatized or outsourced, and owners and operators – at
a minimum – have been afforded considerable regulatory flexibility.
At the same time, governments have been "hollowed out"; they have
been unable to keep pace with the technical sophistication of CI.
Consequently, government officials now lack the knowledge, skill,
time, flexibility, and credibility to keep an eye on the CI owners and
operators who manage risks to CI. Courts and legal processes are
often slow and expensive.

Government finds itself in a conundrum. Polling data suggest that Canadians do not consider security or environmental risks a high priority, and certainly not compared with health care and economic concerns. Yet the public holds government partly if not completely responsible for CI failures, despite the fact that government has less and less control over CI. The public expects its governments to act and will blame them if they do not. In response, before any disaster, governments assume a cooperative stance with industry and use euphemisms to mask unclear accountability, vague and innocuous terms like *information sharing, trust building, collaboration, volunteer, partnership*, and *stakeholder*. In the event of a disaster, the government's position is much more defensive – blame management becomes more pronounced. Given the complexity and the potential political and financial liability, government wants stability in CI but not responsibility for it.

Meanwhile, the media fail to keep a watchful eye on CI risk regulation. Most black swan events generate a lot of media coverage and sometimes a ruthless hunt for someone to blame (especially in the case of terrorist attacks and industrial failures; less so in the case of natural disasters) but disasters and crises are complex and require thoughtful and prolonged examination. Despite this, most media coverage ends the same month it starts and focuses more on personalities and emotive topics than rational risk assessment. For example, the *Globe and Mail* wrote fifteen times more articles about HINI following the death of a seemingly healthy 13-year-old boy than it did about a computer glitch at the Canada Revenue Agency in 2007 that limited government's ability to collect or disseminate funds online, which – unlike the boy's tragic death – had very serious and far-reaching economic implications.

Government is also much more adept at managing its messaging than it was twenty years ago. Despite the rhetoric of markets and competition, which ostensibly underpins the rationale for CI management, many large CI organizations are protected from market competition. Many of the CI sectors – banking, energy and utilities, and health care – are heavily regulated, which creates considerable barriers to potential competition. Moreover, just as some corporations are too big to fail, many large CI organizations are too critical to fail. Governments have a strong incentive to restore CI companies after failures. With few exceptions, this reduces any incentive for companies to invest in protecting themselves against black swans. Companies can further isolate themselves from scrutiny by withholding information from the public under the guise of competition, privacy, or security considerations. As a result, government often doesn't know – or in some cases won't disclose – how seriously companies take security and how effectively they are managing risks in practice.

Forces converge to further empower CI institutions with inordinate control over their own information – forces that include market failures, ill-informed media coverage, governments' diminished capacity for risk policy and management, and companies that are too big and too critical to fail. Meanwhile, the public trusts CI institutions less and less. While some careers end abruptly after CI disasters and share value falls, for the most part organizations maintain power after a black swan event, and sometimes they even gain power. The governance system in place privileges stability, efficiency, and political expediency over transparency and fairness. In an environment in which there is a high degree of complexity and interdependence, government narrows its accountability lest it be caught holding the bag after a failure. Even if government were interested in promoting a learning environment following these events, and it's not evident that it does, it is unclear whether its organizational culture will permit it to learn lessons that go beyond the standard and predictable options, which rarely challenge the organizational patterns that led to the failures in the first place.

We need to learn and adapt so that we can address risks associated with climate change, security, aging infrastructure, and emerging cyber threats. To strengthen our CI, we must strengthen and extend independent audits, report more frequently on performance, share information more widely (including to the general public), manage the risks associated with SMEs, reduce single points of failure, enforce appropriate standards and behaviour in a timely manner, increase mindfulness about security, and distribute risks more fairly.

CIP is not exclusively about government or security; it is about the assets that enable and protect our civilization. We all have a stake in CIP. In Canada and the United States, commitments have been made to spend considerable sums of money on CI. These investments can enable our societies to take a significant step towards smarter, greener cities. CI investments can reflect our values and the communities we wish to build. The planning we do today will take years to come to fruition; we must consider security, climate change, trade, economic challenges, and opportunities of the future to maximize the benefits of today's CI investments. Equally, we must consider how transparent, fair, and accountable our governments are when we build, maintain, and manage these highly interdependent and complex systems; there are no risk-free options.

THE PLAN OF THE BOOK

This book has three parts. The first part contains two chapters. In chapter 2 we situate our research in the existing academic literature. We survey previous work on risk governance, examining how various disciplines have contributed discrete conceptualizations of risk and risk management techniques. More recently, the literature has adopted a holistic approach to risk governance, bringing together a variety of perspectives. Among these new perspectives is Hood and colleagues' risk regulation regime framework, which we explain in relation to two other approaches: Renn and Walker's International Risk Governance Council (IRGC) framework (Renn and Walker 2008) and the Knowledge Commons concept (Hess and Ostrom 2011). Doing so allows us to further illustrate the benefits (and limitations) of using Hood and colleagues' framework.

Having reviewed the relevant literature and described the conceptual framework we will be using, we turn in chapter 3 to a discussion of the current approach to CIP in Canada. We focus on the *National Strategy for Critical Infrastructure* (Public Safety Canada 2009b) and the *Action Plan for Critical Infrastructure* (2009a, updated in 2014) (NS&AP), which were produced collaboratively by the federal, provincial, and territorial governments. The goal of chapter 3 is to set the stage for our case studies by providing information about how governments understand CIP, what their priorities are, and what initial steps they have taken to achieve those priorities.

The second part of the book delves into our two case studies. In chapter 4 we look at the transportation sector, with a particular emphasis on five major subsectors: airports, seaports, rail, trucking, and bridges. In chapter 5 we study the chemical manufacturing industry. We also examine sectors linked to the chemical industry, including water utilities and hazardous-material first responders.

Applying the framework of Hood and colleagues, we describe these sectors in terms of their regime features, that is, as the chemical *regime* and the transportation *regime*.

Building on the data received from our interview participants, we use chapters 4 and 5 to depict the safety and security risk management practices in these two regimes. We examine how each regime collects information, sets standards, and modifies behaviour in pursuit of managing risks and protecting its CI. In the terminology of the risk regulation regime framework, these three components – information gathering, standard setting, and behaviour modification – represent each regime's *content*.

In the third and final section of the book we analyze how the content of each regime is explained by the array of contextual forces acting upon it. In short, we look at how context explains content. We begin in chapter 6 by examining the market failure hypothesis, in many ways the benchmark case for government intervention, which states that governments take regulatory action when markets cannot manage risk on their own. The market failure hypothesis is an appropriate starting point for our analysis because it is explicitly embodied in federal risk management policy. Our analysis unveils mixed support for the market failure hypothesis, suggesting that efforts to address risks to CIP involve more than calculations of market efficiency.

Next we examine the opinion-responsive hypothesis, which states that a regime's content is a product of how the public feels about a sector and how its attendant risks should be managed. To examine the validity of this hypothesis in the case of Canadian CI we draw on a wide range of evidence. In chapter 7, we draw on our interview data, as well as media coverage of recent black swan events and public polling statistics, to identify the degree of correlation between how the public feels about chemical and transportation risks and the regime content we observed in chapters 4 and 5. The media analysis focuses on a variety of black swan event types, including natural disasters, industrial failures, terrorist attacks, terrorist plots, and cyber events. Some of these are specific to the transportation and chemicals sectors and others have a broader reach.

We then turn to the risk psychology literature to draw further conclusions about the role of public opinion in shaping risk regulation. In chapter 8 we focus on the emerging challenge of cybersecurity, examining how risks to information technology systems are framed and how this framing aims to influence how cyber risks are confronted. In chapter 9 we look at the H 1 N 1 disease outbreak in 2009, and in particular how media coverage of the event influenced public behaviour. Together, these case studies provide further evidence about the importance of understanding how risks are framed and how framing relates to public and government responses to black swan events.

We then shift our focus to organizational context. The third contextual hypothesis we examine is the interest group hypothesis, which asserts that regime content can be explained by studying the distribution of power among relevant interest groups. Where an organized interest has a stake in the outcome of a regulatory decision, that group will mobilize its resources to lobby government. The most influential groups will have their priorities reflected in the regime. In chapter 10 we interrogate this hypothesis using the Wilsonian typology, which asks whether observed interest group behaviour aligns with an assessment of the costs and benefits associated with that behaviour. In chapter 11 we offer a different assessment of the interest group hypothesis by using a cultural theory perspective to examine whether regime content can be understood in terms of the organizational cultures predominant in the sectors we studied.

We use the term *black swan* as a shorthand for disasters, or potential disasters. We deviate somewhat from the original author's (Taleb's) understanding of black swans. We agree that there is much after-the-fact accounting for events that is not instructive and that is even misleading. Much of our book focuses on the social construction of risk and blame. Nevertheless, we are perhaps a bit more optimistic than Taleb about our capacity to learn about how to prevent these events by studying what caused these failures in the first place.

We conclude the book in chapter 12 by reiterating our major findings and by assessing the effectiveness of the risk regulation regimes for Canada's C1. As public administration scholars, we are particularly interested in questions of efficiency, fairness, transparency, accountability, stability, learning, and resilience of the risk regulation regimes, all concepts that are addressed in the conclusion.

PART ONE

Situating the Study

In the following two chapters we situate our research in the existing literature on risk management, particularly as it applies to critical infrastructure protection (CIP). In chapter 2 we survey various conceptualizations of risk and risk governance. We begin with the rational actor paradigm, which views risk as probability multiplied by consequence; within this tradition, there is an optimism that these concepts are accessible and can be measured. We also consider definitions of risk from psychology, sociology, and anthropology. Next, we discuss the recent trend in the literature to move towards holistic frameworks that incorporate observations from multiple disciplines into a single understanding of risk governance. Among these new models is the risk regulation regime framework, which provides the theoretical framework for our study of Canadian CIP later in the book. Yet the other frameworks make important contributions as well, many of which we draw on during our subsequent analysis.

In chapter 3 we turn to a discussion of the current approach to CIP in Canada by evaluating the report *National Strategy and Action Plan for Critical Infrastructure* (NS&AP), which is the result of efforts by the federal, provincial, and territorial governments to agree on a common approach to CIP. We evaluate the plan's focus on sharing information and trust and transparency, arguing that the plan is underdeveloped and ill-equipped to achieve effective control over risks to CI. In describing the predominant national approach to CIP, we also set the stage for our case studies in chapter 4 and chapter 5, in which we examine in detail two of the sectors included in the NS&AP.

2

Risk Governance and Critical Infrastructure: Control and Adaptive Capacity

Until the 1980s, the study of risk was dominated by scientists, engineers, economists, and decision analysts. Their views were overwhelmingly influenced by a rational actor paradigm (RAP) (Jaeger et al. 2001, 19–22), in which risk is an objective condition with a rational/individual bias. In this section, we summarize the RAP view of risk and consider the important contributions of psychology, sociology, and anthropology to the risk debate. As an organizing framework, we use the risk rationality diagram (Renn 2008, figure 2.1) to explore traditional and alternative approaches to the study of risk. We then focus on holistic risk frameworks that allow for competing risk rationales and use van der Heijden's (2005) three paradigms to organize our discussion. These paradigms show the trade-off between control and adaptive capacity in responding to risks. Also, they underscore the importance of organizational learning and the power and influence of organized interests.

FOUR RATIONALES FOR RISK

According to Renn, the first – and dominant – view of risk is the RAP (box A). In box A, risk is objective and understood through the lens of the individual. Box B, largely the domain of psychologists, views risk through an individual's lens but assumes that risk is subjective (e.g., personal, intimate). Box C, largely the domain of sociologists, some natural scientists, and many business schools, also assumes that risk is objective but views it through structural or organizational settings. Box D, largely the domain of sociologists and anthropologists, understands risk to be constructed but

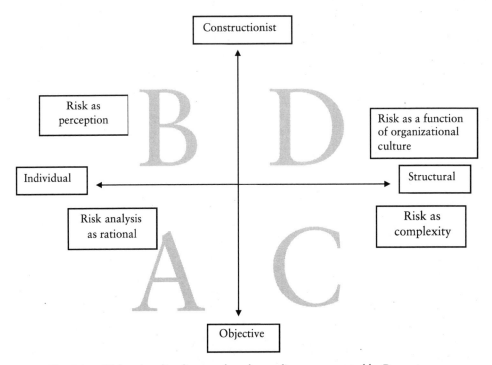

Figure 2.1 Risk rationality diagram, based on a diagram presented by Renn at the Social Contexts and Responses to Risk Inaugural Conference, January 2005, at the University of Kent at Canterbury. An updated version can be found in Renn (2008).

through a structural setting. The following discussion examines each of these four boxes.

Rational Risk Analysis (Box A)

Risk frameworks developed within a RAP seek to explain the relationship between action, uncertainty, and consequence. The method usually includes mathematical models, underpinned by a consistent and coherent rationale for decision-making. The models are necessarily simplified representations of reality with the aim of capturing the key features of the problem. The methodology can include the values of stakeholders and expert judgment as well as historical data to inform the model. Moreover, assessing the adequacy of the resulting model plays an important role in the process.

Starr (1969) and Lowrance (1976) are among the most significant early contributors to this particular approach. Their definition of risk – probability multiplied by consequence – is perhaps the most famous. In this view, technical risk analyses are intended to reveal, avoid, and/or modify the causal agents associated with unwanted effects. Until the early 1980s this understanding of risk was largely uncontested (Adams 1995, 8). Certain tools lend themselves to a RAP approach to risk. Probabilistic risk assessments (PRAs) offer a method for analyzing and predicting the failures of complex technological systems by reducing the systems to their operating component parts. Risk estimates of a system's failure are typically based on fault tree and event tree methods (Jaeger et al. 2001, 90).

While models based on RAP will make use of data to estimate frequencies, rare events necessarily have little or no event data. There are data-driven methods to estimate the likelihood of black swans on the basis of the existing frequency of white swans (see Quigley and Revie 2011) or on the basis of associations with similar events (Quigley, Bedford, and Walls 2007). Regardless of whether a data-driven approach or an expert judgment approach is used, model construction requires experts.

Formal risk modelling is a growing practice in critical infrastructure protection (CIP). Engineers and computer scientists identify entities and interdependencies; the models can include data on probability, vulnerability, consequence, and time elapsed from system failure. The goal of the model is to demonstrate the consequence that one system failure will have on other interdependent systems. Ontario and Quebec have each developed elaborate models in this tradition. (For Ontario, see the government of Ontario's Infrastructure Modelling Program [Government of Ontario (n.d.)] and for Quebec, see Robert and Morabito [2011].)

The RAP approach to understanding risk has been criticized on several grounds. First, what people perceive as unwanted effects or consequences differs according to their values and preferences; a challenge in supporting any solution to a decision problem is the ranking of options, which will not reflect everyone's preferences. Secondly, models based on RAP typically require data yet it is difficult to obtain reliable data for these models. To start, modellers assume people can express themselves accurately in numerical terms. Moreover, the interaction between human activities and consequences is more complex, and perhaps subtle, than the average probabilities captured by most risk analyses. Moreover, when data are unavailable for these models, which is often the case when we are exploring rare events (e.g., acts of terrorism), they are estimated; estimations have errors associated with them. What's more, models are built on past experiences, as is usually the practice in actuarial science. These models will fail to predict new or rare events because the assumptions of the past do not necessarily hold. Thirdly, the institutional structures for managing and controlling risks are prone to organizational failure, which may increase actual risks (Jaeger et al. 2001, 86).

From a normative standpoint a RAP embeds key assumptions. To start, a RAP assumes that we can understand complex technological systems and that a reductionist approach is the best way to understand them. Motivation, organization, and culture are ignored (Jaeger et al. 2001, 91). Moreover, a RAP approach upholds the privileged position of the one who designed the model (i.e., the expert); it values expert views over lay views. Finally, risk minimization and even resilience are not necessarily the only ends in mind; equity, fairness, and flexibility are also plausible and potentially desirable goals but they are frequently overlooked (Jaeger et al. 2001, 86).

Risk Perception (Box B)

Burns (2012) argues that it is important to understand risk perception for two reasons: (1) risk perception helps us to understand and predict people's behaviour, and (2) awareness of how perceptions are constructed helps improve communication between technical experts and lay people. The psychometric paradigm – the theory and technique of mental measurement – draws on the work of cognitive psychologists such as Slovic, Fischhoff, and Lichtenstein (1982) to conceptualize risks as personal expressions of individual fears or expectations. In short, individuals respond to their perceptions whether or not those perceptions reflect reality. The study of risk perception has grown in popularity over recent decades and challenges the assumptions that underpin the RAP approach to risk (for example, see Pratt 1964; Arrow 1971; Slovic 1987; Jaeger et al. 2001; Pennings and Grossman 2008; Lachlan and Spence 2010; Pachur, Hertwig, and Steinmann 2012). The psychology of risk literature identifies several biases in people's ability to draw inferences in the face of uncertainty. Risk perception can be influenced by personal control (Langer 1975), familiarity (Tversky and Kahneman 1973), exit options (Starr 1969), equitable sharing of benefits and risks (Finucane et al. 2000), and the potential to blame an institution or person (Douglas and Wildavsky 1982). Risk perception can also be influenced by how a person feels about something, such as a particular technology or a disease (Alhakami and Slovic 1994). People also show confirmation bias (Wason 1960), which suggests they seek information to confirm, not to challenge, how they feel.

Risk perceptions are often faulty, when we consider consequence and probability (Slovic et al. 1982). Risk cannot be directly observed; rather, people construct their risk perceptions on the basis of their understanding of hazards in everyday life. People often make judgments about risk using incomplete or erroneous information. They also rely on biases or heuristics to comprehend complexity. Heuristics are cognitive tools people use to analyze risk and complexity (Slovic et al. 1982). In some ways, heuristics are helpful; they allow people to render simplistic understandings of complicated subjects. However, they can also oversimplify or distort our understanding. Heuristics conform to two primary dimensions: (1) the unknown factor and (2) the dread factor. The unknown factor makes people more concerned with risks that are not observable or known to science (Slovic et al. 1982). In contrast, the dread factor makes people more concerned with risks that are uncontrollable and may have catastrophic consequences (Slovic et al. 1982).

One of the most common heuristics is availability. Under the influence of the availability heuristic, people tend to believe that an event is more likely to occur when they are able to imagine or recall it easily (for examples, see Slovic et al. 1982; Folkes 1988; Betsch and Pohl 2002; Tversky and Kahneman 1973; Maldonato and Dell'Orco 2011). For instance, fear of shark attacks increased dramatically after the release of the movie *Jaws*, despite the fact that shark attacks had not suddenly become more probable (Slovic et al. 1982). By contrast, the availability heuristic can also lull people into a false sense of security about the risks associated with everyday tasks. Availability is one of the most important heuristics for understanding risk perception (Sjöberg 2000). For instance, the availability heuristic makes people concerned about terrorist attacks despite the fact that – like other many high-profile risks – terrorist attacks are extremely rare (Gierlach, Belsher, and Beutler 2010). This phenomenon is referred to as probability neglect (Slovic et al. 2005). When probability neglect is at work, "people's attention is focused on the bad outcome itself, and they are inattentive to the fact that it is unlikely to occur" (Sunstein 2003, 122).

A psychometric approach to risk provides more insight into the effect of media than a rational approach. The media tend to report the dramatic over the common but more dangerous (Soumerai, Ross-Degnan, and Kahn 1992) and tend not only to sensationalize (Johnson and Covello 1987) but also to sensationalize the most negative aspects of events (Wahlberg and Sjoberg 2000). The academic literature on media and terrorism focuses largely on Islamic terrorism, the American media, and the repercussions of 9/11. It criticizes the media for failing to perform its watchdog role by objectively vetting government rhetoric, especially concerning the War on Terror.

Complex Risk (Box C)

There are two main schools of thought on the safety and reliability of complex technological and social systems: (1) high-reliability organizations and (2) normal accident theory (NAT). The literature on high-reliability organizations argues that hazardous technologies can be safely controlled by complex organizations if the correct design and management techniques are followed, such as strong and persuasive leadership, commitment and adherence to a safety culture (including learning from mistakes), creating redundancies, and increasing transparency with respect to accountability and operations (La Porte and Consolini 1991; La Porte 1996; Weick and Roberts 1993; Weick and Sutcliffe 2001). In contrast, the NAT literature, which is an extension of chaos theory, holds that accidents are inevitable in organizations that are socially and technically complex. NAT advocates argue that the discipline required of a high-reliability organization is unrealistic. Systems fail because of their inherent fallibility and the non-responsive nature of bureaucratic organizations. Efforts to increase accountability result in the shifting of blame. Indeed, safety is only one priority, which competes with many others (Sagan 1993; Vaughan 1996; Perrow 1999).

Black swan theory aligns with NAT. Black swan theory was developed to explain why low-probability events are difficult to predict, yet can have a huge impact on the world that the vast majority of people fail to recognize (Taleb 2007). In the field of risk governance, the term *black swan* is routinely used as a metaphor to describe low-probability (i.e., rare or unexpected), high-consequence events. As explained in chapter 1, it is in this sense that we will use the term *black swan* throughout this book.

Recently, the literary debate over safety culture has shifted from single organizations to networks of organizations, because of growing technical, social, and organizational interdependencies, and from safety and reliability to resilience. The construct of resilience allows for the possibility of massive systems failures because of complex interdependencies and seeks proactive and reactive strategies to manage the consequences of failures (Clarke 2005; Boin and McConnell 2007; Roux-Dufort 2007; Roe and Schulman 2008). Fischbacher-Smith (2011) suggests that the evolving speed, scale, and extent of modern hazards has caused policy-makers to turn to the concept of resilience to address the challenges involved in predicting, preventing, and mitigating such hazards. He argues that the term *resilience* has two interpretations, one from engineering (i.e., how a system bounces back from shocks) and the other from systems biology (i.e., the adaptability of the system). Fischbacher-Smith (2011) concludes that the engineering approach is inappropriate for the risk portfolios of Western governments but that additional research is needed on how best to apply adaptive management approaches in different settings and how to reduce the construct of resilience to a single measure.

The concepts and controversies that underpin the debate on high-reliability organizations and NAT continue to inform the sociology of risk literature today. The search for security is a dynamic process that balances mechanisms of control with processes of information search, exchange, and feedback in complex multi-organizational settings. This dynamic process is guided by public organizations and seeks participation from private organizations, not-for-profits, and informed citizens (Comfort 2002; Aviram and Tor 2004a; Aviram 2005; Auerswald et al. 2006; De Bruijne and van Eeten 2007; Egan 2007). The risk debate has now expanded from avoiding failure to coping with it. NAT is commonly deployed to explain specific failures, such as the 2008 financial crisis (Palmer and Maher 2010), or how the political economy of Japanese municipalities affects their support for nuclear power (Aldrich 2013). In Casler's (2014) study of post-*Columbia* NASA, he concludes that no large public organization can embrace all of the characteristics of a high-reliability organization. Sheps and Cardiff (2011), in contrast, cast system resilience as a third way of understanding accidents alongside NAT and high-reliability organizations. Writing in the health care context, they conclude that clinical and organizational context must include resilience thinking, "which accepts that harm is potentially inherent in all facets of care and encourages adaptability, receptivity to weak signals and open communication in order to enable corrective action based on local experience" (155–6).

Risk as Organizational Culture (Box D)

Cultural theory is useful for interpreting how different organizational types respond to risk (Douglas 1982, 1992; Hood 1998). Cultural theorists see risk as a danger or threat to a value system that is embedded in institutional arrangements, not as a calculable probability. Douglas (2001, xix) notes: "Certainty is only possible because doubt is blocked institutionally. Most individual decisions about risk are taken under pressure from institutions." Douglas describes a person's value system in terms of the grid/group theory that she developed. Grid measures the strength of rules and social norms and is largely about regulation (1982, 191–2). Group measures the extent to which community constraints are imposed on an individual and is about integration (1982, 191–2).

Grid/group theory measures regulation (grid) and social integration (group) to determine value systems and the preferred institutional arrangements flowing from them, leading to the characterization of four cultural types: hierarchists, individualists, egalitarians, and fatalists. Each type has a preferred governance arrangement and particular blind spots and vulnerabilities.

On the basis of Douglas and Wildavsky's (1982) grid/group typology, Hood (1998) and Thompson, Ellis, and Wildavsky (1990) explore the four cultural "types" that emerge and the corresponding forms of governance structures that each would develop. To the hierarchist (high grid/high group), good governance means a stable environment that supports collective interest and fair process through rule-driven hierarchical organizations. Any departure from this rule-bound hierarchy represents risk for the hierarchist. To the individualist (low grid/low group), good governance means minimal rules and interference with free market processes. Individualists understand risk to be government regulation of the economy or the management of public services. To the egalitarian (high group/low grid), good governance means local, communitarian, and participative organizations. For egalitarians, authority resides with the collectivity. Fatalists (low group/high grid) doubt straightforward cause-effect relationships; to them, good governance means management by surprise techniques that circumvent practised or routine responses.

A hierarchical (or bureaucratic) culture is typical of many government agencies. The US Department of Defense's original 1998 Critical Infrastructure Protection Plan identifies six stages to CIP: analysis and assessment; remediation; indications and warnings; mitigation; incident response; and reconstitution (Department of Defense 1998). The plan is orderly and systematic; it assumes that responsibility for gathering the data can be segmented and assigned, and the sum of these data can give a comprehensive view of the risk. The document makes little reference to perspective; it notes that the Department of Defense requires a culture change to become more effective at CIP but fails to define *culture*. In fact, given the systematic nature of the plan, the approach seems entirely consistent with a technical-rational approach that fits within a bureaucratic culture.

When tested empirically, cultural theory has had mixed success (for examples, see Dake 1991; Brenot, Bonnefous, and Marris 1998; Sjöberg 1998). Dake (1991) and Brenot et al. (1998) both found that correlations between culture and bias are weak and of limited predictive value. Oltedal and Rundmo (2007) studied cultural theory and risk perception in the transportation sector and found different risk perceptions among different groups. Grid/group theory has also been criticized on the grounds that the categories in the typology are too limiting. Risk perceptions are far more complex and dynamic than the categories imply (Renn et al. 1992) and cultural theory fails to take the media into account (Zinn 2004, 15). At the same time, cultural theory's capacity to show the recurring debates and irreconcilable difference in these debates has been described as a revolutionary advance in the study of risk (Royal Society 1992); Hood's (1998) use of the theory to explore the recurring debates about how to govern and arrange public services is a particularly recognized study.[1]

Like Hood, we use Douglas's conception of cultural theory as a heuristic device to structure an analysis of risk regulation regimes in different sectors (chapter 11). No organization fulfills all the requirements of any one of the four cultural types. Rather, organizations show tendencies, and these tendencies can be particularly strong in the aftermath of a failure. Knowing this helps one to anticipate who or what an organization will blame when things go wrong and the pressures and demands each sector is likely to make on the regulatory regime.

In sum, despite the dominance of the RAP, several disciplines have contributed to our understanding of risk and its management. Each field brings its own assumptions, tools, and perspectives, contributing to a much richer understanding of risk. Using one approach is narrow; using all approaches is unwieldy. The risk management field has therefore tried to integrate more effectively rich but disparate views.

HOLISTIC AND MULTIDISCIPLINARY APPROACHES TO RISK GOVERNANCE

Over the last two decades, researchers and practitioners have developed holistic approaches to risk governance. These approaches bring observations from different disciplines together, enabling the development of more sophisticated analyses of problems and more robust solutions. At times, different approaches to risk do not mesh well; they highlight but do not necessarily reconcile competing rationales. Nevertheless, holistic and multidisciplinary approaches to risk governance underscore the fact that a solution based on RAP alone will have significant limitations, particularly when it comes to implementation.

Here we analyze three holistic frameworks: (1) Renn and Walker's International Risk Governance Council (IRGC) framework (Renn and Walker 2008), (2) knowledge commons (Hess and Ostrom 2011), and (3) Hood and colleagues' risk regulation regime framework (Hood et al. 2001). We have selected these frameworks for their prominence and because each differs in its approach to risk analysis and management. We will use Van der Heijden's (2005) three paradigms for strategy – rational, processual, and evolutionary – to situate and analyze the three frameworks. Each of the risk frameworks aligns with one of van der Heijden's paradigms and makes different assumptions about the focal point of analysis. The IRGC framework focuses on process and examines the state of knowledge about risk and how to improve it. The knowledge commons examines the state of information infrastructure and how to facilitate learning in an evolving environment. The risk regulation regime framework examines social and economic context and its influence on management. This last framework will structure the analysis in our book.

A PROCESS APPROACH TO RISK: THE INTERNATIONAL RISK GOVERNANCE COUNCIL FRAMEWORK

The IRGC framework focuses on the state of knowledge and process. This framework is normative; it recommends a path for public managers and interested parties. It is similar to an evolutionary approach but allows managers to consider how to intervene. The IRGC framework assumes that organizational success cannot be codified – it is too complex – but that we can make the process of managing risk more skillful. It overlaps with the rational and evolutionary approaches, interweaving thought and action.

Risk governance can be defined as the totality of actors, rules, conventions, processes, and mechanisms concerned with how relevant risk information is collected, analyzed, and communicated and how management decisions are taken. The IRGC framework takes into account different schools of thought on risk for an interdisciplinary approach. Renn divides risk governance process into two broad spheres: assessment, which focuses on knowledge generation, and management, which focuses on decisions and action. The assessment phase includes pre-assessment (which captures existing indicators, routines, and conventions that may prematurely narrow what is going to be addressed) and risk appraisal (which includes technical risk assessments and determining the level of social concern). Tolerability and acceptability straddle both knowledge generation and management; they determine "appetite" for risk given likelihood, consequence, and the level of residual risk allowable after mitigation measures are put in place. Finally, risk management focuses on the actions required to manage risk to an acceptable level. While Renn shows the process as four discrete and sequential steps, it is not necessarily linear or easily compartmentalized; the process is dynamic and iterative as new data come to light, particularly for risks where there are considerable knowledge gaps.

Risk classification determines which phase of the IRGC framework should be the primary focus for governance of that risk (see figure 2.2), which management strategy should be employed, and which stakeholders should be involved. The IRGC framework

divides risks into four classes: simple, complex, uncertain, and ambiguous. Its creators later developed the concept of emerging risk. The
classification of risk is "not related to the intrinsic characteristics of
hazards or risks themselves but to the state and quality of knowledge available about both hazards and risks" (Renn and Walker
2008, 18).

Simple and Complex Risks

With simple risk, predicted events are frequent and the causal chain
is obvious (e.g., car accidents). Simple risks generate reliable data
that help to inform our view about risk; we can be more confident
about the extent to which the threat will materialize and the consequences of that threat. As a result, when policy-makers and scientists
are considering a simple risk, the discussion is largely instrumental;
market failure logic and limiting government intervention (to that
which is optimal in market terms) can be a helpful way to develop a
regulatory approach.

Complex risks[2] exist when there is difficulty identifying and quan-
tifying causal links between a multitude of potential causal agents
and specific observed effects (Renn and Walker 2008, 19). There are
two kinds of complex risks: epistemic, which result from imperfect
knowledge, and aleatory, which result from randomness. Epistemic
risks include those associated with interconnected infrastructure and
for which uncertainty can potentially be reduced through data collection. Aleatory risks include randomness, such as human errors
that occur in managing systems; we know that they happen but we
cannot know when errors will occur.

Complex risks are examined largely on the basis of expert opinion
and formal modelling. Formal models help to explain in rational
terms the interactions between many variables; technical risks associated with the power grid, for example, can be described as a complex
risk. Regularly occurring natural disasters, such as spring flooding,
can also be described as a complex risk. Expert processes can allow
us to focus on the existing data, however imperfect, and in so doing,
increase transparency and remove the politics and sometimes-petty
negotiations. Complex risk problems are the domain of scientists or
medics; these professions are trusted more than most (Canadian
Pharmacists Association 2009) and, therefore, the solutions they generate are more likely to be accepted by the community at large.

Formal models, the tools of the experts, have important limitations. From a normative standpoint, as noted in the discussion above, formal models embed key assumptions. To start, we assume that complex technological and ecological systems are accessible to detailed human comprehension and that a reductionist approach is the best way to understand these systems (Jaeger et al. 2001, 91). Formal models can sometimes completely overlook important social, and even moral, considerations.

While social concern is part of risk appraisal, the analysis of complex risks tends to overemphasize the perspectives of the experts. Lay views are often considered inadequate and ill informed; it is the expert's job to fill the knowledge gaps in the lay views rather than to accept their concerns and anxieties as legitimate. The tools of persuasion can also be suspect. People often have blind faith in numerical analysis and computer models; these processes, however, are subject to bias because information can be manipulated through the manner in which data are presented (Jaeger et al. 2001, 81–2).

Finally, while formal models offer the hope of transparency, rigorous analysis, and optimal outcomes, the models fail to include the more subtle dynamics in decision-making, such as strategic reasoning, power plays, interests, and institutional responses (Jaeger et al. 2001, 82). In this sense, models offer important insights but do not provide a full account of decision-making. Dietz and Stern (1995), for example, note that relatively complex mathematics does not correspond with what we know about human behaviour with respect to decision-making. People are good at pattern recognition, classification, and the application of rules of thumb; this undermines the usefulness of the model altogether and frustrates the experts who developed the model with the intention of reducing the influence of seemingly irrational human behaviours. This gap between the scientists and the lay people, including policy-makers and politicians, annoys everyone and threatens to undermine the legitimacy of each group in the other's eyes.

Uncertain, Ambiguous, and Emerging Risks

Uncertain risks exist where there is "a lack of clear scientific or technical basis for decision making," which "often results from an incomplete or inadequate reduction of complexity in modelling cause-effect chains" (Renn and Walker 2008, 18–19). These limitations diminish confidence in traditional objective measures of risk estimation, and therefore risk management becomes more reliant on "fuzzy" or subjective measures of risk estimation (Renn and Walker 2008, 18–19). Uncertain risks frequently generate surprises or realizations that risk modelling frameworks fail to anticipate or explain (e.g., rare natural disasters, terrorism, and pandemics).

Ambiguous risks result from divergent or contested perspectives on the justification, severity, or wider meanings associated with a given threat (Renn and Walker 2008, 19). With ambiguous risks, there are two types of ambiguity: interpretative ambiguity, which stems from different interpretations of the same results (e.g., use of vaccines) and normative ambiguity, which stems from different beliefs about what risks are tolerable (e.g., nuclear power). For ambiguous risks, broad public consultation is important and solutions are usually provisional until more reliable data become available.

The IRGC has also developed the concept of emerging risk. The IRGC defines emerging risks as new risks, or familiar risks in a new, unfamiliar context or condition (e.g., global financial markets, infectious diseases). Emerging risks are potentially significant but may not be fully understood and assessed; thus, risk management options may not be developed with confidence. As we move from simple and complex risks to uncertain, ambiguous, and emerging risks – such as terrorism, rare natural disasters, and infectious diseases – the data become even more unreliable and contested. Figure 2.2 summarizes the four stages of risk assessment and highlights which stage is most important for a given type of risk. The original IRGC framework did not include emerging risks. This type of risk would have been treated in a similar manner as an ambiguous and uncertain risk.

The Precautionary Principle and Public Engagement

When addressing uncertain, ambiguous, and emerging risks, the IRGC framework recommends taking a precautionary approach, which is not without controversy. Precautionary approaches are potentially expensive, if not altogether contradictory (Sunstein 2005); there are risks if one acts, just as there are risks if one does not. Too often, advocates of the precautionary principle neglect to consider the trade-offs that exist in any risk management plan. Kheifets, Hester, and Banerjee (2001) found considerable variation in how the term *precautionary principle* is used and how the concept

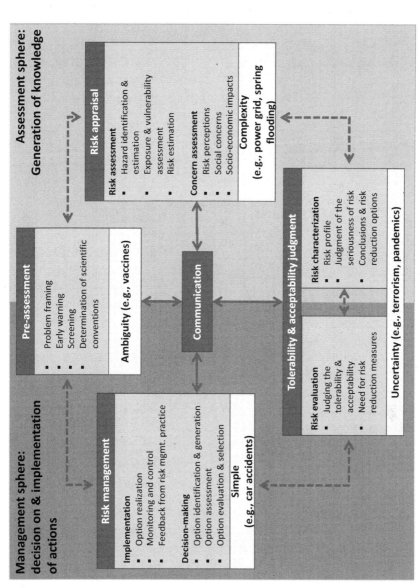

Figure 2.2 The International Risk Governance Council (IRGC) framework (Renn 2008; reproduced with the permission of Springer).

is put into practice. For example, the strength of evidence required to justify action under the precautionary principle varies. The principle may be adopted when there is: (1) "sufficient evidence" that an action or substance is harmful; (2) no conclusive scientific proof one way or the other; or (3) when the substance or action may possibly cause harm (Kheifets et al. 2001). The necessary action can also vary; definitions of the precautionary principle imply a wide range of actions that should be taken, once the strength of evidence requirement has been satisfied. These actions are: (1) prevention or elimination of exposure; (2) adoption of cost-effective action; or (3) mere consideration of action (Kheifets et al. 2001). And who bears the burden of proof? The opponents of a possibly harmful action? Or the proponents of a possibly harmful action (Kheifets et al. 2001)?

Emerging and uncertain risks, such as pandemics, pose particular challenges. While experts can offer a wide range of estimates, they may be unable to anticipate the reach of the risk and to predict with confidence what will be affected by failure. These types of risk create three vulnerabilities. First, our inability to quantify risk credibly gives rise to evaluative and cognitive conflicts among and between experts and stakeholders. Secondly, our imperfect knowledge of the risk can lead to mistakes, such as giving bad advice. Finally, our inability to predict outcomes reliably can result in surprises or shocks to the system. All three of these vulnerabilities can lead to media coverage that emphasizes conflict, guilt, blame, and disaster yet fails to contribute to a better understanding of the risk in question, as we will see in our H1N1 case study in chapter 9. This dynamic can lead to public anxiety and over- and under-reaction.

Indeed, as we consider uncertain, ambiguous, and emerging risks, stakeholder engagement becomes an important part of the risk governance process. With uncertain and emerging risks, policy-makers need to communicate their plans to the community. Public engagement helps to prepare people for volatility. With ambiguous risks, however, policy-makers need to recognize that there are legitimate alternative views. Public engagement helps to build a more robust solution that has broad-based support.

Commentators have raised questions about the extent to which the IRGC framework, in its effort to make the process more accessible, makes the process vulnerable to lobbying (Tait 2008). Moreover, despite the IRGC's goal of making information more available, in some cases, information remains confidential for market or security reasons. Finally, as with many process-oriented approaches to strategy, the IRGC process can be slow. To avoid certain risks, speed is crucial. In sum, for the IRGC framework to reach its full potential, we need to develop fair and efficient strategies for public engagement, including when certain aspects of the response to the risk must remain confidential and/or classified, and ways to adapt to volatile situations.

AN EVOLUTIONARY APPROACH TO RISK: THE KNOWLEDGE COMMONS

Thinking in terms of an evolutionary paradigm can help us to examine the concept of the knowledge commons. An evolutionary paradigm is more dynamic than the other two paradigms; events occur in real time and are interpreted retroactively. This paradigm is based on mutual adjustments and bargaining (it is polycentric). Rather than goal-seeking, this paradigm is ills-avoiding; it evolves away from constraints. The knowledge commons (Hess and Ostrom 2011) is a useful concept for discussing emergent trends in information sharing in a CI context. Within the knowledge commons, knowledge is seen as a shared resource in a complex ecosystem, which requires technical infrastructure and organizational processes to support information search, exchange, updates, storage, and transmission. Users of the knowledge commons update and revise community status profiles in dynamic environments. The knowledge commons captures the notion of better coordination through dynamic information exchange (Ostrom 2005; Hess and Ostrom 2011).

The emergency management field has adopted the knowledge commons and even updated its definition. In a paper examining the aftermath of and recovery from the 2010 earthquake in Haiti, Comfort et al. (2011) define the knowledge commons as a comprehensive, interactive, emergent system to support decision-making and organizational learning by communities in complex, changing environments. Comfort and Okada (2013) also explore the knowledge commons as a tool to assist public managers during extreme events. They note three important characteristics of leadership and communication in extreme events: (1) clear, timely communication between people/organizations; (2) leadership development in "small world"[3] networks of key actors who have specific knowledge, skills, and capacity to act in that specific event or region; and (3) leadership as a collective responsibility that shifts among knowledgeable actors depending on the requirements. Comfort and Okada (2013, 66) conclude that an extreme event "requires an information infrastructure to facilitate the search for, and exchange of, timely, valid information." A knowledge commons provides a powerful way of organizing information (and even a guiding principle) to aid management of extreme events. We now use the concept of knowledge commons to assess the effectiveness of public-sector networks and social media, which ostensibly embody the potential of knowledge commons.

Public-Sector Networks

Emergency management is becoming more knowledge based, complex, and divided among a host of public and private entities. Organizational agility and flexibility are more desirable than organizational size and scale. Studies show that high-end producers rely heavily on personal and organizational networks to learn new information and problem-solving techniques (Agranoff 2008). Agranoff defines public-sector networks (PSNs) as "formal and informal structures comprised of representatives from governmental and nongovernmental agencies working interdependently to jointly formulate and implement policies and programs, usually through their respective organizations" (2008, 322–3). PSNs may exchange information and technology, or they may formally adopt collaborative courses of action and delivery of services.

PSNs improve interagency collaborative processes by bringing administrators and specialists together. They focus on cross-agency problems and enhance multi-agency problem-solving. At their best, PSNs generate the following: new studies, data sets, and enhanced knowledge; efficiencies and increased funding opportunities; revised plans, policies, and programs; and spinoff projects and agreements that enhance network missions and overall public-sector capacity through knowledge mobilization activities. Agranoff (2008) argues that PSNs help overcome the tendency of bureaucracies to define problems narrowly. PSNs develop human capital and offer more complete solutions to complex, multi-agency problems.

Since 9/11 there have been simultaneous pulls towards and away from bureaucratization of security. There has been considerable growth in security-related networks among government departments, orders of governments, and CI owners and operators. PSN growth has been necessary because of dispersed CI ownership, responsibility, and interdependence between CI sectors. PSNs have achieved mixed success. Several constraints limit cooperation, including the need to determine who is accountable to whom and for what. Relatedly, it is difficult to measure and assess performance. There are also issues related to classified and proprietary information that limit information exchange. Bakvis and Juillet (2004) argue that public agencies cannot work completely outside of the bureaucratic form. Such horizontal endeavours require clear issue definition, designation of leads and partners, strong leadership from the centre, good partnerships with the broader policy community, realistic time frames, and dedicated resources. Arguably, PSNs also require momentum.

The United States and Canada responded to 9/11 by centralizing and expanding their safety and security bureaucracies. In response to 9/11, the US government created the Department of Homeland Security, which integrates twenty-two separate agencies; in Canada, the government created Public Safety Canada. Government attempts to integrate bureaucracy more effectively (as opposed to segment) also generate risks. Database integration enabled Chelsea Manning, a former US solider, to obtain enormous amounts of classified data, which she then shared with Julian Assange, the editor-in-chief at WikiLeaks. In short, secure information exchange is easier said than done, and at times it seems more aspirational than achievable. The challenges of information exchange are discussed further in chapter 3.

Social Media

Social media presents an opportunity to examine a much more fluid situation that can be co-constructed in real time by people inside and outside an organization. Social media is often characterized as fundamentally democratic (Loader and Mercea 2011). By reducing the entry costs to mass communication (Whelan, Golden, and Donnellan 2013), social media facilitates a dialogic and interactive dynamic (Schultz and Wehmeier 2010). Social media thus enables interest groups and activists to organize more effectively (Kietzmann et al. 2011). A prominent example is the Arab Spring uprisings that swept North Africa and the Middle East beginning in 2011. The early demonstrations in Egypt, in particular, underscore the "opportunities offered by social media for large-scale mobilization and the organization and implementation of social movements" (Eltantawy and Wiest 2011, 1218). In sum, social media disperses control over content, altering the relationship between traditional media, corporate and government institutions, and the broader public, and it enables new forms of collaborative, participatory interaction.

Information can also be shared quickly through social media. Today, content can spread rapidly "across individuals and communities, growing exponentially with each cycle" (Mills 2012, 163). There are already numerous examples of how social media is changing the way governments and CI operators gather and share information about risks. A study of Twitter use during the 2009–10 HINI flu pandemic indicates that Twitter can be used to "estimate disease activity in real time, i.e., 1–2 weeks faster than current practice allows" (Signorini, Segre, and Polgreen 2011, 7). Social media data can similarly serve as a sensor system for identifying and localizing earthquakes (Crooks et al. 2013) and may also facilitate the identification and tracking of food contamination and food terrorism incidents (Newkirk, Bender, and Hedberg 2012). Social media platforms have been used to enhance government response to several recent natural disasters, including Typhoon Morakot (Huang, Chan, and Hyder 2010), Hurricane Gustav (White et al. 2009), and the 2010 Haitian earthquake (Yates and Paquette 2011), although a study of Hurricane Sandy finds that residents relied on traditional media more than digital media for health and safety information (Burger et al. 2013).

The velocity at which information can be communicated creates opportunities to respond more quickly; however, social media fits awkwardly with traditional bureaucratic accountability. Governments operate under traditional models of accountability, where legislative and media scrutiny incentivizes conservative, risk-averse approaches to online public engagement (Clarke 2012). Accountability considerations also contribute to lengthy, onerous approval processes for proposed online content, limiting the ability of public servants to participate in real-time digital conversations (Schein, Wilson, and Keelan 2010). As Roy (2012, 256) emphasizes, governments have yet to achieve innovation that alters the "execution of democratic accountability in manners that align with the potential of an online and more participative ethos."

Rules and regulations sometimes prevent public servants from participating in online discussions. This potentially marginalizes government and the vacuum it leaves is filled by others. For example, during the 2007 California wildfires, "when people felt that officials were not providing enough information, social media was used extensively to track the location of the fires and notify citizens if their neighbourhood was in danger" (Veil, Buehner, and Palenchar 2011, 115). Increasingly, initial disaster reports come from citizens who happen to be nearby: bystanders tweeted the first images of US Airways Flight 1549 floating in the Hudson River (Hannah 2009). Social media can also empower malicious actors: perpetrators of the 2008 attacks in Mumbai used Twitter posts and live media coverage to identify and locate potential victims (Oh, Agrawal, and Rao 2011).

Although social media makes some types of risk information more readily available, it is unclear if social media is changing how we think about risk and regulation. Twitter, for example, remains a tool for discovering news and opinions from other platforms, rather than a replacement for more comprehensive news coverage and commentary (Bruns, Highfield, and Lind 2012). A key determinant of online behaviour appears to be one's "real life" relationships. Social media is used primarily to maintain offline relationships, rather than to meet new people (Boyd and Ellison 2007; Zhang et al. 2009). Consequently, most social media linkages are shallow, characterized by an absence of serious discussion or exchange of ideas. As Huberman, Romero, and Wu (2008, 8) find in their study of Twitter, "a link between two people does not necessarily imply an interaction between them," and most Twitter links are "meaningless from an interaction point of view." Although there are claims that society is becoming less concerned about privacy, people are still concerned about privacy on certain subjects. For example, many people will not post information on symptoms of an illness they are experiencing on Facebook; it can be too personal and embarrassing.

Similarly, there is little evidence that social media participation has any effect on attitudes beyond reinforcing existing beliefs and opinions. A lot of research on social media focuses on its implications for politics, particularly election campaigns. Findings suggest that social media use is not correlated with perceived political efficacy or campaign interest (Ancu and Cozma 2009; Kushin and Yamamoto 2010) and that campaign organizers view mobilizing their existing supporter base – rather than persuading opponents – as the primary objective of online engagement (Conway, Kenski, and

Wang 2013; Vaccari 2008). According to Raynauld and Greenberg (2014, 418), people who use social media are increasingly turning to Twitter and other online services to "disseminate content and engage in social interaction activities that are compatible with their often narrow preferences and objectives, thus not necessarily of interest to other audience members who might have other concerns." Some non-governmental advocacy groups remain optimistic about social media's ability to promote civic engagement and spur collective action (Obar, Zube, and Lampe 2012); however, the literature suggests that most online interaction resembles a digital echo chamber.

In the context of risk perception, social media may amplify existing anxieties rather than facilitate measured discussion. In other words, rather than changing attitudes about the probability and consequence of risks, social media exacerbates existing risk assessments regardless of their accuracy. Several corporate crises, including the 2007 rat infestation of New York Taco Bell–KFC restaurants, rapidly escalated after videos were uploaded to YouTube, making them "seem more dramatic and alive" by morphing into "mini horror movies" (Mei, Bansal, and Pang 2010, 149). As Rutsaert and colleagues (2013, 88) emphasize, social media "has the potential to develop a seemingly small scale risk into a full-blown … crisis." González-Herrero and Smith (2008, 145) describe this as the "crisis facilitator" function of the Internet, in which the Internet functions "as an agent that accelerates the crises news cycle and breaks geographic boundaries." Coombs and Holladay (2012, 409) further argue that social media has given rise to a new form of crisis, the "paracrisis," which is "a publicly visible crisis threat that charges an organization with irresponsible or unethical behavior."

For CI operators and regulators, social media enhances the disruptive effect of public opinion. When a crisis occurs, information can spread almost instantaneously to enormous audiences. The tenor and content of the resulting dialogue is beyond the control of government and corporate institutions; therefore, other actors can shape the conversation in unflattering or harmful ways. For example, within a week of the Deepwater Horizon disaster, an anonymous, satirical Twitter account, @BPGlobalPR, had accumulated more than 400 times as many followers as the official British Petroleum Twitter feed (Veil et al. 2011). Because of its accessibility, social media and Internet content also has greater permanence than traditional media coverage. Companies cannot remove negative content from the Internet; the web "perpetuates bad news" (González-Herrero and Smith 2008, 151).

Crisis managers must now engage with social media when responding to emergencies. Failure to do so can make companies and governments seem out of touch, insensitive, or unprepared. Increasingly, citizens expect to receive information from, and interact with, emergency responders on social media. Yet maintaining an active presence on social media is not enough – that presence must also be perceived as authentic and accurate. When successful, organizations can use social media to "signal concern with their stakeholders" (Utz, Schultz, and Glocka 2013, 41) and help achieve "the social deconstruction of crises" (Schultz, Utz, and Göritz 2011, 20). At the same time, emergency management professionals must continue to keep in mind traditional media. Research indicates that traditional news sources remain trusted by large segments of the population, often lending offline credibility to crises generated on social media (Pang, Chiong, and Abul Hassan 2014). Even on social media, users are more likely to share a newspaper article than a blog or tweet linking to that article (Schultz et al. 2011). CI operators and regulators are faced with a new and increasingly complex communications environment, in which social media can rapidly magnify public concern for both perceived and actual crises. In this new era, the latent disruptive potential of public opinion continues to grow, underlining with increasing urgency the old axiom that the best way to manage a crisis is to prevent it (Pang et al. 2014, 284).

A RATIONAL APPROACH TO RISK:
THE RISK REGULATION REGIME FRAMEWORK

This framework explains risk regulation according to competing rationales. In their study of risk regulation in the United Kingdom, Hood and colleagues use the concept of regimes to explore different policy areas[4] (Hood et al. 2001, 5). They define regimes as "the complex of institutional geography, rules, practice and animating ideas that are associated with the regulation of a particular risk or hazard" (2001, 9). This broad definition allows for flexibility as Hood and colleagues read across various policy contexts while drawing together a variety of institutional perspectives to understand what shapes risk regulation.

Hood and colleagues hypothesize that context shapes the manner in which risk is regulated, or, as they put it, "context shapes content." *Regime context* refers to the backdrop of regulation. There are three characteristics that Hood and colleagues use to explore context: (1) the technical nature of the risk, (2) the public's and media's opinions about the risk, and (3) the way power and influence are concentrated in organized groups in the regime. These three elements are commonly employed explanations in the public policy literature and can be related, to some extent, to a normative theory of regulation as well as to a positive one (Hood et al. 2001, 61).

Hood and colleagues derive three separate (but overlapping) hypotheses from these three elements. The first hypothesis, the market failure hypothesis, examines the government's intervention as a necessary one given the technical nature of the risk and the inability of the market to manage the risk effectively without such intervention. The second hypothesis, the opinion-responsive hypothesis, examines media coverage and polling data and assesses the extent to which risk regulation is a response to the preferences of civil society. The third hypothesis, the interest group hypothesis, examines the role of organized groups in shaping the manner in which a risk is regulated in the industry.

Hood and colleagues use these three hypotheses to determine the extent to which each context explains the risk regulation content. *Regulation content* refers to the policy settings, the configuration of state and other organizations directly engaged in regulating the risk, and the attitudes, beliefs, and operating conventions of the regulators (Hood et al. 2001, 21). Each of the three critical elements of regime content is characterized further through the three elements of a cybernetic control system – information gathering, standard setting, and behaviour modification (figure 2.3). In this sense, control means the ability to keep the state of a system within some preferred subset of all its possible states. If any of the three components is absent, a system is not under control in a cybernetic sense (Hood et al. 2001, 23–5). We will discuss each of the components in turn.

Information gathering is the capacity to obtain data that can be used to shape regime content. Information may be gathered actively or passively, from outside or within the system (Hood et al. 2001, 22). Standard setting involves establishing goals, or guidelines; in government, standards often take the form of policy. Finally, behaviour modification refers to the preferences, incentive structures,

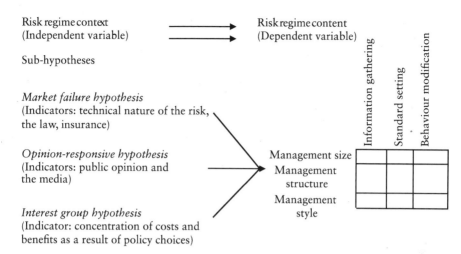

Figure 2.3 Understanding risk regulation regimes.
Source: Hood, Rothstein, and Baldwin (2001).

beliefs, and attitudes that shape systems – the capacity to modify behaviour of participants is the capacity to change systems. The distinction between these dimensions is not always tidy; Hood and colleagues (2001, 21) note, for instance, that information gathering might influence behaviour if people know they are being watched. Each dimension of control may be further considered according to size (the amount and scope of regulation and the resources used to sustain it), structure (the institutional arrangements of regime content, such as public–private sector relationships), and style (the formal and informal codes and conventions that help shape regime content) (Hood et al. 2001, 30–2).

In this book, we will first describe and analyze the management size, structure, and style of information gathering, standard setting, and behaviour modification, essentially populating the right-hand side of figure 2.3 for the transportation sector (chapter 4) and the chemicals sector (chapter 5). Secondly, we will explore the context that influences the control mechanism through three specific lenses, captured by the left-hand side of the table: the market failure context, which might be considered the benchmark or textbook case that charts appropriate government intervention in markets in liberal democratic societies (chapter 6); the broader social context as expressed through public opinion polls and popular media context (chapters 7, 8, and 9); and the organizational context, as expressed through organized groups and lobbyists (chapter 10) and organizational culture (chapter 11). Each of the chapters that explore context will endeavour to answer this question: To what extent can the particular sub-hypothesis being tested explain the risk regulation regime?

The approach of Hood and colleagues' risk regulation regime aligns most closely with a rationalist paradigm. The framework is underpinned by the assumption that there is a rationale for the control mechanism, be it market failure, public opinion, or the influence of organized interests. The framework is also multidisciplinary; it incorporates economics (market failure), social psychology (opinion-responsive), and political science (interests) into its analysis. The cybernetic control method itself (information gathering, standard setting, and behaviour modification) represents a logical categorization of different aspects of control. The style category in the control mechanism incorporates another discipline, anthropology, in its examination of organizational culture.

The basic definition of regimes comes from Krasner's (1983) work; he defines them as a set of explicit or implicit "principles, norms, rules, and decision making procedures around which actor expectations converge in a given issue-area" (185). Two streams of analysis dominate the study of regime formation, that of the utilitarians or liberals and that of the realists (Young 1989). The utilitarians focus on the behaviour of rational utility maximizers. The assumption is that rational actors will reach agreements that are mutually beneficial whenever there is a zone of agreement between the actors. Keohane and Martin (1995) argue that regimes can increase the probability of cooperation by monitoring the behaviour of members and reporting on compliance, reducing transaction costs, and generating the expectation of cooperation among members.

Coming from political science, the realists examine the distribution of power in society as a determinant in understanding collective outcomes. In this stream, the models assume that regimes reflect the configuration of power in the relevant social system. Alter and Meunier (2009) note a growing phenomenon of nested, partially overlapping, and parallel regimes that are not hierarchically ordered. They refer to this as "international regime complexity." A feature that distinguishes international regimes from domestic regimes is the lack of hierarchy within the international regimes – it is more difficult to resolve where political authority resides in the international context. Many scholars have noted that international cooperation can be thought of as a complex system (Young 1996; Aggarwal 1998; Evans, Jacobson, and Putnam 1993).

Alter and Meunier (2009) also note that there are few theories available to guide scholars in thinking about the consequences of this complexity. Scholars tend to focus on the causes of international regime complexity not the consequences. In their analysis of the regime complexity of climate change, for example, Keohane and Victor (2011) explore the idea of a continuum of regimes with comprehensive international regulatory institutions at one end and highly fragmented arrangements at the other. In between the two ends of the spectrum are nested regimes and regime complexes, which are loosely coupled sets of specific regimes. They argue that in areas of structural and interest diversity, such as climate change, policymakers should focus on a strategy of managing a regime complex. They suggest that in areas of high uncertainty and policy flux, activities that are more focused and decentralized will have a larger impact.

Our research, including analysis of the interview transcripts, is structured according to Hood and colleagues' (2001) meso-level risk regulation regime framework. The framework does not include some potentially important contextual influences, such as history (path dependence), ideology, and geography, all of which play a role in risk regulation and critical infrastructure protection, though arguably these concepts can be accommodated by the framework.

Typical of regimes analysis, as Alter and Meunier note, Hood and colleagues' framework is a positive one, not a normative one. In this sense it helps us to see what is happening as opposed to what we would like to see happening. The framework is perhaps less successful at telling us what prompts the regime to change and how one might do it. Black swans can be a disruptive moment for a regime; arguably, they create an opportunity for increased influence of the opinion-responsive hypothesis as members of civil society become much more aware of the vulnerabilities of a system following a disaster.

Unlike the models outlined above, the regimes approach brings power into the centre of the analysis. With perhaps the exception of game theory, the political science literature has contributed little to the risk debate. Ironically, Hood and colleagues conclude that the interest group hypothesis is the most persuasive of the three hypotheses. Hood and colleagues' framework allows us to see a variety of regulatory arrangements at play in different sectors. Bridges, for example, are largely regulated at the regional level while airports and seaports are regulated globally. The framework allows us to see how regulatory complexity, including the number of interested parties, influences the regime in anticipation of and in response to black swans. We will also see the wide range of loosely connected and variously ordered regimes, as in the chemicals sector, whose power dynamics influence other smaller sectors, such as the water sector and emergency services. The framework also brings attention to the negotiations that occur between these regimes in a regulatory space in which the risk and the authority are not always clear. Most of the sectors we examined are regulated by a number of orders of government, from the sub- to the supra-national. Moreover, over the last several decades we have seen a rise in non-governmental organizations and the environmental movement; even if they are not in formal authority, their increased legitimacy has changed the configuration of boards that oversee safety practices in the chemicals sector, for example. What is less clear is how these regimes have accommodated the security community in a post-9/11 world.

CONCLUSION

We have presented three frameworks, each of which provides powerful means to analyze and respond to risk issues. The IRGC framework helps distinguish between types of risk. As a starting point, it is useful to think about our state of knowledge of a particular risk and how this state of knowledge can influence the process and the actors with whom we engage. The IRGC framework emphasizes learning and negotiation, particularly with ambiguous risks. The framework's focus on engagement makes it susceptible to lobbying; the framework is unclear, however, about how to limit the influence of those with knowledge, funding, organizational capacity, and access. Also, despite its emphasis on learning, the IRGC process is vulnerable if a risk is suddenly reframed, which can be the case in disasters. The IRGC framework assumes a degree of stability; reframing is a challenge for it.

The knowledge commons, on the other hand, is less vulnerable to sudden risk reframing. While it may struggle with standards, formal leadership, and deep learning, the knowledge commons engages more seriously with adaptive capacity to exploit emerging social technologies and to develop a more resilient system. The knowledge commons conceives of a highly dynamic environment in which little is assumed and much is in flux. Neither the IRGC framework, nor the risk regulation regime framework, inspires us when we consider the importance of adaptive capacity, which is crucial to the study of black swans. However, the knowledge commons does not manifest itself perfectly through public-sector networks or social media. As we saw in chapter 2, public agencies continue to exist in a bureaucratic framework that constrains the free flow of information. Social media can facilitate the quick exchange of information but struggles to develop, maintain, and enforce standards and behaviour change. It is not always clear that these information exchanges serve the public good. In this sense, the model is nascent.

Indeed, as we will see in chapter 3, the world of CI is fixated on information exchange. The risk regulation regime framework underscores the fact, however, that without standards and behaviour change, the system remains out of control. Our research suggests that behaviour change is particularly difficult to achieve. In addition to capturing the full spectrum of cybernetics, the risk regulation regime framework captures organizational culture and its implications for implementation, which the other frameworks emphasize less. The concept of context, also, is a particularly strong feature of the risk regulation regime framework. The IRGC and the knowledge commons are perhaps less attentive to the role of interests; they both assume a degree of goodwill, which may not be present, particularly when considering the consequences of failure and who gets blamed. As we will see in chapter 10, ignoring the role of interest groups overlooks a contextual factor that is critical in understanding risk regulation.

3

Government and
Critical Infrastructure Protection:
Relevant but Not Responsible

Most – though not all – critical infrastructure (CI) in Canada is owned and operated by the private sector. Canadian governments, like many other Western governments, seek to work closely with the private sector to overcome vulnerabilities. In 2008 the federal, provincial, and territorial governments published *Working towards a National Strategy and Action Plan for Critical Infrastructure* (Public Safety Canada 2008), which articulated a policy framework to enable governments as well as public and private CI owners and CI operators to collaborate on critical infrastructure protection (CIP). Public Safety Canada has since published a *National Strategy for Critical Infrastructure* (2009b) and an *Action Plan for Critical Infrastructure* (2009a, updated in 2014) (NS&AP). Operationalizing a national strategy for CI requires the development of sector-level fora and mechanisms by which to share information on CI vulnerabilities and determine how best to address them. The government has identified ten critical sectors (see below); each sector will have a forum comprising industry and government representatives.

This chapter reviews the government's CI strategy and action plan. The initiative emphasizes trust building, collaborative risk management, and information sharing. We argue that government seeks to be relevant but not responsible. Government's effort to create a space for sensitive information exchange between governments and CI owners and operators is limited by the dynamics of market competition, constitutional, legal, logistical, and institutional constraints. The strategies themselves are focused on large public organizations and large private businesses. There is very little public reporting by which to monitor performance or improvement.

Audits typically show uneven and often slow progress on even some of the most basic measures that are publicly available.

Government's role in operationalizing these strategies has been one of facilitator rather than enforcer. Despite considerable emphasis on information exchange and trust building, both of these concepts are highly ambiguous in the government's published documents. While government may wish to develop communities of practice, there are considerable ethical, legal, operational, and political liabilities that come with learning about the vulnerabilities of CI. Government wants to create opportunities for improvement and nudge organizations in the direction of developing more resilient infrastructure, but it does not want to take responsibility for CI, nor does it wish to undermine the market dynamics of many of the sectors. Government aims to develop trust with CI owners and operators partly by protecting their information from public scrutiny; in this sense, its understanding of trust is narrow and will perpetually constrain the possibility of developing trustworthiness in a democratic context.

EMERGENCY MANAGEMENT AND GOVERNANCE

The institutional arrangements that oversee and support safety and security at the federal level have undergone significant changes over time. National emergency response was a shared responsibility of the Privy Council Office (PCO) and the Department of Defence (Juillet and Koji 2013). Federal and provincial responsibilities for emergency management overlapped, so the governments established a federal–provincial framework captured in the Emergencies Act. One example of how the federal government assists provinces responding to emergencies is the Disaster Financial Assistance Arrangements. Following 9/11, the US government integrated safety and security under the Department of Homeland Security, and the Canadian government followed that lead by integrating a number of safety and security functions in the public safety portfolio. This portfolio has a lead deputy minister, an associate deputy minister, and the department of public safety, which oversees CI policy and includes a number of safety- and security-related agencies, such as the Canadian Security Intelligence Service (CSIS), the Royal Canadian Mounted Police (RCMP), and the Canada Border Services Agency. While Australia and the United Kingdom did not create centralized departments for safety and security, Canada's response was practical given the coordination required with the United States. The United States leads joint training with agencies of the Canadian government; the two governments have numerous agreements, including the Border Initiative, and institutional arrangements that facilitate research and information exchange. During President Barack Obama's first trip to Canada, Prime Minister Stephen Harper noted that a security threat to the United States is a security threat to Canada (Obama 2010). Arguably, the biggest threat to Canada is not terrorism or natural disasters but rather loss of access to the American market. As a result there will always be pressure to coordinate with the American government.

While one might describe Public Safety Canada as Canada's response to the Department of Homeland Security, these two organizations have emerged from different social and political contexts. Following 9/11, security was the top political issue in the United States, which drove a number of policy and funding initiatives. Canada, on the other hand, was not the target of terrorists; increases to its safety and security budget were much more constrained. Public Safety Canada emphasizes safety over security, as its name suggests. It has adopted an all-hazards approach, as opposed to an acute focus on security. The United States has for decades had a stronger emergency management function at the federal level than Canada; while the US Federal Emergency Management Agency has had its ups and downs, the government of Canada has little by way of central coordination of emergency response. Indeed, even as late as 2012 and despite the rhetoric of increased concern over safety and security, the government cancelled the Joint Emergency Preparedness Program established in 1980 and ceased operation of the Canadian Emergency Management College, which had offered training to emergency responders since 1954 (Cohen 2012).

Generally, Canadians are less concerned than Americans about security. Immediately following 9/11, about twenty per cent of Canadians believed the fight against terrorism should be a priority for the government (see chapter 7). By 2003, this number had dropped to under five per cent and for the most part has remained at that level; for Canadians, health care and the economy rank much higher as concerns. In the United States, in contrast, more than seventy per cent of Americans consider security to be a high priority for government (Gallup 2014). Relatedly, Canadians are not as personally connected to security issues. In the United States, one in four

American men has served in the military (Newport 2012); in Canada, fewer than one per cent have served (Veterans Affairs n.d.). Whereas almost all Americans are aware of the Department of Homeland Security,[1] it is doubtful that most Canadians even know that Public Safety Canada exists (Dimock, Doherty, and Gewurz 2013). This low profile seems to be intentional.

Public Safety Canada got off to a poor start and seemed ill equipped to lead a discussion about safety and security in Canada (Rudner 2009). The public safety portfolio is an amalgam of strong organizations with long histories and slightly different (and sometimes competing) mandates, which undermines cooperation. Many of the executive positions were left unfilled for extended periods and budget allocations went unspent (Chung 2009). At times, the portfolio can be an awkward integration. Many public servants in Public Safety Canada have liberal arts backgrounds rather than practical security or military experience, which can undermine their credibility in the eyes of many in the RCMP and CSIS. Security can be highly politicized and have a high profile, which draws ministers, the PCO, the Office of the Prime Minister, and the prime minister into the debate. Increased security concerns have allowed the RCMP and CSIS to argue successfully for more powers and funding (Payton 2015), which arguably strengthens their position vis-à-vis Public Safety Canada.

Public Safety Canada manages CI safety and security at a time when trust in the public service, by industry and elected officials, is low. During the 1980s and 1990s, there was optimism that markets (e.g., competition and price signals) were the most efficient way to provide services; privatization could reduce public service waste and improve efficiency. A vast amount of privatization followed (see appendix 4). Although it was not as extensive as in Australia and the United Kingdom, much of the privatization in Canada was considered a success.

Privatization, outsourcing, and downsizing have important implications for CI. First, much of Canada's CI is privately owned; therefore, to protect CI, the government must engage with CI owners. Secondly, the new public management (NPM) reforms of the 1980s and 1990s led to the belief that private markets are better than governments at providing services to their customers; regulators should intervene as little as possible. As a result of NPM, government agencies have focused on collecting and disseminating information, with voluntary participation from the private sector. Information sharing is a light-touch form of regulation. It also allows government agencies to deftly sidestep responsibility should a CI failure occur. Finally, government downsizing limits the capacity of the public service to build up expertise and challenge industry.

The federal government has formal authority over national emergencies. This authority flows from the federal government's constitutional responsibility for peace, order, and good government; however, provinces are also responsible for emergency response because of their constitutional responsibility for property, civil rights, health care, and local matters (Juillet and Koji 2013, 36). Rudner (2009) argues that the federal government has failed to provide strong leadership on CI and emergency management. At the provincial and municipal levels, Canada's approach to emergency management has evolved in a decentralized fashion (Henstra 2011). Sometimes emergency response at the provincial and municipal levels is formalized through memorandums of understanding, for example, but often the stakeholder relationships are informal and have a largely regional perspective. Many provinces probably have more advanced CI and emergency management plans than the federal government does.

The relative success of the provinces in CIP and emergency management planning is somewhat surprising. Emergency management offices (EMOs) are the central coordinators during an emergency and tend to be small and underfunded (Independent Task Force Sponsored by the Council on Foreign Relations 2003; Cohen 2012; Standing Senate Committee on National Security and Defence 2008). EMOs also tend to be far from the spotlight until there is an emergency and then suddenly they are thrust to centre stage. While they may be able to coordinate a response to an emergency, they often lack expertise on the specifics of any one CI failure. Part of the provinces' success can be attributed to practice. Just like politics, disasters are local and, while rare, some form of crisis usually occurs every year. This compels the provinces to coordinate with municipalities and CI owners and operators. Unlike the popular view of Public Safety Canada, many EMO staff members have backgrounds in the military, policing, or emergency services. EMOs have joint operations facilities. Disasters are often natural events, such as floods, not industrial failures or terrorist attacks. As we will discuss in chapter 7, media coverage of first responders and emergency services tends to be positive during natural disasters; "acts of God" are framed as nobody's fault and therefore EMOS (and government as a whole) often escape criticism or intense scrutiny.

Municipalities largely remain excluded from the federal–provincial dynamic. Juillet and Koji (2013) argue that a path dependency model of traditional federal–provincial dynamics has kept the municipalities out of the negotiations, which has rendered emergency management in Canada less effective (Juillet and Koji 2013, 58).

While most CI in Western countries (e.g., telecoms, banking, and power) is privately owned and operated, ownership arrangements are complex in many sectors; industry and government can sometimes be entangled. Patterns of infrastructure ownership varied across the subsectors we studied. Transportation provides a salient example. The largest seaports and airports are owned by the federal government but managed via a lease, concession, or corporatized commercial entity; smaller facilities may be owned by other orders of government or private companies. In trucking, vehicle ownership is private and fragmented, while most of the infrastructure (both roads and bridges) is owned and maintained by government (there are some private roads and bridges). As for rail, the railroads are privately owned, but in some cases there are running rights held by public companies like VIA or private cargo owners.

A market context does not always lend itself to proactive risk management. Corporate executives and their shareholders – sensitive to market pressures and shrinking margins – are sometimes reluctant to spend money on risk management because its benefits are often indeterminate. Typically, industries exposed to market competition invest in minimizing the risks of operational failures that they are unwilling to tolerate but accept some level of risk. If their gamble fails and they are forced to take their systems offline because of some unexpected problem, then the market will punish them accordingly. Indeed, share values typically tumble after disasters (Capelle-Blancard and Laguna 2010; Carpentier, L'Her, and Suret 2013). Organizations that manage CI are dealing not only with critical social and economic assets but also with assets that are increasingly interdependent. As a result, individual decisions to underspend on risk management pose a risk to the entire infrastructure sector and all those who depend on it. This underspending constitutes a market failure to which government must respond.

THE NATIONAL STRATEGY AND ACTION PLAN
FOR CRITICAL INFRASTRUCTURE

The purpose of the NS&AP is "to build a safer, more secure and more *resilient* Canada" (Public Safety Canada 2009b, 2; emphasis added) by encouraging more cooperation and pre-event information sharing among governments and CI owners and operators. As noted in chapter 2, the term resilience is used in many fields – engineering, psychology, and sociology – and typically refers to an object's, a person's, a community's, or a system's capacity to recover after a shock or respond to and evolve away from a constraint (see, for example, Roe and Schulman 2008; Masten 2009). The NS&AP defines CI as the essential underlying systems and facilities upon which the health, safety, security, and economic well-being of Canadians – and the effective functioning of government – rely. It notes: "Disruptions of this critical infrastructure could result in catastrophic loss of life, adverse economic effects and significant harm to public confidence" (Public Safety Canada 2009b, 2). The NS&AP reflects a macroscopic approach to CIP, suggesting that a common CIP strategy will enhance the resiliency of CI; a common approach will enable partners to respond collectively to risks and target resources to the most vulnerable areas of CI. At the same time, it leaves some flexibility at the sector level.

Sector-Level Fora and Audits from the Auditor General

The NS&AP has three strategic objectives (Public Safety Canada 2009b, 3): (1) to build partnerships, (2) to implement an *all-hazards* risk management approach, and (3) to advance the timely sharing and protection of information among partners. To support these three objectives, governments aim to develop a level of consistency across key sectors, as well as information-sharing tools and delivery mechanisms (such as secure websites). The centrepiece of the NS&AP is the creation of sector networks – one for each of the ten sectors deemed critical to the national infrastructure. Network membership will derive from relevant federal departments and agencies, provinces, territories, national associations, and key members of the private and public sectors. Participation will be voluntary and largely self-funded. Importantly, individual stakeholders will be responsible for implementing a risk management approach that they believe is

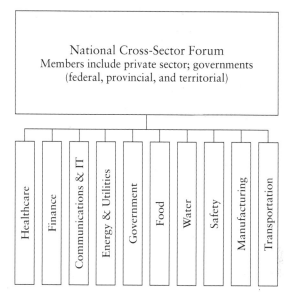

Figure 3.1 National Cross-Sector Forum. Membership includes representatives from the private sector and the federal, provincial, and territorial governments. *Source*: Public Safety Canada (2014).

appropriate for their situation (Public Safety Canada 2009b, 6). In addition, the NS&AP proposes a national cross-sector forum. Figure 3.1 depicts this arrangement.

When the Auditor General of Canada criticized the Canadian government's weak performance in CIP and emergency response, she observed that the NS&AP had been ready for months but had failed to receive cabinet approval. With a few exceptions (i.e., energy, utilities, and transportation), the 2009 audit reported that the departments representing each of the ten CI sectors showed little progress in operationalizing their emergency management plans (Auditor General of Canada 2009). Figure 3.2 identifies the number of milestones that, out of a total of thirty-seven, each sector had reached at the time of the audit.

One discernible trend (other than slow progress) is the distinction between sectors that have experienced infrastructure failures at a transnational level and those that have not. Transportation (e.g., Air India Flight 182, Swissair Flight 111, 9/11, the 2005 London Underground bombings, and the 2004 Madrid train bombings) and

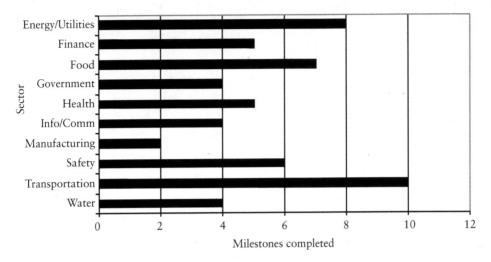

Figure 3.2 Progress of critical infrastructure sectors in implementing their emergency management plans (score out of a possible 37).
Source: Office of the Auditor General (2009), adapted in Quigley (2013).

energy/utilities (e.g., the 2003 Northeast blackout) have made the most progress. There is also considerable interdependence between Canada and the United States in these two sectors.

A flurry of activity ensued from this highly critical audit, including the speedy passage of the NS&AP and the publication of the following documents: the *Canada–United States Action Plan for Critical Infrastructure* (Department of Homeland Security and Public Safety Canada 2010), *Canada's Cyber Security Strategy* (Government of Canada 2010a), *Building Resilience against Terrorism: Canada's Counter-Terrorism Strategy* (Government of Canada 2012), the *Public Report on the Terrorist Threat to Canada* (Public Safety Canada 2013), and the *Action Plan for Critical Infrastructure: 2014–2017* (Public Safety Canada 2014a). Despite the publication of strategy documents, progress has been uneven. In 2012, the Auditor General returned to the subject of security and CI. The 2012 audit was particularly critical of the government's approach to cybersecurity, noting the confusion over the role, profile, and importance of the Canadian Cyber Incident Response Centre (Auditor General of Canada 2012b). While the Auditor General recognized some progress on CIP, particularly in issuing strategy documents and improving communication between government and select CI sectors, he remarked: "Based on Public Safety Canada's monitoring, we found that limited progress had been achieved and that the sector networks are at various stages of maturity. All 10 networks have sector risk profiles and lead departments identified, but 6 did not include representatives from all the industry groups that Public Safety Canada identified as key stakeholders" (Auditor General of Canada 2012b). Despite efforts to develop sector networks, problems persist in participation and engagement.

Provincial Infrastructure Audits

It is unclear precisely how much progress Canadian provinces have made in implementing the NS&AP. Little information about provinces' plans to incorporate changes to their infrastructure strategies is available to the public, and comparisons of improvements to CIP initiatives like that highlighted in figure 3.2 are not possible within or between provinces, given the amount of information currently available. A few provinces have conducted audits of specific aspects of their infrastructure plans in recent years, providing snapshots of their preparedness (or lack thereof) in select areas of CI planning.

Some of these audits have focused on potential emergencies. In 2014, for example, the Auditor General of British Columbia released a report on the province's earthquake preparedness. The report, which found that the province was not ready for a catastrophic earthquake, noted in particular that the province did not have a detailed inventory of critical provincial infrastructure and that its emergency management plan did not include appendices specific to CI needs (Auditor General of British Columbia 2014). Other provinces have conducted incident-specific audits of their infrastructure, as Alberta did following both the 2011 Slave Lake and 2016 Fort McMurray wildfires. The Slave Lake audit repeatedly noted the crucial role that CI had played both during and after the fire, where failed water infrastructure posed a threat to the community's health and safety (KPMG 2012) and where a lack of contingency plans for housing infrastructure left many community members scrambling for shelter during the fire (KPMG 2012). The Auditor General of Manitoba released an audit specific to bridges in the province, noting that almost a third had not been inspected properly (Auditor General of Manitoba 2016). Nova Scotia has been the only province to conduct and release a full audit of the province's progress in implementing the national strategy; in 2016 the Auditor General of the province concluded that there were no tangible plans in place to implement Nova Scotia's infrastructure goals (Auditor General of Nova Scotia 2016).

In one province, Newfoundland and Labrador, the auditor attempted a planned audit of the province's $5 billion infrastructure strategy as well as a review of the Canada–Newfoundland and Labrador Offshore Petroleum Board. The audit could not be completed because the Auditor General was denied access to the province's infrastructure plans and related documents. Key government departments claimed that the documents, which had been released to the auditor in the past, would compromise confidential cabinet decisions. In his 2011 report, the Auditor General noted that his only recourse was to report departments for their refusal to provide key information to the House of Assembly (Auditor General of Newfoundland and Labrador 2011).

In each instance, provincial audits were able to identify key areas in which CI planning had failed in some way, whether in relation to emergency events or broader CI planning. Only the Nova Scotian audit addressed the province's commitments to the national strategy and its conclusions did not provide any reassurances. The audits as a whole provide snapshots of problems in infrastructure planning throughout the country, identifying areas in which initiatives like the national strategy could improve the safety and security of CI projects. Comparisons between jurisdictions, however, are difficult. The audits were conducted largely after emergency events or in response to public concerns about natural disasters; they do not provide consistent benchmarks by which to compare jurisdictions.

Regional Resiliency Assessment Programs

Regional resiliency assessment programs (RRAPS) were developed in the United States and are used by the Department of Homeland Security. They include, among other things, audits that typically provide different scores in a variety of categories that indicate the resilience of an organization, a sector, or a region. There are four main indexes: the Protective Measures Index (PMI), the Resilience Measurement Index (RMI), the Consequences Measurement Index, and the Vulnerability Index.

The PMI, for instance, is meant to measure the ability of CI to resist disruptive events. It divides the evaluation into five categories: physical security, security management, security force, information sharing, and security activity history and background. PMIs take a number of variables and aggregate them per facility. Each facility receives scores from 0 to 100 based on its performance in a variety of categories. PMIs show how the facility's score compares with that of other facilities in the sector. The Department of Homeland Security has developed a dashboard that allows users to add proposed changes to their facilities and see an updated PMI score in real time. RMI, in contrast, measures the resilience of CI, including mitigation measures and response capabilities. RMI measures the ability of a facility or asset to anticipate, resist, absorb, respond to, adapt to, and recover from a disturbance. As for PMIs, data for RMIs are collected via a survey tool and are then used to give a facility an RMI score from 0 to 100. PMI reflects measures taken to safeguard a facility, whereas RMI takes into account natural resiliency, such as local geographic features that may make one site inherently more secure than another. PMI relies more on the interviewees' knowledge of an issue to inform its results and does not incorporate features that the RMI may, like the local economy, population, or environment.

RRAPs are intended to facilitate the exchange of information, communicate standards, and nudge people to improve performance while at the same time protecting individual facilities from having their vulnerabilities disclosed outside their organization. A report commissioned by the Department of Homeland Security notes that these tools have clear strengths, enabling users to compare their organization with others and to understand their organization's weakest CI protection points (Petit et al. 2013a, 2013b).

Public Safety Canada adopted the practice from the Department of Homeland Security. RRAPs represent a significant addition to Canada's Renewed Action Plan, which was updated in 2014. The plan notes: "The goal of the RRAP is to identify and analyze the resilience and interdependencies of critical infrastructure sectors using an all-hazards approach. The RRAP process involves site assessments, training, and exercises. Assessments can be conducted at the individual facility or regional (including cross-border) level. To conduct these assessments, Public Safety Canada will work with appropriate critical infrastructure stakeholders, including provinces/

territories, local authorities, and other partners, which will vary from assessment to assessment. Public Safety Canada will consult sector networks to determine the best areas of focus" (Public Safety Canada 2014a, 7).

The service is offered free of charge by Public Safety Canada, participation is voluntary, and results are not disclosed to anyone outside the organization. In other words, it sidesteps the issue of information being released that might embarrass an organization, benefit its competitors, empower those with ill intention, or scare away customers. The increased transparency at the organizational level – and the comparator data for the sector as a whole – allows managers to have difficult conversations within their organization about how to improve in areas in which they score poorly.

This strength (the fact that the results of the audit are not disclosed) is also a weakness. Despite the attention Public Safety Canada brings to RRAPs in its reports on plans and priorities (2015–16, 2016–17) and the departmental performance reports (2014–15), it is actually difficult to learn much about Public Safety Canada's progress in this area. Public Safety Canada does not publish a method or list the questions it asks in the RRAP audits. Indeed, we acknowledge that our assessment of RRAPs in Canada is somewhat speculative because of the limited public disclosure. Our exposure to the audit results has been limited to informal discussions and a review of a limited amount of online material in Canada and the United States. Neither Public Safety Canada nor the participating organization releases the results of the RRAP audits; even at a sectoral or regional level, we do not know the results. Public Safety Canada is not obligated to follow up with organizations that have undergone an audit, so there is no way to see if they improve over time. There is also no federal funding for infrastructure specifically tied to the results of RRAP audits, so unless an organization has the wherewithal to improve, it may not change much after the audit is complete. Also, RRAP audits frequently rely on the level of knowledge that the user completing the audit has about a given security area. As Petit and colleagues (2013b) point out, the indices and audits place relatively less emphasis on the evaluation of local security factors, whether they make CI easier or more difficult to secure.

There are other issues with the RRAPs. When there is only one organization involved, accountability is clearer; a committed organizational leader can bring about change following a RRAP audit. This

is more difficult at the regional or community level where a number
of organizations may share the responsibility for community resilience but could have different interests and means when it comes to
pursuing resiliency enhancements. The information-sharing component of the audits also seems underdeveloped. The survey asks, for
instance, if organizations share information with CSIS and the
RCMP but it does not ask participants to comment on the quality,
timeliness, and quantity of these exchanges.

Comparing one's organization with the average in one's sector
also raises issues. First, the reference to the average implies that
organizations should strive to at least come close to the average; it is
difficult to imagine that falling below the average would not at least
prompt questions. It is not clear, however, if the average is a good
benchmark when it comes to protecting ourselves against rare events.
Black swans are anomalies; if we follow the pack we will not necessarily be able to address unusual circumstances. Also, the average
score on its own does not reveal if the sector as a whole is doing well
or poorly. In this sense, these reports may give a false sense of security. In addition, in certain Canadian sectors take-up on the RRAP
audits will necessarily be slow because they are extensive evaluations and require a considerable amount of time and commitment.
As a result, when organizations in Canada receive reports about
how they compare with the average in their sector, to make up for
the absence of Canadian data, the indices can include data from US
organizations. This raises questions about whether it is appropriate
to ask Canadian CI owners/operators to meet an average that is
(overwhelmingly) influenced by American organizations that may
have different concerns about subjects, such as security.

Finally, the reports do not distinguish by size of the organization,
which tends to be a key variable in creating good resiliency practices; large organizations have more staff, expertise, and resources
to address risks. Should an airport in Vancouver be compared with
one in Fredericton? Should bridge infrastructure in Montreal be
compared with bridge infrastructure in a remote part of Northern
Ontario? What, if any, are the limitations of such a comparison?
Moreover, knowing the size of the organizations that have completed the audits may give us insight into the reliability of the data
vis-à-vis the sector as a whole. Larger organizations are more likely
to take resiliency practices more seriously. As a result, one wonders
if the organizations that have participated in the audits to date are

larger and likely to have better resiliency practices in place, which
could give a rosier picture of the sector than actually exists. The
absence of available information on the method, the participants,
the results, and reports on progress over time makes it difficult to
draw any meaningful conclusions.

Information-sharing Fora in the United States

The US approach to CIP has had a much wider scope. Since 9/11,
the United States has undergone significant institutional changes,
drawing twenty-three separate agencies together under the aegis
of the Department of Homeland Security and forming a number of
national and state-level organizations. The National Infrastructure
Protection Plan identifies seven main types of coordination structures for CI (Department of Homeland Security 2013a):

1 Sector Coordinating Councils
2 Critical Infrastructure Cross-Sector Council
3 Government Coordinating Councils
4 Federal Senior Leadership Council
5 State, Local, Tribal, and Territorial Government Coordinating
   Council
6 Regional Consortium Coordinating Council
7 Information Sharing Organizations

The Department of Homeland Security attempts to integrate the
security, intelligence, and law enforcement (SILE) community and
creates a vast network that connects all levels of government, as well
as the public with the private sector, and the government with the
SILE community.

The United States differs from Westminster countries in its interactions with the private sector. Australia, Canada, and the United
Kingdom are more likely to have the public and private sectors inter-
acting in CI sector groups. The US government has always been
suspicious of such interactions. As Vogel (1986) once noted in his
comparison of the United Kingdom and the United States, what the
senior civil servant in the United Kingdom considers to be his job,
the senior civil servant in the United States would consider illegal.
The United States tends to formalize interactions between the government and private sector and to distance itself from industry lest it

be accused of anti-trust violations. Sector Coordinating Councils, for example, are private-sector councils with voluntary membership that are "self-organized, self-run, and self-governed" (Department of Homeland Security 2013b). Information-sharing and analysis centers are similar. Arguably the public–private interactions on security are more difficult in the United States than in other countries.

Despite the number of security organizations in the United States, the US government has also struggled. The American Congress has criticized the Department of Homeland Security for its inability to provide performance metrics to demonstrate that investments in security are making Americans safer. For example, a 2012 Senate report on fusion centers[2] observed that personnel were insufficiently trained, there was inadequate physical security and limited capacity to share information at all levels of government, and there was inadequate connection between fusion centers and the Department of Homeland Security. Fusion centers also failed to have a strong physical and virtual presence (e.g., intelligence reports had never been filed). Many of the centers strayed from their original counterterrorism goal to a traditional anti-crime role. Success stories, presented by the Department of Homeland Security, demonstrated that fusion centers were able to thwart domestic crime but did not aid counterterrorism activities; in fact, fusion centers may have hindered national counterterrorism efforts, the Senate concluded, by circulating false information, causing embarrassment, potentially causing international crises, and making false accusations that discredit the centers as a whole (United States Senate Permanent Subcommittee on Investigations 2012). Finally, the Senate report noted that the close affiliation between fusion centers and state/local governments had shifted concerns away from national interests to state and local interests. Overall, the report concludes that fusion centers had not contributed to counterterrorism efforts and were largely ineffective.

INFORMATION SHARING

Information-sharing fora have been developed to deal with two negative consequences of information asymmetries: (1) disasters that could have been prevented had appropriate information been available, and (2) complications in disaster response because information is not available (Pfeifer 2012). In recent years, there has been increasing criticism about the lack of efficiency in existing information-sharing arrangements and some have begun to question "the validity of the entire cooperation concept" of government-led information-sharing networks (Dunn-Cavelty and Sutor 2009, 180).

Government reports and policy documents are often vague with respect to the specific activities encompassed by information sharing. Canada's renewed Action Plan for Critical Infrastructure, for example, refers to information sharing twenty-one times but does not provide much detail about what it entails, despite the NS&AP emphasizing that "partnerships and enhanced information sharing represent the building blocks of the Canadian approach to enhancing the resiliency of critical infrastructure" (Public Safety Canada 2009a). The renewed action plan does refer to the successful launch of Public Safety Canada's CI gateway but it fails to explain the measure by which the launch was successful: was it membership, online participation, or the useful and timely dissemination of information that resulted in successful CIP? The document is further complicated by the fact that it connects information sharing with successful risk management, an ambiguous concept as outlined in chapter 2, and the importance of protecting the information, which is seemingly a contradictory concept.

Despite all the interest in information sharing, the academic literature offers few definitions of the term in the context of CIP (Fleming and Goldstein 2012). Singh and colleagues (2009) focus on end users. They state the goal of information sharing networks as *information assurance*, namely "ensuring the right people get the right information at the right time." Much of the information-sharing literature is focused on articulating information quality or the "degree to which information meets the needs of its users" (Singh et al. 2009). Many authors articulate the various dimensions of *information quality*, which Singh and colleagues describe as timeliness, security, accessibility, completeness, accuracy, coherence, relevance, validity, and format. The importance of each dimension will depend on the type of network and the organization receiving the information (not the group disseminating it).

Fleming and Goldstein (2012) focus on reducing network uncertainty to improve decision-making. They describe information sharing as "the process through which information is provided by one entity to one or more other entities to facilitate decision-making under conditions of uncertainty." On the basis of this definition, Fleming and Goldstein establish several criteria for determining the success of information-sharing arrangements: information sharing should be goal directed, it should involve only actors who can support achievement of the goal, it should be used only for the purpose of achieving the goal, it should reduce uncertainty, and it should reflect the principle that information sharing cannot eliminate uncertainty (Fleming and Goldstein 2012).

Motives for information sharing are not always clearly addressed. Despite Singh and colleagues' emphasis on the end user, presumably governments provide information that satisfies government goals, not industry ones. Sometimes government and industry goals are misaligned. Fleming and Goldstein also struggle with motive. From a rational choice perspective – that is, assuming that actors in the CI policy space are rational utility maximizers – it is unclear whether the arrangement envisioned by Fleming and Goldstein can be achieved at all. According to Willis, Lester, and Treverton (2009), representatives from the private sector are concerned that if they share information, one of any of the following might occur: leaks of proprietary information to competitors, loss of customers or investors if vulnerabilities become public, legal implications of disclosure, and the risk that disclosure will result in new regulatory procedures.

In some cases, however, private-sector firms may accrue some marginal benefit from participating in information-sharing networks. An online platform for sharing risk information could allow firms to identify and mitigate risks before they occur. But even arrangements such as these, where all firms stand to benefit to some degree from information sharing, can become dysfunctional because of the imperatives of competition. As Aviram and Tor (2004b) emphasize, where there is potential for unequal benefits, firms will either refuse to participate or they will participate suboptimally to prevent competitors from realizing larger relative gains. Government agencies face similar impediments: although profit is not an issue, other factors such as organizational reputation and budget mean public-sector institutions may be reluctant to disclose information (see Dawes 1996).

Less problematic from the perspective of information sharing are fora for sharing generic best practices and facilitating interpersonal relationships among CI operators and regulators. As we emphasize in chapters 4 and 5, our interview participants often cited these types of fora as examples of successful information-sharing mechanisms. We received less evidence regarding the success of platforms for sharing detailed information about vulnerabilities. Governments' information-sharing capacity appears to be most effective when the information being shared is helpful but not particularly sensitive, and even innocuous. This general, non-specific approach to information sharing seems to be at odds with Singh and colleagues' and Fleming and Goldstein's respective definitions of information sharing, which emphasize specificity.

Since 9/11, the government of Canada has used legislation to increase its capacity to gather security-related information. The challenge, however, is not in simply obtaining sensitive information but in sharing it. Certain emergencies, such as pandemics, raise an immediate conflict between privacy rights and the public good. The NS&AP proposes focusing on government-to-government or government-to-business interactions. In addition to creating the sector fora, the Canadian government is attempting to facilitate the exchange of sensitive information among CI owners and operators through the Emergency Management Act (EMA). The EMA includes consequential amendments to the Access to Information Act that protect specific CI and emergency management information shared in confidence by third parties with the federal government (Public Safety Canada 2007, 9–10). This can help to reassure private-sector CI owners and operators that information deemed sensitive, either for commercial or liability reasons, will not be disclosed if they share it with the federal government.

The EMA does not fully address the issue of how to exchange sensitive information. Information exchange across sectors can be problematic because data from different sectors may be collected differently and therefore may be incompatible. Moreover, organizations must be able to secure data, which they often do by restricting access to individuals with the appropriate security clearance. Setting up a security clearance process requires time and resources and privileges larger organizations over smaller ones. The EMA also covers federal institutions only. The federal government cannot share confidential information provided by private organizations with its provincial counterparts unless the latter have similar legislation in place.

There is also an expectations gap between the private sector and the intelligence community about the utility of intelligence reports. At a June 2008 Conference Board of Canada CIP event, private-sector representatives said they found classified briefings vague (Quigley 2013). Successful information exchange has to be a two-way street: industry must be forthcoming about its vulnerabilities, and government must also share information with industry (Willis et al. 2009). Until now, government has been loath to do so. This is not necessarily the government's fault. Intelligence work is rarely clear-cut, even for specialists. There are often reams of data, which are only useful when analyzed and interpreted in local contexts and then placed in the broader context of national security (Willis et al. 2009). Much of the intelligence function is informed guesswork and information is therefore usually only shared with caution and caveats. Governments also have to be careful not to overshare information they receive from other governments, lest they lose the trust of their allies. Those in the private sector who go through government security clearance processes expecting a clear understanding of security at the end will probably be disappointed.

While many public servants feel they cannot share information because of legislative constraints, a study by Shore and Schafer (2015) observed that public servants could rarely point to existing legislative constraints to justify their anxiety. Shore and Schafer concluded that public servants were limited by cultural constraints. Incentive structures in the safety and security community do not lend themselves to sharing information, even among federal agencies. If one agency incurs all of the costs of gathering information and then shares the information with another government agency, the latter could claim credit for the outcome. The situation is further complicated by the fact that agencies may have different objectives. Intelligence agencies might wish to use sensitive information for building intelligence; policing and justice departments, in contrast, might wish to use information as evidence to prosecute suspected criminals. It would be difficult to use the information for both purposes simultaneously (Baker 2010). Competing goals potentially limit information sharing, as we saw with the RCMP and CSIS immediately before the Air India disaster (Government of Canada 2010b). There have been calls to declassify more information (Chertoff 2009), but it is unclear that government agencies are always motivated to do so. Among other factors, the fact that individuals have access to classified information validates and confirms their roles and status.

Ironically, despite governments' efforts to create an information-sharing infrastructure, it is unclear that one is always needed. Interviews with private-sector participants in information-sharing

networks in the United States indicate that many do not feel they
need to have access to more classified information sources (Willis et
al. 2009). Organizations believed that classified knowledge and
information often lacks usefulness to the organization because governments did not consider the organization's goals and responsibilities when sharing it. The private sector also shows little concern for
where or how information is obtained, provided that the intelligence
community is able to give reasonable assurance of the information's
credibility (Willis et al. 2009). An additional issue identified by Willis
and colleagues in their study of US information networks is that
senior executives (chief executive officers, chief financial officers,
chief information officers, members of boards of directors, etc.)
often lack the required security clearance and do not participate in
information-sharing fora, opting to delegate participation to an
employee who specializes in security. As a result, if security professionals have access to classified information they deem useful to the
organization they are often unable to share it with those who possess decision-making authority (Willis et al. 2009).

TRUST AND TRANSPARENCY

In working towards a national strategy for CI the first strategic
objective was to build *trusted and sustainable* partnerships (Public
Safety Canada 2008, 3; emphasis added). The words *trusted* and
sustainable were removed from the strategic objective in the final
version but the term *trust* appears throughout the new document
(Public Safety Canada 2009b). The importance of developing trust
between the public and private sectors is mentioned frequently in
many Western governments' CIP strategies (for examples, see
Attorney-General's Department 2003; Centre for the Protection of
National Infrastructure 2006; Department of Homeland Security
2008). Trust increases group cohesion (Jeffcott et al. 2006). In this
case, governments seek to develop trust relationships with and
among CI stakeholders in the public and private sectors to facilitate,
among·other things, the exchange of sensitive information about
vulnerabilities.
    Although social scientists have given considerable attention to the
problem of defining trust, a concise and universally accepted definition remains elusive. As a consequence, the term *trust* is used in a
variety of distinct and not always compatible ways in organizational

research (Rousseau et al. 1998; Kramer 1999). Barbalet (2009) argues that trust is often confused with consideration of legitimacy or loyalty. He suggests that trust must be understood "in terms of a) acceptance of dependency in b) the absence of information about the other's reliability in order to c) create an outcome otherwise unavailable" (2009, 3). Kramer (1999) describes several ways to think about trust: history-based trust characterizes trust as something that evolves over time and is based on past experiences with individuals; category-based trust is based on membership; and roles-based trust is based on one's place or formal authority in an organization. Hardin (2006) argues that the key is trustworthiness – the context that allows trust to develop – and that its value is in making social cooperation possible and even easier. Generally, there are two broad tendencies in defining trust. Some formulations highlight the strategic and calculative dimensions of trust in organizational settings; others emphasize the relational and social context for building trust. The first tradition draws largely from economics and political science; individuals are expected to maximize expected gains or minimize expected losses from their transactions. Viewed through this lens, two elements are critical to understanding the potential for trust: (1) the knowledge that enables one person to trust another and (2) the private incentive for the person to honour and fulfill that trust. This approach has been criticized for being too narrowly cognitive; it gives too little a role to emotional and social influences (Kramer 1999).

If governments assume that this first perspective on trust is accurate, then they should seek to align their interests with those of CI owners and operators. Agranoff (2007, 2008) notes that when there is goal alignment between entities there exists a foundation on which partnerships, like the sector networks, can be built with less formal organizational structure. These relationships can be mutually beneficial. In CIP and emergency management, more generally, these benefits can include inter-organizational training and learning opportunities; identifying key organizational contacts in emergencies; and understanding the emergency management process, including who has the legal authority to make decisions and redirect scarce resources during events (McEntire and Dawson 2007). Indeed, these issues should be a good place for government and industry to start their information sharing and standard setting.

Beyond these first practical exchanges, however, one can imagine instances in which these parties' incentives may not be aligned and information sharing will be more constrained. While governments might wish to obtain information about vulnerabilities in the infrastructure to mitigate the risk of cascading failures, owners and operators of CI may be reluctant to disclose the vulnerabilities of their assets because of the risk to their organization's security, liability, share value, and public image (Willis et al. 2009). There are other challenges. Governments might like industry to take a more proactive stance by adopting certain risk management practices, which industry might see as an unnecessary drain on much-needed resources, particularly in tough economic times.

The second broad approach to trust derives from relational models, which consider social orientation to other people and society as a whole. Here the focus is on social rather than merely instrumental (resource based) motives driving trust behaviour. Most in this second tradition agree that trust is a multi-dimensional concept that reflects an interaction of values, attitudes, and other socio-cultural references (Jeffcott et al. 2006). However, there is no standard definition of trust and therefore no set list of qualities that is required to create a setting conducive to trust building. There are, nonetheless, some trends in the literature.

Peters, Covello, and McCallum (1997) identified three dimensions that people tend to look for in others to develop trust: knowledge and expertise; care and concern; and openness and honesty (cited in Eiser and White 2006). Medical doctors, for example, tend to rank highly in all three categories, which is why they tend to be highly trusted (Royal College of Physicians 2009). These concepts can be applied equally at the organizational level (Gillespie and Dietz 2009). The concept of open communication, in particular, appears repeatedly in research on developing organizational trust (Clarke and Payne 1997) and encompasses free data sharing, inclusive decision-making, and collaborative work (Firth-Cozens 2004; Jeffcott et al. 2006).

Calman (2002) notes that trust comes on foot but leaves on horseback. It is easy to lose because negative information that can diminish people's feelings of trust is more attention grabbing, more powerful, and often more readily available than positive information (Eiser and White 2006). CI failures are particularly susceptible to this bias because they tend to be spectacular and generate considerable media coverage.

Several broad social trends seem to be incompatible with developing trust. Public-sector reform has tended towards market-driven or market-inspired solutions. While the stress on competitive and consumerist logic may conform to our first understanding of trust, it potentially undermines a core component of socially constructed trust, since the motivation of providers is declared to be self-interest in response to market signals, rather than public interest (Taylor-Gooby 2006). In a study of British railways after privatization, for instance, Jeffcott et al. (2006) noted that fragmentation, performance regimes, an increased focus on procedure, loss of expertise, and major accidents all affect the trust relationships across the industry.

If governments assume the socio-cultural approach to trust, none of the three conditions identified above (knowledge, care, and openness) is readily achieved in CIP. To start, the complexity and interdependence of the networks arguably make knowledge claims suspect. As we have shown in chapter 2, with terrorist acts and pandemics, the absence of reliable data makes the magnitude of the risk problem uncertain (Renn and Walker 2008). Even care and concern might be difficult to achieve. Sato (1988) concludes that trust effects weaken as group size increases; participants feel their impact is less in larger groups, which arguably leads to a sense of helplessness or even indifference rather than one of care and concern. Finally, government also faces a trust/transparency conundrum. On one hand, researchers note that open communication is a prerequisite to organizational trust. On the other hand, too much transparency might make owners and operators of CI nervous about disclosing information on vulnerabilities to government. However, government has not yet shown itself to be transparent on these issues. As noted, at a June 2008 Conference Board of Canada CIP event, for instance, private-sector representatives noted that even classified briefings to which they had been invited tended to be vague and unhelpful. RRAP audits also are veiled in secrecy and limited by non-disclosure agreements. There are several constraints that prevent government from sharing information, which will be explored below. Can government generate a context that is conducive to trust building if neither government nor industry can be transparent?

CONCLUSION

CI networks are populated with owners and operators, serving simultaneously the public good and their organizations' private interests, in a highly interdependent context. The concept of information sharing is central to the national strategy, and it is unclear.

While the literature emphasizes timely and relevant information sharing, participants in sector-level fora describe information exchange as very general; they derive some level of comfort from being part of the networks but they are hard pressed to describe specific benefits for themselves or their organizations. Auditors note uneven progress generally in CIP. Government initiatives such as RRAPS have attempted to initiate standards and nudge CI owners and operators in a direction to enhance resilience of CI, which is commendable, but again the absence of public accounting leaves more questions than answers – about performance and accountability.

While most governments refer to trusted *partnerships* with industry, in many cases they may actually be referring to *dependencies*. CIP plans as currently enacted provide governments with an opportunity to be involved in strengthening the resilience of CI without taking responsibility for it. Government takes risks when it aspires to be seen as a trusted partner in this context. CI and emergency events can result in clashes over public- and private-sector accountability structures (Koliba, Mills, and Zia 2011; Koski 2011). Industry responds to its shareholders and is rewarded for taking successful risks. Government has a regulatory role to play on behalf of citizens (and the Crown) to ensure appropriate adherence to standards. Strengthening the relationships between regulators and CI owners and operators can produce stability and collegiality among them but may also result in compromises on transparency and prevent the dramatic changes that may be required (Vogel 1986). The former point about the absence of scrutiny and rigour can apply equally to large, arm's-length Crown corporations, also concerned about image and revenue, as to private companies.

Therein lies perhaps a more serious problem: do people trust the government to regulate organizations that own and operate CI? Polling in most Western countries suggests that trust in government is in decline. In this sense, in trying to build up trust with CI owners and operators, government might be going in the wrong direction. Rather, it should be trying to build up trust among citizens in its ability to regulate CI and those responsible for it. After all, CI is not critical for industry alone but for society as a whole. Ironically, while citizen response is crucial to successful emergency management, the NS&AP is completely silent on citizen engagement and outward accountability. The issue of trust and CI will be discussed further in chapter 7.

PART TWO

Regime Content – Case Studies

In this section, we examine two case studies of CI risk regulation regimes. In chapter 4 we consider the Canadian transportation sector, focusing in particular on five key subsectors: airports, seaports, rail, trucking, and bridges. In chapter 5 we turn to the chemicals sector. We study the regulatory regime for addressing risks to the chemical manufacturing industry, with reference to two other sectors that rely on it: water utilities and first responders.

The data for our case studies come from sixty-eight semi-structured interviews we conducted with CI owners, operators, experts, and regulators between 2011 and 2015. Our interviews were wide ranging, covering an array of topics related to CIP and risk management. We combine the insights gleaned from these interviews with a review of the applicable academic and grey literature.

The objective of these case studies is to describe the features of two prominent CIP regimes in Canada. In the terminology of the risk regulation regime framework, our goal is to document the content of each regime. We do so by analyzing the three components of content deemed necessary for a system to be under control: information gathering, standard setting, and behaviour modification. By cataloguing these features, we enable our analysis in part 3 of the extent to which observed content is explained by contextual factors.

4

Transportation Sector

Canada's transportation system is among the safest and most regulated in the world. Accident rates in all modes of transportation have been steadily decreasing in Canada since 2001 (Transport Canada 2011b, 81, figure s 2). That noted, in certain transportation subsectors our research revealed turf wars, failure to share information, a weak and reactive safety culture, poor oversight, blame shifting, and lax and routine-oriented security practices that failed to adapt to emerging threats.

We have categorized the transportation system by five subsectors: airports, seaports, rail, trucking, and bridges. This categorization is based on the regulatory framework that governs the sector. The categorization of transportation into subsectors allows us to offer a comparative analysis of each subsector. Accordingly, the commentary in the chapter on the size, structure, and style of each of the regime components is given in relative, not absolute, terms. In this chapter, we use Hood and colleagues' (2001) risk regulatory regime framework to structure our descriptions, observations, and discussions of the transportation sector (see chapter 2 for an in-depth description of this framework).

Despite the anxiety that people feel over air travel, we found airports to have robust and confident security operations in place. Information gathering for airports is largely cooperative and collaborative. There are clear, albeit extensive, standards for security, which are developed by Transport Canada in consultation with industry and other stakeholders. Some interview subjects noted that the regulatory regime is sometimes too inflexible and does not take the unique characteristics of each airport into account. Legal and policy concerns have considerable influence on airport staff. Transport Canada is active in behaviour modification, resulting in a robust, albeit at times routine- and rules-driven, control mechanism for the sector.

The other subsectors struggled in different ways. Compared with airport staff, seaport staff felt that information gathering is less collaborative or cooperative. Standards and behaviour modification are driven by the imperative to get products to market as quickly as possible rather than by safety or security concerns. Our interview subjects thought there has been insufficient effort by the federal government to examine the sector as a whole and evaluate vulnerabilities caused by interdependencies. Overall, seaport staff face a number of competing contextual pressures and are less satisfied than airport staff with the regulatory regime. Interview subjects from seaports expressed more concern than interview subjects from other subsectors over risks associated with climate change and extreme natural events.

In trucking, information gathering seems less restricted by formal rules and is less consistent, more dispersed, and intermittent. Standards vary across locations, and behaviour modification depends on private incentives, laws, and, sometimes, membership in voluntary organizations. Interview subjects in this subsector noted that the trucking industry is primarily influenced by markets and their legal dynamics, including the requirement to meet customer needs, insurance concerns, and government road regulations. Interview subjects from the trucking subsector expressed more concern over risks associated with cargo theft and major collisions (which can cause service disruptions) than over other risks.

Bridges are unique in the transportation sector because they are immovable and effectively monopolistic. Bridge staff share information and best practices with staff from other bridges and with emergency services. While there is a strong regulatory regime in place for safety, security is less formal and based on shared best practises and relationships with local law enforcement and staff at other bridges. Bridge staff said that engineering risks and media coverage influence them most when it comes to safety and security and how they spend their time. Bridge staff expressed more concern over risks associated with severe weather events than over other risks.

In the rail subsector, government and industry interactions are influenced by the Class 1 rail companies, which are exposed to varying degrees of competitive pressure. Safety concerns receive more attention than security ones. Small and medium-sized enterprises (SMEs) in this subsector rely on local law enforcement communities and rail associations for information and standards regarding security risks. Railway staff said that regulations and media coverage influence them the most when it comes to safety and security and how they spend their time. Particularly when it comes to security, interview subjects in this subsector expressed concern over risks associated with terrorism and public access points to rail infrastructure. The relationship between rail and government regulators is at once collaborative and strained. Both of these characteristics were in evidence following the Lac-Mégantic train disaster.

In sum, each transportation subsector is different: the subsectors are organized differently; they are concerned about different risks; some have many competitors and some have few; some are cooperative while others are not. At the same time, these five subsectors are part of one interconnected complex system that is both local and global. Most transportation subsectors are preoccupied with efficiency and market pressures but must also recognize the threat of failure. All transportation subsectors try to prepare for risk by building robustness and resilience into their systems and they do so with varying degrees of success.

REGULATORY REGIME CONTENT

Information Gathering

The size, structure, and style of information gathering vary across the transportation subsectors. Compared with the other subsectors, airports are generally highly invested and aggressive in information gathering. Information gathering is partly dependent on the capacity of an airport, which, in general, is a corollary of size (interview subject [Int] 15; Int 13). The largest airports in Canada, classified as Class 1 (e.g., Toronto's Pearson International) tend to have extensive security and intelligence consisting of independent capacities and strong relations with law enforcement, security organizations, and government (Int 1; Int 12; Int 13). Certain Class 1 airports have RCMP detachments located within the airport (Macdonald 2014). Information gathering by governments at Class 1 airports is more complex and involved but also better integrated than at other airports (Int 12; Int 13; Int 15). The smaller Class 2 and 3 airports tend to have less independent capacity. Class 3 airports, in particular, rely heavily on general government bulletins (Int 15).

Information gathering at airports is centred on inspections or compliance audits, the safety management systems (SMS; see the Standard Setting section below), and a variety of multi-organizational fora and advisory committees consisting of government and industry stakeholders. Transport Canada is the lead government department (Transport Canada 2013b) though other federal departments and agencies share responsibility for security, including the Canadian Air Transport Security Authority, which is responsible for airline passenger and baggage screening. The regime style of airports, or operating conventions and attitudes, is at times formal (through institutional mechanisms) but also depends on close working relationships, particularly at the large and better integrated airports (Int 12; Int 13; Int 15; Int 22). Airport operators are very confident that they know who to contact and that they would receive timely information from government concerning safety and security threats to their airports. They also feel that airports have made considerable progress in assessing threats, risks, and vulnerabilities and sharing information with government (Int 12; Int 13; Int 15).

Events such as 9/11 and the Air India tragedy have influenced the way in which airports share information. As the government response to the report of the Air India Inquiry notes (Government of Canada 2010c), progress has been made towards removing past constraints on the flow of information to security agencies. While a "need to know" approach persists with regard to some security information, interview subjects felt that airports have increasingly adopted a "need to share" approach and continue to progress in this direction (Int 13; Int 15). Indeed, the majority of our interview participants at airports did not say that information sharing needed significant improvement.

In contrast, seaports exist in a context of confusing multi-level governance. The Canadian seaport system currently comprises nineteen Canada port authorities (CPAs) that were created under the Canada Marine Act (1998). According to Brooks (2004), this system is akin to a not-for-profit model. CPAs are "federally incorporated, autonomous, non-share corporations that operate at arm's length from the federal government, who is the sole shareholder" (Transport Canada 2013e). Three categories of ports exist in Canada: CPAs, regional/local ports, and remote ports. Regional/local ports are in a position to be better managed by local interests (Ircha 2001). Remote ports are found in isolated communities that are reliant on marine transportation and have a government wharf (Brooks 2007). In CPAs and remote ports, the government plays a strong regulatory role. Remote ports are considered to be a public good, and CPAs are considered to be essential infrastructure to the national ports system (Brooks 2008).

As with airports, information gathering is stronger with larger seaports than smaller ones. CPAs work with Transport Canada as well as the other security organizations. Information is gathered through a combination of inspections and various fora that facilitate the exchange of information. For example, the Interdepartmental Marine Security Working Group helps government agencies share information and includes representatives of seventeen federal departments and agencies (Transport Canada 2013b). Our interview subjects agreed that fora are useful for relationship building and networking (Int 32; Int 33; Int 41; Int 42). Fora allow port staff to engage with government officials (Int 33) as well as with local organizations and marine facilities that are not directly operated by the seaports (Int 30).

Our interview subjects were not entirely satisfied with information exchange about port security. They indicated that port staff need to spend much more time building relationships with stakeholders, including with other ports, emergency services, utilities, and the various services that support port operations (Int 41; Int 42). Port staff were concerned that, while they are prepared for regularly occurring threats, they are less well prepared for rare events (Int 41; Int 42).

Interview participants at seaports underscored many of the key points in the academic literature surveyed in chapters 2 and 3. We heard, for example, that private companies are not always willing to share information with the government (Int 42) and the pressure to get product to market quickly tends to dominate organizational focus. One participant noted that the style of security information sharing is very informal and depends, perhaps too much, on personal relationships within the law enforcement and security community; relationships can be clannish, making them a bit too inwardly accountable and only to those recognized as part of the identified community (Int 42; see Ouchi [1979] for reference to clan control mechanisms). Government and seaports don't seem to trust one another; there is evidence of organized crime and a lack of policing at seaports (Sloan 2012).

The trucking industry in Canada is made up of both corporations and small businesses. While some of these corporations are large, like TransForce with approximately 17,685 employees in 2016, by and large the industry is constituted of smaller companies (Government of Canada 2013; TransForce 2016). This includes for-hire carriers, private carriers, owner-operators, and courier firms, for a total of approximately 56,800 firms (Transport Canada 2011a). From a security perspective, information gathering is much less rigorous for trucking than for airports or seaports. Compared with airports and, to a lesser extent, seaports the trucking subsector has less investment in information gathering. Much of the information gathering regarding security is accomplished by virtue of industry membership in voluntary organizations. Our interview findings suggest that the three programs described in table 4.1 are among the most important for information gathering in the trucking subsector (Int 9; Int 10). Members voluntarily sign up for these programs because membership allows them to conduct their businesses more efficiently.

The style of information gathering in trucking is informal. Trucking companies are more willing than companies in other transportation subsectors to discuss, subject to very few conditions, safety and security at sector fora such as conferences or meetings (Int 9; Int 10). Information about vulnerabilities is usually only shared with government regulators; however, trucking companies seem willing to discuss and compare procedures on issues such as access to buildings or other restricted areas with other trucking companies. Our interview subjects disagreed on the extent to which their subsector competes on safety and security issues (Int 9; Int 10). They were more concerned about the theft of valuable freight than other types of risks. Indeed, cargo theft accounts for major losses in the transportation sector (Burges 2012), as much as $5 billion according to a 2011 study by the Canadian Trucking Alliance (Vescio 2012; Kosowan 2016). Our interview subjects noted that it is important to collect data in a consistent manner to appreciate fully the extent of cargo theft.

Bridges are often under the jurisdiction of the provinces or municipal governments. Approximately one per cent of the bridges in Canada are federally owned (Ircha 2001). Some are also privately owned; the federal railways, for example, maintain over 4,600 rail

Table 4.1 Voluntary certification programs

Program	Description
Free and Secure Trade (FAST)	FAST is a voluntary government–industry joint initiative between the Canada Border Services Agency (CBSA) and US Customs and Border Protection. Members are certified to a standard and then given access to faster border crossings (CBSA 2013a).
Customs-Trade Partnership Against Terrorism (C-TPAT)	Similar to FAST, C-TPAT is a voluntary government–industry joint initiative certifying industry to a standard that gives industries preferential treatment by US Customs (C-TPAT 2017).
Partners in Protection (PIP)	PIP is a voluntary CBSA program in which members agree to certain security standards. CBSA assesses industry on these measures and also provides information sessions on security issues. Members are treated as lower risk by CBSA (CBSA 2013b).

bridges across the country (Transport Canada 2013e). Because of regularly occurring events at the bridges, such as car accidents and suicides, bridge staff are normally in regular contact with emergency services. With respect to formal safety and security practices, information gathering on bridges is structured around inspections. The nature and frequency of bridge inspections vary across provinces, but inspections are predominantly designed to ensure compliance with safety standards. Security information is gathered and shared mainly through multi-organizational fora (Int 2; Int 16) and through strong informal relationships between bridge staff and government officials and between staff from different bridges. Bridges, in general, are monopolistic and therefore do not engage in traditional market competition. As a result, information sharing is strong among bridge owners, operators, managers, and government, both nationally and internationally (Int 2; Int 17). Some of our bridge interview participants were from the United States and the United Kingdom, yet they were familiar with the bridge community in Canada and the presence of a strong information-sharing network that is based on personal relationships (Int 2; Int 17).

The rail subsector contrasts significantly with the trucking and bridge subsectors. While there are thirty-one federally regulated rail

carriers in Canada (Auditor General of Canada 2013), the rail
industry is dominated by its three Class I carriers: Canadian
National (CN), Canadian Pacific (CP) (Int 45), and VIA Rail. As
with other transportation subsectors, size, capacity, and structure
were important themes in our rail interviews. The information-
gathering component is heavily influenced by the structure of the
industry. CN and CP have their own police departments (Int 5),
which allows them to be much more attuned to security issues and
arguably more self-sufficient and bullish in their views. Our interview subjects from Class I carriers felt that information exchange
between the railroads and their police forces is effective. In contrast, smaller railroads and shortlines[1] rely significantly on the
Railway Association of Canada. Many smaller railroads also work
closely with CN and CP for information gathering (Int 45). Class I
carriers are less satisfied with information sharing with government
than are large airports, where operations tend to be well integrated
into government security information-sharing regimes. One interview subject from a Class I carrier stated that much of the information that the government shares with the rail sector is either
redundant (given the information-gathering capacity of its own
police force) or dated (Int 5).

Despite the largely collaborative approach to information exchange
between large rail and government regulators, there are limits to the
cooperation. We see the limits of government reach in an exchange
between former CBC journalist Evan Solomon and Minister of
Transport Lisa Raitt, following the publication of the Auditor General's audit after the Lac-Mégantic disaster.

> SOLOMON: But who's actually responsible? This is, I mean, you
> say the railway companies own the railway beds; I don't think
> people quite appreciate what that means. So let me just … that
> means they have the jurisdiction, they have their own police
> forces actually – in other words, even the government has to ask
> the railway companies, almost by subpoena, to get information
> out of them if they don't want to deliver. Isn't that fair to say?
> They … It literally belongs to their jurisdiction, right?
> RAITT: There is some information they must provide under legis-
> lation. Other information you do make the request for them, and
> if they don't provide it or they don't give you what you want,
> you can resort to obtaining a court order to do so, but that is
> the nature …

SOLOMON: That's incredible, right? That you're the minister and if the railway company doesn't choose to deliver you information even you've got to get a court order from them. That's a bit shocking.

RAITT: But we're satisfied that the important aspects of information that we need to get ... we can get from the railway companies, and they do ... they do cooperate with the regulator, that's Transport Canada, and they do operate safely. So, the Auditor General is clear; this report is not about any kind of assessment of the rail safety in Canada. It is a safe system. What it says is Transport Canada needs to pay more attention to auditing the safety management systems in place, and that's what we're going to do.

SOLOMON: Last question, have you ever as a government had to prosecute a railway company for not giving you timely information about derailments, about what they're carrying, about information? Because this is the key. Have you ever had to prosecute them for not turning over timely information?

RAITT: I don't know, but I will look into it for you.

The exchange above highlights a tension that potentially exists between the rail carriers and the government caused by competing interests, though it is not clear how often rail carriers refuse to provide information. We will return to this interview twice more in this chapter, as it provides equally interesting insights on questions about the safety management system (standards) and ministerial accountability (behaviour modification).

In sum, information gathering can be integrated, efficient (airports), and cooperative (bridges), or redundant (rail), dispersed, ad hoc (trucking), and constrained by competition (seaports, rail). While the Canadian government has spent considerable time working on information sharing, we found that airports and rail were the only subsectors that had institutionalized robust information-sharing practices; bridges had many informal practices, and trucking and seaports had significant gaps in this area.

Standard Setting

One of the most important and controversial trends in the transportation sector is the recent adoption of SMS in federally regulated transportation. At present, airports, seaports, rail, and trucking have all adopted some form of SMS. A SMS is a form of regulation that requires industry to manage its safety risks by developing and implementing its own safety plans, which, in theory, will foster an enhanced safety culture. This approach is similar to a high-reliability organization, as described in chapter 2. Cox and Cox (1991) describe safety culture as the attitude, beliefs, perceptions, and values that employees share in relation to safety in the workplace.

This type of regulation is sometimes referred to as co-regulation. Transport Canada considers SMS to be an extra layer of safety. Many critics of SMS note that they shift the onus of developing safety rules to private actors and allow them to self-regulate, with Transport Canada acting only as an approving authority for their plans. Critics contend that SMS reduces the number of inspectors actually monitoring and enforcing compliance with the rules, which ultimately increases the risk of safety violations. The results of SMS are mixed so far, particularly in rail, where SMS have been used since 2001. SMS play an important role in managing risk in the transportation sector and illustrate the trend towards deregulation in this sector.

There are similarities in the way standards are set across the transportation sector, but there are also some significant differences in the size, structure, and style of standard setting in each subsector. The aviation subsector has extensive legislation and regulations to govern airports and is considered one of the most aggressively regulated industries in Canada (Davis 2001). Table 4.2 shows a list of the legal and regulatory frameworks relating to aviation security (Transport Canada 2013a).

The Air India Inquiry found that there was no single document describing the airport security regime in Canada. Until recently, the aviation security program was fragmented, consisting of a body of disjointed documents. In 2013 Transport Canada rectified this situation by releasing the National Civil Aviation Security Program, which sets out legislation, policies, programs, and regulations on aviation security and attempts to articulate the regulatory regime as a whole. Compared with the other subsectors, the aviation subsector possesses a strong and coherent regulatory regime.

According to the National Civil Aviation Security Program, the government takes a risk-based approach to airport security, meaning higher probability and/or higher consequence events receive more resources and attention. Our interview subjects had mixed feelings about Transport Canada's standards and enforcement. They felt

Table 4.2 Aviation security legal and regulatory frameworks

Name of framework
Aeronautics Act
Canadian Air Transport Security Authority Act (CATSA)
Canadian Aviation Security Regulations
CATSA Aerodrome Designation Regulations
Designated Provision Regulations
Identity Screening Regulations
Regulations Concerning Information Required by Foreign States
Aerodrome Security Measures
Air Carriers Security Measures
Security Measures Respecting Air Cargo
Screening Security Orders

Source: Transport Canada.

generally that Transport Canada is engaged with industry and responsive to its concerns (Int 6; Int 7; Int 11). At the same time, our interview subjects thought that the standard-setting component of the regulatory regime for airports is at times too standardized (Int 12; Int 14). They felt that government should recognize airport diversity when applying the Canadian Aviation Regulations (2012), particularly size differences and differences in how facilities are used (Int 12; Int 13; Int 15). The cost of regulatory compliance is one of the most significant concerns that some airports have about regulations (Int 13). Smaller, regional airports do not want to be treated in the same manner as the larger airports. Table 4.3 lists the top five airports in Canada measured by passengers per year. Airports such as the ones in London, Ontario, and Moncton, New Brunswick, have about 500,000 passengers per year.

The regulations pertaining to seaport and marine security are not as extensive as the regulations for airports. Table 4.4 outlines the legal and regulatory frameworks for marine security.

The Marine Transportation Security Act (1994) is the primary legislation for this subsector. This act creates a security framework that is similar in structure to that of airports, only less aggressive and expensive. It includes inspections, monitoring, surveillance, and enforcement. While Transport Canada is the most significant public actor, several federal departments play roles in regulating seaports. As with airports, standards are influenced by international

Table 4.3 Number of passengers at Canada's top five airports (2015)

Rank	Airport	Total passengers per year
1	Toronto Pearson International Airport	39,638,841
2	Vancouver International Airport	19,690,515
3	Montreal – Pierre Elliott Trudeau International Airport	14,753,247
4	Calgary International Airport	14,578,929
5	Edmonton International Airport	7,466,141

Source: Statistics Canada (2016).

Table 4.4 Marine security legal and regulatory frameworks

Name of framework
Marine Security Legal and Regulatory Framework
Marine Transportation Security Act
Domestic Ferries Security Regulations
Security Measures

Source: Transport Canada.

context. To a degree, the International Maritime Organization's International Ship and Port Facility Security Code standardizes and shares practices.

Operators and managers at seaports find policy direction from government sometimes inadequate (Int 31; Int 32; Int 42). While there are security standards, our interview subjects felt that there are no national standards for cᵢ and that both the responsibilities of government departments and the policy direction are unclear (Int 32; Int 42). Moreover, and in contrast to our airport interview subjects, the interview subjects from seaports felt that government security policies were not developed in a collaborative manner (Int 32). Government regulators are aware of these issues and acknowledge they sometimes face constraints when sharing information with external parties (Int 37; Int 38).

Many of the current standards for seaports are perceived to be a government reaction to 9/11. While ship security has a long history, before 9/11 seaports had not traditionally been as concerned with security as they are now. Seaports started from scratch after 9/11, and they have made considerable progress in a relatively short time. Our interview subjects felt that some of the new security standards are working well, but others are not. Similar to our interviews with airport staff, a seaport representative recommended that government review these regulations to determine which should be kept and which should be discarded or revised (Int 31). There is also a need for clarity with regard to the responsibilities and roles of the various departments. Industry respondents were particularly sensitive to the international context in which shipping occurs, including the international laws, competition, organized crime, terrorism, and geopolitical factors that affect shipping. (See table 4.5 for the number of attacks or attempted attacks on sea vessels between 2011 and 2015.) While most attacks and attempted attacks occur in Asia and Africa, they still increase the concerns of those responsible for Canadian seaport security because the Canadian ports trade frequently with Asia. Industry respondents also felt that these pressures were not always sufficiently recognized by regulators (Int 35). There are also risks associated with passenger travel on cruise ships, ferries, and inland shipping that some felt are not being adequately addressed.

Foreign ownership of ports has been a source of recent controversy in the United States and Australia. The central question is how to balance economic openness with national security and how much control foreign companies should be allowed to have over national infrastructure. The fears over foreign entities owning critical infrastructure generally stem from the belief that foreign companies do not have as vested an interest in security as a domestic company would. On the other hand, proponents note the economic benefits of foreign investment in the economy.

A well-known example of foreign ownership controversy was the proposed sale of port management of six major US seaports to Dubai Ports World, a company based in the United Arab Emirates. A number of prominent politicians and public figures opposed the deal. They argued that foreign governments should not be allowed to own strategic assets and that port security should stay in the hands of American firms. Supporters noted that blocking the sale would be discriminatory towards Arabs and that security would remain a government responsibility as always and would be performed by the United States Coast Guard and US Customs and Border Protection. Because of opposition, the deal was cancelled and the ports were

Table 4.5 Attacks or attempted attacks on sea vessels between 2011 and 2015

	2011	2012	2013	2014	2015	Total
Southeast Asia	80	104	128	141	147	600
Indian subcontinent	16	19	26	34	24	119
South America	25	17	18	5	8	73
Africa	293	150	79	55	35	612
Rest of the world	2	0	0	2	1	5
Total	439	297	264	245	246	1,491

Source: International Maritime Organization (2011–15).

eventually sold to American multinational corporation American International Group.

In the trucking subsector, there is much less standard setting and it is fragmented as compared with airports or seaports (Brooks 2008; Int 48). While there are some national standards, such as the 1987 National Safety Code (Transport Canada 2013d) and standards from the Commercial Vehicle Safety Alliance, regulation is primarily a provincial responsibility and as a result the regulatory regime includes a variety of different regulations across the country (Kahai and Ford 1997). Interprovincial trucking is nationally regulated but is still subject to the regulations of each province that trucks enter. The voluntary certification programs listed in table 4.1 (i.e., FAST, C-TPAT, and PIP) oblige companies to undertake a number of measures to improve their security procedures and adopt good practices, which entitles them to a lower risk classification. Gaining a lower risk status can expedite inspections and border crossings and lead to fewer compliance audits. These voluntary programs (see table 4.1) apply to both trucking and rail.

Inconsistency was a recurring theme in our interviews with respondents from the trucking subsector. For instance, interview subjects cited the lack of uniformity in the credentials required for drivers to gain access to areas such as rail yards or ports. Truck drivers undergo multiple checks, all verifying similar information, to obtain access cards for the locations where they deliver freight. One interview subject noted that this process has been streamlined in the United States (Int 9), although transportation specialists noted execution problems there also.

Standards for bridges are primarily aimed at safety, with relatively less emphasis on security. Our interview subjects did not reference any concrete security standards for bridges in the Canadian or international context. Provincial safety standards and management systems vary (Hammad, Yan, and Mostofi 2007); many provincial standards include safety measures that relate to security but are not expressly security standards. Bridges that fall under the federal International Bridges and Tunnels Act (2007) are the exception. This act does include security measures, but they apply only to the twenty-five vehicular international bridges and tunnels and nine international railway structures that are covered under the act (Transport Canada 2013f). As we see in other sectors, when Canadian agencies interact with American agencies, security standards tend to increase. Our interview participants, both Canadian and international, noted that bridges tend to develop their own security measures by collaborating with the staff of other bridges and adapting standards used by other bridges (Int 16; Int 18). These bridge security measures are shared best practices (Int 2) and not enforced by government. For the majority of bridges, there are few clear security standards or protocols promulgated by government.

Despite the fact that regulatory responsibility for rail is shared by the federal government, provinces, and territories, the federal government has a more pronounced influence in rail and, as such, standards across the country are more uniform (Int 43; Int 44; Int 45). Unlike the airport and seaport subsectors, there is no one legislative act focused primarily on security for the rail subsector: security is based on the Railway Safety Act (1985), the Transportation of Dangerous Goods Act (1985), and the International Bridges and Tunnels Act (2007). The recent adoption of industry-wide SMS as outlined above includes elements of security (Auditor General of Canada 2012a). Railways can develop their own security plans, which are then audited and approved by Transport Canada.

There has been some success. In 2013, the Auditor General's Report on Rail Safety (Auditor General of Canada 2013) stated, "Transport Canada has implemented a regulatory framework for rail transportation that includes a safety management system approach to identify, analyze, and respond to rail safety risks, and it has made progress in working with federal railways to implement safety management systems. It has also made significant progress in addressing many recommendations from the Railway Safety Act review," which occurred in 2007 and made fifty-six recommendations (Railway Safety Act Review Secretariat 2007). Still, any conclusion that the SMS was working effectively in rail would be premature. The Auditor General's report and the Transportation Safety Board (TSB)'s report on the events in Lac-Mégantic have raised concerns about safety practices in rail. One of the main findings of the TSB report on Lac-Mégantic was that the Montreal, Maine & Atlantic Railway (MMA) had a weak safety culture, which prevented its SMS from functioning effectively (TSB 2014). Safety culture is the cornerstone of an SMS. It includes proactive measures to eliminate or mitigate risks. The TSB found that MMA was generally reactive in addressing safety issues and that Transport Canada was slow to follow up. In her interview with Evan Solomon, Minister Raitt explained the government's approach to risk management, emphasizing the necessarily limited resources available for inspections and the vast number of inspections that would be required.

SOLOMON: The question also is trust here. You know the opposition raises the question of the deregulation and the reliance on self-enforcement of regulations from the railway companies. A lot of folks point ... to the jurisdiction problem, that the railway lines own the bridges, they own the tracks, they're not subject to answer to the ministry, even to your ministry. The Transportation Safety Board has to work with the railways to deliver information. If you remember during the Calgary floods you had the mayor of Calgary, Naheed Nenshi, said, "Gee that bridge wasn't even inspected – I didn't know it because it belongs to the railway." Why does the Transportation Safety Board – why do you not have more control over what's happening on those tracks? Should the laws be changed to frankly take jurisdiction away from the big railroad companies?

RAITT: The railway companies own their rail lines and their rail beds. They have to operate in accordance with the Railway Safety Act. We have actually looked at rail safety in the country as part of our government mandate, and we came up with recommendations and changes in the regulations to actually toughen these regulations. And then we invested in more inspectors. We expect railway companies to adhere to the regulations, and when they don't we will prosecute. And that's the system that we do have in place. Added on to that is the need to have a safety culture in all of our railways because with 45,000 km of track, Evan, quite frankly, there is an infinite amount of money we would need for Transport Canada to inspect every day, every company, every piece of rail. That's why you need s m s.

Our interview subjects in the rail subsector noted that safety culture is actually much more pronounced than security culture. One interview participant noted that there simply is not a culture of security present in the rail subsector and that security typically is not a priority. As a result, security is not considered in most strategic planning sessions (Int 45). This is particularly true for shortrail lines, which rely on local law enforcement communities and the Railway Association of Canada for security concerns. As in the trucking subsector, standards in the rail subsector are informal, based on best practices shared among operators, and derived from economic incentives for the subsector to remain trusted (Int 45). The security plans that railways do develop and submit to regulators and industry associations tend to be of a high level and to not conform to any specific standards (Int 5).

In sum, airports have strong standards. Rail and seaports are moving towards more self-regulation, or at least co-regulation between government and industry. In these instances, government approves plans that industry submits and enforces. For bridges, plans are informal; for trucking, plans are inconsistent. In all subsectors, smaller organizations have a harder time meeting standards, which raises important questions about the extent to which standards are enforced among smaller organizations.

Behaviour Modification

In the transportation sector, regulation enforcement is perhaps the weakest component of the regulatory regime. We found evidence of weaknesses in regulation enforcement in the recent Auditor General audits, the report of the Air India Inquiry, and the t s b report on the Lac-Mégantic disaster. Our interview subjects also expressed concerns over regulation enforcement throughout the transportation sector.

The Air India Inquiry (Government of Canada 2010c) found that if an inspection of an air carrier uncovered a security issue there was no authority for enforcement action, other than either a written reprimand or a total revocation of the airline's landing rights in Canada. Thus, regulators could not effectively enforce regulations because they had no appropriate or effective enforcement mechanism. Regulations have since been amended to include a middle ground in the form of meaningful fines.

Nevertheless, problems persist. The 2013 Fall Report of the Auditor General (Auditor General of Canada 2013) revealed significant deficiencies in the inspector's abilities to identify performance gaps in regulatory compliance. The audit found that Transport Canada was not providing sufficient direction for managers on how to develop clear work objectives and performance measures for inspectors. As a result of inefficient direction, the performance assessment process was not effective. Inspectors were having difficulty evaluating performance, recognizing good performance, and identifying performance gaps.

The audit also identified conflict of interest problems for inspectors. The report notes that there was little guidance for inspectors in situations where opportunities arose to work for one of the companies being overseen by Transport Canada. As one of our interview participants noted, inspections were sometimes pro forma, with little real threat of sanctions on a finding of non-compliance (Int 41). The report notes that the organizational culture needs to change to resolve these deficiencies.

Size, structure, and style of behaviour modification vary across the transportation subsectors. While some subsectors have more extensive and formal approaches to enforcing regulations, others have more fragmented approaches and rely on best practices.

Airports have the most extensive behaviour modification component in terms of size. Behaviour modification in airports is structured according to Transport Canada's National Civil Aviation Security Program, which monitors and enforces compliance through inspections and enforcement practices, such as fines or the revocation of operating licences or certificates (Transport Canada 2013a). One interview participant noted that Transport Canada is very active in its oversight of airports (Int 15). Oversight includes an array of activities, such as focused security inspections and testing activities based on risk assessments, compliance results, and threat information. Transport Canada states that its objective is to work collaboratively with airports and attempt to rectify any compliance issues with the least punitive measures possible (2013b). Transport Canada also ensures that airport security complies with Canada's obligations under international treaties (Transport Canada 2013a).

Laws and legal concerns clearly weigh on the minds of airport operators, managers, and regulators. For the most part, airports have business continuity plans and contingency plans and, sometimes, formal agreements with emergency services. When given a list of contextual issues relevant to our risk regulatory regime framework (see chapter 2) and asked which contextual issues influence the manner in which they spend their time with respect to safety and security, interview subjects in the aviation sector scored law or legal concerns higher than any other contextual issue, and they scored these concerns higher than did respondents from the other subsectors.

In seaports, behaviour modification is structured similarly to the way it's structured in airports: through inspections and compliance audits, and a system of graduated penalties for non-compliance. Seaports are subject to random and unannounced audits to confirm compliance with federal rules under the Marine Transportation Security Act (1994). Some of our interview subjects indicated that the aggression and investment in enforcing the regulations were not as significant as in airports (Int 41; Int 42). Interview subjects felt that there were not enough inspections to ensure that ports were actually complying with the rules. Moreover, the inspections lacked rigour and depth. Inspectors often simply inspected the plans in place, in accordance with s m s; they did not inspect the actual physical facility to determine compliance with plans and s m s. The amount of cargo that is actually inspected at seaports has also been controversial. In the United States, about four per cent of cargo is actually inspected; in Canada it is only two per cent (Kenny 2007; Bliss 2012).

This complex regulatory environment, combined with the occurrence of crime and the competitive pressures ports face, creates a great deal of uncertainty and anxiety among seaport staff (Int 29). This point was reinforced by the fact that when asked which contextual pressures influence the manner in which they spend their time, respondents from seaports identified several and could not clearly identify prevailing pressures, including legal concerns, customer concerns, supply risks, contractors, and other technical issues. This clustering of pressures is more pronounced in seaports than in other subsectors. Our interview subjects from seaports expressed more concern over risks associated with climate change and extreme natural events than over other types of risks. Perhaps there is little surprise in this. The total dollar value of damage from Hurricane

Sandy to the Port Authority of New York and New Jersey came to $2.2 billion (Strunsky 2013).

With respect to bridges, there are strong behaviour modification mechanisms in place for safety; however, there is an absence of clear standards for security and no formal mechanism to enforce security standards. One interview participant noted that security is mainly about sharing threat information with security agencies, since bridges are open and vulnerable (Int 16). When asked to weigh which contextual issues influence the manner in which they spend their day, bridge staff said that they were most influenced by engineering risks and by media and public perceptions of the bridges. Compared with respondents from the other subsectors, bridge staff were less concerned about the law, insurance (most bridges are self-insured), or expanding their contacts with other CI owners and operators. Like seaport staff, bridge staff expressed the most concern over risks associated with severe weather events; suspension bridges are vulnerable to high winds. Government transportation officials, in contrast, expressed concern over the aging of the infrastructure and over the amount of bridge infrastructure that has to be monitored and maintained.

In the rail subsector, rail staff expressed concern over the necessarily open nature of rail infrastructure. Trespasser fatalities totalled thirty-three in 2014, and forty-nine on average annually between 2009 and 2014; the data suggest just how accessible rail is.

Transport Canada has been less effective in targeting its oversight at higher risk activities in rail than it has been in aviation. A 2013 Auditor General's report notes that Transport Canada does not collect or use relevant safety performance and risk data to ensure that its oversight activities are targeting the higher risk railways or the most significant safety risks (Auditor General of Canada 2013).

The recent TSB report on the Lac-Mégantic disaster has also shed some light on behaviour modification in rail. While the Auditor General's report noted above found that Transport Canada had implemented most of the fifty-six recommendations made by a parliamentary committee in 2008, the TSB report notes, among other things, that Transport Canada did not audit railways often or thoroughly enough to know how those companies were managing risk (TSB 2014). Rail oversight tends to focus on the Class 1 railways and overlook the Class 2 and 3 railways. The Auditor General's report also found that the majority of the audits that Transport Canada conducted were focused on the country's two largest railways, CP and CN (Auditor General of Canada 2013). Moreover, Transport Canada only conducted about one-quarter of the audits it had planned in the three years leading up to the Auditor General's report. These audits were insufficient to allow Transport Canada to confirm that required processes were effective and that corrective actions were implemented to improve safety.

What is equally noteworthy is the manner in which the government acknowledges these problems. We quote again from the interview between the CBC's Evan Solomon and Transportation Minister Lisa Raitt following the publication of the Auditor General's report on rail safety oversight. In the excerpt, the minister for the most part refers to the elected government, including herself (*we*), as distinct from Transport Canada (*they*). She notes the determined effort the elected government has made to support increased audits and the SMS (e.g., "we provided to the department in 2009 extra funding"). Despite the fact that the elected government had been in power for over five years, she attributes the failings to Transport Canada alone; indeed, it is difficult to detect in the exchange what, if anything, the elected government might be responsible for in relation to the department's past performance. In the second part of the interview, however, when she emphasizes progress and achievements, she includes the elected government as integral to government operations (e.g., "we will implement the plan," and "we have actually increased the number of inspections"). This exchange underscores the malleable and at times opaque nature of ministerial accountability. We will return to this point again in the book's final chapter.

SOLOMON: Why were only one in four safety management audits completed from 2009 to 2013?
RAITT: Well, that's what I asked Transport Canada officials, myself, when the results of the audit were becoming apparent. You know *we* provided to the department in 2009 extra funding to deal with more inspections, to deal with rail safety, and *we* based it on the fact that *we* had a very good independent panel tell us about rail safety in Canada in 2007. So, for us, *we* had fully anticipated and expected that not only is TC doing the compliance work that *they* should be doing with the Railway Safety Act but as well that *they* be working on safety management

system regulations too, and today *we* found from the Auditor General that's not the case. *We* have his recommendations. *We* accept them, and TC has provided a plan, and *we* will implement that plan.

SOLOMON: Alright, but the question here is: does TC need more inspectors after the Auditor General found that it only completed a quarter of its planned audits on the safety management system? What's the plan? Is it more inspectors?

RAITT: The plan is, if you take a look at the plan set out today, that TC has indicated the path forward. *They* have to figure out how many resources *they* need to pull into the safety management system audit side of it. *We* have increased inspectors, though, Evan. *We* have actually increased the number of inspections last year to 30,000 – highest year ever. So *they* are out there doing their work on rail safety and ensuring that companies are adhering to the regulations that *we* passed. On the audit side, though, *they're* not completing audits. It's not acceptable, and as I indicated to them, *we* all agree this is not what Canadians expect.

Since the release of the TSB report and the Auditor General's report, there have been improvements to rail safety. The rail subsector recently adopted new SMS regulations that are aimed at improving the effectiveness of SMS, as well as new regulations that give Transport Canada the authority to fine railways for contraventions of the Railway Safety Act or to suspend or cancel railway operating certificates for non-compliance with safety requirements or SMS regulations. It remains to be seen whether these safety improvements will address the concerns raised by our interview subjects and the reports cited here.

In sum, behaviour modification is arguably the most difficult cybernetic control component[2] to achieve, and it shows. Behaviour modification is expensive, intrusive, and slow. The quality, number, and rigour of inspections, and audits can be wanting; much of this control component is left to CI owners and operators to manage themselves. When things go wrong, blame shifting becomes more pronounced.

CONCLUSION

The transportation system is complex, with many interconnected components, and the institutions that oversee, operate, and manage these interconnected components are fragmented. The government's role tends to be one of meta-governance. It focuses on coordinating markets and overseeing systems that are predominantly owned by non-governmental organizations. This institutional fragmentation creates a conundrum: how can the government coordinate large, interconnected networks of CI, many of which networks have competing interests, without a central command and control system to oversee them?

The successful operation and security of the transportation sector in Canada depends on partnerships, and collaboration between different orders of government and different departments, and between government and private industry. This is partly due to the division of powers in the Constitution Act, 1867, which gives the federal government jurisdiction over international and interprovincial transportation and the provincial governments jurisdiction over intra-provincial transportation, and it is partly due to the fact that the majority of CI is owned and operated by private-sector companies. Indeed, Canada's National Transportation Policy mandates that government and the private sector work together to develop and support an integrated transportation system. Canada's National Transportation Policy also underscores the fact that market competition, complemented by regulation, is the best way to create a transportation system that is both safe and economically viable.

Progress in enhancing risk regulation varies across transportation subsectors. Airports have made the most progress, particularly since 9/11. Airports have built on a tradition of security. Industry, government, and citizen interests are also aligned on airport security issues so it is easy to see why airports were able to make such quick progress.

While there seems to be an alignment of government and industry interests in airport security, seaports exist in an area of confusing multi-level governance with multiple and competing interests. Seaports are immovable, are expected to be competitive, and serve a number of public- and private-sector interests. While they fall under federal jurisdiction, they also depend on services that are the responsibility of the provincial and municipal orders of government. Interview subjects felt pulled in different directions to meet efficiency and security concerns. They felt Canadian government operations at the ports are uncoordinated and regulations create great uncertainty for seaports.

Like seaports, rail also seems to have a somewhat ambivalent relationship with regulators. SMS allow government to leave safety to individual rail companies; in fact, government has failed to carry out most of its audits. Class I rail seems to prefer the autonomy, but it has a profit motive. It has its own security officers, which gives it access to intelligence and decreases its dependence on external agencies.

Trucking is one of the few transportation subsectors that can be highly adaptive. Most CI is in a fixed location, but trucks can relocate and change plans. Trucks would be crucial in any emergency response. This point is not lost on emergency responders. Many organizations include local trucks and school buses in their emergency response plans. What is less clear, however, is the ability and capacity of trucking and school bus companies to meet demand. Indeed, if most organizations are depending on trucks and school buses for emergencies they will be disappointed. There are not enough trucks and school buses to go around, and there is no reliable source of information about how communities would respond collectively to emergencies or how trucks and schools buses would be coordinated.

To date, most bridge security is informal. Bridge failures can also be highly consequential; communities as a whole need to think more carefully about how to respond to bridge closures. Bridge staff also need to think about how to connect more effectively with the communities around them, not just with other bridge staff, and they need to think about how to use technology to collect more reliable data about the use and deterioration of CI.

Each subsector has distinguishing features, but some of the same organizational characteristics that contributed to the Air India tragedy in 1985 also contributed to the Lac-Mégantic rail disaster in 2013. While the two events are different in important ways, both the Air India and Lac-Mégantic reports note that the regulator, Transport Canada, was behind in its oversight of the subsector. During the Air India tragedy, the security focus was on hijacking, despite the fact that Transport Canada had clear information that the current threat was sabotage. Airports did not take steps to adapt the existing aviation security regime to the evolving threat. In the lead-up to the Lac-Mégantic tragedy, Transport Canada was aware of the increased use of rail for transporting crude oil, but it had not adequately assessed the operational risks inherent in the practice. These two disasters provide examples of the government failing to adapt to an evolving threat, or, as one of our interview subjects noted, governments regulators often provide "yesterday's answers to today's questions" (Int 37). Despite the importance of adaptive capacity, regulatory regimes are often stable and self-reinforcing. Indeed, regulatory regimes often lack adaptive capacity, a theme that emerged not only in the transportation sector but also the chemicals sector, the subject of our next chapter.

5

Chemicals Sector

Chemicals are, in many ways, heavily regulated in Canada. Facilities that use, store, and manufacture chemicals are subject to numerous regulations, especially in respect of safety and environmental protection. These regulations cover occupational health, emissions, waste disposal, and a wide range of other subjects. Consumer products must similarly meet a host of statutory and regulatory requirements intended to ensure product safety and protect public health.

With respect to major failures, however, chemical facilities are subject to less oversight, and prescriptive government regulation is rare. Instead, the regime favours flexible, collaborative mechanisms that are often promulgated by industry associations. In practical terms, this means that many aspects of safety and security are left to the purview of individual chemical facilities.

Of the regime's three components, information gathering receives the most attention, encompassing a wide range of monitoring, research, and information-sharing processes. These processes include mandatory reporting requirements for chemical facility operators, information-sharing fora, research initiatives, and communication channels between law enforcement and industry. Informal networks parallel these formal information-sharing networks, emerging and expanding on the basis of personal relationships among colleagues and peers.

Regulatory standards are generally not prescriptive. Standards are designed to facilitate innovation, agility, and cooperation between regulators and industry. Standard setting in the chemical regime exemplifies a high-reliability approach to safety and security, in which processes and structures are designed to be adaptable, responsive, redundant, and dispersed.

Meanwhile, behaviour modification receives little attention, representing the smallest component of the regulatory regime. Few resources are dedicated to ensuring that chemical facilities comply with government regulations and the literature is split on the effectiveness of industry-led enforcement of private standards. For the most part, behaviour modification efforts tend to emphasize compliance over deterrence.

This regulatory environment produces certain tensions. On one hand, the regime is generally responsive to private-sector interests; facilities are allowed the freedom to implement practices tailored to their unique circumstances. These circumstances assist commercial innovation and growth. On the other hand, for small and medium-sized enterprises (SMEs), which are less organized and possess fewer resources and less expertise than large chemical companies, this flexibility may allow lax attitudes towards safety and security to go unchecked. The same is true for municipalities and water utilities, which are geographically dispersed and face resource pressures. Water utilities often look to best practices and standards developed by US and international organizations, because of limited interactions between utilities and the Canadian government agencies responsible for critical infrastructure protection (CIP). First responders call for greater clarity and guidance on standards for storing chemicals.

Similar tensions are generated by the regulatory regime's interactions between industry associations and regulators. By providing de facto authorization to industry standards such as Responsible Care, major industry players are allowed to influence the level and nature of competition in the market, thereby preserving crucial structural advantages. For regulators, maintaining stable and close relationships with large companies provides access to industry expertise and allows regulators to influence private-sector behaviour.

These types of arrangements raise questions about transparency and accountability. Reliance on private standards, in the absence of traditional top-down government regulation, raises the prospect of post-event blame shifting. Without formal agreements to outline roles and responsibilities, it becomes unclear in the aftermath of a major disaster whether the company in question ought to be blamed for failing to implement stronger standards or the government should be held responsible for providing inadequate oversight. The situation is particularly unclear when the regulatory regime is subject to intense public scrutiny and in the hunt for accountability that often plays out in the media following black swan events.

NEPTUNE TECHNOLOGIES
AND BIORESSOURCES DISASTER

The Neptune disaster provides a good starting point for analyzing the Canadian regulatory regime for addressing risks to chemical facilities. Neptune Technologies and Bioressources Inc. is a medium-sized company headquartered in Laval, Quebec. In 2013–14, it employed 117 people and reported revenues of just under $20 million (Neptune Technologies and Bioressources 2014). Neptune operates one facility, in Sherbrooke, Quebec, where it produces dietary supplements containing krill oil, which is rich in omega-3 fatty acids. To extract the oil, Neptune uses a manufacturing process that involves acetone, a highly flammable chemical compound that can harm the nervous system and, at high enough concentrations, lead to unconsciousness (Canadian Centre for Occupational Health and Safety 2015).

On 8 November 2012, company employees shut down the plant for maintenance work. After reconnecting various systems, employees noticed acetone spilling from a processing tank, filling the air with an acetone mist. Frantic efforts to halt the spill were unsuccessful; at around 1:30 pm, an explosion tore through the facility, destroying much of the building. The blast and subsequent fire burned 15,000 litres of acetone, killed three workers, and injured eighteen others. Residents of the surrounding suburb, alerted to the disaster by the violent explosion and plumes of smoke rising over their homes, flooded 9-1-1 with over 100 calls in the first minute after the explosion. Within thirty minutes of the explosion, Neptune's share value had dropped by ten per cent.

The Quebec Commission on Workplace Health and Safety (CSST) led the subsequent investigation.[1] The Commission's report, published in May 2014, highlights three primary causes for the explosion (Beaudette and Marquis 2014, 52–62). First, there were design and process flaws that caused the initial acetone spill when the equipment was restarted. Secondly, the company failed to adhere to the National Building Code and the National Fire Protection Association's Flammable and Combustible Liquids Code, meaning the building was unsuitable for the type of manufacturing process that Neptune was using. Thirdly, the company had inadequate health and safety policies in place, which facilitated poor decision-making by management and heightened the probability of failure.

The CSST's report also highlights that because Neptune was a designated chemical company and a member of a *mutuelle de prévention* – a provincial insurance product that offers cheaper rates for SMES that engage in processes to prevent occupational injuries (Société Mutuelle de Prévention Inc. 2015) – provincial regulations required the company to have in place a hazard identification and prevention plan. Although Neptune had such a plan, it did not address the handling of acetone and had not been updated to reflect significant changes to the building and staff (Beaudette and Marquis 2014, 4, 61). The CSST's report also notes that the company was in the midst of expanding its facility when the blast occurred, although later reports indicate that, despite a $3 million grant for the project from the provincial government, the expansion had not been authorized by Quebec's Ministry of the Environment (CBC News 2012).

The Neptune disaster presents a case of a small chemical manufacturing facility located next to a residential neighbourhood that outwardly appeared to be operating in compliance with regulatory standards: it belonged to a *mutuelle de prévention* and it had in place a hazard identification and prevention plan. In reality, the plan was outdated and incomplete, the company was failing to meet other key standards (including building codes), and its expansion project was unauthorized. Although this approach to safety and security had corresponded for several years with commercial success, it also laid the groundwork for eventual disaster. Similar dynamics exist throughout the sector, and many features present in the Neptune example – an emphasis on competitiveness and efficiency, limited enforcement of standards, a reliance on self-regulation – are key characteristics of the regulatory regime for chemicals.

CHEMICALS SECTOR

Before we examine the regulatory regime and its constituent control mechanisms, it is important to understand the sector itself, including the types of facilities that use, store, and manufacture chemicals. The term *chemicals sector* refers to a broad range of facilities, spread across the entire country and involved in various activities, from producing and storing chemicals to applying chemicals to treat drinking water.

A major segment of the sector is the chemical manufacturing industry itself, which encompasses a complex and diverse array of companies, products, and processes. The literature differentiates the chemical industry in various ways; however, it commonly categorizes it vertically, in terms of layers of ascending product complexity (Ashford and Heaton 1983; Conference Board of Canada 2013; Engelhardt and Maurer 2012; Industry Canada 2011; Mahdi, Nightingale, and Berkhout 2002; Environmental Protection Agency n.d.), horizontally, in terms of product types (Arora 1997; Rubim de Pinho Accioli Doria 2010; OECD 2001; Walsh and Lodorfos 2002), or as some combination of both perspectives (Lenz and Lafrance 1996).

From the vertical perspective, the bottom layer of the chemical industry comprises companies that combine organic and inorganic materials to produce basic chemicals (Ashford and Heaton 1983; Lenz and Lafrance 1996; OECD 2001). In the next layer, companies convert these basic chemicals into intermediaries that are essential inputs into other industries and products. The third layer comprises companies that use intermediate chemicals to make speciality chemicals, such as water treatment chemicals, paints, fertilizers, plastics, or artificial fibres (Lenz and Lafrance 1996). Products in the third layer are also called finished products (Ashford and Heaton 1983). The horizontal perspective, by comparison, divides the industry into product types. Table 5.1 offers a summary of several such descriptions.

The two perspectives, horizontal and vertical, are clearly linked. In fact, many of their categories overlap (e.g., basic and industrial chemicals). Both perspectives provide insight into the diversity, complexity, and interconnectivity of the chemical industry. This complexity and interconnectivity is reflected in the large number of chemical companies and products in North America. Canada alone is home to 2,730 chemical establishments (Industry Canada 2011). Nearly ninety per cent of chemical companies in Canada employ fewer than 100 employees (Conference Board of Canada 2013). In 2001, companies with fewer than fifty employees made ninety-five per cent of the 50,000 chemicals produced in the United States (OECD 2001).

Globally, most of the chemical industry's outputs are basic, commodity-type chemicals (Lenz and Lafrance 1996; Lieberman 1987). In Canada, basic chemicals account for thirty per cent of

Table 5.1 Examples of horizontal descriptions of the chemical industry

Source	Types of chemical products
Arora (1997)	Air separation fertilizers, food products, gas handling, inorganic chemicals, industrial gases, metals, organic chemicals, organic refining, petrochemicals, pharmaceuticals, plastics, paper, textiles, and fibres
Rubim de Pinho Accioli Doria (2010)	Life science (pharmaceuticals, pesticides, biotechnology), consumer care, basic chemicals, and specialties
Lenz and Lafrance (1996)	Industrial chemicals, pharmaceuticals, and other chemical products
North American Industry Classification System (NAICS) (Industry Canada 2011)	Industrial chemicals (NAICS 3251, 3252), agricultural chemicals (3252), pharmaceuticals (3254), and formulated products (3255, 3256, 3259)
Organisation for Economic Co-operation and Development (OECD 2001)	Basic or commodity chemicals, specialty chemicals, life science chemicals, and consumer care products
Walsh and Lodorfos (2002)	Chemicals, pharmaceuticals, and agri-food

industry sales (Conference Board of Canada 2013). Companies producing these chemicals tend to be technologically mature (Ashford and Heaton 1983, 115), large and diversified (Mahdi et al. 2002), and multinational (Rubim de Pinho Accioli Doria 2010). Over the last fifty years, the chemicals sector has seen few changes in the substances it produces; instead of developing new chemicals, companies have focused on process innovation (Ashford and Heaton 1983; Rubim de Pinho Accioli Doria 2010).

Moving up the supply chain, the chemical industry grows increasingly diverse. Chemical companies, however, are small in terms of both the number of people they employ and the volume of chemicals they produce (Vithoontien 2004). This critical infrastructure (CI) sector is marked by "product differentiation, custom tailoring of products for customers, and small scales of production" (Arora 1997, 398). The chemicals produced are often highly profitable, but short-lived in the market (Ashford and Heaton 1983), as well as protected by patents on either the product itself or the manufacturing process (Conference Board of Canada 2013, 1). Chemical companies rely on a handful of customers for most of their orders (Conference Board of Canada 2013), and they engage in risky research and product innovation (Rubim de Pinho Accioli Doria 2010).

As noted above, we use the term *chemicals sector* to refer to the full range of facilities that manufacture, use, or store chemicals. This includes water treatment plants. In Canada, the water sector is similar in many respects to the consumer and speciality product segment of the chemical industry, at least insofar as it is characterized by a large number of small operators. In 2000, the World Health Organization estimated that there were 9,000 public water and waste water treatment systems in Canada. These included 2,500 municipally owned plants serving urban residents and approximately 6,500 privately owned systems providing public services at trailer parks, campgrounds, golf courses, and ski facilities (World Health Organization 2000).

REGULATORY REGIME CONTENT

In Canada, responsibility for chemicals is shared between the federal and provincial governments. The Constitution Act, 1867 does not explicitly assign authority for managing chemicals to either level of government. As a result, the regulatory regime has grown haphazardly, coalescing around an array of federal and provincial legislation on numerous chemical risk-related subjects, including the environment, emergency management, and crime. Municipal land-use planning and private industry standards are also prevalent.

The chemical regime differs from other sectors in its centralization and consistency because Canadian governments possess varying responsibilities across the policy areas relevant to chemical regulation. In a sense, the chemical regime lacks national coherence, exhibiting what Hood and colleagues (2001) might call a diverse and erratic pattern of administrative and institutional geography. The chemical regime is clearly broad and complex. It occupies a policy space that crosses numerous jurisdictions, whose authorities possess varying resources and priorities. Although we refer to the chemical regime as a single construct, in reality it represents a variety of regulations and processes and should not be seen as a top-down, unified entity.

Information Gathering

Information gathering in the chemical regime exhibits a high level of investment and aggression. It includes mandatory reporting requirements for chemical facility operators, information-sharing fora, research initiatives, and communication channels between law enforcement and industry. Given the large number of chemical facilities in Canada, governments rely on these facilities to provide accurate information about the chemicals they are using or storing. Informal networks parallel these formal mechanisms, which emerge and expand on the basis of personal relationships among colleagues and peers.

At the federal level, reporting requirements for chemicals are dictated by the Environmental Emergency (E2) regulations of the Canadian Environmental Protection Act. These regulations were introduced in response to 9/11 (Environment Canada 2003; Shrives 2004, 17). Environment Canada stores information received under the E2 regulations in a database that is only accessible to public safety authorities and the Department of National Defence (Int 63). In some provinces, environmental statutes establish similar reporting requirements for chemical facilities (for example, Ontario's Environmental Protection Act and Quebec's Environmental Quality Act). In addition to information received via these mandatory reporting mechanisms, government-funded research provides a proactive method for learning about chemical risks. For example, the federal government's Chemical, Biological, Radiological and Nuclear and Explosives (CBRNE) Research and Technology Initiative (CRTI)[2] funded research on counterterrorism for chemical, biological, radiological, and nuclear threats (Volchek et al. 2006, 126; Int 56).

Yet not all aspects of information gathering are necessarily aggressive or ambitious. In our interviews, hazardous materials (hazmat) first responders and an emergency management professional said that reporting requirements for fixed chemical sites could be improved. One interview participant explained that firefighters face increased risks when responding to emergencies at facilities where there are few data about the chemicals on site (Int 56). The lethality of the 2013 fertilizer plant explosion in West, Texas, has been attributed, in part, to first responders' lack of knowledge about the quantity of ammonium nitrate at the facility (Int 68; Pell, McNeill, and

Roberts 2013). Two of our interview participants (a first responder and an emergency management official) recommended that provinces create regularly updated repositories of hazmat data (Int 55; Int 60). Improved information sharing is often discussed in the context of transporting chemicals; our interviews, however, show that it is equally important when it comes to storing chemicals.[3]

In the chemical regime, information gathering is characterized by significant levels of third-party or private-sector contributions and a high degree of jurisdictional and system complexity (Hood et al. 2001, 34). These characteristics are evident in the numerous channels for facilitating information sharing between government and industry (and, to a lesser extent, private citizens). Table 5.2 shows a selection of the information-sharing channels and fora mentioned in our interviews, organized according to their membership.

Although not exhaustive, table 5.2 reveals key structural features of the regime's information gathering. First, several fora are multi-jurisdictional. For example, the federal and provincial (and, in some cases, territorial) governments participate in the CI and CBRNE working groups. US information-sharing mechanisms are also prominent. Secondly, industry is involved in most fora on a voluntary basis. For example, Chemwatch (intended to limit the accessibility of illicit drug and explosive precursors) and the Suspicious Incident Reporting (SIR) system involve voluntary partnerships between the RCMP and the chemical industry. Information-sharing fora led by industry (e.g., CAER [community awareness and emergency response] risk communication efforts, Responsible Care committees) are also voluntary, although participation is typically a requirement for industry association membership. Relatively few fora include participation by private citizens. Finally, table 5.2 demonstrates the broad range of policy areas implicated in the control of chemicals. Fora exist on a diverse range of topics, including environmental protection, law enforcement, international trade, and municipal emergency management.

Information gathering – like standard setting and behaviour modification – may also be thought of in terms of style. Style denotes the operating conventions and attitudes of those involved in regulation (Hood et al. 2001, 32). The style of information gathering in the chemical regime is shaped by divergent degrees of operational rule-following and competing perspectives on the extent and reliability of information shared between CI operators and government. For

Table 5.2 Examples of chemical regime information-gathering mechanisms

Mechanism	Government	Industry	Private citizens
	Membership		
American Water and Wastewater Association (AWWA)	✓	✓	
Canadian Water and Wastewater Association (CWWA)	✓	✓	
CBRNE sub-working groups	✓	✓	✓
CBSA Partners in Protection (PIP)	✓	✓	
Comité mixte municipal–industriel (CMMI)	✓	✓	✓
Community Awareness and Emergency Response (CAER) risk communication fora	✓	✓	✓
CBRNE Research and Technology Initiative (CRTI)	✓		
Department of Homeland Security Customs-Trade Partnership Against Terrorism (C-TPAT)	✓	✓	
Federal/provincial/territorial critical infrastructure working groups	✓	✓	✓
Organisation for Economic Co-operation and Development (OECD) Working Group on Chemical Accidents	✓	✓	
Professional associations (Canadian Association of Fire Chiefs, Canadian Institute of Planners, etc.)	✓	✓	
Provincial emergency management fora	✓	✓	
RCMP Chemwatch	✓	✓	
RCMP Suspicious Incident Reporting (SIR) System	✓	✓	
Responsible Care audits	✓	✓	✓
Responsible Care committees		✓	
Water Information-sharing and Analysis Center (WaterISAC)	✓	✓	

Note: CBRNE, chemical, biological, radiological and nuclear and explosives; CBSA, Canada Border Services Agency.
Sources: Int 52; Int 53; Int 54; Int 55; Int 56; Int 58; Int 59; Int 60; Int 61; Int 62; Int 63; Int 64.

example, one interview participant from a water utility stated that strict adherence to security clearance requirements for accessing federal intelligence is a hindrance for small CI operators (Int 52). Similarly, a chemical industry respondent argued that the "for Canadian eyes only" restriction on sensitive information provided by the federal government is impractical because the security offices of many chemical companies are located outside Canada (Int 61).

The perceived quality of information shared by public agencies is also disputed. One water utility manager described the ongoing exchange of information between CI operators and government in positive terms (Int 54), but others said that federal agencies provide only limited information to CI facilities about safety and security risks and best practices (Int 52; Int 59; Int 61). A representative of a chemical industry association stated that his organization had received no contact from the federal government regarding establishment of a CI working group for the manufacturing sector, despite a government commitment to do so (Int 61). In general, industry participants said they would prefer information sharing from regulatory agencies to occur on demand and in convenient, context-specific formats (Int 51; Int 54; Int 59; Int 61). In contrast, interview participants from all sectors reported strong working relationships between CI and law enforcement, including local police, RCMP, and CSIS (Int 52; Int 53; Int 54; Int 58; Int 59; Int 61; Int 64; Int 65).

Information sharing occurs on the basis of both formal rules and informal practices. In the water sector, informal networks facilitated by collegial relationships are more effective than formal information-sharing structures for disseminating accurate and relevant information (Int 51; Int 52; Int 53; Int 54). One interview participant implied that the information shared via these informal networks may exceed what is formally or legally permitted (Int 52). The importance of establishing trust was a common theme in the comments of all participants, as was the notion that fora are primarily useful as an opportunity to build personal relationships (Int 51; Int 52; Int 53; Int 55; Int 58; Int 60; Int 64; Int 65). None of the participants defined *trust*; as we noted in chapter 3, in the academic literature there is a variety of distinct and sometimes incompatible definitions of the term (Kramer 1999).[4] It is consequently unclear whether trust is understood consistently across the regime. Two participants acknowledged that information-sharing networks based primarily on personal relationships are vulnerable to staff turnover (Int 52; Int 58).

In sum, information gathering represents the largest component, and primary focus, of the regulatory regime, encompassing a wide range of monitoring, research, and information-sharing mechanisms. There is an emphasis on formal multijurisdictional and public–private information sharing, but informal and discreet information sharing also occurs on the basis of trusted personal relationships. Interview participants reported largely positive and effective relationships when sharing information *within* organizations (i.e., within industry associations, government agencies, and CI facilities). Participants disagreed, however, on the quality, relevance, and regularity of information sharing *between* CI operators and government agencies responsible for CIP, which may be a product of conflicting expectations with respect to how, why, and to whom information should be disseminated.

Different attitudes towards regulation, and the role of government in general, might help to explain the reasons for some of these conflicts. Water utility operators and firefighters, for example, called for information-sharing platforms where CI operators could freely exchange information and best practices with one another, while interview participants from the chemical industry preferred that context-specific information be provided by government on demand and in industry-preferred formats. The desire for open sharing of information and best practices suggests a preference for flat organizational structures and communitarian decision-making, whereas industry appears to prefer limited government intervention, market efficiency, and corporate autonomy with respect to risk regulation. The responses provided by government regulators, which emphasize the importance of rules and structure in the context of information sharing, suggest a bureaucratic orientation.

Standard Setting

Regulatory size relates to the balance between the state and the market, the degree of "anticipationism" in risk regulation, and the extent of regulatory bureaucracy (Hood et al. 2001, 31). By these measures, the standard-setting component of the chemical regime is small relative to its information-gathering component. Despite the introduction of new government standards after 9/11, the regime continues to exhibit a low degree of policy aggression, meaning standards have limited impact with respect to behavioural change and are intended to be minimally disruptive (Hood et al. 2001). This is not due to oversight or inattention; our interview findings (Int 58; Int 59; Int 63) and the academic literature (for example, Lacoursière 2006; Moffet, Bregha, and Middelkoop 2004, 189–90) agree that the Canadian regulatory model has been shaped by a preference for public–private collaboration and the knowledge that industry standards represent a valid alternative to traditional regulation, particularly where legal authority is distributed across both orders of government. The decision to refrain from prescriptive, top-down standard setting is deliberate.

The scarcity of prescriptive government standards was a common theme in our interviews. Water utility operators reported a lack of standards for storing chemicals (Int 52; Int 53; Int 54), while chemical industry experts reported an absence of government standards for process safety management and site security (Int 58; Int 59; Int 61). Hazmat-trained firefighters called for improved capabilities-based planning among emergency services (Int 55; Int 56), and one firefighter recommended stricter requirements for facilities that store chemicals (Int 56). Water utilities and chemical companies tend to follow guidelines and best practices promulgated by industry associations (Int 53, Int 55; Int 56; Int 59, Int 61), as well as by American agencies (Int 59; Int 61).[5]

Of course, the regulatory regime is not completely devoid of government standards. In our interviews, however, participants expressed hesitation about their value and stringency. Two industry association participants (Int 59; Int 61) stated that members of the chemical industry's Responsible Care program maintain environmental plans that match or exceed the requirements of the E2 regulations.[6] Other research in this area has registered similar scepticism about the effectiveness of the E2 regulations (for example, O'Neill et al. 2009, 6).

Municipal authority over land-use planning is another source of potentially powerful risk management standards (Int 62). However, it can be difficult for municipalities, particularly small ones, to reconcile economic development pressures with risk management considerations to make informed land-use decisions (Int 58).[7] There are few resource materials for communities to consult (O'Neill et al. 2009, 33–4).[8] The placement of chemical facilities is an issue that is "falling through the cracks … and remains a significant gap within the Canadian legislative framework" (Alp 2004, 17). For example, the Toronto Sunrise Propane facility exploded in 2009, killing two and causing the evacuation of thousands, yet its location was in full compliance with municipal zoning laws (Barber 2008). The West Fertilizer Company's facility in West, Texas, also complied with zoning laws (Gillum and Plushnick-Masti 2013), which suggests there may be a similar zoning problem in the United States.

In comparison, interview participants had positive things to say about the current relationship between CI operators and municipal authorities around emergency planning (Int 55; Int 56; Int 59; Int 60; Int 61). Still, provincial emergency management standards apply to *municipal* preparedness, and establish few, if any, mandatory requirements for CI operators who handle chemicals. Moreover, at the federal level, a 2009 report of the Auditor General of Canada found that manufacturing had made the least progress on emergency management of the ten CI sectors (Auditor General of Canada 2009).

As with information gathering, it is possible to think about standard setting in terms of structure, which considers the "extent to which regulation involves a mix of public and private sector actors" (Hood et al. 2001, 31). The concept of structure highlights the role of Responsible Care (RC), the industry's self-regulation initiative and a defining feature of the Canadian chemical regime. Introduced by the Canadian Chemical Producers' Association in the 1980s,[9] RC contains three sets of standards to which member companies must adhere. The RC standards are intended to provide enough flexibility to implement facility-specific practices for safety and security, and they include guidelines for communicating site risks with first responders and community members (Belanger et al. 2009, 21; CIAC n.d.; Int 61; Lacoursière 2006).

In our interviews, industry participants expressed satisfaction with the RC commitments (Int 58; Int 59; Int 61; Int 66; Int 67), although one suggested that improved standards with respect to cybersecurity are needed (Int 61). Government interview participants, including Canadian and American industry regulators and a law enforcement officer (Int 63; Int 64; Int 68), also described the program as effective. However, not all chemical companies are Chemistry Industry Association of Canada members, and non-members have no obligation to subscribe to RC standards.[10]

In any case, government acceptance of industry standards is a prominent feature of the Canadian regulatory landscape. This stems in large part from the Major Industrial Accidents Council of Canada (Int 58; Lacoursière 2006, 311). Jointly funded by government and industry, the council was seen as a consensus-based alternative to the sort of top-down, regulatory approach preferred by most governments in the wake of the Bhopal disaster. Although the council ceased to exist in 1999, its emphasis on working collaboratively towards common objectives continues to influence the development of regulatory standards, serving as the foundation for the E2 regulations and joint municipal–industry emergency planning efforts (Int 58; Int 59; Lacoursière 2006, 313). Similarly, a number of major chemical facilities have recently made voluntary efforts to replace chemicals with less hazardous ones in response to Canada's Chemicals Management Plan, offering further evidence of the collaborative relationship between the private and public sectors (Int 63; Int 68; see also Meek and Armstrong 2007, 613).

In terms of style, meaning the cultural traits, attitudes, and beliefs of standard setters, the regime conveys a preference for limited market intervention. At the same time, the RC program reflects a traditional hierarchical approach to regulation, despite being promulgated by industry: in principle, RC establishes clear rules and lines of accountability that are intended to promote stability.

Standards in the chemical regime are also influenced by the principle of collibration, or "control through opposed maximizers" (Hood et al. 2001, 25). According to this approach, the regulatory regime is calibrated to balance competing principles – risk against cost, for example – by facilitating deliberative processes that enable individual actors to implement controls appropriate for their particular circumstances.[11] One interview participant from the chemical industry attributed this to the small scale of industry in Canada (compared with the United States), which requires government to tailor regulations to specific industrial subsectors or even specific facilities, an onerous and inefficient undertaking (Int 61). RC is characterized by standards that permit flexibility and adjustment. A Chemistry Industry Association of Canada guidance document, for instance, emphasizes that the codes "are deliberately open to interpretation to inspire companies to think more deeply and broadly about the complex issues associated with their Responsible Care commitment" (CIAC 2010, 5).

It may be illustrative here to draw parallels to the literature on high-reliability organizations. According to the high-reliability organization paradigm, safety and security are achieved by inculcating an attitude, or culture, of mindfulness about potential risks. It is more important, in other words, that an organization possess the capacity to identify and respond to emerging failures than it is for the organization to meet a set of rigid standards designed by a distant authority with limited knowledge of the conditions at a specific facility (La Porte 1996; La Porte and Consolini 1991; Weick and Sutcliffe 2001). The Canadian regulatory model contains hallmarks of this approach. Certainly, with RC we see a preference for the dissemination of a certain attitude towards safety and security risk management as opposed to the application of prescriptive standards.

In sum, the regime's standard-setting component reflects a collaborative, consensus-based relationship between government and the private sector. Industry-promulgated standards, such as RC, are prevalent, and the development of new standards by government generally involves extensive consultations with representative industry associations. In permitting facilities a degree of freedom to implement practices tailored to their unique circumstances, the regime is generally responsive to private-sector interests. Water utility operators, however, reported limited interaction with government agencies responsible for CIP. Emergency responders similarly desired greater clarity and guidance with respect to standards for storing chemicals, and better coordination and capabilities-based planning among emergency services when responding to chemical incidents.

Behaviour Modification

The third element of control is behaviour modification, which includes enforcement of standards. Independent audits and reviews are often a good source of information about behaviour modification practices. The E2 regulations, for instance, were subject to a 2011 audit by the federal Auditor General. The findings of that audit described Environment Canada's enforcement program as suffering from poor management, insufficient information about regulated companies, inadequate training for enforcement officers, and failure to follow up on enforcement actions in a fair, predictable, and consistent manner (Auditor General of Canada 2011, 2). In 2011, Ecojustice reported that while the number of Environment Canada enforcement officers had increased since 2000, the number of inspections had remained stable and the number of investigations had declined (Ecojustice 2011, 33–9; see also Girard, Day, and Snider 2010). In summarizing these data, Ecojustice concluded that the figures are low in absolute terms, giving rise to "concern regarding the overall effectiveness of the CEPA [Canadian Environmental Protection Act] enforcement regime" (Ecojustice 2011, 39).[12]

The federal government has published enforcement statistics that provide further insight into the stringency of behaviour modification activities. In 2014, approximately 4,700 facilities used or stored above-threshold quantities of regulated chemicals (Environment Canada 2014a). In fiscal year 2013–14, there were 208 enforcement officers and 176 enforcement analysts.[13] These officials undertook 133 inspections related to the E2 regulations, eighty-eight of which were on site. Assuming each inspection involved a different facility, in 2013–14 the inspection rate for E2 facilities was less than three per cent. Government thus seems capable of targeting only a small proportion of chemical facilities each year. To illustrate this, figure 5.1 shows the number of Environmental Protection Compliance Orders, inspections, and written warnings issued under the E2 regulations each year between 2008–09 and 2013–14.

Inspections and enforcement activities need not target every facility to modify behaviour. Risk-based enforcement approaches can be successful in ensuring adherence to standards. Yet when considered in light of the aforementioned 2011 Auditor General's report, these figures provide further indication that the behaviour modification component of the regime is small and minimally aggressive.

Similar enforcement issues may be present in respect of municipal emergency management. Creedy, Shrives, and Phillips (2005, 378) found that lack of funding and enforcement has led to considerable variation in quality among community emergency plans in Canada (see also Henstra and McBean 2005; Shrubsole 2000). In general, evidence suggests a discrepancy between the preparedness of large, urban centres and small, rural communities (Int 62).

The absence of "command and control" enforcement mechanisms – meaning strict, punitive measures – suggests that the regime may be oriented towards compliance rather than deterrence. Under a compliance model, regulators rely on information sharing and engagement with firms to ensure awareness of standards and to engender a culture that promotes adherence to those standards (Hood et al. 2001, 27). Evidence of this orientation is provided by the numerous information-sharing fora described above. These fora help regulators disseminate information and preferred practices to CI owners and operators, allowing governments to facilitate a

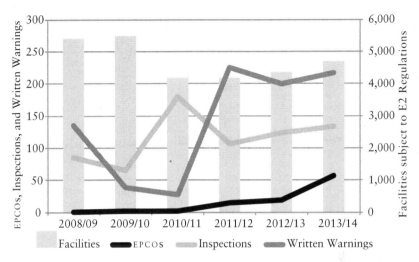

Figure 5.1 Rates of E2 enforcement activities, 2008–14.
Source: Environment and Climate Change Canada (2015). EPCOS, environmental protection compliance orders.

consistent approach to safety and security risk management across the regime. This type of approach can be hindered, however, by the fact that information-sharing fora are typically voluntary and often do not include SMES.

Interview participants offered a variety of perspectives on behaviour modification. A firefighter estimated that twenty per cent of chemical facilities regularly violate standards, either intentionally or because of ignorance (Int 55), and that insufficient monitoring and enforcement are to blame (Int 55; Int 56). In Canada, as well as the United States, chemical facilities are typically operated by SMES (Int 68). A water utility employee suggested that CI operators are occasionally reluctant to implement standards that they deem unnecessary or onerous (Int 54). Two other interview participants, both federal government employees, acknowledged that recent budget changes have had operational implications (Int 63; Int 64).

Others sought to explain the perceived lack of enforcement. Three interview subjects from water utilities argued that safety and security are not well integrated into workplace culture (Int 51; Int 52; Int 54), although safety receives more attention than security (Int 52; Int 54). The priorities of Canadian regulatory agencies have failed to motivate CI operators to focus on security (unlike their American

counterparts) (Int 53) and, according to a chemical industry participant, these agencies have prioritized standard setting over enforcement (Int 59). Industry interview participants generally did not cite
enforcement as a problem, arguing instead that the Canadian industry has a strong record on managing safety and security risks because
of initiatives such as RC.

As we emphasize above, a defining feature of the chemical regime
is the RC initiative. With respect to enforcement, every three years
each member company must undergo an external, inputs-based[14]
audit of its implementation of the program (Int 51; Green and Hrab
2003, 20–5). Additional oversight and accountability for the initiative is provided by the National Advisory Panel (NAP), which is
composed of twelve to sixteen activists and experts not employed
by industry, advocates, and academics (CIAC 2009). The NAP con-
ducts an annual review of the RC initiative's performance and issues
challenges for improvements. Current NAP members possess considerable expertise and experience in corporate social responsibility,
environmental protection, and sustainability. Few individuals with
security experience, however, participate in the RC initiative. In addition, RC uses soft enforcement mechanisms such as peer pressure,
which proponents say creates an atmosphere of mutual accountability and an incentive for laggards to improve performance (Moffet et
al. 2004, 195–6).[15] Green and Hrab (2003) argue that the diffusion
of RC norms, technology, and information among chemical facility
managers serves as an additional, if subtle, enforcement mechanism.

Interview participants with expertise or experience in the chemical
industry (Int 58; Int 59; Int 61; Int 66; Int 67) offered few comments
on the enforcement of RC.[16] In general, they conveyed a sense of
satisfaction with the initiative and indicated that it operates as
intended. One interview subject stated that verification audits are
successful in ensuring that member companies meet RC expectations
(Int 61). When asked questions related to potential enhancements,
participants suggested that member companies could improve their
business continuity planning efforts (Int 61) and that the Chemistry
Industry Association of Canada should review existing standards to
determine if amendments are necessary (Int 59).

The academic literature on the topic of industry self-regulation
suggests that the industry has had mixed results with respect to
enforcement (see Finger and Gamper-Rabindran 2013; Gamper-
Rabindran and Finger 2013; Gunningham 1995; King and Lenox

2000; Prakash 2000). However, this research focuses on the US industry before the implementation of RC's security codes; to our knowledge, there have been no comparable studies on the enforcement of RC in Canada.

At present, RC behaviour modification efforts are focused on improving performance on safety and environmental sustainability issues; security-related concerns are comparatively underemphasized. Evidence of this can be found in the Chemistry Industry Association of Canada's RC verification audits, which are available on the association's website. Fifty-five audits have been conducted since 2010. We queried each report for the frequency of various terms related to three categories: safety, security, and environmental risks (table 5.3). Not every term fit neatly into these three categories. The term *security* was sometimes used in the generic context of maintaining the physical integrity of a facility. Eight reports were in French. For those eight reports, we recorded use of the term *sécurité* under the security heading, even though the term can be used to indicate safety (i.e., the phrase *occupational health and safety* is typically translated as *la santé et la sécurité au travail*). Also, the term *emergency* was rarely clarified in reports, so we could not determine whether the language in question was concerned with emergencies caused by malicious actors, natural disasters, accidents, or some combination thereof.

On average, each verification report contained 16.85 references to sustainability, 20.62 references to the environment, and 26.71 references to safety. Security, meanwhile, received an average of 13.84 references per report (or about ten references, if the eight French reports are omitted). Specific security-related terms, including terror and malicious incident, were hardly mentioned at all. Although preliminary, this analysis calls into question whether security concerns have infiltrated RC to the same extent as safety and environmental concerns, at least when it comes to behaviour modification.

The preceding paragraphs underscore important aspects of the style of the chemical regime's behaviour modification component. They illustrate both the density of formal behaviour modification mechanisms and the government's relatively modest commitment to enforcement. This modest commitment is not due to the attitudes or qualifications of individual regulators or compliance officers but rather to the broader cultural orientation of the regime itself. Hood and colleagues describe this in terms of the toothpaste-tube-like

Table 5.3 Frequency of safety and security terms in Responsible Care verification reports

Term	Total Frequency	Per report Average	Median	Mode
SECURITY:				
Terror*	47	0.85	0	0
Malicious incident	19	0.35	0	0
Security	761	13.84	3	10
SAFETY:				
Accident	155	2.82	0	1
Safe*	1,469	26.71	32	24
Natural disaster	3	0.05	0	0
ENVIRONMENT:				
Environment*	1,134	20.62	11	20
Sustainability	927	16.85	17	17
EMERGENCY:				
Emergency	1,006	18.29	10	14

Source: Calculations are based on data from CIAC (Chemistry Industry Association of Canada) (2014a).

*Includes all terms sharing the identified stem (e.g., terror, terrorist, and terrorism). In the case of the term *terror*, the term *bomb* was also included in the query.

characteristic of regulatory systems: they tend "if squeezed in one place, to bulge out in another" (2001, 15). The "squeeze" (or increased pressure) on information gathering and, to a lesser extent, standard setting, corresponds with a "bulge" (reduction or vulnerability) in behaviour modification and enforcement.

A further challenge to behaviour modification stems from the difference between large and small organizations. Large organizations, such as multinational chemical companies and water utilities in large cities, are generally more compliant than smaller ones. Small firms can find compliance difficult because regulations are often written with large corporations in mind. Indeed, larger CI operators often contribute to the development of regulations, whereas small operators tend to lack the requisite technical expertise or financial resources to participate (Ashford and Heaton 1983; OECD 2001; Walkerton Commission of Inquiry 2002b). Interview respondents noted that smaller facilities often have fewer staff hours to devote to safety and security matters (Int 52; Int 58), and an emergency management respondent argued that small jurisdictions are challenged by the complexity of preparing for chemical hazards (Int 56). Routinized institutional practices are also a limiting factor, as large corporate entities may be better attuned to and organized for the exigencies of prescriptive, bureaucratic standards than small firms operating on a more fluid, competitive, and uncertain basis. In many ways, thinking about chemical risks in terms of large and small actors offers a helpful framework for understanding the regime's approach to behaviour modification, with larger companies and jurisdictions arguably playing a larger role in influencing the development of standards and exhibiting a greater commitment to enforcing them than their smaller counterparts.

With respect to industry enforcement of its own standards, the preferred style of behaviour modification involves collaboration, persuasion, and education as opposed to punitive sanctions. For example, of the fifty-five RC verification audits described above, fifty-two (ninety-five per cent) were deemed to require no further involvement from the verification team.[17] The potential for any RC member to fail an audit thus seems quite low. Moreover, each audit report begins with conciliatory disclaimers, which explain that the external verification process is intended to provide firm executives with "an external perspective ... along with advice," as well as to "identify opportunities for assisting the company" in improving performance (for an example, see CIAC 2013, 5). This is consistent with an approach to compliance that values self-motivated compliance over deterrence.

In sum, behaviour modification appears to be the smallest component of the regime. The academic and grey literature suggests that the resources dedicated to enforcement may be low in absolute terms. This was also the perception among our water utility, emergency management, and chemical industry interview subjects. Enforcement and compliance appear to be particular problems in the case of SMEs, which are less organized (and often do not subscribe to self-regulation initiatives), possess fewer resources and less expertise, and, compared with large organizations (multinational chemical companies, for example), struggle to achieve compliance.

CONCLUSION

We return now to the Neptune tragedy. It is illustrative to consider the main features of the chemical regime in light of the Neptune case, which provides concrete examples of the information gathering, standard setting, and behaviour modification practices described above. In particular, the Neptune example aligns with a key finding of our research, that the Canadian regime values flexibility and particularity over rigid standardization or one-size-fits-all rules. In the case of both government regulation and private standards, the preference is for companies to retain broad discretion to tailor guidelines to the specific circumstances and hazards at their facilities. At the same time, there is little evidence that adherence to standards is closely monitored or enforced. Thus, although Neptune had, on paper, a prevention plan, the plan failed to account for basic risks, such as risks related to handling acetone. Similarly, the CSST report suggests that the Neptune facility may have been operating in violation of the National Building Code since 2002, ten years before the explosion (Beaudette and Marquis 2014, 27).

The regulatory regime fosters commercial innovation and growth. Although there are few public details about the $3 million government grant for Neptune's plant expansion, the fact that the company received this money without first acquiring approval for its new facility from Quebec's Ministry of the Environment hints at the regime's priorities. This is not to say that governments are inclined to support growth at all costs. Rather, it reveals that governments are acutely aware of the highly competitive nature of the chemical industry, including its low profit margins and the constant demand for innovation. In a province like Quebec, where the chemicals sector directly supports almost 22,000 jobs (CIAC 2016), governments have clear incentives to support policies that foster a dynamic and competitive environment for chemical companies.

The Neptune incident reinforces the haphazard and overlapping nature of the Canadian chemical regime. As the CSST report emphasizes, the Neptune facility was subject to the National Building Code of Canada (which incorporates standards developed by the US National Fire Protection Association) as well as various provincial regulatory requirements and Sherbrooke's municipal construction standards (Beaudette and Marquis 2014, 141). Therefore, like all chemical facilities in Canada, the Neptune plant was ostensibly subject to extensive regulation. That these various standards were not applied or enforced in a prescriptive, aggressive fashion underscores our earlier point about the regime's preference for compliance over strict deterrence, in which regulators seek to use persuasion, engagement, or education to modify behaviour.

The Neptune disaster also raises concerns about the voluntary nature of information gathering and sharing mechanisms. Neptune did not belong to any of the major fora surveyed above. We were unable to uncover evidence that Neptune had membership in a *comité mixte municipal-industriel*, which are committees in Quebec aimed at fostering information sharing between industry and municipalities on safety risks and emergency management. Similarly, it appears that Neptune is neither registered in the E2 database, nor a member of the RC initiative. Neptune, like many other firms, operates outside the numerous information-sharing mechanisms implemented to improve communication and collaboration between industry and government.

The Neptune explosion also underscores the difficult balancing act confronting governments in regulating the chemical industry. There are strong incentives for government to enable chemical firms to innovate and grow. Onerous standards and aggressive deterrence techniques can dampen competitiveness, putting at risk an industry that creates thousands of jobs and generates significant tax revenue. Both before and after the explosion, Neptune exhibited the hallmarks of a successful company: in 2014 it opened a new production facility featuring "robust safety measures to ensure the well-being of employees and state-of-the-art equipment to enhance manufacturing practices" (Neptune Technologies and Bioressources 2015). Conversely, without mandatory information-gathering mechanisms supported by effective standards and behaviour modification practices for SMEs such as Neptune, governments are challenged to exert control over the regime. This also facilitates ambiguity about where accountabilities lie when failures occur. To explain why the regime exhibits these characteristics, we turn now to three contextual hypotheses of Hood and colleagues' framework, which direct our attention to the effects of markets, public opinion, and interest groups on regime content.

PART THREE

Regime Context –
Pressures and Explanations

We turn now to a discussion of the three contextual hypotheses contained in the risk regulation regime framework. Each contextual hypothesis provides a different explanation for a regime's content. The contextual hypotheses also provide a basis for comparing regimes against one another, permitting a deeper understanding of variation across regimes.

We begin our discussion of regime context in chapter 6 by focusing on the market failure hypothesis (MFH). MFH is based on the idea that markets are inadequate mechanisms for addressing some forms of risk. Where markets have failed to address a risk, a government should intervene to the extent necessary to address that failure. MFH is formally incorporated in Canadian government policy. The federal government is required to constrain its regulatory activities to cases where markets have failed. But our analysis shows that MFH explains only a portion of the regime content observed in chapters 4 and 5; other contextual factors must therefore be at play.

In chapter 7 we evaluate the opinion-responsive hypothesis (ORH). This hypothesis is based on the assumption that public opinion influences government and business decision-making. Regulatory content will consequently reflect how most people feel about a sector and its attendant risks. To evaluate this assumption, we examine public polling data and media coverage of recent black swan events. We complement our analysis of the ORH by exploring how cyber specialists use popular media to frame our understanding of cybersecurity risks (chapter 8) and how media coverage influenced public opinion with dramatic consequences for government operations during the 2009 H I N I flu outbreak in Canada (chapter 9).

We discuss the third contextual hypothesis, the interest group hypothesis (I G H), in chapter 10. We focus in particular on how cost–benefit analyses of regulatory policy determine why organized interests mobilize resources to lobby decision-makers. In short, when the cost or benefit of regulation is high, organized interests will try to influence the content of that regulation. In chapter 11, we analyze how organizational culture provides additional insight into the role of interest groups by illustrating how organizational design and value systems shape organizational behaviour and learning.

6

The Market Failure Hypothesis:
Markets on the Margins

In this chapter, we examine Hood and colleagues' (2001) market failure hypothesis (MFH). We are interested in the extent to which the Canadian critical infrastructure (CI) regulatory regime can be understood as a reaction to market failures. We begin with the MFH because it is the only one of Hood and colleagues' three contextual hypotheses that is cited by governments in Canada, and in many other countries, as the basis for their regulatory practices. In Canada, governments are explicit that risk regulation is intended to improve outcomes in cases where markets cannot provide socially optimal outcomes on their own. By analyzing the MFH, we are testing whether governments regulate the way they say they do.

The MFH tries to explain regulatory regimes by assuming that government regulation exists because markets are unable to manage a given risk effectively without government intervention. This hypothesis also assumes that well-designed regulation will be proportional to the probability and consequences of a given risk or, in Hood and colleagues' words, the technical nature of the risk. In other words, the assumptions underlying the MFH reflect fundamental economic principles, such as the idea that the private sector will act when it is in its interest to do so but will not provide public goods, respond appropriately to externalities, or address problems associated with information asymmetries and concentrated market power.

To test the MFH, Hood and colleagues (2001) measure the presence of information costs and opt-out costs. Information costs are faced when assessing the probability and severity of risks to which individuals are exposed. Opt-out costs are incurred when avoiding risk exposure through, among other things, insurance markets and civil law processes. Where either information or opt-out cost is high, a market failure is said to exist and the MFH predicts that government will act to reduce the cost. Maximal regulatory intervention is expected in cases where a risk presents high information and opt-out costs.

Our examination of the chemicals and transportation sectors suggests that, in many cases, the MFH helps in understanding government's response to potential black swan events. We find numerous risks for which markets and supporting legal processes function efficiently, meaning that prices encourage actors to behave in a manner consistent with the likelihood the risk and its consequences will occur. In such cases, markets are capable of reducing the likelihood of black swan events on their own, with no need for government intervention. In other instances, we observe high information costs. Terrorism, for example, can be difficult for individual companies to predict. The large number of information-gathering mechanisms in the chemical and transportation sectors aimed at reducing these costs (i.e., making it easier to detect and prevent acts of terrorism) reflects the MFH's predictions. In all of the above examples, the MFH seems to hold true: the level of government intervention in the market is proportional to the capacity of the market to address risks to critical infrastructure.

In still other instances, however, we observe cases where government regulatory policy reflects a preference for limited intervention despite the presence of high information and high opt-out costs. Inefficient insurance and civil law mechanisms are particularly problematic for critical infrastructure (CI), because of the information asymmetries, moral hazard problems, and negative externalities that potentially trigger black swan events. Even where CI is owned and operated by government entities, as is the case for many water utilities or bridges, the type of policy instruments one would expect under an MFH regime are absent. Often, CI operators belong to self-regulation programs, such as Responsible Care. These programs, however, are largely voluntary, exclude many small and medium-sized enterprises, and lack transparency and, at times, rigour.

We conclude therefore that the MFH has mixed capacity to explain government's approach to the chemical and transportation risk regulation regimes. We also identify broader conceptual problems with using market-failure principles to analyze and compare regulatory regimes. A narrow technical understanding of risk, which underlies the MFH perspective, offers limited analytical utility for complex, uncertain, and ambiguous risks. Some events preclude straightforward quantification. For these events, we must consider other factors, beyond rational calculations of self-interest, to grasp how governments and societies choose to regulate risk.

PUBLIC WELFARE AND MARKET FAILURE

The MFH is rooted in the market liberal theory of the state (Dryzek and Dunleavy 2009). This perspective reflects classical economic principles about the welfare-maximizing function of free markets, captured famously by Adam Smith's description of an invisible hand that provides for the efficient distribution of scarce resources through the interaction of rational, utility-maximizing individuals (Rosen, Wen, and Snoddon 2012, 26). Unnecessary state intervention distorts the efficiency of the competitive market, limiting its capacity to achieve social welfare.[1] The state's role is to monitor and intervene as required to support markets in working properly. In short, according to the MFH, the aim of government regulation is to fix market failures.

The MFH is often advanced as a normative idea, described by terms such as the new right, economic rationalism, and neoliberalism. The market failure perspective is a core principle of major political parties in Canada, the United States, the United Kingdom, Australia, and elsewhere (Dryzek and Dunleavy 2009, 100). While in power, these parties have reshaped the structure and activities of government to reflect market liberal priorities.[2]

In Canada, market failure is a key guiding principle of regulatory policy. The Treasury Board Secretariat's guide to cost–benefit analyses of regulatory proposals, for example, emphasizes that governments must intervene to prevent market failures through regulatory policies that restrict behaviours that might lead to negative repercussions (Treasury Board of Canada Secretariat 2007, 2). Unlike opinion-responsive and interest group explanations of regulatory regime content, the MFH is explicitly embodied in government regulatory decision-making. By evaluating the explanatory capacity of the MFH, we are thus also examining whether risk regulation regimes – and specifically government's contributions to those regimes – are consistent with their governments' policy objectives.

In the context of CI, the predominance of market-failure logic corresponds with the privatization and outsourcing of CI. Government is increasingly seen as too bureaucratic, inefficient, self-serving, and lacking in specialized knowledge and experience. Society has an optimistic belief in the virtue of competition and choice. Yet government is not completely absent from CI protection (CIP): particularly since 9/11, the role of government has evolved towards a greater emphasis on promoting resilience and providing reassurance while also helping to facilitate new market opportunities. In Canada, proponents of privatization and market liberalism argue that the role of government is to support rather than control, to leverage resources to expose Canadian companies to international opportunities while simultaneously protecting them against the turbulence and uncertainty of global geopolitics.

Compared with these normative arguments, Hood and colleagues' framework treats the MFH as a potential explanatory tool. Likewise, we are interested in the MFH's capacity to help us understand Canadian risk regulation regimes for CI. In other words, can we explain the CI regime's features (sketched in chapters 4 and 5) by looking at the extent to which markets have failed to control black swan risks in the transportation and chemicals sectors? To answer this question, we will explore the causes of market failures before examining whether the transportation and chemical regimes are designed to address these causes.

WHY MARKETS FAIL

Markets can fail for many reasons.[3] For the purpose of analyzing regulatory regimes, the risk regulation regime framework expresses the causes of market failure in terms of two costs: information costs and opt-out costs. To recap, information costs are faced by individuals in their efforts to assess the level or type of risk to which they are exposed. "An example of low-cost risk information acquisition," write Hood and colleagues (2001, 73), "would be the cost of placing a detector patch above a household gas boiler to monitor carbon dioxide, while a high-cost example would be the efforts made in seeking to assess the risks of a melt-down in a nearby nuclear power plant." Opt-out costs are incurred by individuals seeking to avoid risk exposure through, among other things, civil law processes or insurance. The cost of individually opting out of a hazard can be considered in absolute terms, but it can also be considered relative to a collective opt-out strategy (Hood et al. 2001, 73).

If the MFH is followed, regulations will be substantial only for risks where information costs and opt-out costs are high, and only for the specific control component that is affected by high costs (i.e., gathering information, setting standards, and/or changing behaviour). Conversely, if both information and opt-out costs are low, the market failure approach leads us to expect fewer regulations. If information costs are high but opt-out costs are low, market-failure logic suggests regulations will be high for information gathering but low for behaviour modification. If information costs are low but opt-out costs are high, regulatory size will be low for information gathering but high for behaviour modification. Table 6.1 summarizes the risk regulation regime framework's approach to regulation as dictated by the logic of market failure.

The MFH is built on the rational perspective to risk described in chapter 2. The MFH assumes that the probability and potential consequences of risks can be measured. As Hood and colleagues (2001, 71) explain, the MFH "does not suggest the state will adopt a one-size-fits-all response to each risk domain, but rather points to the ways the state can be expected to deal with each risk on the minimal feasible scale." Other factors, such as how the public feels about a risk or private-sector interests, are not considered when designing regulatory policy. This also means that we can analyze the value of the MFH by considering the extent to which regimes are successful at addressing information and opt-out costs.

TECHNICAL NATURE OF THE RISK

What is the technical nature of the risks confronting CI in the transportation and chemicals sectors? To some extent, the answer to this question is implied by the term we attach to risks: black swans, or high-probability/low-consequence events (see chapter 1 for a definition of the term *black swan*). In general, we are concerned with hazards that are unlikely but, if they occur, could have wide ranging and significant consequences. Still, this broad definition belies important variation across the full spectrum of risks that confront our CI.

In the chemicals sector, products and companies vary in terms of their significance to CI. Some products are easily substituted; others are not. Some manufacturing facilities represent high-consequence single points of failure; others have multiple redundancies. Some chemicals can be weaponized; others cannot. For chemicals that are

Table 6.1 Market failure explanation of regime size

		Cost of gathering information about exposure to CI risks	
		Low	High
Cost of opting out of exposure to CI risks	Low	Minimal government intervention	Government intervention in the form of information-gathering and -sharing
	High	Government intervention aimed at modifying behaviour	Extensive government intervention in the form of prescriptive regulation aimed at all three aspects of control

Note: CI, critical infrastructure. Adapted from Hood, Rothstein, and Baldwin (2001).

prevalent and easily substituted, a major incident at one production site would cause minimal disruption to the supply chain. In other cases, a major incident at a single facility could have international repercussions. For instance, one of our interview participants (Int 59) described the closure of a plant in Louisiana during Hurricane Katrina that produced a chemical required by auto manufacturers. The only other producer of this chemical in North America had halted production to carry out maintenance work. This other producer had to reopen its manufacturing facility on an emergency basis to prevent widespread disruptions to the auto industry.

On balance, the market for chemicals is reasonably stable and efficient; catastrophic events are extremely rare. As a result, information about risk probabilities is difficult to come by and governments have tended to focus their efforts on facilitating information exchange. At the same time, rare, catastrophic events cause considerable social and economic damage to communities (e.g., disasters at Sunrise Propane in Ontario, Neptune Technologies in Quebec, West Fertilizer Company in Texas, and the Union Carbide factory in Bhopal, India, all resulted in permanent devastation).

Similar characteristics are evident in the transportation sector. Ownership can vary from subsector to subsector, as well as within subsectors. The largest seaports and airports are owned by the federal government but managed via a lease, concession, or a corporation; smaller seaports and airports may be owned by other orders of government or private companies. In trucking, truck ownership is widely fragmented while most of the infrastructure used (both roads and bridges) is owned and maintained by government (although there are some private roads and bridges). As for rail, railroads are privately owned, although in some cases running rights are held by public companies like VIA Rail or the owners of private cargo companies.

Most transportation subsectors are subject to considerable government regulation when it comes to safety and security; however, market structures vary considerably in the critical transportation infrastructure, which impacts the vulnerabilities to which the sector is exposed and the manner in which the subsectors respond. As noted above, some subsectors are competitive (trucking), while others are monopolistic (bridges); some are heavily regulated (airports) while others have more flexibility (trucking); some are regulated primarily by one order of government (bridges, airports, and seaports), while others are regulated by several (rail and trucking); some subsectors have considerable redundancies and are adaptive (trucking), while most have critical elements that are static and include high-consequence single points of failure (i.e., seaports, airport, rail, and bridges).

As in the chemicals sector, security threats to the transportation sector vary depending on the subsector, location, and connection to international trade. Security threats can also range from those that capture the public's attention (such as terrorism, drug smuggling, and people trafficking), to those that have perhaps more serious business implications (such as piracy, cargo theft, and cyber crimes), to the mundane and more probable (such as trespassing and petty crime). Many risks relate to the underground economy in Canada, economic and political stability in parts of the developing world, and access to key trade routes in international markets. There are also safety vulnerabilities generated by communicable diseases, aging infrastructure, and human error. Public transportation must be open and accessible, which creates safety and security threats.

Generally speaking, accident rates across all modes of transportation, with the exception of rail in recent years, have been gradually decreasing since 2001. As with the chemicals sector, incidents in the transportation sector that cause major social or economic damage occur relatively infrequently, and accident rates are actually going down (see Transport Canada 2011b). Moreover, although each transportation subsector possesses a unique profile, each subsector has the potential for high-consequence failures (e.g., the Lac-Mégantic disaster).

For both the chemical and transportation sectors, we need to account for the benefits of CI market structures to understand completely the technical nature of black swan risks. Interdependent and global supply chains push down costs and increase choice. Specialization is a basic feature of international trade and leads to CI that exists beyond our national borders: Canada's transportation and chemicals sectors are heavily dependent on the US market and are vulnerable to events and changing conditions around the world. For example, the Atlantic Canadian liquefied natural gas market relies on imports from Trinidad and Tobago, which means that a disaster in the Caribbean, such as a severe hurricane, could have serious implications for Canada and the northeastern United States, which is the ultimate destination of much of Canada's liquefied natural gas. The calculation of risks associated with integration and complexity should also reflect the associated benefits and, conversely, the opportunity costs associated with reducing vulnerabilities by withdrawing from the global economy.

EVALUATING MARKET EFFICIENCY: INFORMATION COSTS

Black swan failures are marginal events, not in the sense that they are insignificant, but rather in the sense that they exist at the outer edge of normal routines. Markets are challenged by the irregularity of some risks because there is little or no information about the likelihood of the event, which makes it difficult for companies and consumers to account for risks in decision-making. As with other sources of market failure, black swan events are not always reflected in prices, meaning market signals do not correlate with the technical aspect of the risk. This is particularly true with risks (e.g., terrorism) that are less easily predicted than others (e.g., seasonal flooding).

In terms of the MFH, black swans present varying information costs. We asked several interview participants to comment on their confidence that chemical or transportation CI operators would receive reliable and timely information in advance of various hypothetical risk scenarios (figures 6.1 and 6.2).

Several factors influence the perceived cost of obtaining information about risks. Interview subjects seemed confident that they would receive reliable information for natural disasters and pandemics.

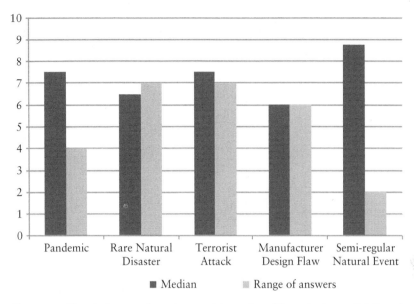

Figure 6.1 Chemicals sector interview participants' confidence in the availability of information before selected risks

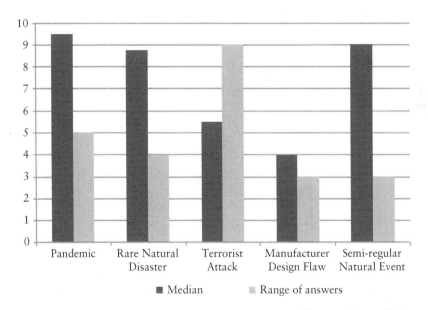

Figure 6.2 Transportation sector interview participants' confidence in the availability of information before selected risks

Interview participants were comfortable, for example, with the mechanisms in place to gather and disseminate information about pandemics; this may be a function of recent efforts by governments to strengthen pandemic preparedness in the wake of SARS and the effort to contain the spread of HINI in 2009 (Int 61; Int 66; Int 67). Participants were also confident that they would receive reliable information about semi-regular natural events, like floods or hurricanes.

Secondly, interviewees from the chemicals sector were less confident that they would receive reliable information about design flaws in their infrastructure. This lack of confidence suggests that complex and uncertain risks raise questions about the cost and difficulty of obtaining reliable information. The mid-level confidence score for terrorism is perhaps unsurprising given the investment by government in programs like the Suspicious Incident Reporting (SIR) system, which are intended to reduce information costs for CI operators. In fact, the presence of these programs suggests that the government response is, at least partly, explained by the MFH.

By comparison, interview participants from the transportation sector indicated greater confidence in the availability of information about rare natural disasters but less confidence in the availability of information about manufacturer design flaws. It is not immediately apparent why this was the case. With respect to natural disasters, perhaps transportation infrastructure is inherently more attuned to weather patterns and natural processes. Similarly, the chemical industry has taken great strides towards improving process safety and may therefore be ahead of the transportation sector in terms of predicting manufacturing failures. Whatever the reason, the results of our interviews with individuals from the transportation sector underscore the notion that information costs vary across the regime.

The preceding discussion uses respondents' confidence in the availability of information as an indicator of information costs. The two concepts are not always related. One can imagine a scenario in which risk information is widely available but poorly understood; we saw this scenario in 2012 when the US National Hurricane Center made assumptions about people's ability to realize the implications of meteorological forecasts in the hours before Hurricane Sandy, which many could not do. This oversight had significant social and economic consequences for businesses and communities (Samenow 2013). In addition, as we explained in chapter 2, there are many complex risks for which a wide array of causal variables has been identified. In such cases, the *cost* of obtaining information about potential causes of failure is low. The potential for non-linear or stochastic interactions between the causal variables, however, means that one's *confidence* in the information (and the stability of the information) may also be low. Modern chemical plants, for example, can be intricate, highly technical facilities. All the individual components of such a facility are well understood, being the result of careful design and engineering. The interaction between these complex parts, on the other hand, leads to multiple and unpredictable points of failure. The availability of risk information thus does not always translate into strong confidence about the probability and consequences of failure.

Information costs may also be understood from the perspective of the general public. In other words, how difficult is it for community members to gain detailed information about major risks posed by chemical facilities or transportation infrastructure in their neighbourhood? The answer is unclear. The Responsible Care (RC) initiative includes site risk communication guidelines, which are intended to help facilitate "a protected, informed community, having both an awareness of the chemical industry's presence and a reasonable comfort level that hazards and risks are under competent control" (Lacoursière 2006, 312). Interview participants from the chemical industry emphasized that program members make an effort to implement these guidelines (Int 59; Int 61). In the transportation sector, several interview participants described deliberate efforts by seaports to communicate risk information to nearby residents (Int 3; Int 4). These interview respondents also noted, however, that security concerns limit the specificity of the information that is made public.

In the risk communication guidelines published by the Canadian Society for Chemical Engineering, companies are encouraged to invite interested citizens – who may have to undergo security clearance – to participate in "a dialogue process involving site operators and [first] responders" (CSChE 2012, 7). Under this model, information exchange is initiated primarily by industry and occurs in an ad hoc fashion. There appears to be no centralized database or website that citizens can access at their convenience for site-specific risk information.[4] Thus, significant information asymmetry – further evidence of market failure – exists both between CI operators and government and between CI operators and citizens.

In general, the chemical industry's aforementioned competitiveness means companies are unlikely to disclose sensitive information to competitors or to the public. Moreover, company vulnerabilities tend to be "dirty little secrets"; industry leaders are reluctant to discuss asset vulnerabilities because of the risk to their organization's security, the risk of liability, the risk to share value, and the risk to the organization's public image. At a minimum, highly competitive industries will almost certainly insist on anonymized data sharing and non-disclosure agreements to preclude proactive disclosure to the public (Quigley 2013).

In the transportation sector, interview participants frequently spoke of constraints that were due to competition (i.e., seaports, rail, and trucking). Interview participants from the seaports and rail subsectors, in particular, showed less willingness or capability to share information outside their organizations. Despite the fact that trucking industry operators compete with each other, interview participants from the trucking subsector showed more willingness to share information, but they were constrained by lack of capacity and incentive.

Competition, however, can be a red herring. Bridges do not compete, and airports do not compete on security (Int 13; Forsyth 2007; Hancioglu 2008). At first blush, it was not surprising to learn that these subsectors shared information more willingly with others within their respective subsectors. Yet monopolies and oligopolies also have a number of reasons not to disclose information about vulnerabilities and many of these reasons are similar to the reasons of more competitive companies (e.g., brand, liability, security). Arguably, monopolies and oligopolies have a greater capacity to control information within their organization; ironically, organizations that are highly competitive and pluralist and that have many suppliers can actually make information more readily available to regulators. If these less competitive monopolies and oligopolies are more likely to share information, this fact can probably be attributed to (1) the seriousness of CI failures, (2) their sometimes more stable and collegial relationship with regulators, and (3) their desire to avoid liability.

Thus, information costs vary across the regulatory regime. Industry and CI operators face a range of both low- and high-cost risks (although risks tend to be consistently higher in the transportation sector than in the chemicals sector). For the general public, accessing information about the risks posed by local facilities can be a high-cost activity, given the time and energy that may be required. Returning to table 6.1, the information costs associated with chemical risks are thus best illustrated as a continuum spanning the horizontal axis, rather than as a single point in either quadrant. Markets are thus reasonably efficient at addressing some information asymmetries but not all.

EVALUATING MARKET EFFICIENCY: OPT-OUT COSTS

Opt-out costs, by comparison, are nearly always high in the chemical and transportation sectors. Even if they could, few, if any, CI operators would choose to opt out completely from risk exposure. The cost of opting out of risks associated with black swan events tends to be high because of the variety of risks and the unreliability of information. Moreover, given the large number of companies across North America, most owners do not believe their sites will be targeted by terrorists or succumb to rare natural disasters (Schierow 2005). As a result, there are limited incentives for owners and operators to invest against a risk they perceive to be small. This sentiment was common among our interview participants, many of whom suggested that terrorism, in particular, was less of a threat to the chemical industry than other risks, including natural disasters and cybersecurity threats (Int 58; Int 59; Int 61; Int 66; Int 67).[5] In other words, there are limited market incentives to prepare for black swans.

A related problem confronts industry standards such as RC. Industry standards are vulnerable to pressures imposed by (1) the chemical market's demand for short-term profit, and (2) the divergence between the interests of large, often transnational corporations and small and medium-sized enterprises (SMEs) (Gunningham 1995, 63). The general public tends to perceive the chemical industry as a single entity but it is not. Companies that devote time and money to implementing RC are at a competitive disadvantage to "free-rider" companies that neglect to adopt voluntary safety and security practices (Gunningham 1995).

In the chemicals sector, substitution represents a possible means for reducing opt-out costs. Substitution means replacing volatile and hazardous chemicals with safer alternatives that achieve the same outcomes. Unfortunately, companies that attempt to replace chemicals with less hazardous ones may find it difficult or expensive to adjust their manufacturing processes, particularly if they are unable to identify alternatives, if alternatives are unavailable, or if other companies in their supply chain have not already made the same substitution (Lofstedt 2013). Although chemical substitution was highlighted by two interview participants (Int 63; Int 68), it remains a potentially high-cost solution that is not always applicable.

Opting out of risk in the transportation sector depends largely on adaptive capacity and redundancies. The critical transportation infrastructure that we studied tends to be open to the public and, with the exception of trucking, fixed in its location. It cannot be easily moved, which creates opportunities for terrorists and criminals and challenges in the face of rare natural disasters. Nevertheless, the transportation sector has a level of redundancy. Trucking, because of its atomistic nature and network structure, has greater adaptive capacity than the other subsectors; there are more routes to access in times of incidents and more service providers. During CI events, major CI sites (such as airports, seaports, and bridges) can redirect traffic to different outlets temporarily. Redundancy has cost implications, however, that can seem to be a waste or unnecessary. Moreover, in a CI event in particular, there will probably be multiple demands on redundant systems; redundant systems that form the basis of a contingency plan in pre-event planning may not be available during an actual event.

Terrorists and criminals are adaptive adversaries. Such adversaries make opting out even more challenging as they (unlike natural disasters) can react to the risk strategies agencies put in place. Managing low-probability security risks in a robust manner can rarely be justified at the company level (Seidenstat 2004); security is usually seen as a negative expense. Market-sensitive organizations will often not take big steps to protect against these events (Jaeger et al. 2001).

Insurance is perhaps the most widely used tool for opting out of risks. As predicted by economists, insurance markets for both chemicals and transportation struggle to operate efficiently because of information asymmetries. Interview participants from the chemicals sector consistently described insurance concerns as having little influence over how CI operators, including water utilities and chemical companies, spend their time on matters of safety and security (Int 51; Int 52; Int 53; Int 54: Int 55; Int 56; Int 57; Int 58; Int 61).

One interview participant suggested that this was because most large chemical companies are self-insured (Int 61). In our transportation interviews, only trucking interviewees described insurance as something that influenced their behaviour.

Black swan risks are notoriously difficult to insure against because there are insufficient data for insurance companies to develop sustainable policies. Ironically, insurance – collective pooling of resources to manage risk – was first created to respond to black swan events on the high seas. Madden (2012, 274) describes early risk sharing by investors: "In the twelfth century ... merchants began adapting the colleganza to allow for *multiple* investors instead of just one ... This single innovation enormously expanded the capital available for overseas trade while diluting the overall risk to investors, who could now diversify their investments instead of staking them on a few high-risk ventures ... Even Venetians of modest means could purchase a small share in a voyage. These small investments dramatically increased the capital available for underwriting overseas trade."

The present-day reinsurance industry works in a similar way by sharing risk among a large number of shareholders; it spreads risks and in so doing limits the risk exposure of any one individual or organization. As J. David Cummins emphasizes, however, "catastrophic events, and particularly mega-catastrophes such as Katrina and the WTC terrorist attack, violate to some degree nearly all of the standard conditions for insurability" (2006, 337). Supply chains are complex, interdependent, and increasingly global. Operations and their failures are difficult to model, which makes it challenging for the insurers to develop and cost reliable insurance policies. This is especially true for terrorism (Boardman 2005), some criminal activities, and rare natural disasters for which data are scarce and unreliable. Despite in some cases being privately owned or at least privately operated, CI is crucial for our collective well-being. As a result, governments are unlikely to let infrastructure, if not the organizations that run it, fail outright, particularly monopolies and oligopolies. Arguably, this creates a moral hazard. After a black swan event, governments may have to assume the role of insurer-of-last-resort and assist in recovery efforts, and they often do.

US flood and terrorism insurance are recent and salient examples of moral hazards; these forms of insurance continue to be subsidized by the US government. Recent black swan events in Canada also suggest that small companies carry insufficient insurance coverage for major losses. The Montreal, Maine & Atlantic Railway Limited (MMA) filed for bankruptcy because of the Lac-Mégantic rail disaster (Van Praet 2013) and, later that year, the federal government announced it would "require shippers and railways to carry additional insurance so they are held accountable" (Krugel 2014).

Challenges related to natural disaster insurance have been attributed in part to the charity hazard problem, which speaks to the belief that individuals, including CI owners and operators, believe that government will step in to provide financial assistance after a disaster. The fact that governments often do so reinforces this behaviour. For example, and as noted, after the 2013 Alberta floods, the provincial government announced the Disaster Recovery Program to cover the estimated $3.1 billion in uninsurable loss and damage suffered by individuals, small businesses, municipalities, and other groups (MNP LLP 2015).

One straightforward way to address the charity hazard problem is to simply mandate through law that all CI facilities purchase insurance. Legal mandates, however, can be unpopular, in particular for extremely low-probability risks. When coupled with insurance subsidies, mandated insurance coverage can also contribute to regressive forms of redistribution. The United States' National Flood Insurance Program (NFIP), for example, provides generous subsidies to primary residences located in flood-prone areas, including waterfront properties. Although precise socio-economic data on NFIP recipients is not easily accessible, a preliminary study by the Government Accountability Office (2013) in the United States indicates that the counties with the highest median home values also tend to have the highest percentages of subsidized policies. In plain terms, under the NFIP, wealthy owners of "older oceanfront homes have received massive subsidies for almost 50 years" (Wriggins 2014, 432). Although Congress enacted reforms to the NFIP in 2012, including the eventual elimination of all subsidies and a transition to pure risk-based insurance rates, many of these reforms were repealed in 2014, leaving in place the subsidy for older homes and primary residences.

Insurance mandates are also difficult to design because of the technical challenges of determining sensible price structures that reflect the potential cost of failure. Moreover, when failures do occur, insurance companies often exit the market because of high losses or bankruptcy (Born and Viscusi 2006). A study on the 2011

Christchurch earthquake in New Zealand reports that insurance-related issues "emerged as a major concern ... particularly in terms of the complexity and time associated with settling insurance claims" (Chang et al. 2014, 6). Disputes with insurers arose as a result of "longer than normal claims development," in part because of disagreement over the scope of insurance policies "and the extent of the damage" (New Zealand 2014, 57). Because of these issues and major financial losses, insurance companies "are trying to reduce their exposure in the New Zealand market," causing substantially higher premiums and deductibles for individuals and businesses than before the earthquake (Chang et al. 2014, 15).

More broadly, the rule of law is also an important mechanism for avoiding risk exposure, but it has limitations. Shore (2008) argues that there is a legal imperative on the part of both government and private enterprise to protect c_i from terrorist events, for instance. Essentially, government and industry need to take reasonable steps (e.g., risk assessments, business continuity plans) to protect c_i. The complexity and interdependence in c_i, however, makes it very difficult to identify the parties that are responsible for c_i failures. Legal processes can also take time. The rule of law is even more limited at the international level. Collaboration between friendly Western nations can be difficult and time consuming because of different legal contexts; collaboration between nations without stable governance – which is sometimes the case on or near critical international trade routes – poses even more substantial challenges. At the same time, cyber law is drawing increasing attention as our reliance on the Internet grows and cyber crimes, such as hacking, become more prevalent. Holding criminals responsible, however, can be complicated in the cyber context. Identifying perpetrators is a time consuming and highly technical process, and litigating cyber crimes is an increasingly sophisticated and resource-intensive undertaking.

Tort law can often provide a solution to market failures induced by high opt-out costs. Where individuals experience harms from liable c_i operators, the law of tort allows the individual to sue for damages. In the case of chemical and transportation c_i, however, tort-law solutions are long, impractical, and expensive.

In 2004, the federal government implemented changes to the Criminal Code that affected how corporations are held accountable for their actions. Bill C-45, the so-called Westray bill,[6] extended the criminal liability of corporations in the field of health and safety

(Creedy et al. 2005, 376–8). It is no longer necessary to prove criminal intent when prosecuting companies for offences such as criminal negligence. Instead, it is enough to show that the company failed to take sufficient measures to prevent the incident. However, these changes to the Criminal Code are rarely enforced and thus have had little effect on corporate behaviour (Bittle and Snider 2011).[7] Criminal and tort-law proceedings often require significant resources and time, so those liable for failures aren't immediately held accountable.

The US government applied pressure to BP after the 2010 Deepwater Horizon oil spill and probably undermined the company's ability to conduct business and even raise private capital. This sort of government pressure does not preclude a legal process but arguably prompts a more immediate response from the company than a protracted legal process. The societal importance of CI also means that an issue that is ostensibly the responsibility of a single company will, given a failure of substantial consequence, inevitably induce government involvement.

A more general issue relates to the opportunity costs of opting out of risks. Precautionary behaviour may reduce exposure to vulnerabilities, but in a competitive environment it also means cutting off opportunities for innovation and profit-making. Risk involves both opportunities and threats, and the cost of excessive caution is reduced entrepreneurialism, which can have implications for companies as well as the broader economy.

EVALUATING THE ACCURACY OF THE MARKET FAILURE APPROACH

MFH can explain some things about the chemical and transportation sectors: (1) the market seems to be reasonably stable and efficient, (2) catastrophic events are extremely rare, and (3) information is difficult to come by and government has tended to focus its efforts on facilitating information exchange. Black swan events cause considerable social and economic damage to communities. Because black swans are low-probability events, market logic would rarely justify investing much in these unlikely, what-if scenarios.

CI events can be catastrophic and can devastate businesses and entire communities. When the survival of the company is at stake, risk can no longer be described as the product of probability and expected monetary losses (Jaeger et al. 2001). When the company is in danger of massive operational failure in the short term, conventional, long-term risk assessments do not necessarily hold. A short-term approach, however, would rarely describe how an organization should approach risk on an ongoing basis.

Reliable risk models are difficult to develop and are not entirely reliable or trustworthy. Several factors point to a context that perpetuates vulnerabilities, including information asymmetries, moral hazard problems, negative externalities, problematic insurance requirements (including inadequate models), and limited tort-law processes. Moreover, the ubiquity of chemicals and transportation infrastructure in modern society indicates high costs for opting out of risks.

In sum, risks in the chemical and transportation sectors present high opt-out costs and both high and low information-gathering costs. This corresponds with the bottom two quadrants of table 6.1. According to the MFH, these costs should translate into either a maximalist, aggressive regulatory system or a regime with a large behaviour-modification component.

A government risk regulation regime underpinned by market failure logic would intervene to reduce both information and opt-out costs. While the current regime does exhibit some degree of government intervention (e.g., in the form of information-sharing mechanisms intended to reduce information costs), various factors can influence the extent to which organizations choose to share information, including competition, incentives, penalties, confidence, willingness, perceived importance of the information, concern over leaks, authority, organizational culture, market sensitivities, ownership, and capacity.

On the whole our research suggests that industry prefers self-regulation, which is largely voluntary, excludes many SMEs, and at times lacks transparency and rigour. Complex and uncertain risks (Renn 2008) and lack of incentives for industry (particularly among SMEs) create a potential moral hazard. Governments must put sufficient standards and behaviour modification practices in place to ensure that owners, operators, and managers take responsibility for their operations and are held accountable for failures. While the probability of certain risks events may be low, the consequences can be catastrophic; weaknesses persist and government does not take a sufficiently aggressive stance to address these weaknesses. In short, the regulatory regime's position does not fully reflect the predictions of the MFH.

There is also the issue of public ownership of CI. Although, as we note above, much of our infrastructure has been privatized in recent decades, public or quasi-public ownership remains a key feature of several specific CI subsectors, particularly in transportation. Arguably, public ownership is indicative of market failure (Shirley and Walsh 2000). Government ownership of CI is necessary in these cases because the private sector has failed to deliver socially optimal outcomes. MFH becomes problematic for analyzing risk regulation in the presence of public ownership because market failure is presupposed: government has already intervened. We pick up on this point again in chapter 10, particularly the notion that the designation of a sector as critical collapses the distinction between the state and industry. The traditional view of a regulator monitoring and intervening where necessary is no longer applicable. Government is already a key player in the sector, operating enterprises in the interest of public welfare. The calculation of information and opt-out costs changes under these conditions with the technical nature of the risk losing capacity for predicting regulatory behaviour.

Our conclusions agree with the findings of Hood and colleagues, who argue that the MFH is "more useful as a method of analytical benchmarking than as a reliable predictor of regulatory content" (2001, 71). This is not to suggest that market forces are unimportant: share values typically tumble after disasters (Capelle-Blancard and Laguna 2010; Carpentier and Suret 2013). But, as noted above, companies rarely see value in investing in the prevention of low-probability disasters. At the same time, while social and economic costs of low-probability events can be high, government is apparently loath to step in and enforce high regulatory standards that could potentially – and arguably unnecessarily – decrease the competitiveness of an industry.

The net effect of this approach, and notwithstanding the traditional government standards, is continued growth in voluntary self-regulation in the industry (Bittle and Snider 2011, 380). As a result, high-consequence risks persist and governments are increasingly prepared to let organizations manage them. While markets may tolerate such risk taking, the public has an aversion to disasters – a point we explore in the next chapter.

CONCLUSION

Every human society has been confronted by the possibility of black swan events. These risks are often an unavoidable feature of a society's institutions or geography. Ancient Egypt emerged as a result of regular flooding of the Nile, which provided fertile soil while at the same time bringing occasional devastation when water levels were too high (wiping out villages) or too low (causing famine). Volcanoes provide nearby communities, such as Pompeii, with fertile land for crops while simultaneously exposing them to dangerous eruptions. Contemporary societies are no different. Vancouver's location on the Pacific coast, for example, is both beneficial, providing access to lucrative trade routes with Asia, and potentially hazardous because of the Pacific Ring of Fire and its faults. Halifax benefits from its proximity to a lucrative lobster supply and transatlantic and South American shipping, but it is vulnerable to seasonal hurricanes.

Technologies also provide social advantages while exposing us to certain types of risk. For instance, the benefits of the Internet are closely connected to its risks: its integration of disparate systems into a single network has improved society in numerous ways while also making it vulnerable to malicious attack or technical failure. CI includes many of humanity's most impressive achievements (e.g., the power grid, telecommunications, modern health care, transportation), which advance our standard of living while simultaneously exposing us to new dangers. Dependence on CI has become an inescapable feature of modern life. This is true for both rich and poor people and for both developed and developing societies. Advancements have been made in addressing certain types of relatively predictable risks (e.g., smoking, drinking and driving, workplace accidents) but black swan events remain a problem for all societies, a problem that transcends many political, economic, and administrative differences between countries.

Ironically, CI failure can also be a source of important advancement and innovation. The Black Death caused a labour shortage that contributed to expanded use of livestock in agriculture, which allowed fewer people to grow more food. In terms of food production, the Black Death enhanced social welfare through the discovery of more efficient production practices (Kelly 2005).

Through CI, black swan events can affect communities, regions, or entire societies. Benefits and costs are determined at a level above the individual. The infrequency of black swan events encourages a societal perspective; a natural disaster may not strike for decades, meaning that generations may pass without realizing the danger. Black swan events pose a distinct problem for markets because they are both irregular and destructive. Effective management of black swan risks requires an intergenerational perspective, because current decision-makers must take into account the long-term consequences of their decisions. The MFH, by comparison, assumes that individuals are short-term utility maximizers, largely unconcerned with costs that may not occur in their lifetime. Even if society were to adopt a long-term view, it is unlikely that risk probabilities would hold steady over time. Climate change, for example, is expected to make certain types of events more frequent (see, for example, Parker 2013).

In addition, markets seem unable to provide for safety and security in the case of CI failure, including in the chemical and transportation sectors. This is often a problem of quantification. Although Hood and colleagues (2001) assert that an MFH approach need not assume that "the danger posed by all hazards ... be expressed in terms of well-understood quantifiable risk," they concede that without at least some numerical expression of a hazard's costs and benefits the MFH approach "lacks all determinacy and could be consistent with almost any state response to risk" (72). At a societal level, it is difficult to quantify the benefits and costs of CI.[8]

Quantification is made especially difficult by the complexity of CI networks. The fact that there are interdependencies among CI facilities makes calculating the cost of failure in one sector an extremely difficult endeavour because failures can cascade across the CI network in unforeseen ways. Efforts to document CI networks are time-consuming and expensive, and their results require constant revision as companies enter and leave the market or otherwise respond to changing market conditions.

Calculations are often little more than vague estimations, preventing a deeper analysis of market efficiency beyond a general statement that some government intervention is required. For our uses, calculations also provide little information about the size, structure, and style of a regulatory regime, features that are necessary for a comparative study of different regulatory regimes. Although reasonably successful at predicting the existence of information-gathering mechanisms, the MFH provides little explanation for how these mechanisms are designed and how effective they are.

Beyond these methodological challenges, it is also unclear whether adopting a market failure perspective is analytically useful at all for thinking about black swan events. Should individuals be faulted for failing to adapt their behaviour to a risk that may never occur in their lifetime? The free market relies on the assumption that rational individuals, making self-interested decisions, achieve efficient outcomes. The idea of market failure presupposes the possibility of inefficient outcomes; MFH requires a clear vision of how a properly functioning market would look. In turn, this vision facilitates the identification of appropriate government interventions for each type of market failure.

It is possible to speak of market failures and of examples of government policy that might address semi-regularly occurring natural events, such as spring floods in New Brunswick, and some forms of technological failure, such as the Toronto Sunrise Propane explosion. The charity hazard problem, for example, exists because individuals assume government will step in to provide financial support after natural disasters. A simple response is to legislate mandatory insurance requirements, but as the probability of an event decreases, so does the extent to which it is possible to evaluate market efficiency. Is it a market failure when individuals do not adjust their behaviour, including by purchasing insurance, to account for an event that may not occur for a century or more? Perhaps it is, in part because our failure to prepare represents a long-term externality whereby our behaviour causes negative effects for future individuals who must deal with the consequences of, say, locating a city on an earthquake fault line.

Even so, as risks become increasingly uncertain, the utility of the market perspective declines. Hood and colleagues (2001) acknowledge this by noting that in many instances, "the practical definition of market failure in terms of information and opt-out costs, to say nothing of distributional impacts, is to a substantial degree a matter of judgement" (88). Where the rarity of an event precludes a straightforward assessment of its technical risk, the MFH cannot provide a clear sense of the appropriate regulatory policy for preventing failure. This deficiency extends beyond failures that stem from inefficiencies related to insurance markets or tort law: externalities that materialize over long periods are similarly difficult to analyze through a market lens.

A related issue is whether the underlying assumption of individual rationality holds up in the face of black swan events. People may not take a purely rational view of risks such as natural disasters. In a paper on charity hazard, for example, Raschky and Weck-Hannemann (2007) cite Kahneman and Tversky's (1982) choice anomalies theory in explaining why individuals choose not to purchase disaster insurance. "This theory of anomalies," they write, "proposes that the standard expected utility theory does not sufficiently describe and predict individual behaviour under uncertainty ... When it comes to natural hazards, individuals do not base their decisions on calculated probabilities, but rather use inferential rules known as heuristics" (Raschky and Weck-Hanneman 2007, 323).

In some cases industry and government have decided to suppress information. In a post-9/11 world, security information is not transparent; concerns over branding also make industry want to keep bad news out of the media and public domain. Recall from chapter 5 that the chemical industry is reluctant to include the public on information-sharing panels. Rational decision-making is unlikely under these conditions.

Market outcomes reflect how people perceive risk, including through evaluations of their susceptibility based on heuristics, which often diverges from what a rational perspective would suggest is the actual technical nature of the risk. Some research has uncovered evidence that, beyond making wrong decisions because of biases, individuals often knowingly expose themselves to harmful risks. For example, an alcoholic or drug addict may know "*before he becomes addicted* that he will regret getting the addiction, but once he is addicted, will not be able to change his behaviour" (Stiglitz 2008, 5). Empirical advances in fields such as behavioural economics lead us to question whether a market failure perspective on risk regulation aligns with how consumers, companies, and governments actually behave.

Typically, we say there is a market failure when risks that we perceive to be meaningful and important are not being addressed. It is only when we decide that an event or hazard is unacceptable, and it occurs, that there is said to be a failure. For black swan events, the MFH involves a post-hoc evaluation of the efficiency of the market. In comparing and analyzing whether the market is controlling a risk, we can only discuss risks for which we have a good sense of the probabilities and the measures needed to reduce them. The set of risks that are "known unknowns," to borrow from Donald

Rumsfeld, is defined by society through the risks that we, as a society, devote time and resources to addressing. This requires an understanding of how people think and feel about risk and the mechanisms and people in place to manage them, which is the subject of our next chapter.

The Opinion-Responsive Hypothesis:
Fascination and Aversion

The opinion-responsive hypothesis (ORH) states that a risk regulation regime is a certain way because that is how those affected by the risks, or the cost of reducing the risks, want it to be (Hood et al. 2001, 90). In short, regime content reflects public preferences and attitudes. As we argue below, congruity exists to varying degrees. Hood and colleagues use media coverage to gauge the concerns of civil society. Black swans generate high-volume media coverage for a short time. In fact, coverage is more nuanced. Different types of events (i.e., natural disasters, industrial failures, terrorist plots, terrorist attacks, cyber events) generate different types of coverage. Media coverage varies in volume, tone, and duration and in the search for accountability. There is surprisingly little rational relationship between the extent of media coverage and the consequences of events. Terrorist attacks and, to a lesser extent, industrial failures generate negative, alarming, and high-volume media coverage. In contrast, terrorist plots and natural disasters generate medium- to high-volume coverage that is mildly negative and at times positive. Media cover cybersecurity very little.

In this chapter, we review media coverage of black swans and examine public opinions of these events and the extent to which people trust government and industry (the owners and operators of critical infrastructure [CI]). We conclude that for a number of social and economic reasons, the media are drawn to black swans. The public is often fascinated and concerned by them. It is less clear, however, whether or not media coverage of black swans reflects public opinion in any meaningful way or whether it translates into sustained interest in changing public policy. Independent inquiries offer the opportunity to learn from past mistakes; however, governments are sometimes unwilling to have independent inquiries because they know that these inquiries will probably lead to negative media coverage and blame. Government's predisposition to avoid independent inquiries constrains our capacity to learn.

PUBLIC OPINION:
CHEMICALS AND TRANSPORTATION

There are numerous reasons why the chemical industry ought to be particularly sensitive to public opinion (figure 7.1) and media coverage. The influence of public opinion and media coverage is particularly evident starting in the 1980s after the Bhopal (King and Lenox 2000, 699) and Seveso disasters, which provided the impetus for the creation for Responsible Care (RC) (Moffet et al. 2004). Public anxiety regarding chemicals has been growing since at least the First World War (van Courtland Moon 1984). In the 1960s, efforts to regulate chemicals gained momentum with the publication of Rachel Carson's now-famous *Silent Spring* and the Cuyahoga River fire (Opheim 1993). The public perceives manufactured chemicals as artificial or "unnatural" (Petrie and Wessely 2002; Trivedi 2012) and public perceptions of chemical companies and regulatory agencies are important (Engdahl and Lidskog 2012). A 1986 public opinion poll indicated that forty-eight per cent of Canadians felt that the chemical industry's risks outweighed its benefits (Wise 1994).[1] More than ten years later, forty per cent of Canadian respondents to an international poll thought that the chemical industry was doing "very little" or "nothing at all" to reduce its impact on the environment.

Other CI operators, such as water utilities, also need to be aware of public opinion and media coverage. As the Walkerton Inquiry report emphasizes, the public assumes that treated drinking water is safe (Walkerton Commission of Inquiry 2002a, 36), and so failures – particularly those resulting in deaths – are troubling, controversial events. Public concern is growing with respect to the sustainability of the country's freshwater supply and the risks associated with activities such as fracking (De Villiers 2003; Pentland and Wood 2013).[2] In cases of perceived negligence, CI operators are subject to public demands for accountability and increased regulatory oversight. Yet it is unclear whether the public would be willing to pay the full cost of improving the safety and security of the water supply.

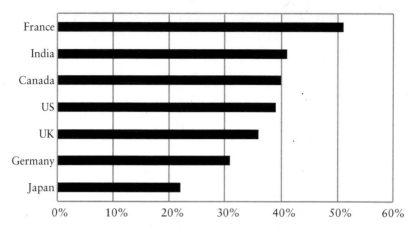

Figure 7.1 Percentage of global survey respondents who reported having a negative impression of the chemical industry, by country. This figure illustrates the percentage of respondents who answered "very little" or "nothing at all" to this statement: "Taking all your knowledge and impressions of the chemical industry into account, I'd like you to tell me how much you feel it is doing to try and reduce any harmful effects its activities have on the environment." Adapted from Schmitt (2000).

Our interview data lend mixed support to the explanatory power of ORH. When asked what factors influence how they spend their time, interview participants identified "citizen concern" as the most influential factor on average. For example, one water utility participant described the public (i.e., customers) as critical from a business perspective (Int 54). Yet this same participant implied that the public has little understanding of the complexity and costs involved in achieving safety and security. By comparison, other industry representatives and firefighters (Int 55; Int 56; Int 61) described the media's influence in terms of its capacity to shape or influence the public's view of how the organization responds to disasters. In other words, their primary concern was how they might be portrayed following a major CI event, as we saw with Montreal, Maine & Atlantic Railway Limited (MMA)'s CEO, Edward Burkhardt, and BP's CEO, Tony Hayward, noted below.

Clearly, people who work in the chemicals sector are cognizant of public opinion and the media. However, it is less clear whether public opinion and the media shape regulations in the chemicals sector. There seems to be a subtle but important difference between, on one hand, striving to avoid controversy and, on the other hand, tailoring risk regulations to public preferences. It is unclear whether industry and government are really trying to ensure that public opinion is adequately represented on decision-making and advisory boards or that the public is informed about the true nature of chemical risks. Relatively few information-gathering fora include the general public and there is no centralized database or website that citizens can access for even minimal site-specific risk information (see chapter 4 for a more in-depth discussion).[3]

ORH is a latent force that shapes the chemical industry's desire to avoid negative media coverage. Industry outreach efforts, such as the RC requirement that member companies undertake proactive community awareness and dialogue processes (CSChE 2012; Int 61), are strategies for shifting public opinion rather than the product of increased demands for transparency. Industry outreach efforts can improve public perceptions of the chemical industry (Heath and Abel 1996); however, Canadian right-to-know legislation has not kept pace with the US laws (Wordsworth et al. 2006). ORH is useful for explaining gaps between public expectations and regulatory content and, by extension, efforts by government and regulators to shape public opinion. However, ORH does not provide a straightforward account of the chemical regime; as Hood and colleagues emphasize, "Gallup-style opinion-responsive government [is] not typical in the government of risk" (2001, 103).

In transportation, regulatory regimes do not necessarily reflect the scale of the hazard but rather the profile of the hazard. When hazards are high profile, there is less resistance to implementing regulations (Lindøe, Engen, and Olsen 2011). The aviation industry is a good example of an industry with high-profile risks. Despite the fact that commercial flights remain the safest way to travel, plane crashes receive a disproportionately high volume of media coverage (Cobb and Primo 2003). Furthermore, industries with high-profile risks can be preferred targets for terrorists (Jenkins 1998). The high level of regulation in the aviation sector may be partially explained by high dread and low control factors (Slovic et al. 2004) and the availability heuristic triggered by such events as 9/11 (Kahneman and Tversky 1982). Airport security functions as an extension of aviation security because airports are the primary access point for airplanes. To engender public confidence in the system, government regulates extensively and the aviation industry cooperates because doing so is clearly in its best interest. Aviation also has a tradition of stringent security practices; in many respects, post-9/11 security practices simply built on this tradition.

Other subsectors in transportation do not receive the same level of attention as airports. Rail can also be a target for terrorists, but we have yet to see the kinds of security checks in trains and subways that we see in airports. Unlike in airports, however, increased security in rail would require a significant change in approach to security, which would increase costs and inconvenience. Further attacks in transportation subsectors could reframe the security issue for the public, especially if attacks have a stronger emotional impact on the public. For example, if pirates (or terrorists) captured a public ferry or cruise ship in Canadian waters, media coverage would almost certainly be higher volume, more alarming, and more immediate than it is now for acts of piracy.

ORH also raises the question about whether (and if so, the extent to which) people wish to live with obvious security practices. In the case of airports, enhanced security creates security theatre (Schneier 2003; Stewart and Mueller 2011), which can be both reassuring and unnerving. By this measure, seaports and rail stations generate different controversies. Unlike airports, seaports and rail stations are often built into the historic landscape, particularly in older cities. Putting fences and closed-circuit TV cameras around modern and remote stations or seaports may not spark the same controversy as putting a fence around transportation facilities in the downtown core of a historic city.

We now open up our discussion beyond our specific case studies to explore media and polling more generally, considering what they tell us about the profile of black swans and whether or not we can draw meaningful conclusions about public opinion and preferred policy positions.

THE MAINSTREAM MEDIA

Several centralizing and decentralizing forces undermine the authority of the mainstream media and raise questions about its usefulness in reflecting the state of public debate on certain issues. First, we will examine decentralizing forces. Today, everyone is entitled to an opinion, as it were. This entitlement is a function of social norms brought about by increased wealth and education, the rise of the rights of the individual, and the relative demise of powerful centralized institutions (De Vries 2000); in a postmodern world, all knowledge claims are suspect and can be challenged. Ironically, the powerful institutions that media played such a prominent role in undermining and challenging – from governments to organized religions to unions (Donohue, Tichenor, and Olien 1995) – have fallen victim to a demographic that now questions the authority of the mainstream media (Pinkleton et al. 2012).

The rise of decentralized technology has played an important role in the news industry. Decentralized technology challenges the notion that there is one authoritative source that controls the news. In the 1980s, editorialists working in London, England, could be counted in the dozens; by the turn of the century, they could be counted in the hundreds; today, there are thousands of editorialists (Tremayne 2012). The Internet and social media have created multiple low-cost channels – including Twitter feeds, Facebook pages, news websites, Instagram, YouTube, and Reddit – in which news is communicated (Gil de Zúñiga, Jung, and Valenzuela 2012). Also, readers are no longer passive recipients of the news; they can reply immediately to articles written by journalists. New media sources have also generated competition through blogs and increased availability of stories. In his report on news and democracy, Greenspon (2017) argues that the amount of competition has resulted in a fragmented audience that no longer shares a common base of knowledge, a base upon which Greenspon believes democracies depend. Today, sensational stories from around the world are immediately available to journalists and readers at a generally low cost. Collectively, these forces have increased competition and chipped away at the authority of and demand for traditional news media.

The media trends noted above have undermined the business model for traditional news media outlets, which struggle to stay alive (Ha and Fang 2012). The mainstream media have all but ceased to hire (Meyer 2009) and mainstream journalists are older, whiter, and more male than journalists working in the new media (Miller 2006). In Canada, one-third of all journalism jobs have been eliminated since 2011 (Greenspon 2017). Mainstream media are trying to compete with journalists on social media who are younger, more tech-savvy, diverse (ethnically, politically, and economically), and arguably less respectful of traditional institutions. These demographics will influence how the news is understood and depicted by journalists and consumed by the audience.

There are also centralizing tendencies that constrain journalists working in traditional media. More and more journalists note that media power is becoming more concentrated through the concentration of ownership. In Canada, almost eighty per cent of print media are owned by just five groups. Similarly, in the United States the top four owners control nearly fifty per cent of the newspapers in the country (Winseck 2008). According to journalists, owners interfere in editorial decisions (Chiang and Knight 2011), fire journalists who write pieces that are not aligned with the editorial positions of the newspaper (Chin 2015), and in some cases are unfriendly towards personalities the paper would like to be friendly towards (e.g., Lawrence Martin criticized Prime Minister Jean Chrétien; McGregor 2011). Centralizing has occurred in digital advertising, too, where over eighty per cent of all ads in Canada are provided by either Facebook or Google (Greenspon 2017). These companies act as news publishers but do not hold the news they promote to journalistic standards, profiting from viral articles with sometimes tenuous links to the truth. Both centralizing and decentralizing tendencies undermine the independence of journalists to write long, probing, thoroughly researched, and thoughtful pieces; articles have to be quick, loud, and low cost. Disasters and crises offer the opportunity for journalists to produce the latter kind of work.

Government communications have become more centralized and sophisticated. While traditional mainstream media are hiring less, the government is expanding its communications departments (Howlett, Craft, and Zibrik 2010). This trend began decades ago and has swept across all Western governments. President Clinton and Prime Minister Blair are notable examples of leaders whose communications departments became bigger, more organized, centralized, politicized, and strategic in their engagement with the media (Negrine 2007) and the public service. In Canada, prime ministers Chrétien and Harper exemplified similar patterns (Kozolanka 2006). Prime Minister Justin Trudeau seems to be following suit.

Despite these reservations, traditional mainstream media still provide important insights for a contextual analysis of the risk regulation regimes that respond to black swans. First, we do not use media coverage to reveal public opinion but rather to understand the flavour of public debate. This approach makes sense because leaders in civil society follow traditional mainstream news sources. Secondly, while traditional media may be trusted less, they are still the most trusted source of news (see table 7.1). Thirdly, mainstream media still have a quality control function. Research suggests that online posts to news stories, for example, are much more negative than public opinion as a whole (Mitchell and Hitlin 2013). Fourthly, the events we selected for our study of media coverage occurred after 9/11; many of them occurred before 2014 when trust in traditional media was still relatively high (see table 7.1.) Fifthly, the "shock and awe" factor that comes with black swans arguably makes them interesting to both new and traditional media.[4]

Finally, disasters provide a glimpse into government that routine operations do not. Because governments have increased efforts to centralize and rehearse their messages, disasters and crises provide media with an opportunity to see government unscripted. How government responds in these unrehearsed moments can be its making or undoing, which is of great interest to the media and their audience.[5]

MEDIA COVERAGE OF BLACK SWANS

We conducted a study of media coverage of selected CI events that have occurred since 9/11. The results of this study are illustrated in figures 7.2, 7.3, and 7.4. Figure 7.2 shows volume of media coverage on the y-axis and government performance assessment (as reported by the media) on the x-axis. (See appendix 1 for further notes on performance assessment.)

We examined media coverage of different types of black swans: natural disasters, industrial failures, terrorist plots, terrorist attacks, and cyber attacks. We examined the *Globe and Mail*'s coverage of Canadian events, the *New York Times*' coverage of American events, the *Daily Telegraph*'s coverage of UK events, and the *Australian*'s coverage of Australian events. We selected these newspapers because they are highly distributed broadsheets in their respective countries. For natural disasters, we selected cases that were extreme but typical of the region (e.g., wildfires in California and Australia). For industrial failures, we selected transportation and chemical examples to build on our case studies. Generally, we tried to select cases that occurred at similar times. Many occurred in 2003, 2006–07, 2013, and 2014. For further notes on the cases, please see appendix 3. Figure 7.2 shows all events in the database, figure 7.3 excludes the outliers (those more than two standard deviations from the mean), and figure 7.4 identifies patterns among the event types from

Table 7.1 Trust among Canadians in news sources,
as a percentage

Media source	2012	2013	2014	2015
Traditional media	75	74	70	62
Online search engines	55	54	62	55
Hybrid media	56	48	55	45
Owned media	38	34	36	35
Social media	32	34	32	35

Source: Edelman (2016).

figure 7.3. In figure 7.4, the dot indicates the mean for the particular event type and the horizontal and vertical lines depict the range – one standard deviation from the mean.

Media coverage of these black swans spikes and then falls away. Of the black swans we looked at, typically about seventy per cent of total coverage occurs in the first month after the event; coverage of almost all events in our database followed this pattern. There can be a second peak in the coverage if there is an inquiry, an audit, a commission, or a trial. This second peak can occur anywhere from six months (inquiries) to two or three years (trials) after the event, and it is usually much smaller and shorter lived than the first peak in coverage. It can also take some time to understand who exactly is responsible for the event. For example, industrial failures are typically very complex, and in almost all cases there is a significant gap between the event occurring and the conclusion of any judicial process. Arguably, this gap decreases the impact of the judicial process and fails to give the public a sense that responsible parties have been held accountable.

Industrial failures, particularly those in transportation, received a relatively high volume of media coverage and included, on balance, many more negative assessments of government performance than positive ones. Our transportation examples include the Waterfall train accident (Australia), the Potters Bar rail accident (United Kingdom), the I-35 highway bridge collapse (United States), the Elliott Lake parking lot collapse (Canada), the de la Concorde overpass collapse (Canada), and the rail disaster in Lac-Mégantic (Canada). The chemicals cases we looked at included the Sunrise Propane explosion (Canada), the Buncefield oil depot explosion (United Kingdom), the Texas City Refinery explosion (United States),

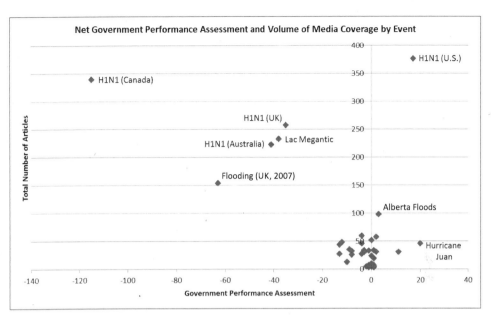

Figure 7.2 Assessment of government performance and volume of coverage for selected events (all events in our database)

the Melbourne chemical spill (Australia, 2005), and the West, Texas, fertilizer explosion (United States).

Industrial failures typically include a somewhat ruthless hunt for accountability (Pidgeon 1997). Despite the high volume of coverage focused on the Lac-Mégantic disaster, it followed the same patterns as the coverage of other industrial failures: highly critical (see table 7.2). Coverage of industrial failures can focus disproportionately on personalities rather than on the technical failure itself. Like cyber events, technical issues are difficult for journalists and readers to understand, and stories on these issues are usually less emotionally engaging than stories that focus on personalities. In the coverage of the Lac-Mégantic disaster, for example, the media focused attention on the role of Edward Burkhardt, the chairman of MMA, especially in the immediate aftermath of the derailment and explosion. At the time, the media seemed more interested in blaming Burkhardt than in discovering what information he might be able to provide about small and medium-sized enterprises (SMEs) and the railroad industry. In one episode of CBC's *Power and Politics*, an entire panel analyzed Burkhardt's perceived mismanagement of public relations.

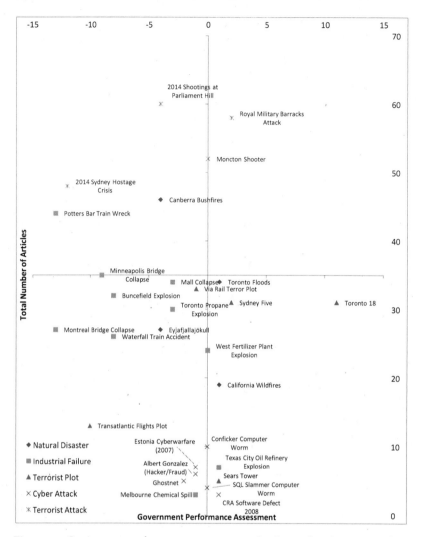

Figure 7.3 Government performance assessment and volume of media coverage by event (excludes events that were more than two standard deviations from the mean)

We have seen this before. Another recent example of "trial by media" is the media coverage of BP and then-CEO Tony Hayward, following the Deepwater Horizon oil spill (Balmer 2010; Smithson and Venette 2013). The media's rabid search for accountability is no doubt a concern for most CEOs in the transportation sector or the chemicals sector.

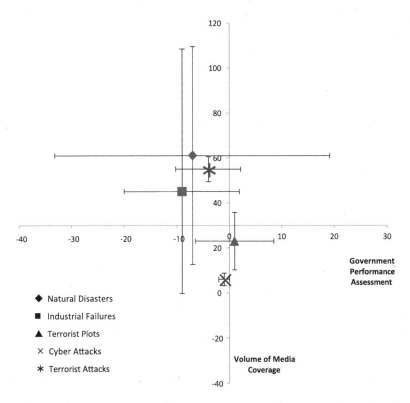

Figure 7.4 Net government performance assessment and average volume of media coverage by type of event. Horizontal and vertical lines show one standard deviation from the mean.

In contrast to the media's treatment of industrial failures, media coverage of natural disasters is usually more forgiving (though usually higher volume), although coverage can vary from event to event (see table 7.3). The natural disasters we examined included the Canberra bushfires (Australia, 2003), Hurricane Juan (Canada), the California wildfires (United States, 2007), spring flooding (United Kingdom, 2007), the Eyjafjallajökull volcanic eruptions (Iceland), the Alberta floods (Canada, 2013), and the Toronto floods (Canada, 2013).

Media coverage of natural disasters is replete with stories of people doing their best in the face of adversity, volunteerism, and of people helping others. The media perceives people to have less control and therefore the blame is less acute. This perception is ironic because many policy decisions are taken well in advance of natural

Table 7.2 Performance assessments and volume of coverage for industrial failures

Event	Net	Number of articles
Lac-Mégantic rail disaster	−85	233
Potters Bar train wreck	−35	44
Waterfall train accident	−8	26
Montreal bridge collapse	−6	27
Melbourne chemical spill	−3	3
Buncefield explosion	−1	32
Elliott Lake mall collapse	−3	34
West fertilizer plant explosion	0	24

disasters that help or hinder our capacity to respond to them (Steinberg 2000), and natural disasters actually kill more people and cost more money than industrial failures (Caruson and MacManus 2011). Media coverage of natural disasters is typically more negative when there is political conflict. Hurricane Katrina, for example, had overt political conflict between the political parties; most natural disasters do not (Barnes et al. 2008).

Sometimes black swans are difficult to categorize. In the case of the Fukushima nuclear disaster, for example, we saw an event that started as a natural disaster – the tsunami that hit the coast of Japan. Coverage was largely sympathetic, focusing on the victims and the devastation to the affected communities. The event became reframed, however, when the nuclear plant started to fail (Hassard et al. 2013; Imtihani and Mariko 2013). The coverage became much more negative; it focused on government corruption and incompetence. Measured in dollars and lives lost, the nuclear power plant disaster was a much less significant part of the story than the natural disaster but the power plant disaster came to dominate the media coverage.

Terrorist attacks dominate media coverage, particularly when the attack is in a Western country and captured in real time. At the same time as the Boston Marathon bombing, there was an explosion in a fertilizer plant in West, Texas. The Boston Marathon bombing killed three and injured 264; the West Fertilizer explosion killed fifteen and injured 160. Despite the human suffering in both events, the Boston bombing dominated media coverage at the time. The cases we looked at included the Royal Artillery Barracks attack (United Kingdom),

Table 7.3 Performance assessments and volume of coverage for natural disasters

Event	Net performance asssessment	Number of articles
Canberra bushfires	–4	46
Hurricane Juan	20	46
UK flooding	–63	154
California wildfires	1	19
Toronto floods	1	34
Alberta floods	3	98
Eyjafjallajökull eruption (Iceland)	–4	27

the Moncton shooting (Canada), the Parliament Hill shooting (Canada), and the Sydney hostage crisis.

These acts of terror generated high volumes of coverage and neutral to negative performance assessments of government. From a rational standpoint, this makes almost no sense. The media play an important role in informing the public during a black swan event but the coverage goes well beyond that; we consume media like we do crime fiction. Alternative framings – which might focus on the perpetrator's psychiatric state (as opposed to solely framing the perpetrator as a terrorist) or broader contextual issues such as gun control – are marginalized in the early stages of the media's response.

Terrorist plots and attacks are different in important ways, and this is reflected in the media coverage. Irrespective of how much advanced planning security officials have done, terrorist attacks catch security officials off guard. Their response is hurried. Security officials have to pursue the perpetrators and contend with the emergency itself (e.g., victims). Within minutes of an attack, security officials will be asked about myriad issues, including who is responsible, why the intelligence community was not better prepared, and the effectiveness of coordination between domestic agencies and other national governments. The list goes on.

Arguably, and as we saw in the Boston Marathon bombing when over 9,000 security officials pursued the perpetrators (Botelho 2013), the Parliament Hill shootings, and the attacks in Paris in 2015, the nature of the attacks leads to a level of transparency with respect to government performance; the public sees aspects of how security officials respond during such a crisis, which can seem disjointed and chaotic. There are also victims, which creates highly emotive media coverage. Finally, the public is not necessarily passive. As we saw in Boston, Ottawa, Sydney, and Moncton, members of the public – victims, bystanders, local businesses, and online communities – helped to identify suspects. In some cases, the public's help was not welcome (or anticipated), as we saw when one person tweeted the location of the police officers tracking the Moncton shooter (Royal Canadian Mounted Police 2014) or was misinformed, as in the case of the online community identifying suspects in the Boston bombing who turned out to be innocent (Sanchez 2013)

Failed terrorist plots are different from terrorist attacks. In the former, security services can control information much more effectively. In the case of failed terrorist plots, the government is more likely to be the primary source of information for the media (Quigley, Quigley, Mills, and Stallard 2013). The cases we looked at included the Sydney 5 (Australia), the Sears Tower plot (United States), the Toronto 18 (Canada), the transatlantic flights plot (United Kingdom), and the VIA Rail terror plot (Canada).

With terror plots, the government can hold press conferences where it decides what to say, when to say it, who attends, what the presenters wear, and whether or not to place national symbols, such as flags, in the background and in so doing associate the event with issues of national identity and pride. The government can also choose which aspects of its response to emphasize. For instance, the government may emphasize areas where intelligence service has improved, such as inter-agency and international collaboration. Indeed, government officials frame failed terrorist plots in the charges they lay and in so doing connect the issue with broader international events, such as the War on Terror.[6] Generally, failed terrorist plots are seen as a good news story for security officials, and the public is a passive recipient of information.

Successful risk management depends on our capacity to learn from early warning signs. Yet there is ambiguity about the meaning of failed terrorist plots. On one hand, they generate positive coverage for security services because the security services have detected and presumably stopped the terrorists. On the other hand, it is unclear if plots are symptomatic of more widespread problems among segments of the population and if other plots are in progress. Also, because the failed terrorist plot is never carried out, it raises questions about the guilt, innocence, and intentions of the alleged terrorists. Would they have actually gone through with the plot? Some scholars have argued that the *Globe and Mail*'s coverage of the Toronto-18 plot was alarmist, distortionary, and irresponsible (Miller and Sack 2010; Morano 2010; Smolash 2009). In the Toronto 18 plot, there was a four-year gap between arrests and the trial. While the media's coverage of police and government was largely positive, over time doubts emerged about the credibility of the charges. The duration of criminal proceedings thus contributed to questions about the efficacy of the judicial process and raised questions concerning accountability and performance of law enforcement. It takes years to arrive at a verdict in such cases, well after the initial media coverage is over.

In stark contrast to industrial failures, natural disasters, terrorist attacks, and failed terrorist plots, cyber events receive almost no media coverage. Our database also includes several cyber events. The country of origin is at times impossible to detect. Our cases included the sQL Slammer Worm, the Albert Gonzalez data thefts (United States), Estonia cyberwarfare, the Canada Revenue Agency software defect, the Conficker computer worm, Ghostnet, and the Sony Pictures hack (United States).

In 2007, the Canada Revenue Agency uploaded a corrupt patch that forced it to take its systems offline for about 10 days, which prevented the government from collecting money online for those 10 days. Arguably, this was a significant event not only because it impacted government revenues but also because it revealed vulnerability in the government's system. Yet the media showed little interest. In February 2011, a cyber attack infiltrated key central government agencies, including the Treasury Board Secretariat, the Finance Department, and the Department of National Defence (Weston 2011). As a result, the government took several systems offline for weeks. Many public servants were without even basic email service. The government had spent years drafting cybersecurity plans, which had been approved for over a year. Despite this, the government's computer network remained vulnerable and the government response – effectively taking everyone offline – was unimaginative and unimaginable.

Again, the media showed little interest. Despite the increased anxiety over cybersecurity by Western governments (Obama 2015; UK Office of Cyber Security 2011; Australian Government 2010), the patterns in media coverage are not necessarily changing. US Senator

John McCain famously described the cyber attack on Sony as the first cyber war and declared the United States the loser (Sheppard 2014). Despite Senator McCain's claims, the media did not cover the cyber attack on Sony any more or very differently than it did the other cyber stories in our database. Cyber still seems to struggle to get traction in the media.

Cyber events receive more coverage if the media can identify a culprit, which is not always easy in cyber attacks. When the media can identify an individual as being primarily responsible (e.g., Edward Snowden, Julian Assange, Chelsea Manning, and Jeffrey Delisle), this generates a compelling human interest story and generally results in more media coverage. Cyber events are by and large nameless and faceless: accountability is unclear, there are rarely interesting photos, and technical issues are frequently difficult for journalists to explain and for readers to understand. These attributes reduce social amplification by the media and correspond to a lack of public interest (Pidgeon, Kasperson, and Slovic 2003).

One type of cyber event does receive media coverage: cyberbullying. For instance, the death of Amanda Todd, a young Canadian who committed suicide after enduring considerable online bullying, received a great deal of media attention, including over 70 articles in the *Globe and Mail* in the six months following her death. Similarly, the death of Rehtaeh Parsons, a teenage girl who committed suicide following sustained cyberbullying, received comparable media attention. Within two weeks of Parsons' death, her parents travelled to Ottawa with the premier of Nova Scotia to meet with the prime minister to discuss cyberbullying (CBC News 2013). Events tend to attract considerable media coverage when they focus on a vulnerable individual and many personal details are available. We will discuss the challenges associated with cybersecurity issues in more detail in chapter 8 and the depiction of vulnerable youth in the media in chapter 9.

PROBLEMS WITH POLLING

Are polling data useful in understanding people's views about risks, black swans, and accountability? Like media, polling has become a regular feature of modern life and has also undergone changes. Over the last two decades, technology has greatly reduced the cost and time of conducting polls and as a result polls have become extremely common, on a variety of subjects. Polls are used by politicians, governments, non-governmental organizations, media, and small businesses. The media publish polls because people like to see them and they are usually inexpensive to produce.

Despite technological improvements, there are questions about the methods and accuracy of polls. A random sample of land lines is no longer representative, since many now use cellphones (Grenier 2013). The 1991 Telephone Consumer Protection Act in the United States, for example, prohibits use of automatic dialing to call cellphones; pollsters have to dial manually, which increases costs and decreases sample sizes and accuracy. People are also much more reluctant to participate in polls than in the past. Participation rates dropped from eighty per cent in the 1970s to eight per cent in 2014. Pollsters wonder if those who choose to participate in polls have commonly held opinions or are outliers (Zukin 2015).

While the cost of certain types of popular polling may be decreasing, the cost of quality and accurate polling is actually increasing; as a result, we see fewer high-quality polls (Zukin 2015). Ostensibly, polling allows governments to understand the public's views on issues. When used to guide government actions, polls can increase the democratic legitimacy of the government's actions. Somewhat ironically, opposition members criticize governments for polling too often; they claim too much money is spent on polls and that governments govern by polls or by focus group because they lack the conviction to make more difficult and controversial choices lest their immediate popularity suffer, or because they want to test different framing strategies for more controversial and divisive policies. Figure 7.5 summarizes trends in government polling in Canada. In 2008, the number of government polls dropped because of the Federal Accountability Act (enacted in 2006), new contract regulations (which came into effect in 2007), and a series of other measures to reduce government spending on public opinion research that came into effect in 2008 (Public Works and Government Services 2009).

PUBLIC ATTITUDES TOWARDS GOVERNMENT, INDUSTRY, AND BLACK SWANS

Black swans generate unique challenges. They get attention from the media and the media focus on the victims, generating highly emotive coverage. Black swans can also generate very positive coverage of

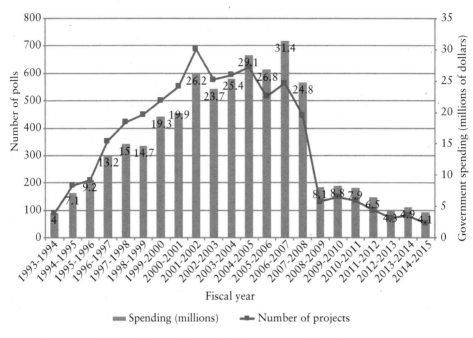

Figure 7.5 Public opinion polling by the Government of Canada, 1993–2015

communities helping one another in a time of crisis. This type of media attention and coverage can change public opinion, but it is difficult to know whether the change will be permanent and whether shifts in public opinion will translate into support for policy change. Policy can take months if not years to change and usually requires some sort of trade-off in benefits. Ninety-eight per cent of Canadians may believe the earth's climate is changing (Graham 2012), for example, but only fifty-three per cent believe that the 2013 floods in Alberta and Ontario were caused by climate change (Star Staff 2013), and less than a third of Albertans were in favour of the provincial government's policy to cover all domestic costs related to the Alberta floods that the insurance industry would not cover because the houses were built in flood-prone areas (Wood 2013).

Attitudes towards terrorism are equally complex, and they are less volatile than one might think. During Canada's federal election in September 2015, a Syrian boy drowned while fleeing the conflict in Syria with his family. Immediately, the boy's photo was projected around the world and had a strong emotional impact. Despite that impact, days after the photo was published, Canadians were divided about what to do about the Syrian refugee crisis; a plurality supported the more cautious approach of the Conservative government over the proposals of the Liberal party and the New Democratic Party (Angus Reid Institute 2015a; Hannay 2015; Vincent 2015). The Conservatives had cautioned that Syria and the surrounding region had significant security problems, and screening of refugees had to be handled carefully lest people with criminal records and ill intention enter Canada. Six weeks later (after terrorists attacked Paris) fifty-four per cent of Canadians were opposed to admitting Syrian refugees (IPSOS 2015) and sixty-two per cent of Canadians believed – contrary to the position of the newly elected Liberals – that Canada should either continue its current level of involvement in the fight against ISIS or increase Canada's involvement (Angus Reid Institute 2015b). Despite dramatic new events, Canadian public opinion was relatively stable throughout.

Irrespective of how Canadians responded to these polling questions, it remains unclear whether Canadians believe security or the environment is a priority. Immediately following 9/11, security concerns increased; at that time, twenty per cent of Canadians believed that security should be a priority for the government. Most Canadians were satisfied with the Canadian government's response to 9/11, although ethnic minorities were decidedly less so (Department of Justice 2015). Most Canadians were unfamiliar with the policies or laws that the government enacted as a result of 9/11; they were more likely to comment on increased airport security (EKOS 2007). Security concerns decreased after 2003 but rose again (slightly and briefly) after the arrest of the Toronto 18 and the Iraq War; many believed that a terrorist attack was more likely and that Canadian security officials were prepared (EKOS 2007).

Since then, few Canadians have identified security or the environment as a priority; more have identified the environment as a priority but neither security nor the environment rivals the economy or health care as priorities for most Canadians. This pattern of concern has existed for some time – 9/11 was an anomaly. Recall that in the 1990s the Defence budget was cut back severely. These cutbacks contributed to a variety of crises, ethical lapses, and general malaise in the military (Perry 2015). Canadians were largely indifferent to these cutbacks.

Similarly, Canadians' views about the environment have been ambivalent. In the 1990s, the Canadian government did little to meet its Kyoto targets, instead preferring to meet booming demand for the country's natural resources. There seemed to be little political consequence; the Liberal party won four consecutive elections. In the 2009 election, the opposition Liberal party proposed a carbon consumption tax that was widely rejected.

Given the dominant position of economic and health care concerns (figure 7.6), event framing becomes crucial. Terrorism constitutes an ambiguous risk because although we may know what has happened we do not necessarily know what it means. For example, there was a debate after the 2014 Parliament Hill shootings where the Conservative government and the RCMP emphasized that Michael Zehaf-Bibeau was a terrorist whereas the opposition parties argued that he was mentally ill. Polls suggest that Canadians were evenly divided on the question of Bibeau's status (Maloney 2014).

The public can also be divided on the implications of industrial failures. While industrial failures generate uniformly negative media coverage, it is unclear whether this translates into meaningful policy. Following the train disaster in Lac-Mégantic, fifty-eight per cent of Canadians saw pipelines as the safest way to transport crude oil, whereas eighteen per cent saw rail as the safest mode of transport. In Alberta, more people perceived pipelines as safer (seventy-five per cent); Albertans were set to benefit financially from more oil exports. Ironically, only fifty-two per cent of people in Quebec – where the Lac-Mégantic rail disaster occurred – perceived pipelines as safer than rail for transporting oil. In fact, municipal politicians seemed hesitant to accept certain changes to rail transportation following the Lac-Mégantic rail disaster (Annis 2014). Many small towns depend on rail transportation to ship goods, which can be crucial for the local economy (Annis 2014; Wahba and Gordon 2013). In the next election, Lac-Mégantic was hardly mentioned by the media or politicians.

A more salient question, perhaps, is this: Do people trust the government to do the right thing in the face of uncertainty and complexity? Trust in government has plummeted in Western countries and nowhere is this trend more pronounced than in the United States. The Pew Research Center has tracked trust in government since 1958 (Pew Research Center 2015). In 1964, seventy-seven per cent of Americans trusted the government to do the right thing "just about always/most of the time"; this was the high point. With the exception of a few spikes, the number has decreased since then, hitting an all-time low of nineteen per cent in November 2011. If we

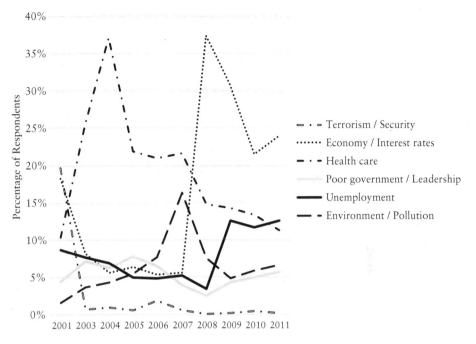

Figure 7.6 Most important problems facing Canadians today. Adapted from the Canadian Opinion Research Archive. Data for years 2001 through 2009 are based on third quarter results; 2010–11 data were only collected once per year, and no data were available in 2002. Respondents were asked: "In your opinion, what is the most important problem facing Canadians today?"

look at more recent patterns, we see that trust in government among Canadians is not high, but it is consistent and slightly higher than among citizens of other Western countries and the global average (see table 7.4).

Most CI is owned and operated by the private sector. Table 7.5 shows levels of public trust in business. Generally, Canadians trust the private sector as much as they do government. Again, Canadians seem a bit more trusting than the citizens of other Western countries, and while the number of people who trust industry is not high, it is relatively stable. After the financial markets collapsed in 2008, it is unsurprising that people in most Western countries had less trust for industry in 2009.

We see more variation in trust for certain organization types and particular sectors. In the developed world, family businesses and

Table 7.4 Level of public trust in government, via the Edelman Trust Barometer (respondents aged 35–64 years)

	Level of trust, %								
	2009	2010	2011	2012	2013	2014	2015	Mean	SD
Canada	51	47	52	56	58	51	49	52	4
Australia	53	41	52	47	43	56	49	49	5
United Kingdom	41	38	43	38	47	42	43	42	3
United States	30	46	40	43	53	37	41	41	7
Global	44	47	52	43	50	45	48	47	3

Note: SD, standard deviation.
Source: Edelman (2016). The Edelman Trust Barometer (ETB) uses telephone surveys to conduct its polling. Its polls are conducted in the fall of the preceding year (e.g., the 2011 ETB was conducted between 11 October 2011 and 28 November 2010). They survey "informed publics" in multiple countries. The criteria for "informed publics" are as follows: college educated; household income in the top quartile for their age in their country; read or watch the news several times per week; and follow public policy in the news several times per week. Results in tables correspond to participants' response to the question "How much do you trust government to do what is right?"

Table 7.5 Level of public trust in business, via the Edelman Trust Barometer (respondents aged 35–64 years)

	Level of trust, %								
	2009	2010	2011	2012	2013	2014	2015	Mean	SD
Canada	45	57	50	56	58	62	47	54	6
Australia	43	47	54	57	48	59	48	51	6
United Kingdom	45	49	44	38	56	56	52	49	7
United States	36	54	46	50	62	58	60	52	9
Global	49	54	56	53	59	59	57	55	4

Note: SD, standard deviation.
Source: Edelman (2016). The Edelman Trust Barometer (ETB) uses telephone surveys to conduct its polling. Its polls are conducted in the fall of the preceding year (e.g., the 2011 ETB was conducted between 11 October 2011 and 28 November 2010). They survey "informed publics" in multiple countries. The criteria for "informed publics" are as follows: college educated; household income in the top quartile for their age in their country; read or watch the news several times per week; and follow public policy in the news several times per week. Results in tables correspond to participants' response to the question "How much do you trust business to do what is right?"

SMEs are highly trusted – between 2013 and 2015, seventy-two per cent to seventy-six per cent of respondents said they trusted them – whereas large private companies and state corporations are not particularly trusted – forty-five per cent to fifty-three per cent of

Table 7.6 Level of public trust in critical infrastructure
sectors

Sector	Subsector	Trust (%)
ICT	Technology	79
	Telecommunications	63
Food	Food and beverage	67
Energy	Hydraulic fracturing	47
	Renewables	70
	Natural gas	57
	Utilities	54
	Oil	50
Manufacturing	Pharmaceuticals	60
	Chemicals	57
Finance	Financial services	51
	Banks	53

Note: ICT, information and communication technologies.
Source: Edelman (2016).

respondents said they trusted them (Edelman 2016). Table 7.6 shows
the level of trust by several critical sectors in a 2014–15 global survey. Large sectors, in which a handful of companies dominate, are
not particularly trusted (e.g., banking, oil, and utilities). Sectors that
are more dispersed, such as food, are trusted, as are renewable
energy companies.

The public trusts the technology sector the most, and by a good
measure. This sector creates enormously popular products and the
way it advertises itself generates extremely positive images. Most
people do not worry about online security, but risk experts do. In
the Society of Actuaries' 2014 annual survey of emerging risks, people who work in the insurance and risk industry downgraded economic and environmental risks and upgraded both geopolitical and
technological ones. For the first time since the society started the
survey in 2008, cybersecurity/interconnectedness of infrastructure
topped the list of emerging risk concerns at fifty-eight per cent
among those surveyed.

In sum, Canadians are highly concerned about the economy and
health care, somewhat concerned about the environment, and not
particularly concerned about security. Black swans receive considerable media coverage, which creates an opportunity for policy change,

but it is unclear whether media coverage changes people's views. It is also unclear that the general public is prepared to support policy changes in light of black swan events. Trust in government and industry is generally low, although Canadians appear to trust their government more than people in other Western countries trust theirs. The Canadian government has not strayed far from public opinion on many environmental and security issues.

CONCLUSION

In the immediate aftermath of a black swan event, particularly industrial failures, governments and industry scramble to reassure the public by promising new and more stringent safeguards and reporting requirements. For example, the Lac-Mégantic rail disaster has led to several announcements regarding new federal regulations. ORH offers a convincing explanation for government and industry behaviour in the wake of black swan events. After a major disaster, normal standards and operating procedures are subject to intense scrutiny by hungry media in search of a culprit and a voyeuristic public that is fascinated and outraged. It is unclear, however, whether new standards announced in the immediate aftermath of a disaster translate into improved regulatory outcomes over the long term. This is particularly true when an incident is not reviewed by a formal public inquiry or commission. The absence of an inquiry limits the potential for organizational learning.

The value of public inquiries is illustrated by comparing the government response to the 2008 Sunrise Propane explosion in Toronto with the 2005 explosion at the Buncefield oil storage depot in Hertfordshire, England. In both cases, the insurance and legal issues took several years to resolve. After the Buncefield explosion, however, the United Kingdom promptly initiated an independent investigation into the cause of the failure. The independent investigator maintained a comprehensive website with detailed information about its activities and its findings, including numerous interim reports (see, for example, Buncefield Major Incident Investigation Board 2008). This investigation was transparent and provided an opportunity for benchmarking and learning. In contrast, the Ontario Office of the Fire Marshal prepared what it described as a "technically complex" internal report that was only available to the public in redacted form upon request (Ministry of Community Safety and Correctional Services 2010). Without a public inquiry, neither media nor the public can learn how organizations incorporate lessons from previous failures. The absence of an independent public inquiry also restricts opportunities for democratic oversight of the regulatory regime and prevents society from holding those responsible to account. Neither Hurricane Juan nor the Lac-Mégantic rail disaster – both sizeable and costly disasters – had independent public inquiries.

Public opinion is sometimes volatile. For Canada, our research confirms that in some cases people change their views in the short term following and in light of disasters, as Canadians did after 9/11. This sometimes dramatic change in opinion represents a disruptive moment for the regime, which can displace temporarily the normal state of affairs and produce progress towards a regime that better reflects the interests and concerns of civil society. Regime disruptions present opportunities to overcome path dependency, entrenched interests, and inertia, but they also can lead to overreaction. When media outlets focus on highly emotive issues (and neglect more probable and consequential risks) they can attract attention and motivate change to the regulatory regime. This focus can also lead to narrow and misguided risk assessments. Canadians' trust in SMEs, for example, may be misplaced. As noted in the previous chapter, SMEs have less capacity to manage operational failures and are also less likely to have adequate insurance. Canadians also have high trust in the technology sector, despite the rising concerns over cybersecurity and the largely unregulated space in which the Internet operates.

Our research suggests that media coverage of natural disasters is less likely than media coverage of industrial failures to lead to dramatic changes. Ironically, natural disasters kill and cost more than industrial failures; planning decisions that make us vulnerable to natural disasters are made well before disasters occur. Interview subjects from seaports and bridges noted that natural disasters concern them the most. In contrast, media coverage of industrial failures tends to blame individuals or to look for a "bad guy" to blame. This approach overlooks the more systemic issues that might underpin the true vulnerabilities in industrial failures. We need more complete information in the public domain to address knowledge gaps and help the public and media develop informed opinions on security issues. The alternative is an ill-informed, emotionally driven reaction to risk, examples of which we see in the next two chapters, which examine the exaggerated claims of cybersecurity specialists and the media in the aftermath of the death of a seemingly healthy boy of H1N1.

8

"Cyber Gurus":
How Professionals Frame Cyber Threats

There is a tension at the centre of our relationship with technology. On one hand, there is incredible optimism that information technology can simultaneously improve service delivery, cut costs, and enhance democratic participation (Layne and Lee 2001; Sharif 2008; Roy 2012). On the other hand, there is burgeoning information technology (IT) security literature that warns that our increasing dependence on technology is becoming a liability because the technology can be so easily attacked by those with malicious intent, and the critical infrastructure (CI) and services that depend on it can be so easily discontinued (Clarke and Knake 2010). Indeed, these actors and actions, it is claimed, can undermine our democratic processes and bring into question the legitimacy of our democratically elected leaders, as we saw in the 2016 US presidential election, during which it is alleged a group of hackers associated with Russian Intelligence infiltrated the Democratic National Committee's computers (Lipton, Sanger, and Shane 2016).

Much of the research on computer security and CI protection (CIP), however, focuses on the ways in which organizations secure their networks and information in the supply chain (Kolluru and Meredith 2001; Faisal, Banwet, and Shankar 2006; Von Solms and Van Niekerk 2013). Less attention has been paid to how organizations construct and understand cybersecurity risks. Our failure to pay attention constitutes a risk in itself. It is not enough for systems to be secure; they have to seem secure (Bertot, Jaeger, and Grimes 2010).

This chapter has three purposes. The first is to provide an understanding of how cybersecurity risk is constructed. We will draw on the "management gurus" literature, which explains how consultants, academics, and authors who profit from selling solutions to complex organizational issues persuade audiences that their ideas are useful. Secondly, we use the techniques Nørreklit (2003) employed in her rhetorical analysis of *The Balanced Scorecard* to analyze cybersecurity discourse in ten recent publications (see table 8.1 for a complete list). The publications range from popular print media to TED (Technology, Entertainment, Design) Talks to academic and technical articles. We are particularly interested in examining the extent to which cybersecurity specialists are using management guru techniques and manipulating common cognitive limitations to overdramatize and oversimplify cybersecurity risks in the popular press. We examine the policy challenges that emerge as a result of the present framing of cybersecurity risks. The ultimate goal of this chapter is to question the effectiveness of how we talk about and raise awareness of cybersecurity issues and what policies we should adopt to address potential weaknesses in governance of cyberspace that are aggravated further by the present cybersecurity discourse.

THE PSYCHOLOGY OF RISK AND THE TECHNIQUES OF MANAGEMENT GURUS

Under the influence of the availability heuristic (see chapter 2), people tend to believe that an event is more likely to occur if they are able to imagine or recall it easily (for examples, see Slovic et al. 1979; Folkes 1988; Betsch and Pohl 2002; Tversky and Kahneman 1973; Maldonato and Dell'Orco 2011). Recall that we noted in chapter 2 that fear of shark attacks increased dramatically after the release of the movie *Jaws*, despite the fact that there was no empirical evidence to suggest that shark attacks had suddenly become more probable (Slovic et al. 1979). By contrast, the availability heuristic can also lull people into a false sense of security regarding the risks associated with everyday tasks, such as in the workplace or the home. Availability is considered one of the most important heuristics for understanding risk perception (Sjöberg 2000). For instance, the availability heuristic makes people more concerned about terrorist attacks despite the fact that, like other many high-profile risks, terrorist attacks are extremely unlikely (Gierlach et al. 2010). This phenomenon is referred to as probability neglect (Slovic et al. 2005). When probability neglect is at work, "people's attention is focused on the bad outcome itself, and they are inattentive to the fact that it is unlikely to occur" (Sunstein 2003, 122). In other words, people tend to overemphasize the consequences of risks while minimizing or even ignoring the probabilities.

Management Gurus

The term *management guru* refers to the authors, publishers, editors, consultants, managers, commercial seminar organizers, and professors who offer advice on business and management (Kieser 1997). These management gurus are primarily interested in "how management knowledge is created, processed into saleable products and services, how it is marketed, communicated to customers, and how it is consumed by them" (Huczynski 2006, 2). The field has also attracted business and management academics critical of the ambitious prescriptions offered by management gurus. The management guru literature can therefore be understood as both a reaction against and response to the popular literature on business and management.

There are three key themes in the management guru literature: how guru ideas become popularized, their unique appeal to managers, and common techniques. Management gurus are considered influential because they inspire managers to implement their solutions to solve complex organizational problems (Huczynski 2006). A key finding of the literature is that these cures come and go over time. Kieser (1997) likens the rise and fall of management trends to the fashion industry. He notes, "at the start of the fashion, only a few pioneers are daring enough to take it up. These few are joined by a rising number of imitators until the fashion is 'out' and new fashions come on the market" (Kieser 1997, 51). In addition to explaining the rise and fall of management trends, this metaphor is helpful for capturing the influential role that aesthetics play in management trends. Røvik (2011) argues that the rise and fall of management trends can also be compared to the life cycle of a virus. The virus theory helps to explain what happens to organizations once they have been "infected" with a new organizational idea. Organizations typically go through the stages of "infectiousness, immunity, replication, incubation, mutation, and dormancy" before the next fad takes hold (Røvik 2011, 635). Finally, organizations do not build immunity to management fads over time. Despite the fact that guru ideas have only a modest impact on actual working life, managers always seem prepared to entertain the next trend.

One of the central questions of the management guru literature is why managers are particularly susceptible to guru ideas, especially given their limited practical results. Ahonen and Kallio (2009) argue that guru ideas are a form of cultural expression. From this perspective, the management model is the Holy Grail onto which "all seemingly good values and ideas have been projected" (Ahonen and Kallio 2009). Much like the quest for the Holy Grail, the search for the ideal management model is more important than the model itself. The concept of search also represents many ideals in liberal Western democracy, such as the never-ending quest for "efficiency, success, and welfare" (Ahonen and Kallio 2009, 433). As such, the search for the best management ideas serves a therapeutic role for managers and gurus alike. Other researchers explain the appeal of gurus through their impressive performances. Clark and Salaman (1996) liken these performances to that of a witch doctor because gurus give "a 'dramatic realization' in which the performer conveys to an audience that which they wish to express" (91).

The management guru literature also accounts for how popular management ideas become influential. Rhetoric is a common and influential technique. For example, Hood and Jackson (1991) argue that persuasion fuels organizational change more often than objective facts. In their view, speakers attempt to establish their theories as the most credible, not necessarily the most truthful. To this end, Hood and Jackson (1991) identify six salient features of administrative arguments: their universal appeal, contradictory nature, instability, use of recycled ideas, reliance on soft data and logic, and competition with rival ideas through aesthetics rather than evidence. Berglund and Werr (2000) support Hood and Jackson's (1991) typology, adding that management gurus rely on the use of contradictory business myths or ideas to adapt their arguments to suit any need or audience. Furthermore, Keulen and Kroeze (2012) bring attention to the way management gurus frame their arguments using historical narratives or anecdotes to express the soundness of their ideas. Using anecdotes is also a persuasive method to position management gurus as the purveyors of practical knowledge in contrast to the theoretical knowledge offered by academics. This positioning lends management gurus affinity with managers as "one of us" (Huczynski 2006). Government is not immune to this trend either. The public sector was most famously captured by the "reinventing government" movement, which rested on the assumption that governments and the public sector should learn from the private sector (Osborne and Gaebler 1992; see also Moore 1995; Osborne and Plastrik 1997).

Management guru techniques and heuristics are powerful tools. The psychology of risk literature and management guru literature are connected to this chapter by the way gurus are able to overdramatize or oversimplify complex organizational issues. Their objective is to inspire managers – usually using rhetorical arguments – to implement their solutions to solve complex organizational problems. Often these problems are based on issues related to the efficiency, success, or welfare of an organization. As the next section will demonstrate, these themes are also prevalent in the cybersecurity discourse.

DEPICTIONS OF CYBERSECURITY THREATS

From a risk governance perspective, cybersecurity threats might be described as uncertain risks (Renn 2008). Uncertain risks occur where there is "a lack of clear scientific or technical basis for decision making" (Renn 2008, 18). Despite the increase in popular discourse about cybersecurity, there is reason to be careful about overestimating the probability of risks and to ensure we understand the motivations behind different actions. Today, there are four main depictions of threats in the cybersecurity literature:

- *Cyber terrorism* – Terrorism is commonly defined as "the purposeful act or the threat of the act of violence to create fear and/or compliant behavior in a victim and/or audience of the act or threat" (Stohl 2007, 229). Cyber terrorism means that these acts are committed using technology.
- *Hacktivism* – Refers to "the marriage of hacking with political activism" (Stohl 2007, 236).
- *Cyber crime* – Refers to criminal offences committed online or through other forms of information technology.
- *Cyber warfare* – Refers to "the role of information technology as an enabler of warfare" (Colarik and Janczewski 2012, 39).

While these are four prevalent types of cybersecurity issues, evidence suggests that the threat is exaggerated and oversimplified for some. Many note the lack of empirical evidence to support the widespread fear of cyber terrorism and cyber warfare, for instance (Lewis 2003; Stohl 2007; Cavelty 2007; Hansen and Nissenbaum 2009; Rid 2013). Others suggest the field is simply not transparent (Kaplan 2016). According to Stohl (2007), there is little vulnerability in CI that could lead to violence or fatalities. Moreover, there are few actors who would be interested in or capable of exploiting such vulnerabilities. In relation to cyber terrorism in particular, cyber attacks are more expensive to carry out than traditional forms of terrorism, limiting the utility of cyber attacks compared with other available measures (Stohl 2007). Instead, technology is most often used by terrorists to provide information, propagate their cause and grievances, solicit financial support, network with like-minded terrorists, recruit, and gather information (see, for example, Stern and Berger 2015). In other words, "terrorist groups are simply exploiting modern tools to accomplish the same goals they sought in the past" (Stohl 2007, 230).

Hacktivism is much more common than cyber terrorism. Typically, hackers use "virtual sit-ins and blockades; automated e-mail bombs; web hacks and computer break-ins; and computer viruses and worms" to draw attention to their cause (Stohl 2007, 236). Hacktivism encompasses the politics necessary to categorize these kinds of attacks as cyber terrorism; however, the objective of hackers is more often to cause mischief for the targeted organization rather than to cause violence or death. Cyber crime is also a major issue, but it is more problematic in terms of law enforcement and business (Lewis 2003). The most common forms of cyber crime include "insider threats, extortion, industrial espionage, and loss of financial data or intellectual property to outsiders" (Lewis 2003, 39). Despite their relative frequency, threats from hacktivism or cyber crime are either overshadowed by or misrepresented as cyber terrorism. This misrepresentation increases awareness of black swan threats, such as cyber terrorism, while decreasing attention for more common cybersecurity risks like hacktivism or cyber crime.

RHETORICAL ANALYSIS OF THE CYBER DISCOURSE

On the basis of Nørreklit's (2003) rhetorical analysis of the argumentation in Kaplan and Norton's *The Balanced Scorecard,* we structure our analysis according to the categories below.

- *Appeal to the audience* – appeal to the audience's *ethos* or trust in the credibility of the source, to the audience's *pathos* or emotions, or to the audience's *logos* or logic (Aristotle and Kennedy 1991). The genre of text will typically influence the type of appeal used.
- *Stylistic devices* – use of popular tropes in the guru field including analogies, metaphors, similes, metonymy, hyperbole, irony, antithesis, loaded adjectives, and imprecise and intertextually based concepts.
- *Argumentation model* – involves three basic elements: a claim, data, and a warrant (Walton 1996). The *claim* is the point of view the source wishes the audience to accept. *Data* are the evidence the source uses to support the claim. Finally, the *warrant* is often implicit and combines the claim and data. It represents the assumptions the source makes (Nørreklit 2003).

The ten articles in table 8.1 were chosen on the basis of their publication date (between 2010 and 2012), the medium in which they were published, and their relevance to the study at hand. We tried to include publications from a variety of sources (i.e., the popular print media, technical experts, and academia). The authors of these ten pieces come from diverse fields and are politicians, public servants, journalists, CEOs, academics, and computer scientists.

The limits of this analysis include the small number of publications that we examined, the sampling method, and the data collection. The number of cases used here impacts the generalizability of this study. The sampling method, a nonprobability method called quota sampling, also influences the results. Using quota sampling, the population of cybersecurity discourse was separated into distinct and mutually exclusive categories or subgroups. We then selected publications from each subcategory according to predetermined proportions (i.e., data selection was non-random).

The benefits of this method are that all relevant categories were represented and there was greater variability among the publications than random sampling might have achieved. The downside of this method is that we made a subjective judgment about which publications to include in the study. We may have inadvertently chosen cases that appeared to support our hypothesis while excluding those that did not. While this potential source of bias is a valid concern, quota sampling is the most appropriate method for this research. We are

Table 8.1 Cases

Author(s)	Date published	Title	Type	Country
Richard A. Clarke and Robert Knake	December 2010	*Cyber War: The Next Threat to National Security and What to Do About It* (introduction and chapter 1)	Book (non-fiction)	United States
Richard Clarke	16 February 2012	Cyber-attacks Can Spark Real Wars	Newspaper article (*Wall Street Journal*)	United States
Misha Glenny	18 May 2012	Canada's Weakling Web Defenses	Newspaper article (*Globe and Mail*)	Canada
Joe Lieberman	17 October 2012	The Threat is Real and Must be Stopped	Newspaper article (*New York Times*)	United States
Con Coughlin	14 October 2010	Cyber Guards or Soldiers: Which Do We Need Most?	Newspaper article (*Daily Telegraph*)	United Kingdom
Misha Glenny	July 2011	Hire the Hackers!	TED Talk (journalist)	United States
Avi Rubin	October 2011	All Your Devices Can be Hacked	TED Talk (academic)	United States
Nicholson, Webber, Dyer, Patel, and Janicke	2012	SCADA Security in the Light of Cyber-warfare	Scholarly article	United Kingdom
Laura Mather	21 April 2011	Cybersecurity Requires a Multi-layered Approach	Technical magazine article (*Info Security Magazine*)	United States
Tony Busseri	12 March 2012	It's Time to Take Cybersecurity Seriously	Technical magazine article (*Wired Magazine*)	United States

Note: SCADA, supervisory control and data acquisition.

primarily interested in whether rhetoric is being used by cybersecurity specialists and in which ways. While this is an initial study into the use of management guru techniques in cybersecurity, a larger study would be a fruitful topic for future research.

Appeal to the Audience

The most common type of appeal used in the publications is to pathos; seven of the ten publications used it. The three academic/technical pieces do not (Nicholson et al. 2012; Mather 2011; Busseri 2012). There are several emotional appeals at play. The first is based on fears about people's lack of control and technology's potential to cause catastrophe, both themes that generate negative risk perceptions according to risk psychology literature. For instance, some of the publications note the potential for digital devices to be infected with viruses without users' knowledge and the possibility that sensitive information can be stolen or lost online (Clarke and Knake 2010; Glenny 2011a). The articles conflate the characteristics of living and non-living entities to convey a sinister and motivated entity that has immediate global reach and is indifferent to inflicting human suffering or financial loss. This is captured most effectively in the description of "zombies" (see table 8.2).

Four of the publications associate cybersecurity with warfare, which, according to the risk psychology literature, generates high dread. Technology is characterized as a tool of modern warfare with effects as devastating as conventional or even nuclear warfare (Clarke 2012; Coughlin 2010). There are several references to technology as a weapon, the Second World War, the Cold War, weapons of mass destruction, and the War on Terror (Clarke and Knake 2010; Clarke 2012; Coughlin 2010; Nicholson et al. 2012). China and Russia, in particular, are shown to use technology in clandestine ways, such as for spying on Western governments and private businesses for the purposes of crime and industrial espionage. Three publications note instances in which technology was used as a form of conventional warfare as well (Clarke and Knake 2010; Coughlin 2010; Nicholson et al. 2012) (table 8.3).

Further evidence of the use of technology for conventional warfare includes the Stuxnet computer worm that the United States and Israel used to disrupt the Iranian nuclear program in 2010 and Russia's use of technology in its 2008 conflict with Georgia (Clarke

Table 8.2 Computers as "zombies"

Author(s)	Example
Clarke and Knake (2010)	"Sometimes the zombie computer sits patiently waiting orders. Other times it begins to look for other computers to attack. When one computer spreads its infection to others, and they in turn do the same, we have the phenomenon known as a 'worm,' the infection worming its way from one computer through thousands to millions. An infection can spread across the globe in mere hours" (p. 14).
Misha Glenny (TED Talk in May 2011)	"A bedrock of cybercriminality is the 'distributed denial of service' attack, in which tens of thousands of zombie computers enslaved by viruses to a command-and-control machine will lay siege to a company's or organization's system."

Table 8.3 Cyberspace as a "battlefield"

Author(s)	Examples
Clarke and Knake (2010)	"In anticipation of hostilities, nations are already 'preparing the battlefield.' They are hacking into each other's networks and infrastructures, laying in trapdoors and logic bombs – now, in peacetime. This ongoing nature of cyber war, the blurring of peace and war, adds a dangerous new dimension of instability" (p. 31).
Coughlin (2010)	"But there is also a growing body of opinion, within both military and intelligence circles, that future threats are as likely to take place in cyber space as on the battlefield."
Nicholson et al. (2012)	"It is understood that attacks and defence issued by nation states take place over networks rather than by physical means such as army personnel, vehicles and barracks" (p. 421).

and Knake 2010; Nicholson et al. 2012). Coughlin (2010) begins his article with a hypothetical "clickskrieg" between the United Kingdom and China, an example we analyze further in the stylistic devices section of this chapter. These examples emphasize the use of technology to disable communications and power systems on a large scale. The publications do not, however, show technology inflicting the sort of direct physical harm associated with conventional weaponry or nuclear attacks. Furthermore, there is a sense that the West, especially the United States, is falling behind the technological capabilities of countries like China and Russia (see table 8.4), which recalls

Table 8.4 Cold War parallels: Russia and China are most advanced and should be feared

Author(s)	Example
Coughlin (2010)	"On the one hand, there is the danger posed by countries such as China, which has invested enormous resources in trying to use the internet to infiltrate Western governments and institutions, in order to acquire information on military capabilities and sensitive commercial information that can be used to Beijing's advantage."
Misha Glenny (May 2011)	"After all, you never know whether your hacker is working for Russian organized crime, an Indian manufacturer, or the People's Liberation Army. Relative to other Western countries, Canada's cyber defences lack funding and a coherent strategy."
Misha Glenny (July 2011)	"In China, in Russia and in loads of other countries that are developing cyber-offensive capabilities, this is exactly what they are doing. They are recruiting hackers both before and after they become involved in criminal and industrial espionage activities – are mobilizing them on behalf of the state. We need to engage and find ways of offering guidance to these young people, because they are a remarkable breed."
Nicholson et al. (2012)	"As was demonstrated by the Chinese and Russian spies in Gorman (2009) it is clear that other nations are perpetrators and their reasons include industrial espionage and military purposes. As evidence is beginning to show, these actions demonstrate that elements of future wars are likely to be fought in cyberspace" (p. 422).

the arms race of the Cold War (Coughlin 2010; Glenny 2011a, 2011b; Nicholson et al. 2012).

Finally, there are also associations made between technology and terrorism, often in the form of attacks on c_i (see table 8.5) (Clarke and Knake 2010; Clarke 2012; Glenny 2011b; Lieberman 2012; Nicholson et al. 2012; Coughlin 2010; Busseri 2012). Yet the cases only cite the potential for cyber terrorism; in fact, there have yet to be any recorded incidents on this scale (Clarke 2012). As one author notes, terrorists may wish to use technology for such purposes but they currently lack the skills (Nicholson et al. 2012).

Few examples of cyber terrorism align with the literature's definition of terrorism. Only one case demonstrates that technology has been used for ideological purposes, a necessary feature of a terrorist attack. Glenny (2011b) argues that the hacker group Anonymous

Table 8.5 Critical infrastructure depicted as vulnerable

Author(s)	Example
Clarke and Knake (2010)	"If they take over a network, cyber warriors could steal all of its information or send out instructions that move money, spill oil, vent gas, blow up generators, derail trains, crash airplanes, send a platoon into an ambush, or cause a missile to detonate in the wrong place."
Clarke (2012)	"If the hackers turn their attention to disruption and destruction, as some have threatened, they are likely to find the controls for electric power grids, oil pipelines and precious water systems inadequately secured. If a hacker causes real physical damage to critical systems in that region, it could quickly involve governments retaliating against each other with both cyber and conventional weapons."
Lieberman (2012)	"The threat of a cyber attack on our electric grid, water supply system, financial networks, or oil and gas lines is anything but hype. I have been concerned about this threat for years, and the evidence has grown exponentially that sophisticated adversaries could paralyze the nation with targeted cyber attacks on critical networks."
Nicholson et al. (2012)	"Whilst none of these incidents have been officially reported as attacks on SCADA systems they demonstrate the dependence of critical infrastructure on these systems and illustrate the widespread impact that could occur should an attack on a critical infrastructure take place. The possible damage that such a cyber attack could cause is comparable to that of a physical attack such as 9/11" (p. 423).
Coughlin (2010)	"At the press of a mouse button, power stations, water firms, air traffic control and all government and financial systems are shut down. In the space of a few minutes, the entire nation has been paralysed."

Note: SCADA, supervisory control and data acquisition.

uses technology as a form of anarchism. Anonymous has limited its actions to mischief thus far, a characteristic more common in hacktivism than cyber terrorism. There is one case of technology being used to inflict direct physical harm as part of a computer scientist's experiments. Most of the discussion of cyber terrorism follows the critical literature's prediction that cyber terrorism is often confused with cyber crime or hacktivism.

The publications also display appeals to the audience's ethos (trust in the credibility of the source) and logos (logic). Given the complexity of cybersecurity issues, it is perhaps unsurprising that many of the authors of these ten publications have technical expertise in the field of computer science (Rubin 2011; Nicholson et al. 2012; Mather 2011; Busseri 2012). The publications also feature current or former US politicians and public servants with experience in national security and bipartisanship, such as Joe Lieberman and Richard Clarke (Clarke and Knake 2010; Clarke 2012; Lieberman 2012). This experience helps to establish credibility.

Logos is most apparent in the academic article by Nicholson and colleagues (2012), the TED Talk by Rubin (2011), and the technical op-eds by Mather (2011) and Busseri (2012). While these pieces also argue that cybersecurity is a threat, they primarily make their appeal through empirical evidence about the likelihood and impact of such attacks. They also define the ways in which technology can be used to initiate cyber attacks, accurately differentiating between hacktivism, cyber crime, and cyber terrorism. Finally, they offer technical solutions to combat future cyber attacks.

By contrast, Clarke and Knake (2010), Clarke (2012), Coughlin (2010), and Glenny (2011a, 2011b) emphasize the consequences of cyber attacks and attenuate their probability. They also rely on anecdotal evidence (as opposed to empirical evidence) to advance their arguments and frequently conflate cyber warfare and cyber terrorism with hacktivism and cyber crime. Finally, they offer vague solutions to thwart cybersecurity threats. Indeed, these four authors raise awareness about the potential problems with cybersecurity but fail to offer solutions.

Stylistic Devices

The cybersecurity literature analyzed here uses metaphors, antithesis, and irony, in particular. We will describe these three common stylistic devices in detail. The most predominant metaphor used in the publications is the idea of cyberspace as a battlefield (see table 8.3). From this perspective, information technology is a new weapon that can be wielded with devastating consequences. The technical and popular pieces depict cyber warfare differently. In the technical pieces by Mather (2011) and Busseri (2012), the notion of cyber warfare is used to explain common attacks on networked computers. The experts are most concerned about the types of attacks that emanate from hackers and cyber criminals. The focus of these pieces is therefore to alert the technical community about emerging threats, draw attention to existing vulnerabilities, and share good practices on how to detect and prevent cyber attacks. By contrast, the popular pieces are more concerned with technology being used for traditional terrorism purposes, such as attacking CI (see table 8.5). These publications also warn about the potential of technology to become incorporated into conventional warfare. This fear is played out to dramatic effect in the opening of Coughlin's (2010) article: "The year is 2025 ... Chinese cyber warriors launch a 'clickskrieg' against mainland Britain. At the press of a mouse button, power stations, water firms, air traffic control and all government and financial systems are shut down. In the space of a few minutes, the entire nation has been paralysed."

In this metaphor, technology has serious and sinister potential. This idea is reinforced through other pieces, in which the authors liken the destructive potential of technology to other well-known incidents, such as the Second World War, Pearl Harbor, the Cold War, or 9/11. Recalling the power of the availability heuristic, this metaphor creates an association between technology and well-known traumatic events, making it seem as if technology could cause similarly devastating consequences. While the publications call for action to prevent such catastrophes, they offer little to no empirical evidence that technology can be used to prevent catastrophes.

The use of antithesis is also prevalent in four publications, three of which use the battlefield metaphor (Clarke and Knake 2010; Clarke 2012; Coughlin 2010; Rubin 2011). The contrast between conventional warfare and cyber warfare used in Coughlin (2010), for example, gives the impression that cyber warfare is replacing conventional warfare. This depiction conveys the notion that we are at a critical moment in time – that cyber warfare is somehow different and more advanced than conventional warfare, and that an exclusive reliance on conventional warfare to protect CI is misguided and in fact creates important vulnerabilities.

Finally, the use of irony is prevalent in six of the publications. This stylistic device is used to argue that people have benefited from advances in information technology but are now more vulnerable because of it as well. Individuals, governments, and organizations can never truly keep their cybersecurity defenses up to date because of the rapid pace of technological innovation and change and because this technology is fully embedded in our society (Clark and

Knake 2010; Glenny 2011a, 2011b; Lieberman 2012; Mather 2011; Busseri 2012). Irony is used to justify the ongoing need for cybersecurity solutions, invoking a perpetual mission to improve.

Argumentation Model

The publications display three common logical fallacies. The first involves the conclusions they draw based on inductive argument. Clarke and Knake (2010) argue that because a certain country experiences devastating and disruptive attacks, all cyber attacks will be devastating and disruptive. This inductive argument ignores probabilities. Four publications use the second logical fallacy, *argumentum ad populum*, which is an appeal to the authority of the many (Cathcart and Klein 2007; Clarke and Knake 2010; Glenny 2011a, 2011b; Coughlin 2010). Glenny (2011a), for example, argues that Canada needs to have a government-run computer emergency response team because "it is the only major Western country not to have one." In other words, if every other country is doing it, Canada should as well. Glenny (2011b) also argues that Western countries should hire hackers to run their computer security systems because countries like Russia and China have already done so. The third logical fallacy, which is present in two publications, is implicit warrant. Clarke (2010), for example, argues that if something is old, it must be of no use. Glenny (2011a) employs an implicit warrant when he argues that, first, because Canada's computer energy response centre guards the country's critical national infrastructure, it needs to be "in government hands" and, secondly, because it involves national security, Canada's military should manage cybersecurity. Table 8.6 summarizes our findings.

Our analysis found that the publications align with many of the literature's predictions. The availability heuristic was found to be at play in the way that the publications create associations between technology and high-dread events like terrorist attacks. Many of the publications conflate cyber terrorism with hacktivism and cyber crime. They also show that traditional management guru techniques are being used to overdramatize and oversimplify cybersecurity problems. The academic piece (Nicholson et al. 2012), the TED Talk by a computer scientist (Rubin 2011), and the technical pieces (Mather 2011; Busseri 2012) succeed in making the argument that technology has introduced new vulnerabilities into our lives.

Table 8.6 Summary of key findings

Case	Appeal to audience	Stylistic devices	Argumentation model ('√' is a check mark; it indicates "present" or "affirmative")
Clarke and Knake (2010)	Ethos √	Metaphor √	Inductive argument √
	Logos	Antithesis √	Argumentum ad populum √
	Pathos √	Irony √	Implicit warrant
Clarke (2012)	Ethos √	Metaphor √	Inductive argument
	Logos	Antithesis √	Argumentum ad populum
	Pathos √	Irony	Implicit warrant √
Glenny (2011a)	Ethos	Metaphor √	Inductive argument
	Logos	Antithesis	Argumentum ad populum √
	Pathos √	Irony √	Implicit warrant √
Lieberman (2012)	Ethos √	Metaphor √	Inductive argument
	Logos	Antithesis	Argumentum ad populum
	Pathos √	Irony √	Implicit warrant
Coughlin (2010)	Ethos	Metaphor √	Inductive argument
	Logos	Antithesis √	Argumentum ad populum √
	Pathos √	Irony	Implicit warrant
Hire the hackers! Glenny (July 2011)	Ethos	Metaphor √	Inductive argument
	Logos	Antithesis	Argumentum ad populum √
	Pathos √	Irony √	Implicit warrant
Rubin (2011)	Ethos	Metaphor √	Inductive argument
	Logos √	Antithesis √	Argumentum ad populum
	Pathos √	Irony	Implicit warrant
Nicholson et al. (2012)	Ethos	Metaphor √	Inductive argument
	Logos √	Antithesis	Argumentum ad populum
	Pathos	Irony	Implicit warrant
Mather (2011)	Ethos	Metaphor √	Inductive argument
	Logos √	Antithesis	Argumentum ad populum
	Pathos	Irony √	Implicit warrant
Busseri (2012)	Ethos	Metaphor √	Inductive argument
	Pathos	Antithesis	Argumentum ad populum
	Logos √	Irony √	Implicit warrant

However, the types of vulnerabilities that appear to be most frequent are those emanating from hacktivism and cyber crime. The arguments about the dangers of cyber terrorism and cyber warfare are less compelling.

The publications warn about the dangers of cyber terrorism and cyber warfare using traditional management guru techniques to make their case (Clarke and Knake 2010; Clarke 2012; Glenny 2011a, 2011b; Lieberman 2012; Coughlin 2010). This trend is seen in their arguments' contradictory nature, instability, use of recycled ideas, and reliance on soft data and logic – four of the six features of administrative arguments identified by Hood and Jackson (1991). As such, it is possible that the dangers of cyber terrorism and cyber warfare cited in these publications are indeed being overdramatized using traditional guru techniques.

CONCLUSION

This chapter has discussed four types of cybersecurity risks: cyber crime, hacktivism, cyber terrorism, and cyber warfare. The perpetrators of each type of event are driven by different motives and have access to different resources; the probability that each will occur is different and the solutions to each will also be different. Equally, public officials should be mindful of the metaphors they employ. Our research suggests that the metaphor of cyber as a battlefield, for example, is overused and inaccurate. This metaphor implies that the risk should be understood in military terms and chiefly as one of survival as opposed to a trade-off between costs and benefits; this distinction has a potentially powerful impact on the manner in which one approaches a risk problem. When the survival of the firm is at stake, risk is no longer a trade-off between costs and benefits; rather, there are minimum conditions that must be met (Jaeger et al. 2001). This extreme position is rarely the case with CI, however. For the most part, owners and operators of CI balance threats with opportunities. Industry is not immediately concerned with the traditional concerns of departments of defence, such as in international espionage or warfare. Rather, industry is more concerned, as Lewis (2003) points out, about insider threats, extortion, industrial espionage, intellectual property, the protection of financial data, and learning good practices from others in its sector.

Many of the popular pieces we examined emphasize extreme consequences and overlook, suppress, or exaggerate probabilities depending on the point the authors wish to make. Not all risks are equal. When, for instance, should government strategies and operations be guided by "worst case scenario" thinking? Precautionary approaches to managing risks are expensive and, at times, illogical and contradictory (Sunstein 2005). There are also opportunity costs. Government policies that ban staff from using social media for security reasons, for instance, prevent public servants from engaging in relevant and important popular discourse that concerns their policy areas (Roy 2012; Fyfe and Crookall 2010; Conabree 2011).

A major determinant in the successful adoption of e-government is acceptance of information communication technologies by public servants and the public (Bertot et al. 2010). Cyber is still in its infancy. Managers frequently rely on each other for quality information and support in understanding cybersecurity threats (Quigley, Burns, and Stallard 2013). Cyber gurus seek to profit from the public sector's lack of information technology expertise and comfort by providing consulting services that claim to simplify complex technological issues.

It is difficult to determine what influence cyber gurus actually have. Despite the burgeoning management guru theme, it is unclear that IT managers in the public sector are convinced by the claims of management gurus at present. Generally, IT managers are motivated by the potential for IT innovation. In one recent study, IT managers expressed concerns about risks associated with data integrity, intellectual property, privacy, reputation, and the trustworthiness of security information (Quigley, Burns, and Stallard 2013).

Over time, our thoughts on cyberspace will mature. If we consider the environmental movement, for example, it took decades to arrive at our present policies. Cyber needs to undergo this same transformation. All of our critical assets depend on the successful functioning of the Internet: supply chains depend on it, children play on it, and adults shop on it. Yet, unlike any other critical system upon which society depends, cyberspace exists largely without safeguards. In the same way that regulation in roads, aviation, and medicine enhances their value to the community, cyberspace might also (ultimately) benefit from such regulation and education.

How to think about cyberspace is a long-term proposition and must involve the public. Most cybersecurity failures, such as credit card fraud, lack the characteristics of a "good" media story (e.g., "catching a bad guy") and therefore tend not to be included in popular media coverage (Fowler and Quigley 2014; Quigley and Mills

2014; see also chapter 7). Lately, we have seen a rise in coverage of cyber bullying (Smith and Steffgen 2013). The government needs to use these types of cyber events to raise awareness and to improve our understanding of the risks associated with the Internet. We need to emphasize probability, not just consequence, and the reasonable steps one can take to protect oneself. "Child as victim" generates considerable media coverage and it can often be highly emotionally charged (Hood et al. 2001; Fowler and Quigley 2014); this kind of highly emotional coverage is not without consequence for public services, as we will see in the next chapter.

9

Pandemic Pandemonium:
Canada's Volatile Response to H1N1

On 26 October 2009, Evan Frustaglio, a seemingly healthy 13-year-old boy, died in Ottawa, Canada, from the H1N1 flu virus, just as Canadian health services were starting their vaccination programs. His death featured prominently in the news media. Within hours, parents rushed to get their children vaccinated (*Globe and Mail* 2009). Despite having encouraged people for months to receive the vaccine, governments and health services appeared to be unprepared for a surge in demand for the vaccine; long lineups formed in front of clinics across the country (Canadian Medical Association et al. 2010). The limited supply of vaccine meant that most provinces chose to administer vaccines to priority groups only, which further aggravated the situation. In the aftermath of this vaccine shortage, there were different views about who was to blame – if anyone – for long lineups and parents' anxiety. In October 2009, seventy-eight per cent of Canadians believed "the media hyped and exaggerated the threat of H1N1" (PHAC 2010, 55). This fact exposes a paradox: if people were confident that the media exaggerated the threat, why was there such a surge in demand for the vaccine? Despite considerable attention, many questions about H1N1 and the social responses to it remain unresolved (Grube 2013; Liang 2011; Waterer, Hui, and Jenkins 2010; Fineberg 2014).

In the last fifteen years a number of pandemics have generated considerable attention – Ebola, SARS, and bird flu, for example. The chance of developing these illnesses is extremely low yet the media give these events considerable coverage. They have many of the characteristics that generate anxiety among the population. As psychologists note (Burns 2012), people are typically more concerned about risks that are unobservable, unknown to those exposed, have immediate effects, and are relatively unknown to science. People dread risks that seem uncontrollable, globally catastrophic, inequitable in their reach, and individually catastrophic, that pose high risks for future generations, that are difficult to reduce in terms of exposure, and that are increasing and involuntary in nature. Because pandemics are so unlikely to affect people and typically occur so far from home, people's experience with them – how they understand and respond to them – is influenced significantly by media coverage. This is not without consequence. While these illnesses may be extremely rare in practice, public reaction can have serious social and economic consequences.

In this chapter, we look more closely at media coverage of H1N1 in Canada in 2009. We examine the claims that media exaggerated the threat of H1N1 and answer four main questions. First, how do people experience and respond to health risk? The psychology of risk literature identifies several biases in people's ability to draw inferences in the face of uncertainty, which creates significant challenges for health officials working in public health, disease prevention, and pandemic response. We also examine the sociology of risk literature to determine how the media frame the death of children and the challenge this presents for public bureaucracies attempting to organize a response.

Secondly, was media coverage of H1N1 unusual? The media amplify some risks and attenuate others (Combs and Slovic 1979; Mazur 1984). The Public Health Agency of Canada (PHAC) report implies, however, that the media coverage was unusual and therefore could not have been anticipated by health agencies. This report suggests the coverage skewed public perception of H1N1 and disrupted the governments' response.[1] H1N1 generated considerable media coverage – much more than is typical of other black swans (Quigley and Quigley 2013). We will compare H1N1 coverage by leading broadsheets[2] in other countries to determine whether there was something unusual about media coverage of H1N1 in Canada. Specifically, we will compare media coverage of H1N1 in Canada's leading national broadsheet, the *Globe and Mail* (G&M), with the coverage of this flu in the United Kingdom's *Daily Telegraph* (DT) and Australia's the *Australian*. Australia and the United Kingdom are also Westminster systems with publicly funded universal health care systems that mounted H1N1 operations.

Thirdly, and as a corollary to the previous question, how were governments depicted by the media? In other words, what did the media criticize the Canadian governments about? To answer this question, we will conduct a content analysis of G&M's H I N I coverage. For our analysis, we developed a three-by-three matrix that combines elements of a cybernetic control model (i.e., information gathering, standard setting, and behaviour modification) with the three justifications of Hood and Jackson's (1991) administrative argument (i.e., efficiency claims, accountability claims, and stability and learning claims); cybernetics helps to identify the focus of the media's criticisms, and administrative argument shows us how the media framed and justified its criticism.

Finally, what lessons does this pandemic provide for health care officials about media and managing responses to uncertain risks? Pandemics have killed millions and have had profound and permanent social and economic consequences (Barry 2004; Benedict 1996; Kelly 2005; Rosen 2007; Vince 2013). Still, we can overreact. In 1976, for example, the US government orchestrated a national response to a pandemic that never emerged. The response resulted in unnecessary illnesses and, arguably, death from the vaccine (Neustadt and Fineberg 1983).[3]

Dealing with uncertain risks requires a willingness and capacity to adapt. Adaptive capacity requires health officials to collect, validate, and share information quickly and to prompt appropriate behaviour change. The government depends on the media in such events. As we saw with H I N I, this can be a challenge when the media and the public are moved by a singular, tragic event. At the same time, simply declaring that the media "hyped and exaggerated the threat of H I N I " is an example of naïve blame shifting. Government plays an important role in setting public expectations; if it fails to meet those expectations it jeopardizes its own credibility and the credibility of its pandemic plan. Government must therefore anticipate amplified media coverage of uncertain risks and learn to cope better with media coverage. Otherwise, important vulnerabilities remain. Before addressing our four questions, we will provide a brief overview of H I N I in Canada in 2009.

H I N I IN CANADA

Timely information is important when responding to, and trying to contain, communicable diseases. Because people are increasingly mobile, disease surveillance must span large geographic areas, yet remain timely, accurate, and comprehensive. Outbreak detection is complex; data must flow up and down organizational hierarchies. In Canada, this challenge is complicated by the fact that provincial and federal governments share responsibility for health, and it is not always clear where the line is drawn between the two orders of government (Deber 2014, 10). Even within provincial jurisdictions, there are a variety of institutional arrangements over public health and pandemic response (Deber 2014, 13–14). Many provinces have divided their health responsibilities among regional authorities, whose geographic boundaries may not correspond to municipal boundaries. The responsibilities of regional authorities vary across the country. These complex and varied arrangements generate challenges, including externalities, unfunded mandates, and data ownership and coordination issues (Macdougall et al. 2014). In addition, circumstances change; pandemics can spread or contract. The degree to which they spread or contract will depend partly on people's willingness to follow the advice of medical professionals (e.g., advice to get the vaccine). Therefore, predications about the spread of the disease as well as plans and professional advice that address the disease must change as events unfold.

The Canadian governments have had a regularly updated pandemic plan since 1988. In 2003, they were roundly criticized by three separate commissions as being inadequately prepared and coordinated to respond to SARS (National Advisory Committee on SARS and Public Health 2003; Expert Panel on SARS and Infectious Disease Control [Ont.] and Walker 2003; Campbell 2004; Macdougall et al. 2014). The coordination problems during SARS were part of a long history of inadequate public health infrastructure to support coordinated responses to national health emergencies (National Advisory Committee on SARS and Public Health 2003). The three commissions variously noted a lack of integration of emergency-related data, information-sharing infrastructure, data quality and reporting standards, emergency response coordination, and agreement on a common list of notifiable or reportable diseases across jurisdictions (Macdougall et al. 2014).

HINI first occurred in Canada when four students from Nova Scotia and two men from British Columbia returned to Canada from Mexico (Manitoba Health 2010). In 2009, a total of 8,507 people were hospitalized for influenza (both HINI and seasonal) in Canada, compared with 2,614 in typical flu seasons (Picard 2010). In all, 428 people died of H1N1. In contrast, approximately 8,000 people died in 2007–08 of seasonal flu and pneumonia (PHAC 2010). That noted, H1N1 affected young people at an unusually high rate; in the early stages of the illness' spread, the median age of patients was 18 years (Alphonso and Galloway 2009). This low median age indicates a very serious influenza.

In April 2009 (following the start of the first wave of H1N1 in Canada), the federal government launched a public awareness campaign. Health officials anticipated that the second wave of H1N1 – in the fall of 2009 – would be much more serious. The campaign focused on "infection prevention behaviours, personal preparedness and a call to action for Canadians to get vaccinated" (PHAC 2010, 54). The federal government published fifty guidance documents and distributed 10 million brochures, 1.7 million guides, and 4 million alert notices to travelers (54); held almost fifty press conferences between 24 April and 15 December (55); and received 6.4 million visits to its website and had over 200,000 downloads (55). The federal minister of health and chief public health officer played prominent roles in this awareness campaign (Standing Senate Committee on Social Affairs, Science and Technology 2010). Generally, all orders of government worked to coordinate communications (Standing Senate Committee on Social Affairs, Science and Technology 2010).

The plan for vaccine administration changed over time. In early fall 2009, H1N1 was not as wide a threat as health officials had anticipated; as a result, health officials decided to delay vaccination to give more time for trials and vaccine production. From September to mid-October 2009, vaccine demand was low and polls suggested public apathy (Mittelstaedt 2009). In late October, there was a surge in demand for the vaccine just as there was a problem with supply (Nova Scotia Department of Health and Wellness 2010). The surge in demand occurred immediately after the death of Evan Frustaglio, which received considerable media attention. Production problems caused a shortage, which created a "rush" for the vaccine; in most provinces, health officials resorted to administering the vaccine to priority groups alone (PHAC 2010, 73), such as children and pregnant women. In early December, the supply increased and the vaccine was once again available to the general public. There were vaccination queues, but apathy returned and governments were once again trying to convince people to get the vaccine. Ultimately about

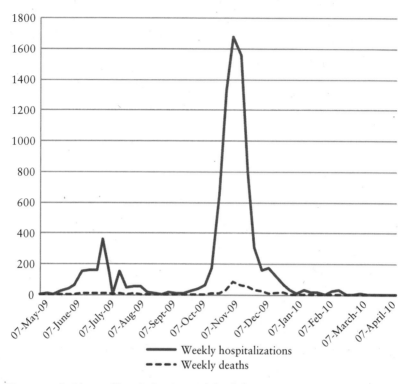

Figure 9.1 Incidents of hospitalization and death from H1N1 (2009) in Canada
Source: PHAC (2017)

forty-five per cent of Canada's population received the vaccine, one of the highest vaccination rates in the world (PHAC 2010, 70). Figure 9.1 depicts the two waves of infection.

H1N1 occurred frequently, and more seriously, among Indigenous populations, particularly in the first wave (Curry 2009; White and Bascaramurty 2009). Some Indigenous leaders expressed concern that the appropriate medical equipment was not provided to Aboriginal communities and that the vaccine program was rolled out too slowly (Hunter 2009). In one incident, Health Canada was criticized for sending an unusually high number of polyethylene bags (cadaver bags or "body bags") to First Nations communities in northern Manitoba. Northern First Nations leaders returned the bags to Health Canada's office in Winnipeg. Garden Hill First Nation Chief David Harper called the deliveries an insult (Alphonso and Ha 2009). The federal minister of health directed health officials to investigate the issue and found that nursing stations were advised by senior officials to order supplies generously, but that there was no ill intention (PHAC 2010).

There is no specific reference to the death of Evan Frustaglio in the PHAC report on Canada's response to the 2009 HINI pandemic. Rather, there are two indirect references. As part of the background material, the report notes: "Media coverage of HINI was extensive and, at times, overwhelming. In October 2009, a survey found over three-quarters of Canadians (78%) believed the media hyped and exaggerated the threat of HINI, representing a 10-point increase from perceptions in July. Correspondingly, just over half of Canadians (53%) surveyed in the same month (October 2009) felt the general public's level of concern was exaggerated while close to four in ten (37%) felt the level of concern was consistent with the risks" (PHAC 2010, 55).

And in the conclusion, the report notes: "There is a need to plan for different scales of pandemic response, dependent on the severity of the virus but recognizing that, even when there is a lower risk of morbidity and mortality with certain strains of a pandemic influenza, there will always be tragic cases that may move public opinion and therefore must be accounted for in a low-risk pandemic situation" (PHAC 2010, 92).

The report concludes that all health-related government agencies in all orders of government must improve their science communication to various audiences. However, the report gives no indication of how to improve science communication or with which audiences (e.g., media, the general public, First Nations communities) the government needs to improve communications.

RISK EXPERIENCE AND RESPONSE

Uncertain and emerging risks, such as HINI, pose unique challenges. Experts can offer a wide range of estimates; however, they might still be unable to appreciate fully the reach of the risk and to predict with confidence what will be affected by a failure to manage the risk effectively. Despite the International Risk Governance Council (IRGC) framework's focus on risk communication, it offers little guidance on the role the media play in framing uncertain risks for a lay audience. This is surprising. Media have considerable influence over how people perceive risks (Fischhoff 1985, 1995; Kitzinger and Reilly 1997). As we noted in chapter 2, the method of communicating uncertain risks creates three vulnerabilities in particular. First, our inability to quantify risk credibly gives rise to evaluative and cognitive conflicts among and between experts and stakeholders. Secondly, our imperfect knowledge of any given risk can lead to mistakes, such as giving bad advice. Finally, our inability to predict outcomes reliably can result in surprises or shocks for which we are not prepared. All three of these vulnerabilities can lead to media coverage that emphasizes conflict, guilt, blame, and disaster but that does not necessarily contribute to a better understanding of the risk in question. As the risk psychology literature suggests, uncertain risks can lead to public anxiety and over- (and under-) reaction.

DISEASE PREVENTION
AND PUBLIC HEALTH CHALLENGES

Disease prevention efforts can be an effective use of resources in many instances (Wyden et al. 2014). Despite this, it is difficult to secure commitment to disease prevention. Prevention reverses the normal clinical practice. It often starts at the population level and then translates to the individual. Rather than dwell on the pathology of an individual's disease, disease prevention focuses on the risk in the population as a whole. Many challenges work against broad-based disease prevention acceptance and action (Fineberg 2013): it is difficult to prove conclusively that disease prevention is successful; when it is successful, it is quietly successful over time (in other words, it lacks the drama that generates media coverage and public attention); disease prevention rewards are delayed, and not accrued necessarily to the payer; professional advice can be inconsistent; and permanent, long-term (and unpopular) behaviour change may be required.

There are other psychological biases that may work against public health initiatives. The relationship between people's anxiety levels and their willingness to engage in preventive or containment measures is well documented (for examples, see Tausczik et al. 2011; Hilton and Smith 2010; Jones and Salathé 2009). Government recommendations during a pandemic are more likely to be followed by those who perceive the risk of infection to be greater. On the surface this appears to be good news for government health officials. Unfortunately, the relationship between people's anxiety and the probability of them dying or becoming debilitated by a threat is quite weak (Jones and Salathé 2009). From a probability point of view, people often feel anxious about the wrong things. Medical advice may also conflict with personal, cultural, or religious beliefs. (For a recent example, see the Ebola case in 2014–15 as described in Manguvo and Mafuvadze [2015] and Landen [2014].) Furthermore, there is a bias against errors of commission (Fineberg 2013): people often have more regret if they take an action (e.g., if they take a vaccine) that results in illness than if they fail to take action (e.g., if they fail to get a vaccine) and become ill because of their failure to act. In other words, people accept certain (avoidable) harms as "normal." Finally, people do not identify with "statistical lives"; they are moved by human stories. Additionally, the successes of public health initiatives suffer from a dilution of benefit, whereby the perceived benefit is diminished because the public no longer observes the consequences of the disease (Poland and Jacobson 2001).

Media reactions to the death of Frustaglio in late October 2009 expose the scope of the challenge when addressing uncertain risks. While the novelty of one death might initially attract media attention, the death of one person does not change the probability that one is going to develop a disease. Responding to such a low-probability event in a proportionate manner, however, depends on a rational actor paradigm in which probability and consequence are objective and obtainable measures (Jaeger et al. 2001), which is not the case with uncertain risks. While it can be challenging for governments to communicate with lay audiences about low-morbidity pandemics, governments at the time of the H1N1 pandemic gave mixed messages. As late as August 2009, the federal minister of health declared, "What may come this fall is something that could test all of us, possibly to a limit we have never experienced" (PHAC 2010, 47).

A psychometric approach to risk provides more insight than a rational approach to understanding the effect that media has on risk perception. The media tend to report the dramatic over the common, but more dangerous (Soumerai et al. 1992). The media tend not only to sensationalize (Johnson and Covello 1987), but also to sensationalize the most negative aspects of events (Wahlberg and Sjoberg 2000). The media connect with people at an emotional level. Public perception of risk can be explained as a function of two components, hazard and outrage (Sandman 2012); hazard refers to the technical expert risk assessment of the event, while outrage refers to the emotional reaction people have concerning the event. Many event characteristics can affect the magnitude of outrage, including strong media presence, an identifiable victim, and the negative effect on vulnerable members of society (Sandman 2012). Hazard, outrage, and event characteristics furnish a useful framework for studying risk communication in health controversies (Burgess, Burgess, and Leask 2006).

A particularly powerful moment in the H1N1 episode in Canada was the death of Frustaglio just as the vaccine was released. Sociologists have focused on how the media stage and amplify death and grief and the social context in which it is interpreted. The moral panics literature (Cohen 1972; Goode and Ben-Yehuda 1999) examines episodes that include broad social concern, disproportionate response, and volatile public opinion. Moral panics also encompass an element of the "taboo," such as the death of a child. The media play a crucial role in interpreting and staging death scenes for public consumption (Walter, Littlewood, and Pickering 1995). Child deaths are frequently interpreted through the lens of maternal grief, exploiting their emotional and symbolic significance (Weaver and Jackson 2012). There is also a utopian bias that underpins most coverage – no child should ever die prematurely. Mitchell and colleagues (2012) note that the death of a child is one of the most disruptive and profound types of loss; it produces deep, intense, and prolonged grief, particularly in affluent societies. In the West, the death of a child is "an unspeakable contravention of the 'natural' order of things, particularly in 'modern' society" (14).

The rational ordering of public bureaucracies is ill equipped to deal with the death of a child. The governments' interest in fairness, regulation, and process cannot easily accommodate problems of profound human grief. In many emotionally charged events the media and social commentators rush to impose meaning, which leads to a selective search for accountability and an eagerness to lay blame. The *Columbia Journalism Review* (1979) notes that issues involving children are often "ambiguous, complicated and touchy," and that stories about kids can be "nasty, intrusive and potentially sensational" (as cited in Hennink-Kaminski and Dougall 2009, 3). More generally, in reference to crises and disasters, Pidgeon argues that "despite the inherent complexity and ambiguity of the environments within which large-scale hazards arise and the systemic nature of breakdowns in safety, cultural myths of control over affairs ensure that a culprit must be found after a disaster or crisis has unfolded" (1997, 9). In other words, while the death of Frustaglio generated the initial coverage, an aggressive and selective hunt for a culprit was likely to follow.

MEDIA COVERAGE OF H1N1

The volume of H1N1 media coverage was three to ten times greater than the volume of media coverage for other black swans (Quigley and Quigley 2013; Quigley and Mills 2014; see also figure 7.2). Table 9.1 shows statistics on H1N1 hospitalizations and deaths in Canada, the United Kingdom, and Australia. While H1N1 was more serious in Canada than in the United Kingdom or Australia, there are three reasons why the comparison between these three countries is still valid. First, the differences are within an order of magnitude. H1N1 caused a large number of deaths and hospitalizations in each country and generated considerable media coverage. Secondly, the respective health sectors[4] and governments prepared their responses without knowing what the eventual death and hospitalization rates would be. Finally, while we recognize there are differences between these countries (e.g., proximity to Mexico, where the pandemic started), H1N1 was largely the same problem at the same time. These similarities allow us to control many extraneous variables in our comparison, which is generally difficult to do with black swan events in different countries.

For our analysis, we selected the most widely distributed national broadsheet in each country. Our sample comprises all articles in the year following 25 April 2009 that included the term(s) most commonly used to refer to the event. We eliminated any articles that were not principally about H1N1. Content analysis of the articles was carried out in two stages. First, we reviewed articles to determine whether key actors were assessed positively, negatively, or neutrally (N/A was also an option). We assigned a value of +1, −1, or 0 to each article depending on whether it was on balance a positive, negative, or neutral performance assessment for each key sector. We then calculated the net sum. Each order of government[5] was assessed separately (if one article had a negative assessment of both the federal and provincial governments, then it was assessed −2).

As outlined in the introduction of this chapter, we created a three-by-three matrix to assess what the governments in Canada were

Table 9.1 Comparison of selected H1N1 statistics for three countries

Country	H1N1-related hospitalizations	H1N1-related deaths	Population in 2009 (in 100,000s)	Hospitalizations per 100,000	Deaths per 100,000
Canada	8,678	428	33.7	257.51	12.70
United Kingdom	5,376	474	61.8	86.99	7.67
Australia	4,992	213	21.9	227.95	9.73

Source: Quigley, Macdonald, and Quigley (2016).

criticized for by the media. First, we used a cybernetic definition of control to determine on which control components governments were being criticized.

For the second aspect of the matrix, we adopted the three justifications of Hood and Jackson's (1991) administrative argument: sigma, theta, and lambda justifications. Sigma-type justifications (efficiency claims) are based on precepts about matching resources to tasks for defined circumstances. These arguments relate to waste limitation, the pursuit of efficiency, and avoiding muddle and confusion. Theta-type justifications (fairness claims) are based on precepts about how to ensure fairness, mutuality, and the proper discharge of duties. These justifications relate to fair treatment, bias avoidance, pursuit of accountability, and avoidance of abuse of office. Lambda-type justifications (stability and learning claims) are based on precepts about how to ensure resilience, even in adverse conditions. These justifications relate to reliability, adaptive capacity, and robustness. Circumstance guides which administrative argument we employ to criticize government performance (e.g., an issue of efficiency, if identified previously in a similar risk event, could also be categorized as a failure of stability and learning). In all cases, reviewers were instructed to choose the best fit.

While the volume and distribution of coverage in the news sources were similar before Frustaglio's death, there was some variation. After an initial peak in coverage through July, the *Australian* coverage slowed. The Australian flu season occurs between May and October; there may have been a sense of urgency in April/May, but by August it became clear that the pandemic would not pose a serious threat in Australia. There is also variation in how child mortality is reported. The *Australian* rarely reported the death of children and did not focus on the specifics of any one child (with one exception in

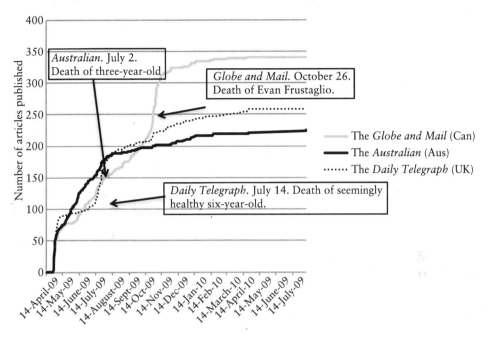

Figure 9.2 H1N1 cumulative coverage in selected broadsheets over time

which the death of one child prompted two articles in the *Australian*). There is a somewhat stronger parallel between the G&M and the DT in how child death is reported. The DT's coverage spiked between mid-June and mid-August. There were four articles about the death of a seemingly healthy 6-year-old – Chloe Buckley – which, like the case of Evan Frustaglio, contributed to a surge in media coverage. While the number of articles about Buckley's death in the DT was lower than the G&M's coverage of Frustaglio's death, the DT stories focused largely on vulnerable youth.

Figure 9.2 shows just how dramatically the G&M coverage increased following the death of Frustaglio and the release of the vaccine. Between 27 October and 26 November, eighty-six articles were published. This number represents twenty-five per cent of the articles published, all within a month.

Notwithstanding the spike in coverage after Frustaglio's death, only sixteen articles referred to the death of a youth in the G&M, and only twelve of those articles referred to Frustaglio in particular.[6] Frustaglio's death seems to have heightened awareness of the risks associated with H I N I just as the vaccine became available. The vast majority of media coverage, however, focused on the performance of governments in response to the surge in demand for the vaccine.

The domestic health sector tended to receive neutral assessments and a relatively small mix of positive and negative assessments, which netted to zero. In contrast, assessments of governments varied dramatically. The G&M included several negative assessments of government (–82); the DT and *Australian* had moderately negative assessments (–23 and –27, respectively). Figure 9.3 shows the performance assessments of governments in each of the three newspapers. In the G&M, sixty-three per cent of the negative assessments can be attributed to the federal government and thirty-seven per cent to the provinces. In comparative perspective, media coverage in the G&M was unusual. It is unclear whether this was due to an overzealous G&M, an overanxious population, or a poorly prepared government response. The dramatic increase in negative performance assessments coincided with the cadaver bags incident in September but became much more pronounced after Frustaglio's death in October.

Globe and Mail Criticisms of the Canadian Government

Of the 339 articles published in the G&M, forty-eight per cent (161) included negative performance assessments of governments. There were 201 negative performance assessments in total. We categorized criticisms according to cybernetic control and the administrative argument that journalists used to frame their criticisms (see table 9.2). The most common criticism concerned the intersection between behaviour modification and stability and learning, constituting thirty-two per cent (64) of all criticisms. Efficiency and behaviour modification (28) and each of the three argument types concerning standard setting (32 efficiency; 32 fairness and accountability; 27 stability and learning) ranged from sixteen per cent to thirteen per cent of the total negative performance assessments. These criticisms might be grouped as the second most common. Few criticisms concerned information gathering, which is ironic given its importance to public health initiatives.

To detect variations in negative performance assessments over time, we divided the G&M's coverage into four periods: before the first wave (25 April to 3 May); the first wave (4 May to 31 July); the

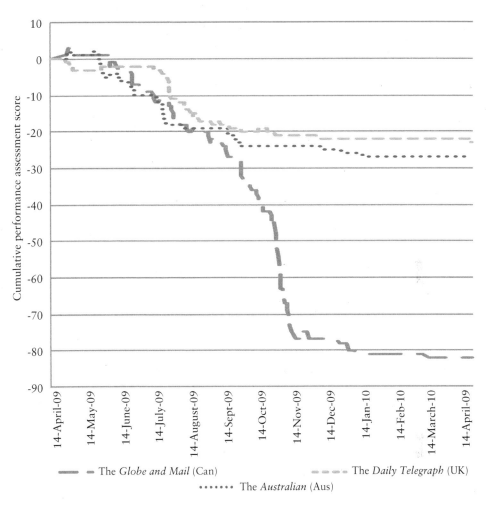

Figure 9.3 Cumulative performance assessment of all orders of government during the 2009 H1N1 pandemic (by broadsheet and date)

interim period (1 August to 30 September); and the second wave (1 October to 25 April). Standard setting and behaviour modification were very similar throughout all four periods, although behaviour modification passed standard setting during the second wave. As noted, information gathering got little attention. When we consider which administrative argument was used to frame criticism (figure 9.4) we see that most criticisms were framed as criticisms of stability and learning. From the interim period onward, however,

Table 9.2 Classification of articles by cybernetic control and administrative argument

Administrative argument	Cybernetic control			
	Information gathering	Standard setting	Behaviour modification	Total
Efficiency	5 (2.5%)	32 (15.9%)	28 (13.9%)	65 (32.3%)
Fairness and accountability	4 (2%)	32 (15.9%)	7 (3.5%)	43 (21.4%)
Stability and learning	2 (1%)	27 (13.4%)	64 (31.8%)	93 (46.3%)
Total	11 (5.5%)	91 (45.3%)	99 (49.3%)	201 (100%)

Source: Quigley, Macdonald, and Quigley (2016).

criticisms were framed less as criticisms of stability and learning and more as efficiency concerns. In short, there seem to be two distinct periods in the criticisms: the knowledge generation stage, which is concerned largely with learning, and the implementation stage, which is concerned with stability, learning, *and* efficiency. Growing concern over efficiency can be detected before the death of Frustaglio and the cadaver bags incident.

CONCLUSION

Uncertain and emerging risks create communication challenges for health officials. Their inability to predict the likelihood of events within a narrow range – as well as to articulate the possible consequences – conveys knowledge gaps from which people can draw the wrong inferences; these inferences can lead to exaggerated concern and heightened anxiety. Arguably, Frustaglio's death reframed the H I N I story from a pandemic that was under control to one that could prove fatal to healthy youth. This reframing affects all stages in the IRGC framework: social concern increased; tolerance and acceptability decreased; circumstances required a risk-management process that was adaptive and immediate. In essence, the problem health officials were addressing before Frustaglio's death changed after his death. The governments and their plan were in a highly vulnerable position: they had been strongly encouraging people to receive the vaccine but now the governments did not have enough vaccine. H I N I shows both the volatility of media coverage around uncertain and emerging risks and the consequences of this volatility. Media coverage cannot easily be predicted but it can have considerable impact on demand for public services. Coverage can also be

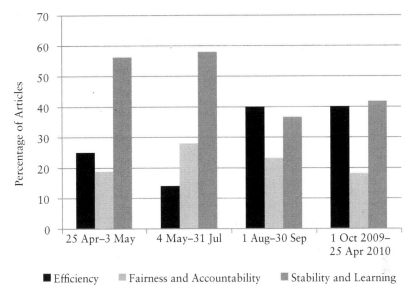

Figure 9.4 Percentage of articles categorized by the administrative argument used to frame criticism in the media coverage of the H1N1 pandemic.
Source: Quigley, Macdonald, and Quigley (2016).

highly negative about government performance, which can undermine the credibility of the governments' plan. For these reasons, governments must carefully consider how to prepare for high-volume, volatile media coverage.

While media may influence government reactions, it is also true that government communications can influence media. It is clear from the H1N1 outbreak that governments play a role in influencing how media and populations respond to messages about uncertain and emerging risks. For months, governments had contributed to heightening awareness of H1N1. A large public bureaucracy had been working on pandemic response since SARS in 2003 (Liang 2011). H1N1 communications included press conferences, alert notices, brochures, downloads, and a website. While PHAC implies the media overreacted to H1N1, evidence suggests that the governments also reacted strongly.

Our media analysis shows that the health sector received much more favourable coverage than governments. Medical practitioners are trusted more than elected officials and civil servants (Freed et al.

2011). Crisis response led by political figures can generate more negative coverage (Eisenman et al. 2007): the motives and competence of politicians are suspect, and members of opposition parties may attack the position of elected officials for political gain. This erodes trust in the process (Kramer 1999; Hardin 2006).

Government's lack of preparedness for the public reaction is surprising. While the death of Frustaglio seems poorly timed from a health services operational perspective, it should not have been a surprise that a young person would die of H I N I in the fall of 2009. Moreover, there are many things that could have alerted health services to the possibility of media and public overreaction: healthy young people were vulnerable (high dread); the disease was indiscriminant (uncontrolled); there was not enough vaccine ready (few escapes/exits); the national media published a powerful photo of a child (probability neglect); and governments were expected to have obtained enough vaccine (ability to blame an institution). PHAC publishes guidebooks on a variety of topics, yet its report does not list any on the subject of child death or dealing with the media (PHAC 2010, 45–6).

The communications challenge is significant. Government cannot dismiss the emotional weight of a child's death. While the death may not tell us much about the probability of a disease spreading, it has a strong emotional impact and will probably draw media attention. Ominous descriptions, such as the one conveyed by the federal minister of health in 2009, heighten anxiety. No doubt governments did much to reduce concerns when Frustaglio died but by then it was too late; the government had contributed to increasing public anxiety for months.

The H I N I example also points to the potential value in improved collaboration between governments and the media. In late 2009, the federal government could have tried to persuade the media to report on the considerable evidence that was then emerging from Canada and abroad that H I N I should not cause alarm (Schabas and Rau 2009). There are also considerable data on child death and illness that could have helped to convey the point that risks associated with H I N I were much lower than risks we face every day.[7] Importantly, health officials could have shown evidence that vaccines work and that a significant percentage of the population would ultimately receive the vaccine in a timely manner. And there are other actions the population can take to reduce the spread of a disease, such as washing hands regularly. Finally, editorial boards make decisions about how to report stories. The coverage of the *Australian* and the D T was much less alarming than the coverage of the G & M. The governments had the opportunity to coach the media over time, not strictly following the death of Frustaglio when anxiety levels were high, as many of the same journalists covered the story for several months. Relatedly, governments can do more work with organizations designed to improve scientific communication in the media, such as the Science Media Centre of Canada (2013) and the Evidence Network of Canadian Health Policy (n.d.).

In the early stages of the H I N I pandemic, criticisms were framed as stability and learning criticisms, relating to capacity to learn and adapt, even in adverse conditions. While these criticisms remained frequent throughout the pandemic, we saw a rise in efficiency criticisms from August onwards. There may be a temptation to focus on learning and to be optimistic that we can learn to understand the problem and maintain a stable operation. As the second wave of the pandemic approached, however, there was concern over operational effectiveness. Measures of success in operational and learning phases are not the same. Moreover, the G & M coverage suggested that there were operational problems and that they predated Frustaglio's death.

The best way to address increased demand for health services is with an effective response that meets public expectations. Achieving such a response requires that plans possess adaptive capacity and a diversity of means to accomplish mission-critical tasks. Future scenario exercises are a good way to increase adaptive capacity. Uncertain risks, in particular, can benefit from scenario exercises because the external driving forces (supply and demand of vaccines) are neither predictable nor under the complete control of health authorities (for examples of scenario exercises, see van Asselt et al. 2010; van der Heijden 2005).

Adaptive capacity does not come naturally to public bureaucracies. Despite decades of public management reform to improve the delivery of public services (Aucoin 1998), the H I N I vaccination program seemed insensitive to the manner in which people organize their lives. People had to stand in line for hours to receive the vaccine. There are few public services today with such a standard of service. It was not difficult for the media to find stories that resonated with the public: parents having to take the day off work to get their children vaccinated (C B C News 2009), line jumping by people who were not in risk groups (Wente 2009), and family doctors that did not provide vaccinations because of bureaucratic obstacles (Alphonso, Priest, and Matas 2009). Frustaglio's death may have increased coverage of H1N1 significantly, but coverage almost certainly would have subsided more quickly had the health service provided more efficient service. It would have helped to have a more decentralized approach, an approach that employed the entire health community, including more family doctors.

Finally, government needs to get better at getting it wrong. The PHAC report claims that the media hyped and exaggerated the threat of H1N1. This claim is unsettling because the report sidesteps, however gently, the responsibility that health-related government agencies have to anticipate media coverage and incorporate it into their plans. Because of our limited knowledge of uncertain risks, we may misinterpret early warning signs, over- (and under-) react, and give bad advice.

It would be disconcerting if government approached the next pandemic with a distrust of the media. This distrust would inevitably lead to less transparency, which would further erode trust in government process (Kramer 1999). Civil servants would become more nervous about engaging with the media, knowing the potentially negative consequences of a high-dread message amplified by the media. Rather, government should work to understand the incentive structures and biases in media coverage and public reaction to these biases, particularly during a highly emotive and volatile event, and account for these features in government pandemic planning. Ultimately, government will still need media to help communicate its message. The rise of social media makes the need for adaptive capacity in the health sector even greater. Next time, the pandemic may be more severe and we may have considerably less lead time, as occurred in Australia when there were only weeks between the initial outbreak and the onset of the flu season.

10

The Interest Group Hypothesis:
The Concentration of Power

This chapter explores the risk regulation regime framework's third contextual hypothesis, the interest group hypothesis (IGH), which supposes that risk regulation is the outcome of interest group pressure. To explain the source and effects of this pressure, the risk regulation regime framework directs our attention to the costs and benefits associated with regulatory decision-making. Depending on the relative concentration of these two factors, different groups will mobilize to influence the regulatory regime by lobbying government. When regulatory action promises concentrated costs or benefits for a specific constituency, its members will organize in support of their preferred outcome. When costs and benefits are widely dispersed, interest groups will pay little attention to regulatory policy.

We apply IGH to the chemical and transportation regimes. Our analysis suggests that both sectors are characterized by client politics, a form of politics that occurs when the benefits of regulation are enjoyed primarily by a single interest group and the costs are shared by many interest groups. Several features of both regulatory regimes are consistent with industry priorities, as manifested by the prevalence of self-regulation programs. Under these programs, industry can implement and enforce standards that promote efficiency and competitiveness. Stringent government regulations do exist, but they are designed through extensive consultation and collaboration with industry. Information gathering is often voluntary and led by industry, and punitive enforcement measures are rare.

The IGH raises important questions about accountability and transparency. It also highlights the risks posed by critical infrastructure (CI) facilities owned and operated by small and medium-sized enterprises (SMEs), which may not belong to industry self-regulation programs nor be able to adhere to government standards. To close this chapter we highlight some potential flaws with the IGH's assumptions in a CI context, which has a different arrangement between government and industry than is assumed by the risk regulation regime framework. We also discuss the conditions under which the opinion-responsive hypothesis (ORH), discussed in chapter 7, can complement our understanding of interest group behaviour, particularly in the immediate aftermath of large failures.

THE STATE, INTEREST GROUPS, AND REGULATORY REGIMES: THE WILSON TYPOLOGY

The relationship between the state and interest groups is the subject of considerable research. Much of this research illuminates how institutional context affects interest group behaviour.[1] To facilitate comparative analysis across different political systems, many cast the relationship between the state and interest groups in terms of a continuum between pluralism and corporatism. Using this approach, a regulatory regime can be categorized according to "the character of the actors involved in the decision-making process and the nature of their relations with the state" (Molina and Rhodes 2002, 308). Pluralism refers to political systems characterized by a high degree of competition between autonomous interest groups. The state plays a neutral role, reflecting the priorities of the dominant interest group. Corporatism, on the other hand, occurs in the presence of formalized arrangements between the state and umbrella associations comprising key industry and labour interests. Compared with the adversarial nature of pluralism, corporatism operates according to a logic of collaboration and bargaining, with an active state engaged in ongoing deliberation with private interests.

The costs and benefits associated with regulation can influence the extent to which a regime is either pluralist or corporatist. Businesses, for example, often compete to influence regulation because their "fortunes could be affected by price control or restrictions on entry to their markets" (Hood et al. 2001, 65). In such cases, a regime is likely to be characterized by aspects of pluralism. Non-business groups also attempt to influence government. For example, environmental organizations lobby governments to strengthen pollution standards. Regulators themselves can be understood as an organized interest group (Hood et al. 2001). Regulators may seek to maximize their departmental budget (Niskanen 1971) or job satisfaction (Dunleavy 1991) or may seek to have their personal preferences reflected in policy (Downs 1967).

The idea of regulatory costs and benefits is central to the IGH. To illustrate the IGH, Hood and colleagues (2001) draw on James Wilson's seminal book, *The Politics of Regulation* (1980) to develop a two-dimensional matrix of interest group configurations, reproduced in figure 10.1.

Each quadrant in the matrix corresponds to a specific type of regulatory politics. When both benefits and costs are diffuse, the matrix predicts majoritarian politics will be present. The wide distribution of both benefits and costs means no group stands to gain from regulation and no group stands to lose. The opposite situation, where both benefits and costs are highly concentrated, produces interest group politics. This situation tends to arise when a regulation threatens to benefit one set of business interests at the expense of other business interests. The segregation of benefits and costs means some groups will win while others will lose. Client politics occur in the presence of regulatory capture, which occurs when regulatory decision-making aligns with the preferences of large industry groups. Client politics differ from interest group politics in that costs are diffuse so no group perceives itself as losing. Entrepreneurial politics exist when a widely dispersed and loosely organized group (the public, usually) benefits from regulation that involves a significant cost for a much smaller set of interests, such as a specific industry sector.

The Wilson typology, and by extension the risk regulation regime framework's IGH, is ultimately about locating the sources of power in a regulatory regime. When power is concentrated among a few small groups, the regulatory regime exhibits client politics and regulatory capture. When power is diffuse, regulations are contested by multiple groups. The former situation approximates a corporatist arrangement and the latter a pluralist arrangement in which the regulatory regime reflects the priorities of the victorious interest group.

Discussions of power can be intrinsically normative; however, our primary purpose is to describe power dynamics. As with the market failure hypothesis (MFH) and ORH, the IGH is a tool for understanding the chemical and transportation regulatory regimes as they exist currently rather than in terms of how they ought to function. By thinking about power – or, in plain terms, about who wins and

		Distribution of benefits of CI regulation	
		Diffuse	Concentrated
Distribution of costs of CI regulation	Diffuse	Majoritarian regime: no clear winners or losers	Client regime: clear winners but no specific groups perceive themselves as losing
	Concentrated	Entrepreneurial regime: clear losers but no specific groups perceive themselves as winning	Interest group regime: clear winners and clear losers

Figure 10.1 The Wilson typology: an interest group explanation of regulatory regime size. Adapted from Hood, Rothstein, and Baldwin (2001). CI, critical infrastructure.

who loses – we hope to better understand why the regulatory regime operates the way it does.

APPLYING THE WILSON TYPOLOGY: THE CHEMICALS SECTOR

Risk regulation in the chemicals sector tends towards client politics, with power emanating primarily from the nexus between industry associations and regulators. This relationship provides concentrated benefits to large chemical companies while producing diffuse costs. We will highlight why this is the case with the following brief discussion of the structure of the Canadian chemical industry.

The Canadian chemical industry is diverse. In 2014, there were 3,182 chemical establishments in Canada, concentrated in Ontario, Quebec, British Columbia, and Alberta (Industry Canada 2015). Although the industry as a whole employs over 77,000 people, nearly ninety per cent of chemical companies in Canada have fewer than 100 employees (Conference Board of Canada 2013; Industry Canada 2011). But this diversity belies an oligopolistic market

Table 10.1 Five largest Chemistry Industry Association of Canada companies, by revenue (2012)

Company	Revenue (in millions)	% of CIAC revenue
NOVA Chemicals	$5,049	20.50
Dow Chemicals Canada	$4,633	18.81
Methanex	$2,673	10.85
BASF Canada	$1,332	5.41
E.I. du Pont Canada	$921	3.74
Rest of CIAC	$14,609	59.31
Total	$24,630	100.00

Note: CIAC, Chemistry Industry Association of Canada.
Source: Calculations are based on data from *Globe and Mail* (2013) and the CIAC (2014).

structure. In terms of revenue, five companies accounted for over forty per cent of the revenues reported by Chemistry Industry Association of Canada members in 2012 (table 10.1).

Sectors related to the chemical industry exhibit similar market concentrations. For example, in pharmaceuticals the combined market share of the top ten companies is 54.4 per cent (Innovation, Science and Economic Development Canada 2013). The fertilizer industry is even more concentrated, with Alberta's Agrium Inc. and PotashCorp of Saskatchewan controlling much of the market; the four largest fertilizer companies control the entire Canadian market (Hernandez and Torero 2011).

Market power is thus concentrated in a handful of large companies. Their monopoly is protected by barriers to market entry (including high energy costs), low profit margins (and therefore the need for economies of scale), and large fluctuations over the business cycle (OECD 2001). Compliance costs for regulation are another barrier to market entry (Mahdi et al. 2002). By retaining regulatory control through Responsible Care (RC) and other programs, industry players are able to influence the level and nature of market competition, thereby preserving crucial structural advantages. These companies are represented by well-funded industry associations such as the Chemistry Industry Association of Canada, the Canadian Chlorine Chemistry Council, the Canadian Association of Chemical Distributors, and Canada's Research-based Pharmaceutical Companies (Office of the Commissioner of Lobbying of Canada 2016a). These industry associations seek to influence federal and provincial regulatory policy. The Canadian chemical industry exhibits the characteristics of a powerful, if loosely organized, lobby.[2]

Self-regulation through industry associations also enables industry to comply with US standards. Given the importance of the US market to the Canadian chemical industry, minimizing border restrictions on Canadian products is a priority.[3] Through self-regulation, industry can relax or tighten safety and security practices to ensure maximum efficiency and competitiveness. In cases where the United States has requested more stringent government standards – the E2 regulations, for example – industry has been an active and enthusiastic participant in drafting new policy (Int 59). The costs of self-regulation, on the other hand, are shared by consumers who face higher prices because of the costs associated with RC compliance. SMES also face higher costs in the form of barriers to market entry.

The academic literature and our interview data generally support this account of the government–industry relationship. One interview subject from the chemical industry said that initiatives such as the Major Industrial Accidents Council of Canada are the standard approach for regulating industry in Canada (Int 58). According to this interview subject, the prevailing regulatory model in Canada involves extensive government consultation with industry, which facilitates the development of mutually acceptable regulatory mechanisms. "A culture of partnership, of working together towards common objectives," writes Lacoursière, "is now well in place and influences the development of regulations" (2005, 353). Echoing Lacoursière, another industry representative explained to us that regulations in Canada generally emerge from compromise and ongoing discussions between government and industry (Int 59). Another interview subject suggested that the federal government prefers to shift regulatory responsibility almost entirely to industry, as in the case of RC, which the interview subject said is viewed by regulators as a suitable alternative to traditional regulatory measures (Int 61).

Development of the E2 regulations is a prominent example of collaboration between government and industry. Recall from chapter 5 that these regulations were implemented in response to the 9/11 terrorist attacks and subsequent pressure to address security risks to North American hazardous materials sites.[4] In drafting the E2 regulations, government consulted closely with a prominent industry association (Int 59). Industry input was largely responsible for the regulation's relative flexibility, manifest in its focus on emergency response plans rather than process safety management.

Since the 1970s and 1980s, environmental groups have played an increasingly important role in industry self-regulation initiatives. As we note in chapter 5, the RC National Advisory Panel includes several prominent scholars, consultants, and activists with expertise in areas such as corporate social responsibility, environmental protection, sustainable development, and human health. Ostensibly, this signals that large chemical companies are willing to improve their safety and environmental records. It is unclear, however, whether advisory committees are able to provide anything beyond high-level guidance to industry associations.

Our analysis indicates that while safety and environmental issues have become a priority, improving security practices has not. In the RC verification audit reports we reviewed, security issues received only modest attention compared with safety and environmental ones (see table 5.3 in chapter 5). We might conclude from this finding that the chemical industry has successfully avoided a transition away from client politics towards interest group politics. By offering targeted concessions, industry associations have avoided a more intense and public struggle with environmental organizations.

Chemical companies, however, are not the only players in the regulatory landscape. Client politics produce costs and benefits beyond the chemicals sector. They affect water utilities and firefighters, and these groups can also be factored into our IGH analysis. As in the case of chemical SMEs, water utilities are numerous. In 2009, there were 2,018 public drinking water plants and 2,113 sewage treatment plants in Canada, not including systems administered by the federal government, including on reserves (Statistics Canada 2009). Private water provision is limited to very small, rural communities, typically "serving fewer than 50 customers in trailer parks, resort areas, subdivisions, or isolated communities" (Brubaker 2003, 5, as cited in Ouyahia 2006, 16). Water is thus primarily a public service, operated by municipalities, by the provinces or, on federal land, by Ottawa.

Water utilities rely on the chemical manufacturing industry for critical water treatment chemicals (Int 52; Int 53; Int 54). Chlorine, for example, is used by many Canadian water treatment plants as the primary disinfectant (Health Canada 2009b). Disruption of the chemical supply to water treatment plants is a key risk facing water utility operators (Int 53; Int 54; Grigg 2003; Meyer 2004; Reid 1998).[5] In a recent federal government business continuity exercise, one Canadian water utility noted that one of their top priorities in an emergency would be to restore access to water treatment chemicals (Int 54). The water utility operators we interviewed source their key chemicals, including chlorine, from domestic suppliers (Int 52; Int 53; Int 54). These water utility operators told us that there are no guarantees in place, from either chemical manufacturing companies or the federal government, that chemical deliveries will resume in the event of interruptions. Where chemicals are sourced from the United States, border closures pose an additional risk to Canada's drinking water supply.

Water utilities generally operate in a non-competitive environment and, therefore, from a financial perspective, have limited incentive to influence regulatory standards. Also, their geographic and size differences preclude easy organization of water utilities into an effective interest group. Their reliance on chemical substances, however, means water utilities are affected by chemical regulatory policy. As a result, the relationship between the chemical industry and government has implications for water utility operators, both insofar as it determines the availability of chemicals and because water utilities store and use chemicals and are subject to chemical regulation for controlling low-consequence/high-probability events.

Our interviews with representatives of the water sector revealed a number of specific issues on which water utilities would welcome a more active government role. Interview subjects noted that water CI seems to be undervalued, leading to a general sense of complacency about black swan events. We were told that many municipalities do not have plans in place to ensure water utilities have access to crucial chemicals in case of a supply disruption. Waste water is similarly overlooked and many jurisdictions are potentially unprepared to deal with untreated waste water during an emergency. More generally, we also heard calls for clearer direction from governments regarding safety and security standards, particularly in the context of CI protection. The absence of safety and security standards has created uncertainty for many water utilities, which have turned to international standards for guidance (Int 59; Int 61).

Our interview data support the IGH's prediction that the regulatory regime for the chemicals sector would be characterized by client politics. Our data also point to the consequences of a corporatist regime for dependent sectors, such as the aforementioned absence of safety and security standards in water, which do not enjoy the same degree of access to policy-makers as well-organized chemical industry associations. The priorities of the chemical industry coincide with a regulatory regime that creates uncertainty and ambiguity for water utilities, many of which lack the resources of large companies and their capacity to influence policy. Water utilities are, in some respects, left to their own devices.

The first responders we interviewed wanted improved standards for chemical storage (Int 56) and enhanced capabilities-based planning among emergency services (Int 55; Int 56). Despite this, firefighters have refrained from organizing public campaigns in pursuit of these objectives. Given the IGH's assumption that interest groups will mobilize to pursue their interests, it is perhaps surprising that firefighters have not leveraged their popularity to pressure governments publicly for improved chemical standards and investments in capabilities-based planning.

There have been relatively few major chemical incidents in Canada. As a result, chemical storage standards may be a lower priority than other objectives, such as higher wages or improved benefits. At some future point, however, firefighters may choose to galvanize public opinion in support of more stringent standards for chemical storage facilities. Should they do this, we would expect the dynamics of the regulatory regime to shift to interest group politics, with ORH also assuming greater explanatory power. Similarly, an event such as the fertilizer plant explosion in West, Texas, in which several firefighters were killed, could galvanize firefighters and public support for more stringent standards in Canada.

In sum, our data indicate that the regulatory regime for chemicals is a form of client politics. Large, well-organized chemical companies maintain a corporatist relationship with regulators, giving rise to a regulatory landscape that provides concentrated benefits to industry association members while spreading costs across a broad range of groups, including chemical SMEs and firefighters. In recent decades, environmental organizations have shaped the regulatory regime, marshalling their resources to influence regulatory outcomes. However, it is unclear whether the environmental movement's lobbying successes correspond to a fundamental shift in the size, structure, or style of the risk regulatory regime. The risk regulatory regime's corporatist dynamic in the chemicals sector also affects other CI sectors; water utilities, for example, rely on chemical manufacturers for water treatment chemicals. In terms of costs and benefits, large chemical companies are the clear winners.

APPLYING THE WILSON TYPOLOGY: THE TRANSPORTATION SECTOR

Like the chemical industry, the Canadian transportation sector operates according to the logic of client politics. Transport Canada is committed to regulating the transportation sector as a single multimodal transportation network (Transport Canada 2015a), but Transport Canada and other federal departments interact in different ways with each of the transportation subsectors we studied (i.e., airports, rail, seaports, bridges, and trucking). Our data suggest that a corporatist dynamic exists between Transport Canada, the primary federal regulator, and the air and rail subsectors. In contrast, seaports and bridges tend to have limited access to regulators and are less able to influence regulatory regime content. For trucking, we found some evidence of regulatory capture but other evidence of a fragmented subsector with limited capacity to influence regulatory decision-making. The concentration of costs and benefits varies across the regulatory regime, reflecting differences in corporate concentration, public ownership, and capacity for collective action.

The airport subsector is highly concentrated and quasi-public. Most passenger and traffic cargo goes through Canada's twenty-six largest airports, which are not-for-profit, non-share capital corporations owned by the federal government but operated commercially by Canadian airport authorities. These authorities are represented by the Canadian Airports Council, which advocates on their behalf with the federal government.[6]

The rail industry is perhaps even more concentrated than the airport industry. While there are thirty-one federally regulated rail carriers in Canada (Auditor General of Canada 2013), the rail industry is dominated by its three Class I carriers: Canadian National (CN), Canadian Pacific (CP) (Int 45), and VIA Rail.[7] These major carriers, plus a number of smaller railways, lobby government through the Railway Association of Canada.

By comparison, Canada's seaports are more competitive, as well as more fragmented with respect to their size, location, and regulatory structure. Canada's large Canadian port authorities (CPAs) do not compete against one another for container traffic, but they do compete extensively with American ports (Statistics Canada 2003). This suggests that Canadian ports' domestic market concentration belies a far more competitive international operating context. The main industry association for Canadian seaports is the Association of Canadian Port Authorities, of which all eighteen CPAs are members.

The bridge sector encompasses a much larger number of organizations than airports, rail, or seaports, with more than 8,700 bridges registered in the National Highway System (Transport Canada 2012a). Bridges are often under the jurisdiction of the provinces or municipal governments, and they are generally non-competitive.[8] There is no single industry association that lobbies on their behalf at the federal level.

In terms of market structure, the trucking sector is even more diffuse than the bridge sector. There are approximately 56,800 companies (Transport Canada 2011a) operating 750,000 medium and heavy trucks in Canada (Transport Canada 2012a). Although subject to some federal government standards, trucking is regulated primarily at the provincial level. Some companies have organized into provincial industry associations, which in turn are represented at the federal level by the Canadian Trucking Alliance, which has approximately 4,500 members (Canadian Trucking Alliance 2016).

Each transportation subsector can be categorized according to its interest group arrangements. Of the five subsectors we studied, rail and airports are the largest and most well organized to influence regulatory policy. This is unsurprising given that a small number of organizations in both of these subsectors enjoy considerable market power and are organized into umbrella industry associations. For airports, Transport Canada's (2013a) stated objective is to work collaboratively with operators on safety and security and to rectify compliance issues with the least punitive measures possible. Several interview participants indicated that Transport Canada is engaged with industry and responsive to its concerns (Int 6; Int 7; Int 11). Airport interview participants described their interactions with government in terms of close relationships that permit both lobbying (Int 12; Int 13) and conversations (Int 1). Regulatory development was characterized as a collaborative process, with government often taking into consideration the views and priorities of industry (Int 11; Int 12).

The rail industry also exhibits corporatist characteristics. Interactions between government and the rail industry are privileged, non-competitive, and influenced by a few large companies. These large companies also influence the subsector as a whole. In addition, government still has considerable direct influence on VIA Rail given that it is a Crown corporation. The Lac-Mégantic rail disaster provides a particularly visible example of the close relationship between government and railways. Transport Canada met with rail carriers following the disaster to discuss regulatory changes, and CP Rail updated its procedures before Transport Canada published the new standards (Transport Canada 2013c). In the media, these standards were criticized for being "vague" and "open to interpretation by the railways," particularly in comparison to new standards implemented by US regulators (Robertson 2015).

Despite the ostensibly strong relationship between government and industry, interview participants from both the airport and rail subsectors expressed displeasure with government standard setting. Interview participants from these two transportation subsectors discussed government standard setting more than interview subjects from the other transportation subsectors. It may be that privileged access brings heightened expectations about the extent to which the regulatory regime ought to align with industry priorities. The airport and rail subsectors may also be more confident about speaking out publicly against government than other transportation subsectors because they have to placate shareholders.

Among airport interview participants, two indicated satisfaction with existing standards, but both suggested that further improvements would be beneficial in some areas (Int 11; Int 15). Other interview subjects felt that the standard-setting component of the regulatory regime for airports is too standardized (Int 12; Int 14). The legislation and regulations governing the airport sector are extensive; indeed, airports are one of the most aggressively regulated industries in Canada (Davis 2001). Interview subjects stressed that government should recognize the diversity in airports when applying the Canadian Aviation Regulations (2012), particularly diversity in size and facilities use (Int 12; Int 13; Int 15). The cost of regulatory compliance is one of the most significant issues for some airports (Int 13). Similarly, rail interview subjects identified government regulation as the single largest risk facing Class 1 carriers (Int 5).

Seaports are competitive and their operators must interact with and adhere to standards applied by multiple orders of government. Moreover, seaport operators and managers sometimes find policy direction from regulators inadequate (Int 31; Int 32; Int 42). While various security standards exist, seaport interview subjects felt that there are no overarching national standards for CI and that lines of responsibility for government departments, as well as policy directions, are unclear (Int 32; Int 42). In contrast to our airport interview participants, seaport interview subjects felt that government security policies were not developed in a collaborative manner (Int 32).

Many of the current security standards for seaports are perceived by seaport officials to be a government reaction to 9/11. While ship security has a long history, before 9/11 ports were traditionally less concerned with security. Some seaport officials have described ports as starting from a clean slate after 9/11 and making considerable progress in a relatively short time. Interview subjects felt, however, that while some of these new standards are working well, others are not.

Seaports see themselves as unique organizations, belonging neither to industry nor to government. They express frustration that they are left out of the security community. The market pressures that they (and seaport businesses) face conflict with what they describe as unpredictable interactions with government. Despite the international nature of shipping, seaports do not identify with a seaport community, and seaport staff feel decision-making is highly fragmented and unpredictable. The lack of seaport security and stable governance in parts of the shipping world creates further uncertainty for seaport operators.

Seaports must interact with a large number of agencies and organizations on safety and security issues (Int 30; Int 31; Int 42). Depending on the port, there may be several local law enforcement agencies involved in port security, as well as a provincial emergency management office, the Department of National Defence, Transport Canada, and the Canadian Coast Guard. This dispersion of regulatory authority means seaports are unable to focus their lobbying efforts on a single organization. Combined with their relatively small number and limited cohesion, this prevents seaports from organizing to pressure government in the same ways that airports and rail carriers do.

The bridge subsector is characterized by strong relationships between individual operators but, compared with other sectors, limited coordination with government on issues related to CI protection. Our bridge interview participants rarely mentioned how often they interacted with regulators, or the nature of their interactions, regarding security standards. Although bridge operators and regulators share information about risks, there is little ongoing dialogue between bridge operators and regulators about the efficacy of standards. In contrast to staff in other transportation subsectors, bridge staff seemed less inclined to spend time expanding their contacts outside the bridge community and more inclined to spend their time learning about the technical infrastructure for which they are responsible. There are parallels between bridges and water utilities. Both are non-competitive and diffuse. Like water utilities, bridges have not organized to lobby government, perhaps because of their geographic dispersion and, in many cases, limited resources.

Finally, in the trucking subsector, we found a complex relationship between industry and government. On one hand, the structure of the trucking industry is highly fragmented, which could make it difficult for operators to coalesce into an organized and cohesive lobby group. Also, this subsector has a large number of SMEs. Our interview subjects stressed that their companies have pronounced sensitivities to market conditions, such as the price of oil and insurance and customer needs.

Inconsistency across jurisdictions was a recurring theme in our trucking interviews. For example, interview participants cited the lack of uniformity in the credentials required for drivers to gain access to areas such as rail yards or seaports. Truck drivers undergo multiple checks, all verifying similar information, to obtain access cards for the locations to which they deliver freight. On the other hand, some interview participants argued that national trucking associations enjoy close relationships with regulators. For example, one trucking interview participant suggested that a national association had very close ties with the federal regulator and that all regulatory changes affecting trucking are addressed by a committee that includes industry membership (Int 8). Another interview participant said that the trucking lobby is among the strongest and most well-organized in the country and that it was able to influence the design of environmental standards to ensure favourable outcomes for industry (Int 35).

The registry of lobbyists maintained by the Canadian Commissioner of Lobbying offers a further point of comparison between transportation subsectors. Between 2010 and 2015, the registry shows that

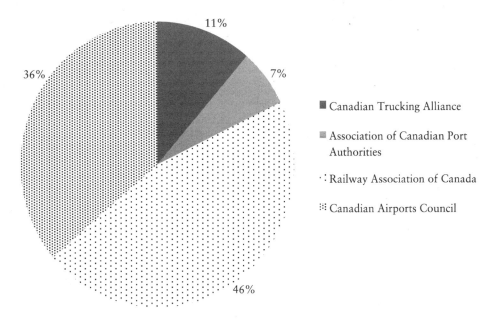

Figure 10.2 Percentage of communications with public office holders, 2010–15.
Source: Office of the Commissioner of Lobbying of Canada (2016b).

Members of Parliament were contacted 246 times by lobbyists representing transportation industry associations (Office of the Commissioner of Lobbying of Canada 2016b). As indicated in figure 10.2, the rail and airport associations together accounted for more than eighty per cent of this activity.

It is also illustrative to look at the frequency of lobbying activities. Figure 10.3 plots the number of communications reported per month by the Railway Association of Canada between 2010 and 2015. For reference, the chart also indicates major rail accidents during the same period.

Figure 10.3 shows large spikes in lobbying activity in the months following major incidents, indicating that the railway industry enjoys some degree of privileged access to the federal regulatory bureaucracy. After the Lac-Mégantic rail disaster, the Railway Association of Canada lobbied public office holders sixteen times between August and October 2013, the highest for any three-month period between 2010 and 2015. Nine of these communications were sent directly to the office of the Minister of Transport; recipients

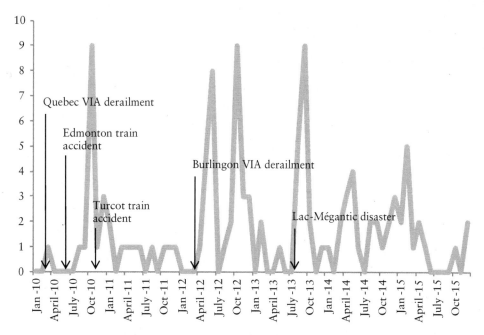

Figure 10.3 Monthly communications reported by the Railway Commission of Canada, 2010–15.
Source: Office of the Commissioner of Lobbying of Canada (2016b).

of these communications included the chief of staff, senior policy advisors, and, on two occasions, the minister.

In sum, our examination of the transportation sector suggests the presence of client politics between regulators and airports and rail, the two transportation subsectors with the most resources. Despite indications from air and rail interview participants that improvements could be made in specific areas, our data show that new regulatory policy is usually made in close consultation with industry. In contrast, the seaport and bridge subsectors struggle to influence government. Interview participants from these groups depicted the regulatory regime as a distant concept, describing it in terms of minimal, unclear, or competing standards, with few opportunities for them to interact with regulators. Finally, our data on trucking suggest that this subsector's access to government may be less stable than that of the airport and rail subsectors.

INTEREST GROUPS AND FEDERALISM

Originally, Hood and colleagues applied the risk regulation regime framework in the United Kingdom, a unitary (if increasingly decentralized) state. Canada, by contrast, is a federal state with potential for overlap and inconsistency between orders of government. Ottawa and the provinces are not always in sync on regulatory matters, as the costs and benefits of regulatory action may vary from government to government. This is also true in the United States.

We heard from one interview participant with expertise in emergency management that in Canada the federal government is leery about imposing obligations on the provinces, and that federalism has thus limited the development of a national emergency management policy (Int 62). This theme is prominent in the academic literature, where research underscores the thorny challenge posed by Canada's unique federal structure and how the provinces are reluctant to relinquish authority to Ottawa to achieve national CI standards (Hay 2006).[9] In preferring to retain control over key aspects of the regulatory regime, the provinces ensure that the regulatory regime remains decentralized and inconsistent. Even without resistance from the provinces, the federal government would struggle to establish and enforce an appropriate control mechanism for the provinces and territories. National emergency management policy is an intricate issue, made even more so by the cluttered state of Canada's intergovernmental agenda. The constitutional division of powers may also illuminate "to a great degree why Canada has relied so much on industry to adopt best practices initiatives like [RC]" (Macza 2008, 12/8–12/9). By endorsing industry standards, federal regulators possess a subtle means of promoting consistency across the regulatory regime without overstepping their constitutional authority or burdening industry.

In the transportation sector, federalism provides an interesting point of comparison between the subsectors. Airports and Class I rail carriers are regulated almost exclusively by the federal government; seaports, trucking, and bridges must interact with a range of jurisdictional authorities, including US agencies for truckers and bridges that traverse the Canada–US border. Jurisdictional complexity is often associated with opacity, trade-offs, and higher transaction costs, as CI owners and operators must divide their resources between multiple regulators, who themselves may have different or even opposing agendas.

There is a correlation between transportation subsectors that are regulated principally by the federal government and the presence of client politics. For airports, which are mainly a federal responsibility, the regulatory landscape is easily mapped, with regulatory powers distributed according to collaborative arrangements between Transport Canada and large airports. For interest groups that must engage simultaneously with multiple orders of government, the calculation of costs and benefits is more complex. In these subsectors, such as trucking, we see a higher degree of competition and greater evidence of pluralism.

CONCLUSION

Our application of the Wilsonian typology highlights cases where elements of the chemical and transportation regulatory regimes align with the preferences of influential industry associations. In the chemicals sector, the regulatory regime's reliance on industry standards and self-regulation shows that large companies influence regulatory policy. At the same time, resourceful and well-organized environmental organizations have forced an ostensible commitment from industry to consider environmental hazards related to natural disasters and industrial accidents, which in turn explains why industry continues to prioritize safety risks over security risks.

In the transportation sector, we detect a clear connection between the interests and priorities of regulators, on one hand, and airports and Class I railways on the other. Although interview participants from these subsectors identified several ways in which the regulatory regime could be improved, overall our data suggest that regulation in the transportation subsectors aims to ensure that regulatory outcomes align with private interests.

The chemical and transportation risk regulation regimes are thus characterized by concentrated power, collaboration, dialogue, and negotiation between government and industry associations. In both sectors, regulatory regimes lack the traditional regulatory tension. The dichotomy between regulator and regulated has been supplanted by a situation in which government is content to use industry self-interest as the impetus for risk management. Companies will implement safety and security measures even in the absence of government standards because consumers demand these measures. By leveraging this tension, regulators work closely with industry associations to negotiate guidelines and standards to influence the behaviour of individual chemical facilities and transportation operators (Dunsire 1993). Government's role is largely rhetorical; it makes claims about its rigorous regulatory practices, but in reality the substantive work of risk regulation is left to industry.

Regulators have not lost sight of the public interest, though. While client politics are often associated with regulatory capture, we hesitate to depict either the chemical or transportation regulatory regimes as being concerned solely with promoting private interests. Our literature review and interview data suggest many reasons why the public interest may in fact be served by a regulatory regime that incorporates the expertise and resources of CI owners and operators and that promotes a close relationship between industry and government. Indeed, government regulators describe how working collaboratively with industry produces mutually beneficial outcomes (Int 60; Int 63; Int 68). Both regulatory agencies and large companies tend to be hierarchical organizations, structured according to rules and clear lines of accountability. These shared organizational characteristics mean they both – regulatory agencies and large companies – act within bureaucratic frameworks. Hierarchical companies prefer to approach risk management by negotiating stable and predictable regulation in a collegial context. They want open and unrestricted access to regulators; they do not want to compete for access. These preferences match government preferences.

The IGH does not hold in all cases; the style of regulation we have described above is neither inevitable nor necessarily permanent. As we argue in chapter 7, black swan events involving chemicals or transportation (or both) often correspond with the displacement of interest group pressures by public opinion. In these cases, the chemical and transportation regulatory regimes are disrupted by intense media coverage and public scrutiny. In some cases, as this attention subsides, the day-to-day functioning of the regulatory regime is restored. For instance, recall that CP Rail published new standards for itself before Transport Canada published its own following the Lac-Mégantic disaster. In other instances, public opinion is forceful enough to effect fundamental shifts to the regulatory regime's underlying structure. For example, following the revelation of toxic contamination in the Love Canal neighbourhood of Niagara Falls,

New York, the United States introduced stringent new environmental regulations in response to heightened public concern (Kahn 2007).

A second challenge to the IGH stems from the nature of CI itself. Originally, the Wilson typology was developed to analyze government regulation of industry. The Wilson typology assumes a clear division between public regulators and the private sector, with the latter operating in a highly competitive environment with a clear profit motive. CI, however, differs in significant ways from this assumption. First, when the government designates a sector as CI it is implied that government will pay attention to the behaviour of companies and organizations in the CI sector to ensure the safety and security of vital national assets. Companies do not get to decide whether or not to lobby government; government is already at their door, inviting them to (or demanding that they) pay attention to safety and security risks. As public goods, CI facilities must factor in the costs and benefits to society of their continued operation.

In some of the subsectors we examine, it is unclear whether the alignment between industry and government is intentional or simply an inherent feature of the subsector. In the airports subsector, for example, the vast majority of airline traffic flows through a small number of large, quasi-public airports that are non-competitive because of structural monopolies afforded by geography. It would be difficult to imagine a scenario in which these airports did not enjoy a close relationship with airport regulators. In this case, the analytical utility of the IGH is less evident because the relationship between industry and government is not a function of a careful cost–benefit analysis and subsequent decision to mobilize, but rather a function of the underlying structural characteristics of the subsector itself. It is partly for this reason that the anthropologist Mary Douglas points not to cost–benefit analysis or the privileged access of some to the policy-making process but rather to the organizational cultural – a function of organizational design – as the key to understanding why organizations respond to risks the way they do, which is the focus of our next chapter.

11

Values and Institutions: Organizational Culture and Risk Response

The British anthropologist Mary Douglas originated cultural theory. She argues that what a person thinks constitutes risk either to oneself or one's community determines who or what the person blames when things go wrong (Douglas 1992). This understanding of blame determines the person's accountability system. Risk, blame, and accountability are informed by a person's cultural values (Douglas 1992). This is the essence of cultural theory.

Cultural theory helps us interpret how different organization types respond to risk (Douglas 1982, 1992; Hood 1998). Cultural theorists do not see risk as a calculable probability, but rather as a danger or threat to a value system, which is embedded in institutional arrangements. Douglas notes: "Certainty is only possible because doubt is blocked institutionally. Most individual decisions about risk are taken under pressure from institutions" (Douglas 2001, xix). Douglas describes a person's value system in terms of the grid/group theory that she developed. *Grid* measures the strength of rules and social norms and is about regulation of people (1982, 191–2). *Group* measures the extent to which community constraints are imposed on an individual and is about integration of people (1982, 191–2).

The theory measures regulation (grid) and integration (group) to determine value systems and the preferred institutional arrangements that flow from them, leading to the characterization of four organizational types: hierarchist, individualist, egalitarian, and fatalist (figure 11.1). In this chapter we use cultural theory as a heuristic device to structure an analysis of different organizations. Each type has certain preferences. Hierarchists focus on rules and specialization, egalitarians focus on community and process; individualists focus on market signals and private incentives, and fatalists focus on randomness. We also assume, like Hood, that organizational culture can be changed by manipulating the degree of regulation and integration in organizations. Hood uses new public management (NPM) reforms of the 1980s and 1990s, such as the rise of public-sector pay-for-performance, privatization, and outsourcing, to exemplify how governments can curtail the hierarchical culture of the post-war bureaucratic state with enhanced individualism in the public sector. While he brings our attention to the NPM example, he also underscores the point that these changes recur over time; he argues that the individualism of the 1980s and 1990s has been present in public service arguments before, and as far back as Jeremy Bentham's duty/interest junction argument of the 1820s (Hood 1998; see also Bentham 1825). In short, no organizational approach is stable, and no category within cultural theory is more modern than any other (Hood 1998). Rather, we should think of public management reforms as a pendulum that swings back and forth, largely between individualism and hierarchy. The change is usually initiated after a collection of failures caused by the inherent weaknesses of the organizational type, increased frustration with these failures, and a collective forgetting over time of the weaknesses of other types.[1]

In this chapter, we categorize the subsectors that we studied as follows: (1) large bureaucracies as hierarchical organizations (i.e., airports, large rail, and multinational chemical companies), (2) bridges, water, fire, and emergency management organizations as egalitarian organizations, (3) small and medium-sized enterprises (SMEs) as individualist organizations (e.g., trucking companies and small chemical companies), and (4) seaports as fatalist organizations. We then use the framework to identify strengths, weaknesses, blind spots and potential improvements for each of the subsectors.

CULTURAL THEORY

Hierarchist: Command and Control[2]

Hierarchists fit comfortably into a bureaucratic framework; control is assumed to reside at the top of the organization; those in the organization follow the commands of those at the top. The transportation sector contains several examples of organizations with

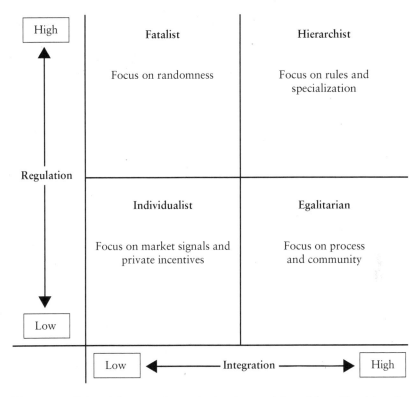

Figure 11.1 Cultural theory and organizational types. Adapted from Hood (1998).

hierarchical tendencies, including airports and large rail. Within the transportation sector, airports have the most hierarchical tendencies. While airports are subject to market pressure, security is highly regulated and key stakeholders are integrated into the regulation process. Airports do not compete on the issue of security nor is the government or industry particularly transparent on security issues. Government leadership is also strongly committed to security. Airports have more formal practices in place, such as with emergency services and specific preordained security processes to follow; these formal practices are typical of hierarchical organizations. When it comes to security, interview subjects at airports said they were more influenced by rules, regulations, and legal concerns than by other factors.

While not as hierarchical as airports, large rail and multinational chemical companies also possess hierarchical tendencies. These large organizations are subject to considerable market pressure because they are competitive, raise money on private markets, and report to their shareholders. Representatives from the chemical industry, for example, noted that customers influence the amount of time they spend on security. Notwithstanding competitive pressures, large rail and multinational chemical companies are not as atomistic and dynamic as the trucking industry, for example. They are large organizations, subdivided, specialized, and highly regulated. As is the case with any bureaucracy, dramatic changes take time. Interactions between government and industry have corporatist characteristics, which is to say they are privileged, non-competitive, and significantly influenced by a few large firms. These large firms also influence the sector as a whole. Representatives from rail companies said that rules, regulations, and laws are the main things that influence how much time they spend on security issues.

According to cultural theory, hierarchists understand good governance to mean a stable and predictable environment (Hood 1998, 75). On the positive side, a small number of large organizations – which is typical in hierarchical arrangements – can be easier to organize than a large number of small organizations. The dynamic present among a small number of large organizations could work particularly well in airports, rail, and large multinationals, where a handful of large organizations dominate the sector. Because of their size, hierarchical organizations are also the most similar to government bureaucracies and are therefore conducive to the formation of a stable relationship between these organizations and government regulators. While large airports, rail, and chemical companies may take different strategic directions because of competitive forces, their size and importance mean they rarely go out of business, which further protects the stability of the transportation and manufacturing sectors. Their considerable resources allow them to secure expertise when required. Generally, these sectors are likely to enjoy stable, trusting, and collegial relationships with government regulators, which can facilitate consensus on risk management priorities for the sectors (Vogel 1986).

Hierarchists have a highly optimistic view of management; when things go wrong, they generate more standards, recruit experts, and engage in formal strategic processes (Hood 1998, 53). To the hierarchist, "leadership at all levels" is rhetorical speech-play; authority lies at the top and filters down from there. At each level of the hierarchy, "responsibility for specific tasks" is a more appropriate way to describe the organization. Such sectors have corporatist tendencies; they can be loath to accept dramatic change unless all interests believe it is warranted or there is a profound external shock to the system; these hierarchical organizations are not known for their flexibility. When things go wrong, hierarchists blame lack of expertise and strategic thinking. Hierarchist organizations can overregulate their staff – whom they can tend to dehumanize in their practices – and in so doing diminish adaptive or innovative behaviour. There is also an assumption that leaders are working in the best interests of the organization, which is not always the case. Because larger industry players dominate their sectors, rules are developed with them in mind. Smaller industry players are too often regulated in the same manner as the larger industry players; nuance is not the strong suit of hierarchist organizations.

Individualist: Competitive Context

SMES in general, and trucking in particular, are best described as individualist organizations. Interview subjects from SMES stressed that SMES are more sensitive than larger enterprises to market conditions, price signals, and customer needs. Because many SMES are local, the regulatory complexity across provinces is less important.

The individualist understands good governance to mean minimal rules and interference with free market processes. Individualists believe that people are self-seeking, rational, and calculating opportunists. Individual responsibility rules supreme and apathy means consent (Thompson et al. 1990, 34, 65). In contrast, individualists perceive government regulation of the economy as a threat. For this organizational type, competition is natural. Individualists are not motivated by the public interest. SMES are highly atomistic; they are less likely to build up redundancies but can be responsive in a CI event provided their private interests are also served and they possess sufficient capacity to serve the public's needs. Unlike large organizations, SMES can easily go out of business with little disruption to the sector or the economy. As a result, SMES are more responsive and adaptive; at the firm level, they are also more disposable.

Despite the individualist's faith in market practices, individualist practices such as pay-for-performance can undermine collective goals and lead to competition, not cooperation. At the same time, because SMES are less well organized than larger organizations, they are less likely to lobby effectively, which means standards are easier for government to impose but consultation and reliable information gathering are harder to conduct. SMES are also more immediately sensitive to price signals than larger organizations. While this means that appropriate incentives can drive desired behaviours, it also means that SMES are more sensitive to cost increases. There are a vast number of SMES working in a competitive context with little direct oversight, which makes it difficult to capture those breaking the law for private gain.

Egalitarian: Community Effort

Non-competitive industries tend towards egalitarianism (e.g., bridges, fire services, emergency management organizations, and water services). There is a strong sense of team or community in non-competitive industries. Interview subjects in these industries noted a collegial relationship with others working in their fields. People in the same fields share similar technical training, which ostensibly suggests higher regulation but can also be a way to distinguish who is "in the club" and who is "out." The training also comes with symbols, such as uniforms, which further reinforce a team identity. Many rules and cultural norms are inaccessible to outsiders but the members know when these rules and norms have been broken. In contrast to other organizational types, many egalitarian organizations are disinclined to spend their time expanding contacts outside the community and more inclined to spend their time working within their community and learning about the technical infrastructure for which they are responsible.

The egalitarian understands good governance to mean local, communitarian, and participative organizations. For egalitarians, authority resides with the collective. Moreover, egalitarian organizations are flat, or at least there is minimal difference between top officials and the rank-and-file. While on the surface police, firefighters, and military personnel seem to work within strongly hierarchical organizations, in fact, there is a strong sense of team at the street level.

Egalitarian organizations are keenly aware of the important role they play in supporting their communities. Notwithstanding this awareness, cultural theory suggests that egalitarian organizations would tend to be inwardly accountable to their team and to their profession. There is a high level of commitment to the team and its mission. In such communities, organizations do not necessarily resist information gathering, standard setting, and behaviour modification but it is important who delivers messages and how messages are delivered. Egalitarians are much more likely to learn and adapt on the basis of lessons from specialists in their own subsector. Generally, this predisposition is effective because risks associated with egalitarian fields are often highly technical. For instance, bridge masters and industrial engineers are best placed to address risks to CI in the transportation sector. The team thinking that is prevalent in egalitarian communities can sometimes get in the way of innovation and making new connections beyond their immediate network. Changes can be slow and rules are often informal (and not always apparent to outsiders). If organized on too large a scale, egalitarian organizations are susceptible to breakdowns and fracturing.

Fatalist: Conflicting Priorities

Seaports are regulated but isolated, and as a result they exemplify fatalist tendencies. They do not see themselves as private organizations or government organizations. Seaport representatives express frustration that they are left out of the security community, which includes RCMP, CSIS, and Border Services, for example. Both seaports and port businesses face market pressures and efficiency concerns that conflict with what they describe as unpredictable interventions from government. Despite the international nature of shipping, seaports do not identify with a port community. Unlike bridge staff, seaport staff usually feel little connection – only competition – between ports. Unlike airport staff, for whom there is a strong sense of cohesive leadership nationally and internationally on security, seaport staff feel that decision-making is highly fragmented and unpredictable. In parts of the shipping world, the lack of seaport security and stable governance creates further uncertainty for seaport operators.

Fatalist forms of governance are random, which undermines incentives to build strong teams. Unlike hierarchist organizations, which are optimistic about management potential, fatalist organizations are skeptical. It is not surprising that interview subjects from the seaport sector, as fatalists, question the accuracy of information, doubt many of the standards, and recognize that their behaviour must change as the wind blows. Of all the organizational types, fatalist organizations are least likely to plan for a hypothetical event. Seaport employees are unlikely to take drastic actions during a security breach because of doubt that their overseers will support their decisions after the fact. Fatalist organizations operate in a low-trust environment. Figures 11.2 and 11.3 summarize our discussion of the four organizational types.

CHANGING ORGANIZATIONAL CULTURE

We now use the framework to consider the strengths, weaknesses, and blind spots of the sectors and changes they can make to improve their approach to critical infrastructure protection (CIP).

Command and Control Context

Command and control security has generated mixed results. After 9/11, there was a clear consensus among industry and government that airport security had to be improved (Frederickson and La Porte 2002). Government and industry security are more integrated than they were before 9/11, and international airports have much stronger lines of communications with other airports and security services. In contrast to other CI sectors, however, airports had embedded the concept of security into their practices since the 1947 Chicago Convention (ICAO 2016). Building on this security tradition, airports merely had to reinforce existing practice within their organization. Also in keeping with this hierarchical bias, airports and government regulators created more rules with which airport security agents had to comply. These regulations attempt to control the behaviour of the front-line security agents. A recent incident in the Edmonton International Airport is telling. A passenger tried to bring an explosive onto an airplane, but he was caught; airport security removed the pipe bomb and documented and reported the event to the RCMP, and the passenger was fined. The passenger claimed it was an accident and he was allowed to continue his travel (Rusnell and Russell 2004). The Edmonton airport's security agents were criticized for not following the rules (Canadian Press 2014), despite the fact that security agents exercised judgment and ultimately made the right decision. Such criticism pressures security agents to follow rules without using their judgment. Given that terrorists are adaptive

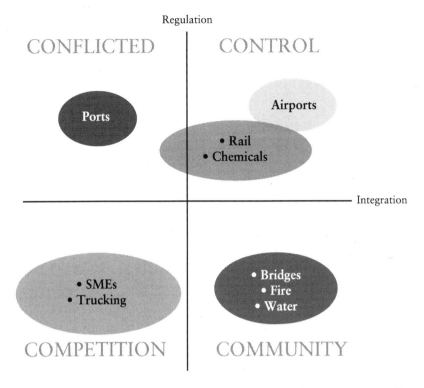

Figure 11.2 Regulation and integration. Adapted from Hood (1998). SMES, small and medium-sized enterprises.

agents, security agents also need to be able to adapt to events as they arise, rather than just follow prescribed and inflexible rules. Research suggests airport security promotes the latter approach over the former (Kirschenbaum 2012). Standard application of rules raises other challenges. Small airports, for example, are exposed to fewer risks than large airports and yet they are subject to the same high standards for security. Smaller airports are concerned about the costs associated with security practices, many of which they see as excessive (Int 1).

Command and control security has also been inconsistent across the sectors we studied. While airports have enhanced their security practices, the chemicals sector has been less committed. Responsible Care (RC) grew largely out of a response to the environmental movement in the 1970s and 1980s and events like the Cuyahoga River catching fire, the Three Mile Island partial nuclear meltdown, the

Regulation

The fatalist	The hierarchist
Trust: low trust dynamic **Risk:** unpredictability **Strength:** resilience and skepticism	**Trust:** rules, management **Risk:** overly formal regulation, not adaptive, "big" failures, sweeping indiscretion under the rug **Strength:** stability, capacity
The individualist	The egalitarian
Trust: incentives **Risk:** cutting costs, exposure to operational risk, single points of failure, capacity **Strength:** adaptive	**Trust:** community members **Risk:** outward accountability, community buy-in, efficiency concerns **Strength:** supportive

Integration

Figure 11.3 Trust, risk, and strength. Adapted from Hood (1998).

Bhopal gas tragedy, and the nuclear meltdown in Chernobyl. As a result, RC boards have strong environmental representation but they have little security representation. They have also been slow to adopt more transparent practices. This is still the case sixteen years after 9/11, reinforcing our observation that these institutions are slow to adapt. In contrast to airports, the chemical industry has generally not supported increased security practices, and vulnerabilities have resulted (Spellman and Bieber 2009); in the United States, the Government Accountability Office (GAO 2004) has noted this industry's lack of cooperation. Moreover, because the regulation of chemicals is largely in the provincial domain in Canada, it is difficult – as with any other provincial issue – to develop a national consensus. As a result, different hierarchies coexist but are not integrated, which necessitates negotiations between hierarchies and makes organizations vulnerable to conflict and to sweeping indiscretions "under the rug." Similar challenges exist in the rail subsector. In the immediate aftermath of the Lac-Mégantic disaster, CP and CN quickly adopted new safety practices; in this instance, there was a clear convergence of interests between Transport Canada and the major rail carriers.

Still, it is also clear that these organizations do not share safety and security information with each other as often as they might; the relationship is at times strained. It is also clear that major rail carriers have been slow to adopt a safety culture and even slower to adopt a security one.

These organizations could be improved by more aggressive and transparent third-party audits. Even the reach of the Auditor General is limited by the fact that he can only audit public agencies; private-sector CI owners and operators are not subject to these audits. The Auditor General's audits do raise important questions, however, about how rigorous the auditing process is by Transport Canada.

Competitive Context

The smaller and more atomistic the sector, the more sensitive it is to market dynamics. Among the CI sectors we examined, trucking and SMEs in the chemicals sector were most sensitive to price signals. Provided there are appropriate incentives, individualists are highly adaptive; adaptability is crucial and rare, particularly in the transport sector because of the fixed nature of most critical transportation infrastructure. Security practices can be improved by strengthening the incentive structure for security; incentives will be more successful if customers demand security than if security is regulated by government. To date, trucking companies have been more concerned by excessive (and redundant) security checks (at borders, for example), insurance rules and costs, labour disruption, cost and availability of gas, and cargo theft.

Government should work closely with industry groups to understand how to collect more reliable information from sectors and how best to coordinate responses during a CI event. Lately, government has successfully coordinated information sharing with organizations that depend on, and sometimes own, their own trucking fleet (e.g., Walmart). This approach to coordination may not be as successful in more remote communities where Walmart is not present.

Government should also consider carefully how to integrate SMEs into their information-sharing processes. In many instances, SMEs are seeking practical information, not classified information, about how to respond to CI failures and how to get reliable information. SMEs are usually more interested in when the power will be up and running and when the roads will be cleared than the identity of suspected terrorists. It can be useful to develop a strong SME network before CI events occur. There are some models that have been successful. The UK government developed one such model in the run-up to the 2012 Olympics; the Cross-sector Safety & Security Communications hub is a voluntary body that includes SMEs in the City of London. It deals strictly in unclassified information, avoiding intractable problems over security clearance.

Security failures, however, are largely seen as a market failure. SMES are critical to supply chains, particularly in manufacturing, and for delivering many services to small communities. Because they frequently work on the smallest profit margins, SMES are unlikely to have business continuity plans or disaster insurance coverage (Boardman 2005). For businesses of any size, there is a trade-off between opportunities and dangers, so risks are not seen in isolation. The Lac-Mégantic rail disaster brought many of these risk and opportunity trade-offs into focus: smaller train operators entered the market to meet increased demand for crude oil; staff numbers on the train were kept to the minimum; and Montreal, Maine & Atlantic Railway Limited (MMA) had inadequate insurance to cover its losses (Kemp 2014). Indeed, vulnerabilities go beyond the SMES themselves. As noted in chapter 7, despite the magnitude of the rail disaster in Lac-Mégantic, mayors from small towns were quick to underscore the importance of railway lines to their communities and their preference that rail lines not be diverted (Annis 2014). For many small towns, railway lines transport goods that allow companies to be in the town. Therefore, these rail lines are crucial to the town's economy (Annis 2014; Wahba and Gordon 2013).

Community Context

Many organizations that are important to emergency management have strong egalitarian tendencies (e.g., firefighting, bridge, and water organizations). Employees of egalitarian organizations have a high level of commitment to their organization and to their community (however defined). These organizations are generally not motivated by profit. This ethos is particularly helpful in emergencies, where cost–benefit analyses are not the order of the day; saving lives is. "All for one and one for all" is a helpful attitude in emergency contexts. Members of egalitarian organizations are frequently the heroes in the aftermath of disasters (e.g., firefighters in 9/11, fallen soldiers in conflict, police killed in the line of duty).

Egalitarian rhetoric obscures a more complex reality. Not surprisingly, most interview respondents from egalitarian organizations emphasized community engagement and wanted to do more community engagement. But who is part of the community, and what is the nature of this engagement? Is it about pushing information out or an interactive community dialogue?

For egalitarian groups, as with many team dynamics, one is either on the team or not. This can be empowering as everyone works in lockstep during an emergency; however, emergency services must have a positive relationship with the community they are trying to assist. Egalitarianism fosters high trust among those community members and low trust towards those who are not deemed a part of the community.

The level of trust people have in representatives from organizations depends on past experiences (Kramer 1999). In Northern Ireland, police officers were not regularly rotated out of extreme conflict positions; this fostered a warlike mentality among the officers towards community members (ICP 1999). In the United States, we have seen numerous breakdowns in social order because of perceived injustice towards the African-American community by the police. The Canadian government has seen conflict with members of the Afro-Caribbean, Islamic, and Indigenous communities, as well as other mass political movements, such as Idle No More, environmentalism, and libertarianism.

To establish credibility with different communities, emergency services must reach out to these communities. We have seen examples of this recently with the RCMP working with the Muslim community on radicalization (Cullen 2014). It helps if one has a diverse workplace in the first place. Key organizations in emergency services have struggled in this regard; despite repeated efforts to make military and police more reflective of the population, police forces continue to be predominantly white and male (Freeze 2010). Emergency management offices (EMOS) in Canada are similarly non-representative; they draw many people with policing and military backgrounds but few from more diverse fields, such as health and social services, and nursing in particular. Nurses have many of the skills necessary for emergency management, particularly with regard to prioritization and performing under pressure. The nursing profession is also more diverse and is experienced at ongoing and proactive community engagement (Canadian Nurses Association 2016).

Egalitarian organizations are inwardly accountable but not outwardly so. As such, EMOs must have regular contact with CI owners and operators to satisfy the need for face-to-face accountability. In time, EMO staff and CI owners and operators will collectively establish norms, patterns, behaviours, and relationships that will help during an emergency response. For the purpose of democracy and good government, however, EMO staff and CI owners and operators must also have standards on which to report publicly; these standards must be validated by an external, independent body, which will stir controversy but also reinforce transparency. Systematic transparency is crucial during a CI event, when accountability can be obscured. Egalitarians are unlikely to say negative things about one another (inwardly accountable), because going against the group is frowned on in egalitarian systems. Learning after an event is also constrained because media coverage – particularly during natural events and terror plots – tends to be exaggerated. Sometimes media coverage is too flattering and sometimes it is overly critical. In either case, it constrains the opportunity to learn. Independent public audits were carried out after fewer than half of the black swans for which we examined media coverage. This is particularly important given that these egalitarian organizations are usually monopolies. As such, there is no other entity with which to compare their performance to determine whether or not they did a good job.

Egalitarian organizations can encourage innovative approaches to safety and security by developing team-based rewards for good ideas and can benefit from scenario planning that tests their ability in non-routine events during which they interact with non-routine partners. Finally, the informality of egalitarian organizations can make them opaque; staff should formalize security practices and thereby make them more transparent, teachable, and transferable. The lack of availability of formal emergency management training and education – particularly at the university undergraduate and graduate degree level – exacerbates this problem of lack of transparency.

There are some good examples of resource sharing in the context of egalitarian organizations' national efforts to coordinate CBRNE (chemical, biological, radiological and nuclear and explosives) units, for example. Egalitarian organizations are also good targets for government funding and grants. These organizations tend to be underfunded and largely focused on cost containment. As security problems are seen as low probability and often an unnecessary drain on resources, many organizations will tend to neglect security unless they receive special support. Finally, information sharing can be improved by providing infrastructure to support team-based information exchange. Because of the high trust level between community members, they are very likely to share information with others in their sector, especially given that they are not competing with other organizations in their field. This is not the case in most other organizational types.

Conflicting Priorities

Seaport security is airport security's poor cousin. It is illustrative to reiterate our findings about seaports from chapter 4: seaport security gets less attention and funding than airport security yet arguably the challenges for the former are no less daunting than for the latter. Seaports are critical supply chain hubs, as seventy per cent of the world's imports are moved by sea (Burns 2013). Ports compete against one another for business and therefore have to keep goods moving as efficiently as possible. At the same time, ports are exposed to considerable threats associated with the underground economy, economic and political stability in parts of the developing world, and access to key trade routes in international markets. Safety vulnerabilities are also generated by communicable diseases, aging infrastructure, and human error. The somewhat open and accessible nature of seaport operations also creates safety and security threats.

To date, academic research has focused on developing rational economic models and methods to improve the delicate balance between port security and efficiency (Helmick 2008; Burns 2013; Psarros, Skjong, and Eide 2009). Problems persist. For example, Wengelin (2006) argues that Swedish ports are composed of multiple layers of actors with their own interests and agendas, with no one in control. This fragmentation undermines efforts to create and enforce strong port security measures. In the United States, some have argued there has been progress since 9/11 but much more needs to be done (Haveman, Shatz, and Vilchis 2005). The US Government Accountability Office remains unconvinced that there has been

progress. It has asked for concrete evidence that security investments make a difference and has found the evidence inconclusive
(Government Accountability Office 2014).

In 2007 the Canadian Senate observed, "Canada's ports ... need
a shift in culture, away from various fiefdoms acting in their own
interests toward owners, shippers, unions and shipping companies, all of whom pretend to act in the Canadian public's interest"
(Standing Senate Committee on National Security and Defence
2007, 2). In this report, the Senate concluded that Canada's ports are
"riddled" with organized crime, and nobody seems to be doing much
about it; these problems, the report noted, are typically shrugged off
as the cost of doing business (Standing Senate Committee on
National Security and Defence 2007, 2).

Ports need to be better integrated into the broader security community, and a stronger, more unified port community needs to be
developed. This could be accomplished by transforming seaports
from fatalist organizations into more hierarchical organizations. To
make seaports more hierarchical, governments would need to integrate ports more completely into the formal security apparatus that
includes government departments with responsibility for security.
Integration would require stronger leadership on port security from
those with formal authority to lead. Security would have to be a
clearer priority for seaports, and ports would have to train staff on
formally articulated security practices. This training would help port
staff see security as a strategic priority; goals and performance would
also be tracked formally, a point the Government Accountability
Office has struggled with in the United States. There would also have
to be better coordination between the federal, provincial, and municipal orders of government. While seaports fall under federal jurisdiction, they cannot be successful unless they coordinate with the
communities in which they operate, which necessitates coordination
between all orders of government.

There are weaknesses to making seaport culture more hierarchical.
In addition to undermining commercial goals, further integration
into the bureaucratic infrastructure would reduce adaptive capacity. Adaptive capacity is important when preparing for emergencies,
particularly when guarding against terrorism and criminal activity.
Criminals and terrorists are adaptive agents and security plans need
to adapt along with them. As noted, there is evidence of organized
crime at seaports (Sloan 2012), and hierarchists are not known

for their adaptive capacity. The Canadian Senate (Standing Senate Committee on National Security and Defence 2007) noted that seaports continue to be exploited by organized crime to move contraband, in particular illicit drugs, in and out of Canada. Progress has been made in the area of security, and the level of security at seaports is closer than it has ever been to the level of security at airports, but there is still much that needs to be done (Standing Senate Committee on National Security and Defence 2007). Governments either have to more aggressively confront organized crime at seaports or they have to recognize that by integrating ports more fully into the security apparatus, they risk information being shared inadvertently (or in a clandestine manner) with organized crime. Relatedly, a government bureaucracy would, at best, risk leaving private businesses operating at the seaport with limited access to security-related information given the government's reluctance to share sensitive information with non-government entities and, at worst, leave those businesses out of the security community altogether. The hierarchist is most likely to manage these risks by creating formal confidentiality agreements, prosecuting those who break these agreements through the legal system, classifying information and staff, and scrubbing identifiers before sharing data.

Government can also improve governance by stressing more egalitarian qualities, such as strengthening a sense of port community. Unlike bridge staff (Int 2; Int 17), for example, seaport staff felt very little kinship with staff at other ports and information sharing among them was limited; in lieu of kinship, they felt competition. One could strengthen the community by creating more meetings, conferences, common training, and staff exchanges between ports. Ports would collaborate on shared research projects and bid together on opportunities. Ports would brand themselves as Team Canada and have a team approach on national trade missions. If government wished to incentivize better performance, it would work with the seaports to determine collective goals and reward ports collectively. Information would flow more freely between ports: ports would develop an information-sharing platform to exchange ideas on good practices, lessons identified, and emerging risks. Rules concerning safety and security would be developed by the port community itself, not imposed by external sources. Our interview subjects felt that the most significant threats they faced derived from climate change and natural disasters, yet these risks were too often overlooked. Egalitarian communities believe in face-to-face account-ability and therefore would meet regularly to hold one another to account on safety and security practices. A security breach for one would be a security breach for all. A similar dynamic would prevail within the seaports themselves: there would be security committees comprising seaport operators and private-sector tenants. These com-mittees already exist, of course, but emphasis would be placed on building a committed consensus on the security subject, not simply sharing information.

Just as in the case of a command and control approach, the sea-ports would probably become less efficient if they used the egalitarian approach; egalitarian structures, like hierarchical ones, are not known for adaptive capacity, creativity, or entrepreneurialism. Egalitarian organizations are also inward looking; it would be difficult to hold an egalitarian seaport to account to outside sources, like Transport Canada, that may actually have formal authority. For this reason, there would be a tension in simultaneously pursuing hierarchical and egalitarian tendencies. Seaports would be distrustful of outside advice or direction. Organizations that put a premium on personal relation-ships and face-to-face interactions can be difficult to organize on a large scale. Organization would be particularly difficult for a country the size of Canada, as well as at the international level. Egalitarian cultures are susceptible to fracturing because of irreconcilable differ-ences among members with different priorities and contextual pres-sures. Egalitarianism does, however, create the opportunity for local partnerships in a region, such as Atlantic Canada, provided ports can overcome their impulse to compete with other local ports rather than cooperate. At the level of individual seaports, owner/operator–tenant committees would also struggle to overcome their competitive impulses and share information more freely. Figure 11.4 summarizes the concerns and solutions for each type.

CONCLUSION

A cultural theory analysis of CI sectors allows us to do three important things. First, it allows us to distinguish between the organizational types, and in so doing, identify strengths, weak-nesses, and blind spots in the governance of each sector. Secondly, if we assume that organizational culture is derived from regulation and integration, then we have concepts that can help us to change

Regulation

Concerns: prioritization **Solutions:** adaptive capacity, scenario planning, and further integration into a community	**Concerns:** over-regulated, expensive, transparency, concentration/single points of failure, and "big" failures **Solutions:** learning culture, oversight, institutional conflict, the capacity for "big" changes
Concerns: capacity, single-points of failure, and self-interest in a crisis **Solutions:** coordination and incentives	**Concerns:** outward transparency and organizing on larger scale **Solutions:** support the community and information-sharing infrastructure

Integration

Figure 11.4 Concerns and solutions. Adapted from Hood (1998).

organizational culture. For example, our discussion in this chapter highlighted opportunities to strengthen security culture at seaports either by integrating them more fully into the security apparatus in Ottawa, and thereby making them more hierarchical, or by deliberately strengthening the relationship between ports, thereby making ports more egalitarian. Each type of governance has its limitations but these changes can go some way to addressing significant blind spots in the seaport subsector.

Finally, cultural theory helps us to see the tensions at the heart of CI governance. While CI sectors may be highly interdependent, the organizational design of many sectors is quite different, which makes coordination, cooperation, and accountability more difficult to achieve. Cultural theory also suggests that when things go wrong, the tenuous relationships that organizations have in place to facilitate coordination will probably fall apart. This tendency would undermine any attempt to have national CI strategies. Cultural theory also suggests that the sector-by-sector approach that government has adopted for CI will probably result in a wide range of practices and norms that will reinforce the uniqueness of individual sectors and make bridging the gap between sectors even more difficult. These gaps increase the probability that disasters will occur and that responses will be poorly coordinated.

12

Conclusion

In this book we have applied the risk regulation framework of Hood and colleagues to study critical infrastructure protection (CIP) in Canada. We have paid particular attention to the regulatory regimes in two sectors, chemicals and transportation. We have also reviewed the social construction of risk in the popular media and the cyber domain and for the 2009 H1N1 outbreak. Our goal has been to examine the context in which CI exists and the extent to which different market, popular, and institutional pressures influence the risk regulation regimes that manage the risks associated with CI. We have used black swans, in particular, as a lens through which to examine these risk regulation regimes. In this chapter we review our key findings. We conclude by discussing the effectiveness of these regimes according to three different measures: their efficiency; their transparency, fairness and accountability; and their capacity for stability and learning.

THE STATE OF RISK REGULATION IN CRITICAL INFRASTRUCTURE SECTORS IN CANADA

The primary focus of risk regulation efforts in CI appears to be the gathering of information. While information gathering may be constrained by privacy and competition concerns, it embodies higher degrees of policy aggression than other regime components, meaning governments often take an active role in researching, monitoring, and collecting data about risks as well as in setting up the institutional arrangements to support information gathering. Governments have made large investments in information-gathering mechanisms, and private-sector CI operators are often subject to reporting requirements – sometimes mandatory, often voluntary. We learned that information-gathering programs and institutions vary with respect to their rule orientation; some, such as airports, operate on the basis of formal information-sharing precepts, which can overregulate staff, whereas others, such as seaports, rely on informal personal relationships, which risks leaving key players out.

We detect here the influence of the knowledge commons concept discussed in chapter 2, which encourages the creation of information-sharing systems aimed at facilitating organizational learning, coordination, and adaptive capacity during low-probability/high-consequence events. It is not clear, however, that the information exchange is meaningful or successful. While our interview participants were nearly unanimous in their endorsement of information-gathering and -sharing tools, calling them important mechanisms for building trust and ensuring shared approaches to risk management, they often could not articulate concrete benefits of these tools. More often they talked about *feeling* reassured by being part of a community and getting to know key players, and they talked about the value of briefings, even if they were often general in nature. Indeed, where such information-sharing mechanisms do not exist, we found that industry often pushes governments to create them. While these fora make people feel more confident, the academic literature suggests information sharing should be more specific and goal oriented than it is currently. It is also clear that different sectors enjoy different degrees of access to information: large airports and rail, for example, tend to get better access than small and medium-sized enterprises (SMEs).

Knowledge commons struggle also with standards and behaviour change. Information gathering alone does not control a system. Governments can spend inordinate time and resources gathering information or planning to gather information. These activities allow government to keep busy without getting into the more difficult and controversial business of standard setting, which also leads to making people accountable for achieving specific goals, and prompting and monitoring behaviour change. Government auditors in Canada and the United States chastise government agencies for their inability to show progress in CIP and emergency management; there are at present too few meaningful and publicly available performance metrics. Peel the onion and it gets even more complicated. Knowledge

commons assumes a degree of goodwill but it is not clear that goodwill is present among participating organizations. There are numerous reasons to withhold information – security, liability, share value,
and public image, to name a few. Recall that while many regulators
claimed there were legal barriers preventing public agencies from
sharing information that had to be addressed through policy and
legislative mechanisms, Shore and Schafer (2015) concluded there
were, in fact, few legal impediments and that information sharing
was limited more by organizational culture, which is upwardly
accountable, not outwardly accountable. Finally, when government
and CI owners and operators share information, the assumption is
that by sharing information everyone will act in accordance with the
public good. This is not necessarily so. Public- and private-sector
interests are not necessarily aligned, nor are the interests of the competing CI owners. In short, while most government agencies refer to
information sharing, it is unclear if they have made (or will make)
meaningful progress in a market or bureaucratic context.

The regime gets weaker from here. Standard setting is characterized by less policy aggression and a preference for flexibility and
compromise over conventional command-and-control instruments.
Under this model, governments set broad guidelines, which are
interpreted and applied by industry associations or individual firms
in the manner best suited to their circumstances. The results are
industry-led (or industry-influenced) standards that usually become
the minimum requirement for market entry. The chemical industry,
for example, has programs such as Responsible Care (RC), and transportation subsectors are increasingly adopting safety management
systems in which responsibility for managing safety risks is placed on
industry. While we can describe safety management systems (SMS) as
a form of flexible risk management, which leaves those with the most
knowledge to manage the complex risk context, they can also be
seen as a form of blame shifting; by allocating responsibility for the
sometimes ambiguous concepts of SMS to the owners and operators,
government takes cover from responsibility for failures. Audits conducted through regional resiliency assessment programs (RRAPs) are
a recent means by which to address traditional tensions. The audits
share sector-level information with individual organizations without disclosing organization-specific information; they nudge organizations in the direction of improving standards by communicating
average performance in key safety and security practices.

When government intervention does occur, it is often in the wake of major failures, when public opinion and media coverage are focused on the regime and there is pressure to implement new standards. Such standards are nearly always developed in consultation with industry. With the exception of seaports, where trust between government and the ports is highly strained, in none of our interviews did we hear of an example in which government introduced new standards without significant input from appropriate industry associations. Yet the influence of these associations means that new standards generally favour the capacities and priorities of large companies and organizations, with smaller and less well-organized CI facilities left to implement ill-fitting requirements, as we saw with smaller airports. Standard setting in Canada can also be fragmented because of the division of powers between the federal and provincial governments. In subsectors regulated primarily by the federal government, such as airports, standards seem to be more uniform and stringent. Canadian standards are heavily influenced by international organizations, too, as well as by countries such as the United States, which is requiring foreign exporters to adhere to its domestic security standards.

Behaviour modification appears to represent the smallest component of the regime. We heard from many interview participants that governments dedicate relatively few resources to legislative and regulatory enforcement. Conducting inspections, applying penalties, prosecuting lawbreakers – these activities demand significant investments and large bureaucracies. In an era of fiscal restraint, governments prefer alternative tools for ensuring that CI facilities are operating safely and securely. Information sharing represents one such alternative. By promoting the dissemination of norms and preferred practices, and mechanisms such as RRAP audits, regulatory agencies seek to shape the behaviour of private sector actors. But without recourse to meaningful sanctions, it is unclear whether this approach provides the desired level of protection, particularly when adherence to recommendations, guidelines, and best practices clashes with firms' profit- or revenue-generating imperatives. We also learned that information sharing is not viable for SMEs and other facilities that do not belong to industry associations or government–industry round tables and fora. In the case of industry-led standards, by comparison, we found mixed evidence regarding the efficacy of enforcement mechanisms. Our interview participants were generally convinced that programs such as RC and RRAP audits influence member behaviour; academic literature is divided on the success of RC, and there is insufficient evidence in the public domain to draw conclusions about RRAP audits.

SUMMARY OF KEY FINDINGS: MARKET FAILURE HYPOTHESIS

The market failure approach invites us to consider the technical nature of a risk and the extent to which it is addressed by existing markets. Where there is evidence that markets left to their own devices do not adequately protect society, government is expected to intervene. Central to this approach is the concept of proportionality: the stringency and extent of government action should match the type of failure being addressed.

The risk regulation regime framework measures the presence of market failure in terms of opt-out costs and information costs. A government risk regulation regime underpinned by market failure logic would intervene to reduce costs along both dimensions. For example, where risk avoidance requires significant restrictions on personal behaviour, government should provide measures to reduce our collective exposure to that risk. Similarly, where it is difficult to obtain data about the probability of a risk, government should invest in research and information-sharing initiatives.

In the case of CI, we found clear evidence of market failure with respect to preparing for low-probability/high-consequence events. This is not unexpected because firms have little incentive to invest in preparing for events that are unlikely to occur. Using the terminology of the risk regulation regime framework, we detected high opt-out costs and both high and low information costs. Chemicals and transportation are both ubiquitous in modern life. Eliminating low-probability/high-consequence events means limiting corporate risk-taking, which is an important source of innovation and profit. Traditionally, insurance has been the way in which the economy manages such risks but it is only a partial solution. It is difficult to establish reliable policies because catastrophic failures are rare and difficult to model and predict. In some cases, insurance companies are slow to pay because of the cost; payment of flood and terrorism insurance, for example, typically depends on some degree of government intervention.

Information costs are more variable and the probability of some risks is easy to calculate. The exceedingly slim likelihood of dying in a plane crash, for instance, is well known. But not all such information is in the public domain. Determining exposure to, say, industrial failures in one's neighbourhood requires detailed information that is usually not readily accessible, such as local dangerous goods transportation patterns and the type and volume of chemicals stored nearby. It is unlikely that a layperson could interpret the information and make an informed choice anyway.

Given the technical nature of low-probability/high-consequence events that could affect Canadian CI, the market failure hypothesis (MFH) tells us that we should observe an active government presence in the form of "high regulatory aggression" (Hood et al. 2001, 74). In some cases, our data fit this prediction. The chemical and transportation sectors, for example, both contain significant investments by government in information-gathering mechanisms. Class 1 airports, for example, have extensive intelligence-gathering capabilities, and ports and bridges are subject to mandatory inspections. Chemical facilities must similarly adhere to mandatory reporting requirements and many participate in voluntary information-sharing programs, such as the RCMP's Suspicious Incident Reporting system. At the same time, however, private firms retain leeway to limit their sharing of proprietary information or details of specific vulnerabilities. Some small CI operators may fail to report information at all because of resource constraints.

In terms of opt-out costs, the evidence is less equivocal: there is a clear preference for industry public–private collaboration, self-regulation, and private standards. Rather than enforce prescriptive standards, regulators are comfortable – or at least prepared – to let the private sector manage risks to CI. Government is to play a coordinating role, although in Canada even this function is constrained at times by the exigencies of federalism. Yet the regime is not without benefits. Firms retain flexibility to adopt risk management techniques suited to their particular circumstances. Export-oriented industries are able to align their standards with foreign requirements. Governments also have the option to punish organizations should they be responsible for CI failure. This potential to punish is an important stick that the government carries at all times. That noted, the legal processes can be very long and expensive for both sides; no one wants a lawsuit. And, as noted, we found more evidence of government's failure to inspect and failure to follow up than evidence of government aggressively holding laggards to account. Overall, we found that the MFH is only partially applicable to the CI sectors we examined. The technical nature of low-probability/high-consequence risks is not the sole, or even the primary, explanatory variable for regime content.

SUMMARY OF KEY FINDINGS: OPINION-RESPONSIVE HYPOTHESIS

The opinion-responsive hypothesis (ORH) directs our attention to the correlation between regime content and public preferences and attitudes. According to this hypothesis, regulatory efforts will focus on the risks of most concern to citizens. Studying the validity of this argument requires measuring public concern, which can be done in various ways and none are without controversy. Public polling offers one source of data, as does media coverage. In chapter 7, we considered both of these sources, as well as input received from our interview participants.

Canadians have low and decreasing levels of trust for large organizations, many of which own and operate CI, and for government regulators. Canadians trust SMEs and the technology sector more than other sectors by a good margin. They have reservations about the chemicals sector, in particular.

Our evidence indicates that the chemical and transportation sectors are sensitive to public opinion but to varying degrees. The chemical industry is aware of the public's anxieties; concerns about the effect of the Bhopal disaster on public perception were an impetus for the introduction of the RC program. Concern over public opinion about chemicals also extends beyond the manufacturing industry to other sectors that use chemical products. The introduction of chemical substances into the water supply – fluoride, for instance – is viewed by some as a particularly troubling, controversial action. Sensitivities in the transportation sector towards public opinion were mixed. Staff at airports, rail companies, and seaports were more concerned about regulations and interactions with government than public opinion, staff at trucking companies were concerned about meeting customer needs, and staff at bridges were concerned about maintaining public confidence.

Media coverage of black swans is usually high-volume but short-lived and not necessarily very informative. For many of the events we tracked, transportation events received more coverage than chemical events. Media coverage was also influenced by the personalities involved in the event. When a perpetrator or victim could be more clearly identified and, in the case of perpetrator, blamed, there was more media coverage. In the case of HINI, the death of Evan Frustaglio just as the vaccine was released triggered massive media coverage and scrutiny of government health operations that put the HINI operation and the pandemic plan at risk. Media coverage of the Lac-Mégantic disaster was also extensive and highly critical. The coverage was not strictly focused on personalities; however, the railway's CEO, Edward Burkhardt, did receive considerable coverage. In addition to considering his potential culpability for the disaster, the media paid close attention to his behaviour following the incident. Tony Hayward, the CEO of BP, underwent a similar "trial by media" in the wake of the 2010 Deepwater Horizon oil spill. In contrast, despite growing concerns in the defence, insurance, and IT security industries brought on by risks associated with the Internet, people like their technology and trust the technology firms that provide it; there seems to be little popular appetite for increased regulation of the Internet. While it is increasing, negative media coverage is still rare in the technology sector compared with other CI sectors.

As with the MFH, we saw mixed support in our evidence for the opinion-responsive explanation of regime content. Canadians do not seem to be particularly concerned about security and therefore a regime that focuses largely on information gathering and spends relatively less time and money on standards and behaviour change may be consistent with the ORH. The psychology literature would also suggest that people are concerned about aviation safety and, again, we see a regime that is consistent with those popular concerns. The alignment becomes more problematic when we consider the chemicals and rail industries; these sectors have produced consequential events but governments have tended more and more towards industry self-regulation.

Public opinion appears to operate as a latent force. It surfaces in the wake of disasters, providing opportunities for regulatory change as governments and industry scramble to address heightened public concerns. Sometimes new standards and enforcement procedures are introduced that align with public opinion, but often regimes return to their previous equilibrium as media coverage subsides.

The effect of media coverage, in fact, emerged as a key finding of our analysis. In particular, among the disasters we examined, there appears to be a preference among media organizations for coverage and even voyeurism rather than scrutiny, and this seems to be influenced by the pressure to provide big-bang, low-cost, and sentimental coverage of events. Natural disasters typically generate dramatic but sympathetic coverage; industrial failures, in contrast, generate a ruthless and narrow hunt for accountability. These pieces tend to focus on personalities at the expense of highlighting systemic flaws in the regulatory regime. The media business model privileges stories about individual corruption, conflict, negligence, action, or loss, leaving limited resources for investigations into complex technical issues that may persist elsewhere in the regime. Despite government's growing anxieties over negative media coverage, through its increased communications capacity it seems to be more adept at managing the media than responding to it. We therefore question not only the extent to which the media itself serves as a major influence on the regulation of low-probability/high-consequence events but also whether it is fulfilling its responsibility to inform the public on important public policy issues.

SUMMARY OF KEY FINDINGS: INTEREST GROUP HYPOTHESIS

The interest group hypothesis (IGH) draws on political science to frame regulatory regimes in terms of the distribution of capabilities (i.e., power) among actors in a given policy domain. Traditionally, this approach has been used to explain why individuals or firms organize to lobby government. The costs and benefits associated with new regulations are the independent variables. When benefits or costs (or both) are concentrated, actors are expected to organize to either support or oppose new regulation. These groups generally comprise firms or civil society groups, such as environmental activists or consumer advocates. Regulatory content is said to reflect the preferences of whichever group is better funded and organized.

As did Hood and colleagues (2001), we adopted a broader view in our analyses of the types of organized interests that are relevant to understanding risk regulation. Beyond firms and civil society groups, we considered the preferences of domestic regulators, foreign governments, and international organizations. In the Canadian context, we also acknowledge the constraints imposed by federalism, and the extent to which the different orders of government may have different or competing priorities. Evaluating the utility of this approach involves identifying the winners and losers of regulatory decisions and then determining how regularly one group is victorious over others.

In chapter 10, we argued that the IGH offers a strong explanation for the features we observed in the chemical and transportation regimes. Specifically, we saw a high degree of alignment between industry preferences and government preferences in subsectors where firms are represented by well-organized and well-funded industry associations or where there are only a small number of non-competitive operators. The preferences of these groups often override public concerns (i.e., the ORH) and are incorporated into regime content despite their potential for causing market failures (i.e., the MRH). The regime thus embodies the dynamics of client politics, in which regulatory instruments are developed and implemented in close coordination with the affected groups. In cultural theory terms, these groups are hierarchical and bureaucratic.

These arrangements are often viewed in negative terms as a form of regulatory capture, meaning that government simply implements the priorities of the most influential interest group. Our evidence, however, offers a less pessimistic take on the implications of client politics. As underscored by the governance literature, expertise and capacity are no longer located solely, or even primarily, in government bureaucracies. By maintaining close relationships with chemical and transportation companies, regulators can access and leverage the technical knowledge possessed by industry officials. Through qualified acceptance of self-regulation programs, regulators at the federal level are also able to influence industry behaviour in areas under provincial jurisdiction, enabling a higher degree of uniformity to be established across the regime.

In addition, domestic collaboration between industry and government helps facilitate Canada's global competitiveness. In both the chemical and transportation sectors, international standards are becoming increasingly important. Countries such as the United States are resorting to extraterritorial application of security standards to address vulnerabilities in cross-border supply chains. The

C-TPAT program (C-TPAT 2017), for example, requires firms in other countries to meet American standards and undergo audits by the Department of Homeland Security. Equally, the Department of Homeland Security has trained water service providers in Canada. To remain competitive, Canadian companies must retain the flexibility to meet these types of international standards. There is a competitive advantage for Canada in allowing its industry to self-regulate to adopt the practices best suited for maintaining access to foreign markets, particularly the United States.

A related issue is the degree to which globalization has constrained the ability of governments to regulate in a manner that does not accord with global norms and commitments. The *quid pro quo* of free-trade agreements, for example, involves exchanging improved access to foreign markets for acceptance of shared standards on tariffs and, increasingly, regulatory practices. Formal regulatory power remains vested in governments, but the operation of this power in the countries we studied tends to align with international obligations. In North America this trend is particularly pronounced, as Canada and the United States continue to prioritize the compatibility and, in some cases, full harmonization of their regulatory regimes. Recall from chapter 3 that the Canadian CI sectors that have made progress are those in which the trading relations between Canada and the United States are strongest.

Each of the three hypotheses illuminates important aspects of the regulatory regimes we studied. Figure 12.1 summarizes our findings about the chemical and transportation regimes. It shows how the main features of each contextual hypothesis translate into regime content.

The relationship between content and context is dynamic and iterative rather than linear. In this book, we have concentrated on showing how contextual factors influence regime content. But it is worth reflecting on how the opposite can also occur: decisions about content can alter the contextual factors surrounding the regime. Changing laws and regulations, for example, have a direct impact on the operation and efficiency of markets. In the case of terrorism, efforts by the US government to implement terrorism insurance signal to the market that it has a role to play in addressing terrorism risks. Yet the decision to provide heavy subsidies for terrorism insurance, plus many other insurance instruments, means insurance markets operate in a distorted fashion. Similarly, public concern about environmental conservation has contributed over time to a greater

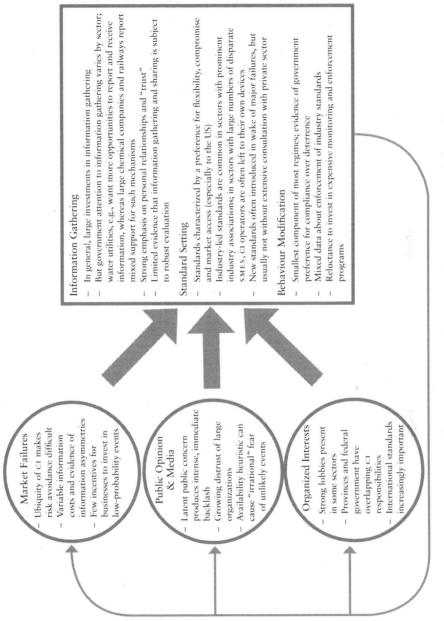

Information Gathering

- In general, large investments in information gathering
- But government attention to information gathering varies by sector; water utilities, e.g., want more opportunities to report and receive information, whereas large chemical companies and railways report mixed support for such mechanisms
- Strong emphasis on personal relationships and "trust"
- Limited evidence that information gathering and sharing is subject to robust evaluation

Standard Setting

- Standards characterized by a preference for flexibility, compromise and market access (especially to the US)
- Industry-led standards are common in sectors with prominent industry associations; in sectors with large numbers of disparate SMEs, CI operators are often left to their own devices
- New standards often introduced in wake of major failures, but usually not without extensive consultation with private sector

Behaviour Modification

- Smallest component of most regimes; evidence of government preference for compliance over deterrence
- Mixed data about enforcement of industry standards
- Reluctance to invest in expensive monitoring and enforcement programs

Market Failures

- Ubiquity of CI makes risk avoidance difficult
- Variable information costs and evidence of information asymmetries
- Few incentives for businesses to invest in low-probability events

Public Opinion & Media

- Latent public concern produces intense, immediate backlash
- Growing distrust of large organizations
- Availability heuristic can cause "irrational" fear of unlikely events

Organized Interests

- Strong lobbies present in some sectors
- Provinces and federal government have overlapping CI responsibilities
- International standards increasingly important

Figure 12.1 Main observed features of regime content and context in the transportation and chemicals sectors.

emphasis by government on environmental regulation of the private sector. The creation of the Environmental Protection Agency was motivated in many respects by public outcry over events such as the Cuyahoga River fire. In turn, the expansion of government regulation contributed to a reconfiguration of the costs and benefits associated with environmental protection. New opportunities for rent seeking emerged as industries sought to impose harsher standards on their competitors under the guise of achieving environmental policy objectives such as reducing greenhouse gas emissions. Adler (1996, 27) catalogues several examples of such rent seeking, including the Environmental Technology Council, the industry association for companies that recycle and treat hazardous waste, which lobbied the Environmental Protection Agency to require that common hazardous products, such as fluorescent bulbs, be covered by hazardous-waste regulations. In this case, public opinion influenced regime content, which in turn contributed to a realignment of the interest group pressures acting on government.

Generally, the growth and increased sophistication in government communications over the last decades influenced how lay people perceive risks and black swans, and how, in turn, governments respond to them. Since SARS in 2003, governments have had larger health bureaucracies in place ready to respond to a pandemic. In other words, the institutional arrangements to amplify pandemic risks that we described in chapter 9 were in place well before the 2009 HINI outbreak. Governments also play a significant role in shaping our understanding of risks associated with terrorism. As noted in chapter 7, governments make many decisions about how to frame and announce terrorism arrests. More broadly, the expansion of government communications also reshapes the relationship between government and the media, particularly in light of the diminishing staff and resources at many media organizations. In this environment, news agencies often rely on government media releases as the basis for new articles.

In short, while the framework is structured for us to examine how context shapes content, in fact, we can also think of the regime in a more dynamic manner, in which content influences context. The extent to which government influences the context does seem limited, however, and the opportunities seem to be fewer and fewer, which is the point of our final discussion.

THE ROLE OF GOVERNMENT
IN CRITICAL INFRASTRUCTURE PROTECTION:
FROM STRONG MAN TO STRAW MAN

As we conclude, we now turn to a discussion of how government could take steps to improve its regulation of CI. We will assess the effectiveness of the risk regulation regimes in light of the three justifications of Hood and Jackson's (1991) administrative argument that we introduced in chapter 9 (sigma, theta, and lambda considerations), and we will point to areas where governments could improve their risk regulation of CI. Recall that sigma-type justifications (efficiency claims) are based on precepts about matching resources to tasks for defined circumstances. These arguments relate to waste limitation, the pursuit of efficiency, and avoidance of muddle and confusion. Theta-type justifications (fairness claims) are based on precepts about how to ensure fairness, mutuality, and the proper discharge of duties. These justifications relate to fair treatment, bias avoidance, pursuit of accountability, and avoidance of abuse of office. Lambda-type justifications (stability and learning claims) are based on precepts about how to ensure resilience, even in adverse conditions. To a degree, the same aspects of the regimes can be discussed under more than one heading; the concepts are also interrelated: increasing efficiency might decrease transparency, for example.

The Efficiency of the Regimes

With respect to sigma justifications, CI cannot be assessed strictly in terms of its likeliness to fail or harm; it also represents opportunity. Consider the most important advances of the twentieth century: the power grid, nuclear technologies, cars and national highways, high-speed rail, the Internet, personal computers, cellular technology, radio and television networks, airplanes and airports, a national health system, advanced water purification and distribution, and global banking. Governments played key roles in the development of the technology, the policies, and legal agreements, and the infrastructure that supports them. The risk-taking involved in developing these technologies contributed to a vastly improved quality of life. Traditionally, much of the CI would be considered public goods; most of it is now owned, operated, and/or managed by the private sector with varying degrees of government involvement (see appendix 4 for a list of CI privatizations in Canada since the 1970s).

Private organizations reduce costs to realize profits; these actions can increase risks. We saw this in the Lac-Mégantic derailment, the Sunrise Propane explosion, and the parking lot collapse in Elliott Lake, Ontario. Increased robustness and redundancy in the form of extra material, staff, or processes result in additional costs; precautionary approaches to risk are generally expensive, not just in terms of implementing the system but in terms of the opportunity cost.

The private sector, however, does not have a monopoly on CI failures. While governments are more concerned with cost containment than profit, black swan events also occur in the public sector. Publicly owned bridges collapse, as we saw with the de la Concorde overpass in Montreal (Gohier 2011). The water supply in Walkerton is also a publicly owned utility (Walkerton Commission of Inquiry 2002a). Indeed, the poor state of public infrastructure, such as in transit and water supply, is an ongoing concern (Federation of Canadian Municipalities n.d.).

The traditional market method of insuring against failures in CI can be unreliable. In the immediate aftermath of the Christchurch earthquakes, insurance providers were key in supporting businesses that suffered losses. As described in chapter 6, as time went on, however, payments became slower and more contested (Chang et al. 2014); SMEs with the least capacity to shoulder such losses suffered the most. Eventually, insurance agencies began reducing their exposure to the New Zealand market, leading to higher premiums. Following the Toronto and Alberta floods in 2013, the insurance industry cautioned that the increasingly frequent natural disasters cannot be adequately covered by existing insurance policies and agreements. The industry has also raised concerns about the interdependent nature of CI and the overall lack of insurance and insurance policies in the cyber domain (see Society of Actuaries 2014.)

We need to ensure that people understand what they are insured against and contribute more for more comprehensive policies. SMEs do not hold enough insurance to cover the costs of catastrophic loss, as we saw in Lac-Mégantic. Most people are not covered for flooding and it is unlikely they are even aware of this fact (Philippi and Osberghaus 2016). Allowing people to build in flood-prone areas will inevitably lead to calls for financial assistance from government when homes flood, as we saw in Alberta. These policies disproportionately benefit the better off, not the vulnerable (Wriggins 2014). In light of a dramatic event such as a flood, there will always be considerable pressure on politicians to cover such costs, and politicians will capitulate. Indeed, in the post-mortem of the 2013 Alberta floods, the report observed that politicians frequently misunderstood the Disaster Recovery Program and kept making promises that were not part of the program (MNP LLP 2015). These types of events demonstrate how unstable and elusive the concept of risk tolerance is; people accept risks in the abstract but are much less tolerant once they see and experience the consequences of such an event, particularly one that is framed in sympathetic terms by the popular media. While no government will ignore the plight of desperate people in a crisis, nor should it, we cannot make policies on the fly in the midst of a crisis, characterized by highly emotive media coverage. In the age of big data, we need to ensure we are getting access to more information and building more reliable models for insurers. We also have to ask those who assume risks to pay more of the insurance to cover their losses, even if they do not cover the full amount. We also need smarter urban development that better takes these risks into account.

Several recent studies point to potential solutions to persistent challenges in the insurance industry, including many of the problems surveyed above. One solution is to invest more resources in enforcement of mandatory insurance schemes (Michel-Kerjan and Kunreuther 2011). Even when insurance is required by law, many people choose not to purchase it. Governments should complement enforcement with communications initiatives aimed at building risk awareness and a better understanding of the financial implications of insurance decisions (Monti 2009; Surminski and Eldridge 2015). To promote long-term planning, disaster insurance should be sold as a multi-year contract attached to a property rather than the homeowner (Michel-Kerjan and Kunreuther 2011; Surminksi and Eldridge 2015). In the case of government-run insurance programs, government authorities could purchase private reinsurance and catastrophic bonds to reduce the financial burden that major disasters place on public coffers (Michel-Kerjan and Kunreuther 2011). In federal states such as Canada, research suggests that when federal governments refuse to insure the full amount of losses after a disaster, they promote larger subnational investments in infrastructure protection (Goodspeed and Haughwout 2012). Together, this research points to a number of potentially effective methods for improving insurance markets.

While the law provides a necessary legal framework with which to hold people to account, courts are slow when addressing CI failures and black swan events. The technology is complex and there are often many people involved; it is increasingly difficult to determine who is responsible for what, and when negligence, for example, becomes a criminal act. In the case of large companies, such as with the *Exxon Valdez* and the Deepwater Horizon oil spills, it can take years to resolve these issues, and large companies have the means to drag out such processes. Cases involving SMEs are by no means quickly resolved; disputes over damages associated with the 2008 Toronto propane explosion were not resolved by the courts until 2016 (Loriggio 2016). A similar point can be made in cases of terrorism; the complexity of the case prevents justice from moving in good time. It took over twenty years for the results of the Air India Inquiry to be published; even with the Toronto 18, it took four years for the cases to be heard. The absence of claims under the Westray legislation raises question about the effectiveness of its provisions. The time it takes to hear these cases distances and disempowers regular citizens from the process. People lose faith in the system and become unable to connect perpetrators with guilt and consequence.

There are alternatives. The Deepwater Horizon spill offers a powerful example: the US government publicly pressured (and scolded) BP to allocate funds for the Gulf cleanup and rehabilitation (Robertson and Lipton 2010). Had BP not complied, its future would have been uncertain, which would have made it difficult for it to raise money on capital markets and could have been the end of the company.[1] This approach seems to be gaining momentum. In a different context, we have seen President Donald Trump use Twitter as a new bully pulpit to pressure organizations to comply with his preferred outcomes. He criticized Lockheed Martin, for example, for F-35 cost overruns; his comments resulted in a $4 billion drop in Lockheed Martin's share value and a subsequent offer by Lockheed Martin to reduce the cost of the program (Thielman 2016). He criticized US-based Rexnord for relocating a plant from Indiana to Mexico; Rexnord's stock subsequently fell by eight per cent (Schwartz 2016). There is no doubt that the method is quick and has effect; some have argued that the strategy may prompt executives to act with more care and corporate social responsibility. At the same time, others have suggested it is a form of blackmail that operates outside the law and bureaucratic procedure. It is also not clear that it will have any real, long-lasting economic impact (Schwartz 2016).

Prompt inquiries that function in a timely and transparent manner can help to show the public that progress is occurring, as we saw after the Buncefield explosion and the Waterfall train accident. The 9/11 Commission published its final report in 2004, under three years after the event. In contrast, the Ontario Office of the Fire Marshal seemed decidedly less interested in informing the public following the Sunrise Propane explosion (*Toronto Star* 2010); its reports were unavailable to the public until a city councillor protested, at which point a highly redacted and technical report of the event was made available on the office's public website. Out-of-court settlements are also a means by which to move things along more quickly, as we saw in the Lac-Mégantic disaster. Out-of-court settlements, however, limit public scrutiny and accountability, a point to which we now turn.

The Transparency, Fairness, and Accountability of the Regimes

In certain publicly owned CI we examined, there was a high degree of transparency. Following events like Walkerton (and the inquiry that followed), we have seen increased transparency in the water sector (Water Security Agency 2015; Office of the Ombudsman 2016). Following the collapse of the de la Concorde overpass in Montreal, there was an extensive public inquiry into bridge infrastructure in the province (Quebec Commission of Inquiry 2008).

Generally, the National Strategy and Action Plan for Critical Infrastructure (NS&AP) is concerned more about cooperation between organizations than transparency; when it comes to issues of security there is very little transparency at all. We see an uneven degree of transparency among those transportation subsectors that have increasing private sector involvement. The Transportation Safety Board (TSB) reports regularly, for example, on safety incidents in the air, marine, pipeline, and rail subsectors. As we noted, however, there is also extensive lobbying of government, particularly in the aftermath of a disaster. The chemicals sector seems to be even less transparent. It is very difficult to get information about the chemicals sector and this goes beyond whether or not citizens sit on community panels – generally, municipalities do not know when dangerous goods are transported through their communities and communities are not informed about where and how dangerous chemicals are stored.

Again, the problem does not lie strictly with the private sector. There is an incentive for municipalities to increase commercial and residential development because it increases the tax base. These new developments can occur increasingly in flood-prone areas, as we saw in the United Kingdom in the 2007 floods (Pitt 2008), and in areas zoned for the storage of chemicals, as we saw in the West fertilizer explosion in Texas, the Toronto Sunrise Propane explosion, and the Neptune Technologies and Bioressources disaster in Quebec. These communities had been zoned years earlier for chemicals, but as the communities grew so did the need for homes, which were built in the same areas. In the aftermath of the explosion in West, Texas, the Chemical Safety Board concluded there were very few standards in place in the United States, for example, concerning residential dwellings and the storage of chemicals (Chemical Safety and Hazards Investigations Board 2013). In the case of the West Fertilizer Company, few (if any) people in the neighbourhood, including the firefighters, knew there was so much fertilizer stored in the facilities.

Are the regimes fair? There is a randomness to black swan events and, as such, there is a strange sense of fairness. Scratch the surface, however, and we see evidence that risks affect some more and differently than others. We know that remote parts of the country have poorer infrastructure and often fewer qualified staff to manage it. We saw this in the water contamination case in Walkerton. Remote regions also have more single points of failure, as we saw when flooded roads prevented food from arriving in Whitehorse in 2012 (Keevil 2012). Poorer people (urban or not) are most affected by evacuations, for example (Strolovitch, Warren, and Frymer 2006); they are least likely to have independent sources of support, such as their own transportation, as we saw in New Orleans during Hurricane Katrina (Masozera, Bailey, and Kerchner 2007). In the post-mortem of the 2013 Alberta floods, one of the few criticisms of government was that it needed a stronger framework for social services in emergencies (MNP LLP 2015).

Large and growing cities have their own challenges. The densely populated downtown areas of Toronto and Vancouver are vulnerable should there be any adverse events, particularly since the number of high-rise buildings has grown. Evacuation of these areas – caused by chemical spills or natural disasters, for example – would be slow and complicated. Evacuation plans across the country are uneven at best (Henstra 2011). They also embed a number of assumptions, such as that people can look after themselves for up to 72 hours (Public Safety Canada 2016), which is unlikely for the vulnerable but also unlikely for many who may seem able-bodied. An Australian report on the effects of flooding in Queensland notes that younger people were disproportionately affected because many "lived in apartments where there was limited storage space for food" and because they "did not know how to cook anything other than pre-prepared meals (which became unavailable during the flooding)" (Australia Department of Agriculture, Fisheries and Forestry 2012, 33).

In a time-sensitive context, difficult prioritization exercises occur. In *Five Days at Memorial*, a book that details the dynamics of a hospital in crisis during Hurricane Katrina, Fink (2013) describes doctors reversing the conventional practice of saving the most in need of assistance to saving the most likely to survive; these decisions were not without controversy, and a grand jury was summoned to deliberate over the case in the years that followed. Pre-event exercises can help improve evacuation; they should include a number of organizations, public and private, and from all orders of government, with appropriate and transparent reporting and performance metrics. Better engagement between the public service and politicians is also useful. In some provinces, for example, health officials briefed Cabinet before the second wave of H1N1 on extreme scenarios and what the decision-making and prioritization process would entail. The intention was to minimize one-off political interventions that might confuse people and undermine the plan. When there was a shortage of vaccine, however, and health officials reverted to the priority groups, politicians did intervene, which resulted in some provinces abandoning the pre-approved pandemic plan, which did cause confusion (Alphonso 2010).

With respect to accountability, Peters (2001) refers to three types: answerability, which refers to rendering an account; responsibility, which refers to following ethical standards and the law; and responsiveness, which refers to responding to the needs of the public. At times, these concepts overlap.

The government's response to the Lac-Mégantic disaster and rail safety audit sheds light on the different ways in which government meets – or fails to meet – Peters' categories of accountability. Transport Canada plays an important role in regulating risks of rail travel and is responsible for monitoring and enforcing rail safety practices. Transport Canada permitted MMA to have a reduced staff complement on the train (Whittington et al. 2013). In the 2013 audit of Transport Canada, the Auditor General noted, "Despite discussions with the industry and progress over the past twenty years, a number of long-standing and important safety issues remain, including trespassing, grade crossings, concerns about the environment, the collection of data on safety performance from federal railways, and the implementation and oversight of safety management systems" (Auditor General of Canada 2013 and chapter 7 of this book). The problems go beyond the specific failures that caused the derailment at Lac-Mégantic. MMA had a weak SMS which did not receive appropriate scrutiny from Transport Canada.

Despite the department's poor performance, a point underscored by the minister, there are limits to the degree of government transparency. Minister Raitt made the following comments in an interview with the CBC's Dave Seglins (CBC News 2015) one year after the event in Lac-Mégantic:

SEGLINS: You used the word "failings." Has there been any accountability within Transport Canada, has anybody lost their job over the way things were or were not enforced on MMA?
RAITT: If you take a look at the current listing of people who are in Transport Canada you'll see there's a marked difference than the people who were in Transport Canada pre-2013. A lot of it was natural turnover, there was a lot of retirements happening, and you know the management of the department lies with the deputy minister, and I think he's done an excellent job of making sure that we have the right group and the right mix of people going forward. I think the department's in a really good place to make sure that the lessons we need to learn from Lac-Mégantic, from the derailment, from other derailments, from the Auditor General's report are going to be implemented, and I have great confidence that they will.
SEGLINS: But were those changes around accountability? Anybody moved in or out because of the way things were or were not?

RAITT: I leave it to the deputy minister to make his assessment of who needs to be in what position, and changes were made.

Minister Raitt did not explain why she was so confident in the new staff. She did not describe a process by which anyone was held to account, or who was held to account and for what. In fact, she obscured the accountability even further by noting that, yes, staff left, but some left because of retirement.

In some respects, this type of answerability represents traditional forms of accountability; the minister takes responsibility and the public service remains behind the curtain. It is ironic, however, because there has been a move away from public service anonymity for more than a decade (Savoie 2003). In any event, as we noted in chapter 4, it was unclear what level of responsibility the elected government was willing to accept for failings, despite the fact that the Conservative government had been in power since 2007, a full five years before the derailment.

This opportunity to avoid responsibility for operational failures existed for Minister Raitt partly because of the opaque definition of ministerial responsibility, which had recently been revised by the Privy Council Office (PCO). Max Paris (2014) describes the revision:

The 2007 guide for ministers, written by the PCO, explained ministerial responsibility this way: 'Ministers are individually responsible to Parliament and the prime minister for their own actions and those of their department, including the actions of all officials under their management and direction, whether or not the Ministers had prior knowledge.' By 2011, there had been a shift in thinking, emphasizing what it is *not*. 'Ministerial accountability to Parliament does not mean that a minister is presumed to have knowledge of every matter that occurs within his or her department or portfolio, nor that the minister is necessarily required to accept blame for every matter,' wrote PCO in an updated version of the pamphlet.

PCO is not a third-party arbiter; it supports the Office of the Prime Minister. There is a conflict of interest. Effectively, the definition includes enough ambiguity that ministers can deny responsibility for operational failures. This style of framing that keeps blame away from the minister is the type of communications strategy that is increasingly common in Ottawa (Savoie 2015). The example demonstrates, however, that despite the intense scrutiny of the audits and the poor performance of the department as well as the trend towards greater public sector accountability, there continues to be important limits on transparency and accountability at the political and staff level.

The government also did not hold an inquiry. While Minister Raitt noted that the event was studied by the TSB and that Transport Canada's safety oversight was audited by the Auditor General, the TSB looked only at the Lac-Mégantic derailment and the Auditor General does not investigate the private rail companies (Transport Canada 2015b). Moreover, neither report provided much by way of public testimony, as we saw in the inquiries held for the Walkerton water contamination, the Elliott Lake parking lot collapse, or, indeed, the Waterfall train accident in Australia, for example, all three of which resulted in far fewer deaths and much less destruction than the events in Lac-Mégantic. In addition, the 2007 Safety Review as well as the Auditor General and TSB reports concluded that there were recurring problems with management and oversight. This is all the more reason why it is surprising that a disaster described by TSB as not being the fault of one person or organization would not warrant an independent and far-reaching examination, especially for a country that depends so much on the transportation of dangerous goods by rail.

In terms of Peters' second type of accountability, responsibility, the government arguably did a better job than it did with answerability, particularly in the aftermath of the event. Minister Raitt and her successor, Minister Garneau, noted that the government had no responsibility for the Lac-Mégantic derailment, which may be legally true but is ironic at the very least, given the government's regulatory role before such events and financial exposure in the aftermath of such events. In fact the government did respond to the event with a number of initiatives, mostly under the watch of Minister Raitt. First, the federal government provided more than $155 million to Lac-Mégantic for reconstruction and other costs associated with the derailment. Secondly, it acted to improve rail safety following the event. In 2013, Transport Canada announced a number of new safety directives immediately following the derailment (Transport Canada 2013c). In 2014, Transport Canada unveiled a new set of regulations that included prohibiting the older-style tank cars that had been used in Lac-Mégantic, imposing speed limits for trains transporting dangerous goods, increasing inspections, and instituting risk assessments for all transportation routes. Shippers were also required to develop emergency response plans for all trains carrying high-risk goods, including petroleum products (Transport Canada 2014). The government also launched consultations aimed at improving the "polluter pays" principle and tasked the House of Commons Standing Committee on Transport with recommending further changes to improve the sector's safety practices. The changes implemented, however, were criticized as "cosmetic" by some (Winfield 2014).

With respect to responsiveness, how the government's response aligns with public expectations is more difficult to determine. There is no question that the public expects a rigorous form of review after an event like Lac-Mégantic, that victims should be compensated for their suffering, and that systems should be put in place to prevent similar incidents. Despite the media coverage, however, it is difficult to determine the level of public concern over the matter. Notwithstanding their concerns over safety, small communities argued to keep the trains coming to their communities because of their important economic value. There is still a high level of public resistance to pipelines, especially in Quebec, despite the fact that they have a better safety record than rail (CBC News 2016). In the last federal election, Lac-Mégantic was hardly mentioned, and the new government was prepared to conclude the settlement quickly without having to accept responsibility. In this sense, the public is implicated in the matter; again, we see a pattern of fascination and aversion but neither of these things fundamentally changes attitudes towards public policy, which has implications for how we approach CI, as we will now discuss.

Stability, Learning, and Resilience

Immediately following 9/11, government officials referred to CIP; today, they are more likely to refer to the resilience of the infrastructure – the capacity to bounce back or adapt – for practical and economic reasons. Protection is a proactive process that includes identifying CI and planning and paying for its ongoing protection. The concept of resilience, on the other hand, allows for failure; it recognizes that not every event can be anticipated and not every asset can be protected. What constitutes CI is often a question of perspective and circumstance. During a flood or hurricane a small bridge connecting an island to the mainland can be considered as important as a major highway, as we saw in Garden Cove, Newfoundland, in 2010 when communities were cut off from food and clean water because the roads were flooded and bridges collapsed (Bailey 2010). The term CI has therefore expanded to include a number of sectors and systems, big and small, many of which are not particularly well defined or accounted for.

Given the financial constraints, it makes sense to use the concept of resilience as a guiding principle, as Canada's national strategy does. When there are failures in CI, we need a capacity to bounce back but not necessarily to the point where the system was before; after all, the system failed. We need a capacity to learn from the failure and bounce back with stronger assets, sometimes referred to as "bounce (or build) back better." Moreover, the term *resilience* is too limited. We need more refined ways to refer to the threats to CI and to respond to them. Part of the solution lies in building systems that are more robust when we cannot tolerate failure, such as with nuclear power, and redundant systems when costs permit, such as with excess Internet capacity. We also need to think about retiring assets, a subject that gets much less attention in the literature and political circles.

Black swans can create an opportunity for positive change, a notion captured famously by Rahm Emanuel during the 2008 financial collapse when he warned fellow policy-makers that they should not let a good crisis go to waste (Seib 2008).

Part of the challenge after a disaster is interpreting and conveying the appropriate meaning of the event. Leaders try to frame the debate and in so doing create heroes and villains. In the chapter on cybersecurity (chapter 8), we saw many examples of cyber gurus underscoring the threat to stability that cyberspace poses to CI. This framing has not really resonated with many organizations or the public; it is too remote and complex, and in any event the benefits of the technology seem to outweigh the risk to most people. The technology sector remains popular, trusted, and largely unregulated. Cybersecurity is getting more traction, however, in departments of defence, and has been for some time (Kaplan 2016); the Society of Actuaries (2014) is increasingly sharing this concern. Industrial failures, on the other hand, result in a ruthless and narrow hunt for accountability that focuses on the people deemed responsible; if you build it, you'd better maintain it, the saying goes. This approach overlooks systemic failures. Natural disasters, in contrast, are framed as acts of God over which we have no control, and therefore accountability seems to be diffuse, evasive even. Neither the response to Hurricane Juan in Nova Scotia in 2003 nor the response to the flash floods in Toronto in 2013 had an independent audit. The response to the 2013 Alberta floods did have an audit but it was narrowly focused on emergency management and the conclusions were largely flattering. In fact, natural disasters are the black swans that cost the most every year (Insurance Information Institute 2016) yet governments often receive positive performance assessments following them. Broadening the scope of these reports to include past policy decisions that created the vulnerabilities in the first place would be helpful. Attacks in the name of radical Islam are framed as evidence of growing and pervasive terrorist threats. Evidence of how limited this threat is, or alternative explanations for this behaviour, such as psychiatric disorders, are given considerably less attention.

Organizational culture matters when it comes to identifying and responding to risks. SMES – individualistic in design and orientation, in cultural theory terms – are difficult to accommodate in CI planning: they are trusted by citizens but in fact they do not have the resources, insurance, contingency plans, or security clearance to have robust CI plans in place. On balance, the failure of a SME is usually inconsequential to the overall functioning of a community. As a result, SMES are often overlooked in CI planning. Governments could share information more widely with SMES as the UK government does. Despite government's anxiety over sharing classified information, most SMES are not normally interested in classified information if it has no immediate relevance to their business operations; they are more concerned with practical operational information. Governments might also invest in infrastructure to support knowledge commons in more egalitarian, non-competitive sectors, such as the water and bridge subsectors. Investments here could help facilitate information exchange in sectors in which funding is low but the willingness to share information with like-minded people is strong.

The organizational dynamic in many CI sectors is bureaucratic. These organizations are stable, hierarchical, and rules oriented; they are upwardly accountable, not outwardly so. They are underpinned by a form of corporatism that allows government regulators and CI owners and operators to work collaboratively. The overall lack of transparency we found in many sectors is a way to reinforce stability. In a UK study of trust in government, the authors concluded that increased transparency eroded trust in government because the media only covered and amplified the story when there was conflict or a failure to achieve standards (Taylor-Gooby 2006). Ironically, then, transparency in a particular media context does not necessarily increase trust in government. This leads to one of the more unsettling conclusions of this book – that lack of transparency bolsters the stability of the system. If the risks were more apparent and reported more widely, like divulging the amount of chemicals stored in suburban areas or heightening the threat level for terrorist attacks, people might be unsettled by this information without knowing what corrective actions to take.

As we have underscored throughout the book, more independent audits would help to hold CI owners and operators and government regulators to account but audits themselves are not a panacea. The term *lessons learned* in these audits is overused and unhelpful; we should instead refer to *lessons identified*. There is often little evidence that lessons have resulted in meaningful systemic changes, particularly in the short term, and even if people do learn lessons it is not clear that they have learned the right ones or that they are prepared to make the fundamental changes that would generate different results; people's optimism about learning lessons is an expression of hope over experience. Studies of organizational culture suggest that organizations learn lessons consistent with the survival of their organizational culture; they are often deaf to lessons that challenge it. In a sense, stability and learning can be competing concepts. In other words, organizations learn only what they need to in order to be stable. It is not unusual, for instance, for an audit to conclude that an organizational failure occurred because of lack of expertise, leadership, and process. These are core characteristics of a bureaucracy. Public-sector auditors usually reinforce bureaucratic characteristics; they do not challenge them. Auditors rarely conclude, for example, that public organizations require more flexibility, more creativity, more outward accountability, or a greater commitment to the community they serve. In other words, oversight requires more diversity than simply bureaucratic auditors. Audits can, however, make more and a broader range of information available in the public domain for increased scrutiny by legislators, academics, advocates for victims, the growing number of think tanks and non-governmental organizations, and the public in general. Indeed, auditors should make more of their source data available for others to use and analyze. Auditors – as well as concerned citizens' groups – should also track more aggressively the progress government agencies and CI owners and operators are making with respect to recommendations, as we saw following the audit of the Waterfall train accident in Australia. Similar websites – clear and accessible – should be established following disasters to monitor progress against all recommendations; this monitoring should continue until the organizations have addressed the recommendations.

Moreover, our infrastructure planning needs to take into account not simply today's threats but also the threats and opportunities of the future. The Canadian governments plan to spend as much as $800 billion over the next decade on infrastructure. The federal government plans to double its contribution to $180 billion over the next twelve years; its spending will focus on infrastructure renewal and upgrades, as well as new projects relating to social, green, and transit-based infrastructure (Government of Canada 2016a).

Canada needs a more transparent, better informed, and more integrated approach to infrastructure planning. Infrastructure planning is slow and expensive; it must start with a sense of what we think the future looks like and in which ways we might be able to influence and adapt to that future. New Zealand, for example, has a 30-year strategic infrastructure plan (New Zealand Government 2015); no such plan exists in Canada. Government decision-making concerning infrastructure investments is opaque and constrained by coordination and governance challenges (Craft et al. 2013; Hammerschmid and Wegrich 2016; Rajabiun and Middleton 2013; Rossi 2014; Tamtik 2016). These factors narrow the focus of infrastructure policy, causing governments to overlook the benefits of a more ambitious and integrated approach.

Infrastructure investments, particularly in emerging technologies such as driverless cars, high-speed commuter trains, and mobile and wireless systems, will not just accommodate the needs of future communities, they will shape them. This new investment has the potential to elevate Canadian infrastructure, paying dividends in improved sustainability, increased productivity, and substantial value to individuals, organizations, and communities across the country. It will also change the risk profile for communities and CI sectors.

One theme that recurs in many post-event audits is government's inability to see new problems and adapt its behaviour and institutional arrangements accordingly. We saw elements of this lack of adaptive capacity in security services before the Air India bombing and in safety practices at Transport Canada before the Lac-Mégantic derailment almost thirty years later. Failed foresight increases risks in times of instability, innovation, and technological development. Climate change will bring about enhanced risks associated with natural hazards, such as floods and droughts (World Meteorological Organization 2007). New global trade agreements and new trade routes in the North will create new opportunities but also new security challenges (Smith and Stephenson 2013; Hall et al. 2014; Ibáñez et al. 2010; Rinaldi, Peerenboom, and Kelly 2001). Pipelines and hydraulic fracking can generate new wealth but also give rise to environmental extremism and adverse geological effects. Our access to a largely unregulated Internet will continue to introduce new efficiencies, flexibility, and dangers at the national and local levels.

Our ideological biases and bureaucratic arrangements frequently segment innovation, environmental threats, and security threats, but there is much to be gained from thinking of these concepts jointly. Scenario planning in the tradition of van der Heijden (2005) accepts that many variables that drive change exist outside an organization's control; his approach to scenario planning can help to increase an organization's adaptive capacity, particularly among bureaucratic agencies that are premised on false assumptions of internal command and control. In addition, the emergence of smart technologies will allow us to collect more accurate data and make better decisions about which assets should be maintained and expanded and which ones should be retired.

What is clear is that the government will continue to depend on the private sector in the area of CI. Of the federal government's planned spending, $35 billion will be used to establish an infrastructure bank to finance projects with the private sector and other orders of government (Government of Canada 2016b). Government hopes to take advantage of industry's expertise, cash reserves, entrepreneurialism, and innovation to help Canada become a greener and more tech-savvy society. To meet its infrastructure goals, government seeks to entice managers of large investment funds to invest in public infrastructure. To secure these investments, government will have to relinquish control of the assets, in whole or in part, to make them appealing. Given popular resistance to user fees and various aspects of privatization, it is not clear how popular views will be reconciled with private interests, how transparent and fair the decisions will be (Enoch and Stadnichuk 2015), and where the public good resides. To date, there seems to be little public consideration about how infrastructure investments change not only the level of risk but also the type of risk to which Canadians will be exposed, and how that might influence infrastructure planning, ownership, investment, management, and reporting.

The federal government's national strategy for CI seeks to improve resilience by increasing trust between government and the owners and operators of CI and, in so doing, improve the conditions for information sharing, trust building, and better risk management. Government may be pursuing trust with the wrong people. It is not industry whose faith government has to earn. Government should be trying to increase trust with the citizenry, a group largely overlooked in the NS&AP.

Government has a regulatory and formal leadership role to play. By sitting at a round table as a partner, as government frequently describes itself, government potentially compromises its ability to play the role of enforcer and loses sight of its accountability to the public.

Managing the infrastructure file requires humility, ambition, and courage. It requires humility because of the complexity of the technology and the awesome forces of nature, both of which can bring about devastation that no manufactured system can fully mitigate. It requires ambition because these same technologies can be transformative; they can generate new wealth and opportunities for people and communities across the country. It requires courage because there are no risk-free options. Government must include the public as government pursues opportunities and manages threats that emerge to Canada's critical assets. At times, this transparency may result in fractious debate, and the pursuit of these opportunities could indeed result in tragedy. But a more transparent process will contribute to a more just society and informed public, better able to participate in a democracy and deliberate over the choices of an unknowable future.

APPENDICES

Methods

This book is the culmination of several years of data collection and analysis. Our aim has been to produce a comprehensive study of critical infrastructure (CI) risk regulation regimes in Canada. In pursuit of that goal, we have applied a mixed-methods approach involving both qualitative and quantitative research techniques. We used diverse yet complementary methods to capture the full range of contextual factors that influence regulatory content.

INTERVIEWS

The first stage of our primary research occurred from 2011 to 2013. With the support of funding from the Social Sciences and Humanities Research Council of Canada, we conducted and transcribed forty-seven semi-structured interviews with CI regulators, owners, operators, and experts. In 2013, after obtaining further funding support through Public Safety Canada's Kanishka Project, we conducted an additional twenty-one interviews.

During both interview stages, we identified potential interview subjects through a review of the academic, grey, and government literature. Subsequent interview subjects were identified through a snowball sampling technique: at the end of each interview, we asked participants to identify other people we should contact. The majority of our interviews were with Canadians. To provide context, as well as to permit comparative analysis, we also interviewed CI regulators and owners/operators in the United States, the United Kingdom, and Australia.

We tried to achieve balance and equivalence with respect to the institutions and roles of the people we interviewed. In broad terms, we sought to ensure similar breadth of input from government regulators and CI owner/operators and representatives of industry associations. When we note that we interviewed staff responsible for bridges, we mean major suspension bridges.

We found that federal government employees were less likely than private-sector representatives to accept interview requests. Federal public servants were also less likely to speculate on issues perceived to be outside their area of expertise or responsibility. This could be due to the strict accountabilities that bind public servants.

We complemented the data received from these sources with data from interviews with CI experts, including academics, consultants, and retired industry representatives. These individuals, who are removed from the immediate pressures facing regulators and CI owners/operators (e.g., public-sector accountability, profit), yet possess deep insight into risk regulation, provided a useful perspective on critical infrastructure protection (CIP). Their input also provided the basis for initial triangulation of our other interview data; we could compare their data with that of regulators and CI owners/operators to identify areas of potential controversy, dispute, or uncertainty.

The interviews were conducted in a semi-structured format, in which the interviewer was free to divert from the prepared questions to develop ideas and explore points raised by participants during discussion. We recorded most interviews. We typed transcripts of each recording and sent them to participants for their review. The names of all interview subjects and the transcripts are confidential. We committed to the Dalhousie University Research Ethics Board and to our interview subjects that we would not use direct quotations from our transcripts without the explicit consent of our participants.

We used a mixed-methods approach to analyze the interview data, employing both quantitative and qualitative methods. The quantitative analysis consisted of descriptive statistics, including simple means and response percentages. The small sample size of interview subjects in any one subsector would preclude the use of any rigorous statistical analysis to support generalizations of the findings. At the same time, we found it useful when conducting semi-structured interviews to ask participants to score contextual pressures that influence how they spend their time, for example. While not generalizable, the scoring allowed interview participants to distinguish more succinctly the impact of the different pressures. We present the data as indicating the relative importance of the contextual influences as assessed by these individual interview subjects, and we use the data as a departure point for analysis and discussion.

The qualitative portion of our mixed-methods approach involved using a grounded theory-based approach to extract and organize themes from the interview transcripts. Using as a starting point the broader framework of Hood and colleagues (2001) and a comprehensive literature review, we parsed the transcripts to identify common ideas and arguments, as well as comments that stood out for being unique or in conflict with the views of other participants. We gradually distilled these findings into larger themes, which allowed us to identify the contours of our argument.

MEDIA ANALYSIS

For the media analysis presented in chapter 7, we reviewed 2,510 newspaper articles from four different newspapers. These articles covered ci failures in a variety of categories: natural disasters, industrial failures, terrorist plots, terrorist attacks, and cyber attacks.

We conducted this analysis in two stages: we reviewed 1,857 articles between 2011 and 2013 and an additional 653 articles in 2015 and 2016. We accessed the articles using the Factiva database to search a leading national newspaper in each country: the *Australian*, the *Globe and Mail*, the *Daily Telegraph*, and the *New York Times*. These are all high-distribution newspapers and opinion leaders in each of the respective countries. We identified our sample by drawing on all articles that appeared during the year following the date each event began and that included the term(s) most commonly used to refer to the event. We eliminated any articles that were clearly not principally about the event. These types of events tend to appear in large numbers of articles during the year in which they occurred, but the references to the events are often "asides" in articles that are principally about something else.

To analyze the content of the articles, we counted the number of articles that referred to various key search terms. The key search terms were selected on the basis of conventional items that were relevant to public administration and risk management. We also determined whether key actors – such as government and owners and operators in critical sectors – were assessed positively, negatively, or neutrally. (N/A was also an option.) To summarize the performance data, a value of +1 was assigned to each article that was on balance a positive assessment for each key sector and a value of –1 was assigned to each article that was on balance a negative assessment (neutral assessments were assigned a value of 0.) We then calculated the total net sum, adding the number of positive and negative assessments together. When assessing government performance, we assessed each order of government separately. In other words, if one article had a negative assessment of both the federal and provincial government, then it was assessed as −2.

All non-H1N1 articles were analyzed during February and March 2010 (n = 1,857 articles) or during May, June, and July 2015 (n = 653 articles). We reduced the impact of the bias in assessments by using several strategies. As noted, we assessed all the articles during a short and fixed period of time. We also developed a standard template and applied it to all articles. All results were stored in a Microsoft Access database that we developed and maintain. In most cases, one research assistant classified the articles in the *Australian*, one classified the articles in the *Globe and Mail*, one classified the articles in the *Daily Telegraph*, and one classified articles in the *New York Times*. The group also met at the start of the project and periodically thereafter to review articles together, to introduce a further level of consistency.

To test the inter-rater reliability of all aspects of coding, ten per cent of the articles were double coded independently. In the first set of articles (n = 1,857), 186 were assessed by a second reviewer. Using Cohen's kappa coefficient we found an inter-rater reliability agreement of κ = 0.66 for government performance assessment. This corresponds to a substantial level of agreement. In the second set of articles (n = 653), sixty-six articles were coded by a second reviewer. The agreement among the coders in the second sample was lower for government performance assessment, κ = 0.37. Nevertheless, the coders agreed on seventy-one per cent of the articles; this would constitute a fair level of agreement.

We worked on the H1N1 case separately from the other cases. In January 2011 we retrieved 819 articles about H1N1. We used Factiva to search the *Globe and Mail*, the *Australian*, and the *Daily Telegraph*. Our sample comprises all articles in the year following 25 April 2009 that included the term(s) most commonly used to refer to the event. We eliminated any articles that were not principally about H1N1. Content analysis of the articles was carried out in two stages. First, and as above, we reviewed articles to determine whether key actors were assessed positively, negatively, or neutrally (N/A was also an option). We assigned a value of +1, −1, or 0 to each article depending on whether it was on balance a positive, negative, or neutral assessment for each key sector. We then calculated the net sum. Each order of government was assessed separately (if one article had a negative assessment of both the federal and provincial government, then it was assessed −2).

Following this initial assessment, we created a three-by-three matrix to assess what the governments were criticized for. Once we had created the categories, one reviewer analyzed the 339 relevant H1N1 articles in the *Globe and Mail*. The review occurred from December 2013 to January 2014. A second reviewer conducted an independent analysis of 10 per cent of the articles. Once again, we used Cohen's kappa coefficient to determine whether there was significant bias in the reviewer's analysis; we found a high level of agreement. The agreement on the selection of administrative argument was 0.7366; the agreement on the control mechanism was 0.7612 and the agreement of both the administrative argument and the control mechanism was 0.648.

Interview Participants

Code	Role	Sector or subsector	Location	Date
Int 1	Industry association	Aviation	Canada	December 2011
Int 2	Owner/Operator/Manager	Bridge	United States	September 2011
Int 3	Government regulator/Official	Other	United Kingdom	Not recorded
Int 4	Government regulator/Official	Ports	United States	December 2011
Int 5	Owner/Operator/Manager	Rail	Canada	July 2011
Int 6	Owner/Operator/Manager	Rail	United States	November 2011
Int 7	Owner/Operator/Manager	Surface transport	Canada	July 2011
Int 8	Industry association	Surface transport	Canada	June 2011
Int 9	Owner/Operator/Manager	Surface transport	Canada	July 2011
Int 10	Industry association	Aviation	Australia	February 2012
Int 11	Government regulator/Official	Aviation	Canada	September 2011
Int 12	Owner/Operator/Manager	Aviation	Canada	October 2011
Int 13	Owner/Operator/Manager	Aviation	Canada	October 2011

Code	Role	Sector or subsector	Location	Date
Int 14	Owner/Operator/ Manager	Aviation	Australia	February 2012
Int 15	Industry association	Aviation	Canada	August 2013
Int 16	Owner/Operator/ Manager	Bridge	Canada	June 2011
Int 17	Owner/Operator/ Manager	Bridge	United Kingdom	November 2011
Int 18	Owner/Operator/ Manager	Bridge	United Kingdom	September 2011
Int 19	Owner/Operator/ Manager	Bridge	United States	August 2011
Int 20	Government regulator/Official	Other	Australia	January 2012
Int 21	Government regulator/Official	Other	Canada	August 2011
Int 22	Government regulator/Official	Other	Canada	December 2011
Int 23	Government regulator/Official	Other	Canada	Not recorded
Int 24	Government regulator/Official	Other	United States	October 2011
Int 25	Government regulator/Official	Other	Canada	August 2011
Int 26	Government regulator/Official	Other	Australia	October 2011
Int 27	Government regulator/Official	Other	United Kingdom	March 2012
Int 28	Government regulator/Official	Other	United Kingdom	November 2011
Int 29	Transportation specialist	Other	United States	July 2013
Int 30	Owner/Operator/ Manager	Ports	Canada	June 2011
Int 31	Owner/Operator/ Manager	Ports	Canada	August 2011
Int 32	Owner/Operator/ Manager	Ports	Canada	July 2011
Int 33	Owner/Operator/ Manager	Ports	United States	December 2011

Code	Role	Sector or subsector	Location	Date
Int 34	Owner/Operator/Manager	Ports	United States	September 2011
Int 35	Industry association	Ports	Canada	July 2011
Int 36	Industry association	Ports	United States	September 2011
Int 37	Government regulator/Official	Ports	Canada	July 2011
Int 38	Government regulator/Official	Ports	Canada	July 2011
Int 39	Government regulator/Official	Other	United States	September 2011
Int 40	Government regulator/Official	Ports	Canada	August 2011
Int 41	Owner/Operator/Manager	Ports	United States	July 2013
Int 42	Owner/Operator/Manager	Ports	Canada	July 2013
Int 43	Government regulator/Official	Other	Canada	August 2013
Int 44	Government regulator/Official	Other	Canada	September 2013
Int 45	Owner/Operator/Manager	Rail	Canada	September 2013
Int 46	Government regulator/Official	Other	Canada	August 2013
Int 47	Government regulator/Official	Other	Canada	August 2013
Int 48	Transportation specialist	Ports	Canada	July 2013
Int 49	Government regulator/Official	Surface transport	Canada	July 2013
Int 50	Government regulator/Official	Other	United States	August 2013
Int 51	Owner/Operator/Manager	Water utility	Australia	July 2011
Int 52	Owner/Operator/Manager	Water utility	Canada	July 2011
Int 53	Owner/Operator/Manager	Water utility	Canada	July 2011

Code	Role	Sector or subsector	Location	Date
Int 54	Owner/Operator/Manager	Water utility	Canada	June 2011
Int 55	First responder	Emergency management	Canada	June 2011
Int 56	First responder	Emergency management	Canada	June 2011
Int 57	Government regulator/Official	Regulatory agency	United Kingdom	November 2011
Int 58	Expert	Chemical industry	Canada	July 2013
Int 59	Industry association	Chemical industry	Canada	July 2013
Int 60	Government regulator/Official	Emergency management	Canada	July 2013
Int 61	Industry association	Chemical industry	Canada	August 2013
Int 62	Expert	Emergency management	Canada	August 2013
Int 63	Government regulator/Official	Regulatory agency	Canada	August 2013
Int 64	Government regulator/Official	Law enforcement	Canada	August 2013
Int 65	Government regulator/Official	Law enforcement	Canada	August 2013
Int 66	Industry association	Chemical industry	United States	August 2013
Int 67	Industry association	Chemical industry	United States	August 2013
Int 68	Government regulator/Official	Regulatory agency	United States	October 2013

"Other" denotes that the interview subject had responsibility for more than one subsector. This occurred most often in the transportation sector.

Media Events Studied

Year(s)	Event	Description
2002	Potters Bar train wreck	A passenger train derailed at high speed in Potters Bar, England, injuring seventy-six people and killing seven. The derailment was blamed on poor maintenance of the railway.
2003	SQL Slammer worm	This computer worm began spreading on 25 January 2003. Within 10 minutes, SQL Slammer is estimated to have infected ninety per cent of vulnerable computers around the world, significantly slowing Internet traffic and causing disruption to government, industry, and media networks.
2003	Canberra bushfires	A major wildfire in the Australian Capital Territory was triggered by lightning strikes and extremely dry, windy conditions. The bushfires injured 490, killed four, and caused extensive damage to the outskirts of Canberra.
2003	Waterfall train accident	The derailment of a train near Waterfall, Australia, injured forty and killed seven. The crash was blamed on a combination of mechanical and human errors that caused the train to enter a curve in the tracks at almost double the speed limit.
2003	Hurricane Juan	This tropical cyclone made landfall in Halifax, Nova Scotia, on 27 September 2003 as a Category 2 hurricane. Described as the worst storm to hit Halifax in over a century, it caused over $300 million in damages in Nova Scotia and Prince Edward Island and eight deaths.

Year(s)	Event	Description
2005	Melbourne chemical spill	A presumed gas leak at Melbourne Airport left tens of thousands of passengers stranded; fifty-seven people were treated for nausea, vomiting, and shortness of breath (forty-seven of whom were hospitalized). No chemical or toxic leak was found, leading some psychologists to believe it was a case of mass sociogenic illness (i.e., mass hysteria).
2005	Texas City Refinery explosion	A massive explosion at a B P oil refinery in Texas City, Texas, injured 170 and killed fifteen. The explosion was blamed on a series of technical and organizational failings.
2005	Sydney Five terrorism plot	Five men plotted to conduct terrorist acts in Sydney, Australia, in retaliation for perceived attacks against Islam. All five were convicted in October 2009 and later received prison sentences ranging from 23 to 28 years.
2005	Albert Gonzalez data thefts	Computer hacker Albert Gonzalez stole over 170 million credit cards and identification documents in a series of data thefts between 2005 and 2007. Gonzalez was sentenced to 20 years in prison in 2010.
2005	Buncefield explosions	A series of explosions at the Hertfordshire Oil Storage Terminal in England resulted in a major fire that burned for several days. The explosion was blamed on a faulty level gauge that caused a fuel tank to be filled beyond its capacity, although management deficiencies at the facility were also identified as contributing factors. The explosion, said to be the largest in peacetime Europe, and subsequent fire injured forty-three people.
2006	Sears Tower plot	A Florida-based religious cult plotted to destroy the Sears Tower in Chicago. The group was infiltrated at an early stage by the F B I, which provided money on the pretense that it was funding from foreign terrorists. Of the seven accused in the plot, five were ultimately convicted on various terrorism-related charges.

Year(s)	Event	Description
2006	Toronto 18 plot	Eighteen people, including fourteen adults and four youth, plotted to carry out a series of attacks in southern Ontario. Among other things, the group planned to storm various public buildings and assassinate government officials. Ten of the adults and one youth pleaded guilty or were convicted at trial, receiving sentences from 2.5 years to life imprisonment.
2006	Transatlantic flights plot	Approximately twenty-four people in the United Kingdom plotted to detonate liquid explosives onboard aircraft flying to the United States and Canada. Eight men were eventually convicted and jailed in relation to the plot. The plot led to the introduction of strict new controls on the amount of liquid permitted on commercial flights.
2006	de la Concorde overpass collapse	The overpass over Quebec Autoroute 19 near Montreal collapsed. In the accident a nearly 20-metre section of the overpass fell onto traffic below, crushing two vehicles, injuring six people and killing five. The collapse was blamed on design flaws, including a failure by the original engineers to estimate traffic volumes.
2007	California wildfires	A series of separate wildfires burned between March and October 2007. Among the worst in California's history, they injured 160 people and caused fourteen deaths. Approximately 1 million people were evacuated from their homes.
2007	Estonia cyber warfare	A series of highly sophisticated cyber attacks were conducted against Estonian government, industry, and media organizations. The attacks occurred during a dispute between Estonia and Russia over the location of a Soviet-era war memorial in Tallinn, the Estonian capital. Estonia accused Russia of the attack, although no proof of formal Russian involvement has been found.
2007	United Kingdom floods	Major flooding occurred across the United Kingdom in June and July 2007. The flooding was linked to thirteen deaths and is estimated to have caused £6.5 billion in property damage.

Year(s)	Event	Description
2007	Canada Revenue Agency software defect	A software update, called a patch, inadvertently disrupted Canada Revenue Agency's ability to receive electronically filed tax returns for 43 hours. Several more days were required to fix the problem. In total, the agency's software was affected for 10 days, during which time 2,100 temporary employees were laid off without pay and taxpayers were unable to file their taxes online.
2007	I-35W bridge collapse	The I-35W Mississippi River bridge in Minneapolis, Minnesota, collapsed during rush hour. The accident, blamed on a design flaw, injured 145 people and killed thirteen.
2008	Sunrise Propane explosion	There was a series of explosions at the Sunrise Propane facility in Toronto, Ontario. The blasts contributed to the deaths of two people and forced thousands of evacuations from nearby homes. The explosions were caused by a truck-to-truck propane transfer, which Sunrise had previously been barred from performing by the Ontario Technical Standards and Safety Authority.
2008	Conficker computer worm	This computer virus, first discovered in 2008, targets computers running the Microsoft Windows operating system. The origin of the virus is unknown. Conficker is believed to be one of the largest ever computer worm infections, affecting an estimated 9 to 15 million computers around the world.
2009	GhostNet	This cyber-spying operation was discovered in March 2009 and was later found to have infiltrated government, industry, and media networks in 103 countries. The source of the spy network is unknown, although its command and control infrastructure is said to be located in China. GhostNet was blamed for a massive cyber attack against the Canadian government in 2011.

Year(s)	Event	Description
2009–2010	HINI (United States)	An outbreak of influenza A virus subtype HINI was first confirmed in the United States in March 2009. By May 2009, the pandemic had spread to all fifty states. In the United States, the outbreak resulted in 115,318 state-reported confirmed cases of HINI and 3,433 deaths. The end of the pandemic was declared in August 2010.
2009–2010	HINI (Canada)	An outbreak of influenza A virus subtype HINI was first confirmed in Canada in April 2009. By June 2009, the pandemic had spread to all provinces and territories. In Canada, the outbreak resulted in 40,185 laboratory-confirmed cases of HINI, 8,678 hospitalizations, and 428 deaths. The end of the pandemic was declared in August 2010.
2009–2010	HINI (United Kingdom)	An outbreak of influenza A virus subtype HINI was first confirmed in the United Kingdom in April 2009. In the United Kingdom, the outbreak resulted in 28,456 confirmed cases of HINI and 474 deaths. The end of the pandemic was declared in August 2010.
2009–2010	HINI (Australia)	An outbreak of influenza A virus subtype HINI was first confirmed in Australia in May 2009. In Australia the outbreak resulted in 37,484 confirmed cases of HINI and 187 deaths. The end of the pandemic was declared in August 2010.
2010	Eyjafjallajökull eruptions	A series of volcanic events at Eyjafjallajökull, a mountain in Iceland, produced an enormous cloud of ash over northern Europe, causing the greatest disruption to air travel since the Second World War.
2012	Elliot Lake mall collapse	The Algo Centre Mall in Elliot Lake, Ontario, partially collapsed; portions of the rooftop parking deck caved in on the building, injuring twenty and killing two. A technical inquiry into the collapse found that poor waterproofing of the parking lot had allowed water and road salt to leak into the building, causing extensive corrosion of its steel frame.

Year(s)	Event	Description
2013	West, Texas, fertilizer plant explosion	There was a fire and subsequent explosion at the West Fertilizer Company plant in West, Texas. The explosion occurred after firefighters had arrived at the scene, resulting in injuries to 160 to 200 people and fifteen deaths. A technical investigation blamed the company for inadequate chemical storage practices and for failing to notify authorities of the chemicals on site. A criminal investigation later concluded that the initial fire had been intentionally set, although no suspects have been charged.
2013	VIA Rail terrorism plot	Chiheb Esseghaier and Raed Jaser conspired to attack Via Rail passenger trains. Esseghaier, a Tunisian, and Jaser, a stateless person of Palestinian descent, were arrested in April 2013, convicted, and sentenced to life in prison in September 2015.
2013	Royal Artillery Barracks attack	British Army soldier Lee Rigby was murdered near the Royal Artillery Barracks in southeast London by Michael Adebolajo and Michael Adebowale, who said the attack was revenge for the killing of Muslims by the British military. Adebolajo and Adebowale were both found guilty of murder and sentenced to life imprisonment.
2013	Lac-Mégantic explosion	A train carrying crude oil derailed in downtown Lac-Mégantic, Quebec, resulting in the explosion of multiple tank cars. The accident, caused by a brake failure, destroyed more than thirty buildings, released 5.6 million litres of crude oil into the environment, and caused forty-seven deaths.
2013	Toronto floods	Heavy rainfall and subsequent flash flooding in Toronto, Ontario, caused widespread power outages and shut down significant portions of the city's transportation infrastructure. The flooding was later named the costliest disaster in Ontario history, with insured property damages estimated at over $850 million.

Year(s)	Event	Description
2013	Alberta floods	Widespread flooding triggered by heavy rainfall occurred across Alberta in June 2013. Rising waters in several rivers ultimately displaced over 100,000 people, led to over $5 billion in property damage (making it the costliest disaster in Canadian history up to that point), and caused five deaths.
2014	Moncton shootings	A series of shootings targeted at police in Moncton, New Brunswick, was carried out by Justin Bourque, resulting in the death of three Royal Canadian Mounted Police officers and serious injuries to two others. Bourque claimed the attacks were a rebellion against government oppression.
2014	Parliament Hill shootings	A series of shootings in Ottawa, Ontario, was carried out by Michael Zehaf-Bibeau, who had expressed opposition to Canadian foreign policy and a desire to join the civil war in Syria. Zehaf-Bibeau murdered Corporal Nathan Cirillo at the Canadian National War Memorial before entering the Parliament of Canada, where he was killed in a shootout with security personnel.
2014	Sydney hostage crisis	An attack and hostage-taking was carried out in a Sydney café by Man Haron Monis, who had declared allegiance to the Islamic State. After Monis killed a hostage, police raided the café, resulting in the deaths of Monis and an additional hostage.
2014	Sony Pictures hack	The hacking of Sony Pictures using malware resulted in the public release of internal e-mails, salary information, and films. The hack, attributed to a group called the Guardians of Peace, was said to be sponsored by North Korea, allegedly in response to a comedy movie, *The Interview*, about the assassination of Kim Jong-un.

Significant Privatizations in Canada, 1975–2011

The following table lists significant privatizations in Canada between 1975 and 2011. It is adapted from a report by Boardman and Vining (2012). The report defines privatization as "the transfer of a corporate-like entity from government ownership and control to the private sector. It involves the transfer of an on-going business (or service), not just the sale of assets. Following privatization, the primary goal typically becomes profit-maximization" (Boardman and Vining 2012, 2).

Date	Company	Sector	Former owner	Buyer	Proceeds ($M)
1975	Alberta Energy Company	Oil and gas	Alberta (crown corporation)	Two public offerings	75
1985	Northern Transportation Company Ltd.	Marine shipping	Canada (crown corporation)	Inuvialuit/ Nunasi Consortium	53
1986	Saskatchewan Oil and Gas Corp.	Oil and gas	Saskatchewan (crown corporation)	Five public offerings	402
1986	de Havilland Aircraft Canada Ltd.	Airplane manufacturer	Canada (crown corporation)	Boeing	99
1986	Canadian Arsenals Ltd.	Munitions manufacturer	Canada (crown corporation)	SNC Group	5
1986	CN Route (CN subsidiary)	Truck transportation	Canada (crown corporation)	Transport Route Canada Inc.	29

Date	Company	Sector	Former owner	Buyer	Proceeds ($M)
1986	Canadair Ltd.	Air transportation	Canada (crown corporation)	Bombardier Inc.	143
1987	SOQUIP Alberta	Oil and gas	Quebec (crown corporation)	Sceptre Resources Ltd.	195
1987	Northern Canada Power Commission (Yukon)	Electric utility	Canada (crown corporation)	Yukon Power Corp.	76
1987	Teleglobe Canada	Telecommunications	Canada (crown corporation)	Memotec Data Inc.	612
1988	BC Hydro's mainland natural gas division	Natural gas distribution	British Columbia (crown corporation)	Inland Natural gas	741
1988	Saskatchewan Power Corporation's (SaskPower) oil and gas business	Oil and gas	Saskatchewan (crown corporation)	Saskatchewan Oil and Gas (Saskoil)	325
1988	Air Canada	Transportation	Canada (crown corporation)	Two public offerings	708
1988	Northwest Tele Inc. (CN subsidiary)	Telecommunications	Canada (crown corporation)	BCE Inc.	200
1988	Terra Nova Telecommunications Inc. (CN subsidiary)	Telecommunications	Canada (crown corporation)	Newfoundland Telephone Company	170
1988	CNCP Telecom	Telecommunications	Canada (50% owned mixed enterprise)	Canadian Pacific Ltd.	235
1990	Alberta Government Telephones (Telus)	Telecommunications	Alberta (crown corporation)	Two public offerings	1,766

Date	Company	Sector	Former owner	Buyer	Proceeds ($M)
1991	Petro-Canada	Oil and gas	Canada (crown corporation)	Four public offerings	5,693
1991	Nordion International Inc.	Health sciences	Canada (crown corporation)	MDS Health Group Ltd.	165
1992	Novatel's systems business	Telecommunications	Alberta (crown corporation)	Northern Telecom Ltd. (Nortel)	38
1992	Novatel's cellular telephone manufacturing	Mobile telecom	Alberta (crown corporation)	Telexel Holding Ltd.	3
1992	Nova Scotia Power Corp.	Electricity generation	Nova Scotia (crown corporation)	Public offering	816
1992	Suncor	Oil and gas	Mixed enterprise	Public offering	299
1992	Telesat Canada	Satellite communications	Canada (53% owned mixed enterprise)	Alouette Telecommunications Inc	155
1992	CN Shortline in Nova Scotia	Rail shipping	Canada (crown corporation)	RailTex Inc.	20
1992	Co-enerco Resources Ltd.	Oil and gas	Canada (crown corporation)	Two public offerings	75
1993	Syncrude Canada	Oil and gas	Mixed enterprise	Murphy oil (5%)	502
1995	Vencap Equities Alberta	Financial services	Mixed enterprise	Onex	174
1995	CN Exploration (CN subsidiary)	Oil and gas	Canada (crown corporation)	Smart on Resources Ltd.	97
1995	CNR (Canadian National Railway)	Rail shipping	Canada (crown corporation)	Public offering	2,079
1995	Canarctic Shipping Comp.	Maritime shipping	Canada (mixed enterprise)	Fednav Ltd.	0.3

Date	Company	Sector	Former owner	Buyer	Proceeds ($M)
1997	Manitoba Telephone Systems	Telecommunications	Manitoba (crown corporation)	Public offering	860
1998	Theratronics International Ltd.	Health sciences	Canada (crown corporation)	MDS Inc.	15
2002	Ontario Power (four hydroelectric stations)	Electricity generation	Ontario (crown corporation)	Brascan Ltd.	340
2011	AECL's Commercial Division	Nuclear power	Canada (crown corporation)	SNC-Lavalin Group Inc.	15

Notes

INTRODUCTION

1 A forty-eighth person, an employee of emergency services, also died as a result of the event.
2 A seventh person was charged with offences relating to the Fisheries Act.
3 Public Safety Canada captures the chemicals sector as a subsector under the manufacturing sector. In the book we refer to the chemicals subsector of the manufacturing sector simply as the chemicals sector.
4 See appendix 3 for descriptions of these events.
5 The rational approach to risk, in its simplest formulation, evaluates risk significance by multiplying probability by consequence.
6 The term is a reference to the long-held belief that all swans were white because of the absence of any observations of non-white swans until the discovery of Australia – and black swans – in the late seventeenth century.
7 When we mention that we interviewed staff responsible for bridges, we mean major suspension bridges.

CHAPTER TWO

1 Hood's (1998) book won the 1998 Mackenzie Book Prize for the best book in political science.
2 Here, when Renn refers to complex risk, he refers to our state of knowledge about the risk. When we refer to the objective/structural quadrant of Renn's risk rationality diagram (see figure 2.1), we mean organizational complexity, which involves the number of units included in managing a risk, and the relationship between these units.

3 According to Shirky (2008), there are two characteristics of small-world networks. First, small groups are densely connected. In a small group the best pattern of communication is that everyone connects with everyone. Secondly, large groups are sparsely connected. "A Small World network cheats nature by providing a better-than-random trade-off between the number of links required to connect a network, and that network's effectiveness in relaying messages" (Shirky 2008, 215).

4 Hood and colleagues (2001, 37) examined (1) attacks by dangerous dogs outside the home; (2) lung cancer caused by radon gas at home and (3) at the workplace; (4) cancer caused by benzene from vehicle exhaust and (5) at the workplace; (6) attacks on children by pedophiles; (7) injuries and deaths from vehicles on local roads; and (8) health from pesticides in food and (9) in water.

CHAPTER THREE

1 In a survey, only one per cent of Americans did not recognize the Department of Homeland Security. We are not aware of any polls regarding the role of Public Safety Canada.

2 Fusion centers were created in the United States by the Department of Justice and the Department of Homeland Security to promote information sharing between federal agencies and between different orders of government.

CHAPTER FOUR

1 "*Shortline* railways are a fundamental component of the country's rail network, feeding and delivering traffic to and from mainline railways, originating more than 20% of all CN and CPR's freight carload traffic, and moving billions of tonne-kilometres back and forth from Class I railways" (Transport Canada 2012b).

2 See chapter 2 for a discussion of cybernetic control components.

CHAPTER FIVE

1 In French, the Quebec Commission on Workplace Health and Safety is known as la Commission des normes, de l'équité, de la santé et de la sécurité du travail.

2 The CRTI's mandate was recently amalgamated into the Canadian Safety and Security Program (DRDC 2013).

3 Data in the Canadian Disaster Database indicate that fixed site incidents occur approximately as frequently as transit incidents (Quigley and Bisset 2014).

4 Kramer (1999) describes many types of trust, including personal, rules-based, roles-based, and process-based trust. Trust is often confused with other concepts, such as loyalty, for example.

5 These include standards established by the Department of Homeland Security's C-TPAT program, the United Nations Chemical Weapons Convention (Int 61), and the American Institute of Chemical Engineers (Int 59).

6 Beyond the reporting requirements outlined in the previous section, the E2 regulations require that facilities prepare an environmental emergency plan (Int 63). These plans must identity and address the full range of hazards present on site, as well as prevention, preparedness, response, and recovery measures.

7 According to data in the Canadian Disaster Database (Public Safety Canada 2014a), more than half of the chemical incidents in Canada between 1900 and 2008 occurred within the boundary of a population centre (Quigley and Bisset 2014).

8 In general, the federal government stopped promoting best practices for community planning in the early 1980s (Millward 2006, 481). MIACC published several guidelines in the mid-1990s, but they are seldom referenced today (Hosty 2008).

9 Today it is managed by the Canadian Chemical Producers' Association's successor organization, the Chemistry Industry Association of Canada.

10 Some research has found that large firms are generally successful at imposing industry-wide standards on smaller companies (for example, see Engelhardt and Maurer 2012). However, the extent to which these smaller companies actually *commit* to the initiative's principles is in dispute.

11 This is in contrast to a homeostatic approach, in which acceptable-risk thresholds are applied uniformly across the entire system (Hood et al. 2001, 26).

12 Others have raised similar questions about implementation and enforcement at the provincial level. Krajnc, for example, points to the reduction in abatement and enforcement officers at the Ontario

Ministry of Environment as a contributing factor in the 1997 fire at the Plastimet recycling facility in Hamilton (2000, 120). In Alberta, many environmental impact assessments contain large informational gaps, and many fail to consider extreme weather events (Weinhold 2011, A130).

13 In addition to the E2 regulations, these officials enforce the Canadian Environmental Protection Act, 1999, and its forty other regulatory instruments (Environment Canada 2014b).

14 An inputs-based audit focuses on whether companies have the appropriate systems in place, not whether they are achieving desired compliance or environmental protection outcomes (Green and Hrab 2003, 25).

15 For example, each quarter the CEOs of RC member companies meet in six regional leadership groups to discuss performance; the potential embarrassment of reporting to peers that one's company has failed to meet even the minimum standards serves as a compliance motivator (Moffet et al. 2004, 196; see also Conzelmann 2012, 205).

16 Not all chemical companies are members of the Chemistry Industry Association of Canada and the RC initiative.

17 Two of the three audits where follow-up was deemed necessary involved the same company.

CHAPTER SIX

1 In *The Road to Serfdom* (2007), Hayek offers among the most well-known and widely cited defences of the market failure approach. On moral grounds, he justifies a limited role for government in economic decision-making. Hayek argues that central planning inevitably diminishes liberty by directing all human activities according to a single plan, which must privilege some values and preferences above others. Yet even Hayek was not opposed to all forms of government regulation: "To prohibit the use of certain poisonous substances or to require special precautions in their use, to limit working hours or to require certain sanitary arrangements, is fully compatible with the preservation of competition. The only question here is whether in the particular instance the advantages gained are greater than the social costs which they impose. Nor is the preservation of competition incompatible with an extensive system of social services – so long as the organization of these services is not designed in such a way as to make competition ineffective over wide fields" (86–7).

2 The Conservatives in Britain under Margaret Thatcher, for example.

3 In economic terms, these reasons can be grouped into two categories: market power and nonexistence of markets (Rosen et al. 2012). The first category, market power, occurs when consumers or companies can affect market prices. The second category, nonexistence of markets, involves cases where markets for certain goods or services fail to emerge at all (Rosen et al. 2012, 37). This may happen because of information asymmetries, that is, situations where one side of a transaction is better informed than the other. Market nonexistence is also a problem in the case of externalities and public goods.

4 Environment Canada's E2 database shows only the addresses of regulated companies.

5 The term *cybersecurity* refers to a diverse range of strategies aimed at mitigating an even broader range of malicious cyber activities, such as interstate cyber warfare, cyber terrorism, "hacktivism," and corporate intellectual property theft (Quigley, Burns, and Stallard 2013). Despite this fact, only one interview participant specified what they meant by the term *cybersecurity*; other participants used it in a general sense.

6 In 1992, an incident at the Westray coal mine in Nova Scotia caused the death of twenty-six miners. The subsequent public inquiry revealed "an almost wilful avoidance of basic safety by the mine operator coupled with a 'do nothing' attitude by the provincial safety inspector overseeing the working conditions at the mine" (Creedy et al. 2005, 376).

7 In a comprehensive study of Canadian criminal laws relating to corporate crime, Bittle and Snider (2011) note that between 2004 and 2010 there were only three charges and one conviction under the new provisions. They argue that Bill C-45 and other attempts to criminalize corporate negligence have been undermined by the prevailing "consensual/cooperative" model of corporate regulation, which is animated by the "erroneous belief that corporations will self-regulate under the influence of market forces" (Bittle and Snider 2011, 380). In addition, a new consulting market has arisen in Canada, in which lawyers and occupational safety experts advise companies on how to avoid responsibility under the Westray amendments, effectively non-criminalizing workplace accidents (Bittle and Snider 2011, 381).

8 Despite these challenges, some initial efforts have been made. The US Army Corps of Engineers, for example, estimates that the return on investment for its projects that strengthen CI is generally 8 to 1. Still, a broader quantification of the value of CI to society in general remains elusive.

CHAPTER SEVEN

1 A study by Dow Chemical at around the same time found that within 6 km of Dow's plants, people held opinions about the company that differed from their opinions about the industry as a whole. Beyond 6 km, people's image of Dow was influenced by their views on the industry as a whole (Moffet et al. 2004, 177).

2 According to the International Risk Governance Council framework (Renn 2008), uncertainty associated with fracking may contribute to risks, perhaps in the form of civil unrest, stemming from public distrust or hesitation regarding its perceived hazards.

3 A related concern is the need to balance trade-offs between safety and security. The potential benefits of improving public awareness must be weighed against the risk of inadvertently providing to malicious actors sensitive details about CI. Concern about this issue was prominent after 9/11, when it was determined that the previous decade's push for online transparency had made available on the Internet "details about public utilities and nuclear plants, blueprints for public buildings, and the design structures of bridges and tunnels, as well as storage of chemical and hazardous materials" (Feinberg 2002, 272).

4 Edelman (n.d.) defines these media thus. Traditional media: "the traditional delivery vehicles of print or broadcast"; hybrid media: "the dot.com versions of traditional media and media that is born digital like the *Huffington Post*"; social media: "includes Facebook, Twitter feeds and YouTube channels"; owned media: "includes a brand or company's website and apps – vitally important because every company should be a media company."

5 For example, the government of Spain lost its re-election bid following the Madrid train bombing (Powell 2016). On the other hand, the mayor of New Orleans was re-elected following Hurricane Katrina (Lay 2009). Similarly, the mayor of New York City was named *Time* magazine's Person of the Year after 9/11 (Pooley 2001).

6 While the Canadian government described the Ottawa shooting as an act of terrorism, opposition parties framed the issue as one of mental health (Smith 2014).

CHAPTER NINE

1 Formal responsibility for health care in Canada is shared by the federal, provincial, and territorial governments. Each provincial and

territorial government has different institutional arrangements, which may include municipalities. When we refer to *governments*, we are referring to federal and provincial governments (including municipal arrangements). When we refer to *government*, we are referring to the concept of governing. For the media analysis in this chapter, *government* also refers to federal government health departments (such as PHAC) or provincial health departments. See appendix 1 for additional notes.

2 Broadsheets are a class of newspaper that covers issues in depth and with greater intellectual authority than tabloid newspapers. We selected the most widely distributed broadsheets, not newspapers. This makes a difference in the United Kingdom (i.e., the *Daily Telegraph* vs. the *Sun*).

3 It has been disputed whether or not the 1976 vaccine caused death (Sencer and Millar 2006).

4 For the media analysis in this chapter, *health sector* refers to doctors, nurses, and hospital staff.

5 *Orders of government* refer to, in Canada, federal, provincial, or municipal government, in Australia, federal, state, and municipal government, and in the United Kingdom, central, devolved, and city.

6 A 6-year-old-girl from Brampton, Ontario (whose name was never released to the media) was the first child to die from H1N1 in Canada (Boyle 2009).

7 People do not compare risks easily. For instance, accidents, cancer, congenital malformations/deformations, assault/homicide, heart diseases, intentional self-harm, cerebrovascular diseases, and septicemia all ranked higher as causes of mortality for youth (ages 1–14 years) in Canada in 2008 than influenza/pneumonia (Statistics Canada 2012).

CHAPTER TEN

1 For example, in Canada, strict party discipline and centralization of power in the Office of the Prime Minister mean the primary relationships for Canadian interest groups are with the executive and administrative arms of government, not with individual legislators. Similarly, strict campaign finance laws mean Canadian candidates and parties are less reliant on donations to fund election campaigns than their American counterparts (Young 2004).

2 In the United States and Europe, major chemical companies enjoy similar powers and have long exerted influence over regulatory policy.

Following 9/11, for example, the American chemical industry was successful in preventing the passage of legislation forcing stricter security standards on chemical producers (Karruthers and Hild 2004). Subsequent regulatory changes in the United States, including development of the Chemical Facility Anti-Terrorism Standards program, have taken place following consultation and collaboration with industry (Int 68).

3 Seventy-five per cent of Canada's chemicals exports are to the United States (Industry Canada 2015).

4 Environment Canada implies that pressure from the United States played a role in the introduction of the E2 regulations, noting on its website that the regulations stemmed from "threat assessments conducted in Canada and the United States" following 11 September 2001 (Environment Canada 2002).

5 Although often addressed in the context of developing countries, which may face regular interruptions in access to key inputs, disruption of the chemical supply is nonetheless also a concern for Canadian water utilities as a result of black swan threats.

6 The literature disagrees about the degree of competition among airports. Until the 1980s, the prevailing view was that airports are natural monopolies, enjoying structural advantages that prevent competitors from entering the market. Deregulation in the airline industry has led some academics to re-evaluate this position, with airport costs emerging as a key price determinant for low-cost airlines (Monteiro 2014). On the other hand, airports continue to enjoy considerable market share at the local level, and consumer behaviour research indicates that people are unlikely to use a different, more distant airport, if their local airport raises fees (IATA 2013).

7 The two Class 1 freight carriers, CN and CP, make up over eighty per cent of the Canadian freight rail industry (Cairns 2015).

8 Bridges are generally monopolistic and do not engage in traditional market competition. This is not universally true. The Ambassador Bridge connecting Windsor and Detroit will face competition from the Gordie Howe International Bridge once its construction is complete (Diebel 2016). But most bridges are natural monopolies that operate in relative isolation from one another.

9 This is true of chemical policy in general (i.e., not just as it pertains to safety and security), where constitutional ambiguity has produced a contested and multi-layered regulatory space (Edge 2012); consider, for example, that at present there is no single system in place that

articulates the regulatory situation everywhere in Canada (Eco-Efficiency Centre 2008; Ontario Ministry of Environment 2007).

CHAPTER ELEVEN

1 For additional notes on cultural theory, please see the discussion in chapter 2.
2 Command and control is synonymous with hierarchical bureaucracies.

CHAPTER TWELVE

1 The collapse of B P would have been devastating for the U K economy as a whole because many people in the United Kingdom have part of their pension invested in B P stock. About 1.5 per cent of U K pension industry money was invested in B P shares, which had plummeted in value (Lawrence and Davies 2015).

References

Adams, J. 1995. *Risk*. London: UCL Press.

Adler, J.H. 1996. "Rent Seeking Behind the Green Curtain." *Regulation* 19(4): 26–34.

Aggarwal, V.K. 1998. *Institutional Designs for a Complex World: Bargaining, Linkages and Nesting*. Ithaca, NY: Cornell University Press.

Agranoff, R. 2007. *Managing within Networks: Adding Value to Public Organizations*. Washington, DC: Georgetown University Press.

Agranoff, R. 2008. "Enhancing Performance through Public Sector Networks: Mobilizing Human Capital in Communities of Practice." *Public Performance & Management Review* 31(3): 320–47.

Ahonen, A., and T. Kallio. 2009. "On the Cultural Locus of Management Theory Industry: Perspectives from Autocommunication." *Management and Organizational History* 4(4): 427–43.

Aldrich, D.P. 2013. "A Normal Accident or a Sea-Change? Nuclear Host Communities Respond to the 3/11 Disaster." *Japanese Journal of Political Science* 14(2): 261–76.

Alhakami, A.S., and P. Slovic. 1994. "A Psychological Study of the Inverse Relationship between Perceived Risk and Perceived Benefit." *Risk Analysis* 14(6): 1085–96.

Alp, E. 2004. "Hand in Hand: An Informed Look at the Relationship between Risk-Management and the New Emergency Response Planning Regulations under the Canadian Environmental Protection Act, Section 200." *Canadian Chemical News* 56(2): 11–13. http://www.cheminst.ca/sites/default/files/pdfs/ACCN/BackIssues/2004%20-%2002%20February.pdf

Alphonso, C. 2010. "$2-billion Mass Flu Immunization Program a Bust, Figures Reveal." *Globe and Mail*, 3 Jun. http://www.theglobeandmail.

com/news/national/2-billion-mass-flu-immunization-program-a-bust-figures-reveal/article1372103/

Alphonso, C., and G. Galloway. 2009. "Flu Disproportionately Targets the Young and Healthy." *Globe and Mail*, 17 July. http://www.theglobeand mail.com/news/national/flu-disproportionately-targets-the-young-and-healthy/article4289098/

Alphonso, C., and T.T. Ha. 2009. "Expecting Flu Assistance, Reserves Get Body Bags from Ottawa." *Globe and Mail*, 16 September. http://www. theglobeandmail.com/news/politics/expecting-flu-assistance-reserves-get-body-bags-from-ottawa/article1202910/

Alphonso, C., L. Priest, and R. Matas. 2009. "Flu-shot Clinics Struggle to Keep Up with Demand." *Globe and Mail*, 29 October. http://www.the globeandmail.com/life/health-and-fitness/health/conditions/flu-shot-clinics-struggle-to-keep-up-with-demand/article4215191/

Alter, K.J., and S. Meunier. 2009. "The Politics of International Regime Complexity." *Perspectives on Politics* 7(1): 13–24.

Ancu, M., and R. Cozma. 2009. "MySpace Politics: Uses and gratifications of befriending candidates." *Journal of Broadcasting & Electronic Media* 53(4): 567–83.

Angus Reid Institute. 2015a. *Syrian Refugee Resettlement: Tight Timelines are Key Driver of Opposition to Ottawa's New Year Plan.* http:// angusreid.org/refugee-resettlement/

Angus Reid Institute. 2015b. *Mission against ISIS: Three-in-five Canadians Say Government Should Maintain or Increase Bombing.* http://angusreid.org/canada-isis-mission-november/

Annis, R. 2014. "Lac Mégantic Mayor Wants Oil Train Shipments to Resume." *Vancouver Observer*, 14 March. http://www.vancouver observer.com/news/lac-m%C3%83%C2%A9gantic-mayor-wants-oil-train-shipments-resume?page=0,0

Aristotle, O., and G.A. Kennedy. 1991. *On Rhetoric: A Theory of Civic Discourse.* New York: Oxford University Press.

Arora, A. 1997. "Patents, Licensing, and Market Structure in the Chemical Industry." *Research Policy* 26(4): 391–403.

Arrow, K.J. 1971. *Essays in the Theory of Risk Bearing.* Chicago: Markham Publishing.

Ashford, N.A., and G.R. Heaton. 1983. "Regulation and Technological Innovation in the Chemical Industry." *Law and Contemporary Problems* 46(3): 109–60.

Atkins, E., and V. Stevenson. 2015. "Six Former Railway Employees Charged in Lac-Mégantic Disaster." *Globe and Mail*, 22 June. http://

www.theglobeandmail.com/news/national/ottawa-says-its-laying-new-charges-in-lac-megantic-derailment/article25055238/

Attorney-General's Department. Government of Australia. 2017. *Trusted Information Sharing Network*. http://www.tisn.gov.au/Pages/default.aspx

Aucoin, P. 1998. "Restructuring Government for the Management and Delivery of Public Services." In *Taking Stock: Assessing Public Sector Reforms*, edited by B. Guy Peters, Donald J. Savoie, and Canadian Centre for Management Development, 310–47. Montreal: McGill-Queen's University Press.

Auditor General of British Columbia, Office of the. 2014. *Catastrophic Earthquake Preparedness*. https://www.bcauditor.com/sites/default/files/publications/2014/report_15/report/OAG%20Catastrophic%20Earthquake_FINAL.pdf

Auditor General of Canada, Office of the. 2009. *2009 Fall Report of the Auditor General of Canada. Chapter 7 – Emergency Management – Public Safety Canada*. http://www.oag-bvg.gc.ca/internet/English/parl_oag_200911_07_e_33208.html

Auditor General of Canada, Office of the. 2011. *2011 December Report of the Commissioner of the Environment and Sustainable Development. Chapter 3 – Enforcing the Canadian Environmental Protection Act, 1999*. http://www.oag-bvg.gc.ca/internet/English/parl_cesd_201112_03_e_36031.html

Auditor General of Canada, Office of the. 2012a. *2012 Spring Report of the Auditor General of Canada*. http://www.oag-bvg.gc.ca/internet/English/parl_oag_201204_05_e_36469.html

Auditor General of Canada, Office of the. 2012b. *Report of the Auditor General of Canada to the House of Commons*. http://www.oag-bvg.gc.ca/internet/English/parl_oag_201210_e_37321.html

Auditor General of Canada, Office of the. 2013. *Fall Report of the Auditor General of Canada*. http://www.oagbvg.gc.ca/internet/English/parl_oag_201311_e_38780.html

Auditor General of Manitoba, Office of the. 2016. *Management of Provincial Bridges*. http://www.oag.mb.ca/wp-content/uploads/2016/07/BRIDGESWEBVERSIONJuly2016.pdf

Auditor General of Newfoundland and Labrador, Office of the. 2011. *Report of the Auditor General to the House of Assembly*. http://www.ag.gov.nl.ca/ag/annualReports/2011AnnualReport/AR2011.pdf

Auditor General of Nova Scotia, Office of the. 2016. *Report to the House of Assembly*. https://www.oag-ns.ca/sites/default/files/publications/Full%20Report.pdf

Auerswald, P.E., L.M. Branscomb, T.M. La Porte, and E.O. Michel-Kerjan, eds. 2006. *Seeds of Disaster, Roots of Response*. Cambridge: Cambridge University Press.

Australia. Department of Agriculture, Fisheries and Forestry. 2012. *Resilience in the Australian Food Supply Chain*. Canberra: Commonwealth of Australia. http://www.tisn.gov.au/Documents/ Resilience%20in%20the%20Australian%20food %20supply%20 chain%20-%20PDF%20copy%20for%20web.PDF

Australian Government. 2010. *Cyber Security Strategy*. https://www. ag.gov.au/RightsAndProtections/CyberSecurity/Documents/AG%20 Cyber%20Security%20Strategy%20-%20for%20website.pdf

Aviram, A. 2005. "Network Responses to Network Threats: The Evolution into Private Cybersecurity Associations." In *The Law and Economics of Cybersecurity*, edited by M.F. Grady and F. Parisi, 143–92. New York: Cambridge University Press.

Aviram, A., and A. Tor. 2004a. *Information Sharing on Critical Infrastructure Industries: Understanding the Behavioral and Economic Impediments*. George Mason Law & Economics Research Paper No. 03-30.

Aviram, A., and A. Tor. 2004b. "Overcoming Impediments to Information Sharing." *Alabama Law Review* 55: 231.

Bailey, S. 2010. "Newfoundland Welcomes Military Help Delivering Food, Water After Hurricane Igor." *Western Star*, 24 September. http://www. thewesternstar.com/News/Local/2010-09-24/article-1791422/ Newfoundland-welcomes-military-help-delivering-food,-water-after-hurricane-Igor/1

Baker, S. 2010. *Skating on Stilts: Why We Aren't Stopping Tomorrow's Terrorism*. Hoover Institution Press Publication No. 591. Stanford, CA: Hoover Institution at Leland Stanford Junior University.

Bakvis, H., and L. Juillet. 2004. *The Horizontal Challenge: Line Departments, Central Agencies and Leadership*. Ottawa: Canada School of Public Service.

Balmer, J.M.T. 2010. "The BP Deepwater Horizon Debacle and Corporate Brand Exuberance." *Journal of Brand Management* 18: 97–104.

Barbalet, J. 2009. "A Characterization of Trust, and its Consequences." *Theory and Society* 38(4): 367–82.

Barber, J. 2008. "City Zoned out on Regulation of its Propane Industry." *Globe & Mail*, 2 August.

Barger, C. 2008. *Cleburn County and Its People*. Vol. 2. Bloomington, IN: Author House.

Barnes, M.D., C.L. Hanson, L.M.B. Novilla, A.T. Meacham, E. McIntyre, and B.C. Erikson. 2008. "Analysis of Media Agenda Setting During and After Hurricane Katrina: Implications for Emergency Preparedness, Disasters Response, and Disaster Policy." *American Journal of Public Health* 98(4): 604–10.

Barry, J. 2004. *The Great Influenza: The Story of the Deadliest Pandemic in History*. London: Penguin Books.

Beaudette, R., and J. Marquis. 2014. *Rapport d'enquête: Explosion survenue le 8 novembre 2012 à l'entreprise Neptune Technologies et Bioressources inc. 795, rue Pépin à Sherbrooke, Commission des normes, de l'équité, de la santé et de la sécurité du travail, Gouvernement du Québec*. http://www.centredoc.csst.qc.ca/pdf/ed004016.pdf

Belanger, J., P. Topalovic, G. Krantzberg, and J. West. 2009. "Responsible Care: History & Development." http://www.eng.mcmaster.ca/civil/facultypages/krantz11.pdf

Benedict, C. 1996. *Bubonic Plague in Nineteenth-Century China*. Palo Alto, CA: Stanford University Press.

Bentham, J. 1825. *A Treatise on Judicial Evidence*. Oxford: J.W. Paget.

Berglund, J., and A. Werr. 2000. "The Invincible Character of Management Consulting Rhetoric: How One Blends Incommensurates While Keeping Them Apart." *Organization* 7(4): 633–55.

Bertot, J.C., P.T. Jaeger, and J.M. Grimes. 2010. "Using ICTs to Create a Culture of Transparency: E-government and social media as openness and anti-corruption tools for societies." *Government Information Quarterly* 27(3): 264–71.

Betsch, T., and D. Pohl. 2002. "Tversky and Kahneman's Availability Approach to Frequency Judgement: A Critical Analysis." In *Etc. – Frequency Processing and Cognition*, edited by P. Sedlmeier and T. Betsch, 109–19. Oxford: Oxford University Press.

Bittle, S., and L. Snider. 2011. "'Moral Panics' Deflected: The Failed Legislative Response To Canada's Safety Crimes And Markets Fraud Legislation." *Crime, Law and Social Change* 56(4): 373–87.

Blatchford, A. 2016. "Lac-Megantic Victims Quietly Paid $75-million Settlement by Feds." *Toronto Sun*, 2 May. http://www.torontosun.com/2016/05/02/lac-megantic-victims-quietly-paid-75-million-settlement-by-feds

Bliss, J. 2012. "U.S. Backs off All-Cargo Scanning Goal with Inspections at 4%." *Bloomberg*, 13 August. https://www.bloomberg.com/news/articles/2012-08-13/u-s-backs-off-all-cargo-scanning-goal-with-inspections-at-4-

Boardman, A.E., and A. Vining. 2012. "A Review and Assessment of Privatization in Canada." Calgary: University of Calgary, School of Public Policy. https://www.policyschool.ca/wp-content/uploads/2016/03/boardman-vining-privatization.pdf

Boardman, M. 2005. "Known Unknowns: The Illusion of Terrorism Insurance." *Georgetown Law Journal* 93(3): 783–844.

Boin, A., and A. McConnell. 2007. "Preparing for Critical Infrastructure Breakdowns: The Limits of Crisis Management and the Need for Resilience." *Journal of Contingencies and Crisis Management* 15(1): 50–9.

Born, P., and W.K. Viscusi. 2006. "The Catastrophic Effects of Natural Disasters on Insurance Markets." *Journal of Risk and Uncertainty* 33(1–2): 55–72.

Botelho, G. 2013. "Timeline: The Boston Marathon Bombing, Manhunt and Investigation." *CNN News*, 2 May. http://www.cnn.com/2013/05/01/justice/boston-marathon-timeline/

Boyd, D.M., and N.B. Ellison. 2007. "Social Network Sites: Definition, History, and Scholarship." *Journal of Computer-Mediated Communication* 13(1): 210–30.

Boyle, P., and C. O Grádo. 1986. "Fertility Trends, Excess Mortality, and the Great Irish Famine." *Demography* 23(4): 543–62.

Boyle, T. 2009. "Swine Flu Kills Brampton Girl, 6, in 24 Hours." *Toronto Star*, 23 June. https://www.thestar.com/life/health_wellness/2009/06/23/swine_flu_kills_brampton_girl_6_in_24_hrs.html

Brenot, J., S. Bonnefous, and C. Marris. 1998. "Testing the Cultural Theory of Risk in France." *Risk Analysis* 18(6): 729–39.

Brooks, M.R. 2004. "The Governance Structure of Ports." *Review of Network Economics* 3(2): 68–183.

Brooks, M.R. 2007. "Port Devolution and Governance in Canada." *Research in Transportation Economics* 17: 237-57.

Brooks, M.R. 2008. *North American Freight Transportation*. Northampton, UK: Edward Elgar.

Brown, A. 2007. "Strong Language on Black Swans." *American Statistician* 61(3): 195–7.

Brubaker, E. 2003. "Revisiting Water and Wastewater Utility Privatization." Prepared for the Government of Ontario Panel on the Role of Government (presentation, Public Goals, Private Means Research Colloquium, Faculty of Law, University of Toronto).

Bruns, A., T. Highfield, and R.A. Lind. 2012. "Blogs, Twitter, and Breaking News: The Produsage of Citizen Journalism." In *Produsing Theory in a*

Digital World, edited by R.A. Lind, 15–32. New York: Peter Lang Publishing.

Buncefield Major Incident Investigation Board. 2008. *The Buncefield Incident: 11 December 2005 (The Fnal Report)*. Vol. 1. http://www.hse.gov.uk/comah/buncefield/miib-final-volume1.pdf

Burger, J., M. Gochfeld, C. Jeitner, T. Pittfield, and M. Donio. 2013. "Trusted Information Sources Used During and After Superstorm Sandy: TV and Radio Were Used More Often Than Social Media." *Journal of Toxicology and Environmental Health, Part A* 76(20): 1138–50.

Burges, D. 2012. *Cargo Theft, Loss Prevention, and Supply Chain Security*. Waltham, MA: Butterworth-Heinemann.

Burgess, D., M. Burgess, and J. Leask. 2006. "The MMR Vaccination and Autism Controversy in United Kingdom 1998–2005: Inevitable community outrage or a failure of risk communication?" *Vaccine* 24: 3921–8. http://www.petersandman.com/articles/BurgessLeask.pdf

Burns, C. 2012. "Implicit and Explicit Risk Perception" (presentation, European Academy of Occupational Health Psychology, Zurich, Switzerland, 11–13 April 2012).

Burns, M.G. 2013. "Estimating the Impact of Maritime Security: Financial tradeoffs between Security and Efficiency." *Journal of Transportation Security* 6(4): 329–38.

Busseri, T. 2012. "It's Time to Take Cybersecurity Seriously." *Wired*, 12 March. http://www.wired.com/2012/03/opinion-busseri-cybersecurity/

C-TPAT. 2017. *C-TPAT: Customs–trade Partnership against Terrorism*. www.cbp.gov/border-security/ports-entry/cargo-security/c-tpat-customs-trade-partnership-against-terrorism

Cairns, M. 2015. *Staying on the Right Track: A Review of Canadian Freight Rail Policy*. Ottawa: Macdonald-Laurier Institute. http://www.macdonaldlaurier.ca/files/pdf/MLIRailPolicyPaper02-15-WebReady.pdf

Calman, K.C. 2002. "Communication of Risk: Choice, Consent, and Trust." *Lancet* 360(9327): 166–8.

Campbell, A. 2004. "The SARS Commission Interim Report: SARS and Public Health in Ontario." *Biosecurity and Bioterrorism: Biodefense Strategy, Practice, and Science* 2(2): 118–26.

Canada Marine Act, Statutes of Canada. 1998, c. 10. http://laws-lois.justice.gc.ca/eng/acts/c-6.7/

Canadian Aviation Regulations. 2012, SOR/96-433. http://www.tc.gc.ca/eng/civilaviation/regserv/cars/menu.htm

Canadian Centre for Occupational Health and Safety. 2015. "OSH Answer Fact Sheets: Acetone." https://www.ccohs.ca/oshanswers/chemicals/chem_profiles/acetone.html

Canadian Medical Association, College of Family Physicians of Canada, and National Specialty Society of Community Care. 2010. *Lessons from the Frontlines: A Collaborative Report on H1N1*. Ottawa: Canadian Medical Association, College of Family Physicians of Canada, and National Specialty Society of Community Care.

Canadian Nurses Association. 2016. "Nursing Statistics." https://www.cna-aiic.ca/en/download-buy/nursing-statistics

Canadian Pharmacists Association. 2009. "Canadians Trust Doctors and Pharmacists Most." http://www.newswire.ca/news-releases/canadians-trust-doctors-and-pharmacists-most-538604251.html

Canadian Press. 2013. "Feds: Lac-Megantic Could Be Worst Train Disaster in Canadian History." *Maclean's*, 12 July. http://www.macleans.ca/news/feds-lac-megantic-could-be-worst-train-disaster-in-canadian-history/

Canadian Press. 2014. "Man Who Brought Pipe Bomb to Edmonton Airport Blasted by Judge." *Toronto Star*, 16 January. http://www.thestar.com/news/canada/2014/01/16/edmonton_airport_staff_let_go_teen_found_with_explosive.html

Canadian Trucking Alliance. 2016. "About the CTA." http://cantruck.ca/about-the-cta/

Capelle-Blancard, G., and M.A. Laguna. 2010. "How Does the Stock Market Respond to Chemical Disasters?" *Journal of Environmental Economics and Management* 59(2): 192–205.

Carpentier, C., J. L'Her, and J. Suret. 2013. "Private Investment in Small Public Entities." *Small Business Economics* 41(1): 149–68.

Carpentier, C., and J.M. Suret. 2013. "Stock Market and Deterrence Effect: A Long-Run Analysis of Major Environmental and Non-Environmental Disasters." https://papers.ssrn.com/sol3/papers.cfm?abstract_id=2253272

Caruson, K., and S. MacManus. 2011. "Gauging Disaster Vulnerabilities at the Local Level: Divergence and Convergence in an 'All-hazards' System." *Administration & Society* 43(3): 346–71.

Casler, J.G. 2014. "Revisiting NASA as a High Reliability Organization." *Public Organization Review* 14(2): 229–44.

Cathcart, T., and D.M. Klein. 2007. *Aristotle and an Aardvark Go to Washington*. New York: Abrams Image.

Cavelty, M.D. 2007. "Cyber-terror–Looming Threat or Phantom Menace? The framing of the US cyber-threat debate." *Journal of Information Technology & Politics* 4(1): 19–36.

CBC News. 2009. "Appeal for Calm as Vaccination Continues." 29 October. http://www.cbc.ca/news/canada/montreal/appeal-for-calm-as-vaccination-continues-1.841083

CBC News. 2012. "Quebec Factory in Blast Had Too Much Acetone, Ministry Says." 17 November. http://www.cbc.ca/news/canada/montreal/quebec-factory-in-blast-had-too-much-acetone-ministry-says-1.1171419

CBC News. 2013. "Rehtaeh Parson's Family Has 'Heartfelt' Talk with Harper." http://www.cbc.ca/news/canada/nova-scotia/rehtaeh-parsons-s-family-has-heartfelt-talk-with-harper-1.1310239

CBC News. 2014. "Lac-Mégantic Families Welcome Charges against MM&A Railway Workers." 13 May. http://www.cbc.ca/news/canada/montreal/lac-m%C3%A9gantic-families-welcome-charges-against-mm-a-railway-workers-1.2640891

CBC News. 2015. Full interview with Transport Minister Lisa Raitt. 30 June. http://www.cbc.ca/player/play/2670837141

CBC News. 2016. "Quebecers Leery of Pipeline Safety: Poll." 14 March. http://www.cbc.ca/news/canada/montreal/quebecers-poll-pipeline-safety-1.3489939

Centre for the Protection of National Infrastructure. 2017. CPNI [website]. Accessed 7 July 2017. http://www.cpni.gov.uk/

Chang, S.E., J.E. Taylor, K.J. Elwood, E. Seville, D. Brunsdon, and M. Gartner. 2014. "Urban disaster Recovery in Christchurch: The central business district cordon and other critical decisions." *Earthquake Spectra* 30(1): 513–32.

Chemical Safety and Hazards Investigations Board. 2013. "Chemical Safety Board Ongoing Investigation Emphasizes Lack of Protection for Communities at Risk from Ammonium Nitrate Storage Facilities; Finds Lack of Regulation at All Levels of Government." http://www.csb.gov/chemical-safety-board-ongoing-investigation-emphasizes-lack-of-protection-for-communities-at-risk-from-ammonium-nitrate-storage-facilities-finds-lack-of-regulation-at-all-levels-of-government-/

Chertoff, M. 2009. "Seven Questions for Michael Chertoff." *The CIP Exchange*, Spring. http://cip.management.dal.ca/?page_id=9

Chiang, C.F., and B. Knight. 2011. "Media Bias and Influence: Evidence from Newspaper Endorsements." *Review of Economic Studies* 78(3): 795–820.

Chin, J. 2015. "Andrew Coyne Resigns *National Post* Executive Editorials Role." *Huffington Post*, 19 October. http://www.huffingtonpost.ca/2015/10/19/andrew-coyne-resigns-national-post_n_8332116.html

Chung, E. 2009. "Disasters May Catch Canada Unprepared: AG Report." *CBC News*, 3 November. http://www.cbc.ca/amp/1.785134

CIAC (Chemistry Industry Association of Canada). n.d. "Responsible Care Codes." http://www.canadianchemistry.ca/responsible_care/index.php/en/responsible-carecodes

CIAC (Chemistry Industry Association of Canada). 2009. "About CIAC's National Advisory Panel." http://www.canadianchemistry.ca/responsible_care/index.php/en/national-advisorypanel

CIAC (Chemistry Industry Association of Canada). 2010. "Responsible Care Commitments." http://members.canadianchemistry.ca/Portals/0/site%20files/site%20library/responsi ble%20care/RC%20Guide/codes%20and%20committments/Commitments-EN%20- %20non-booklet.pdf

CIAC (Chemistry Industry Association of Canada). 2013. "Responsible Care Verification Report: Rhodia Canada Inc. October 30–31." http://www.canadianchemistry.ca/responsible_care/uploads/2013_Rhodia.pdf

CIAC (Chemistry Industry Association of Canada). 2014a. "Responsible Care Verification Audits." http://www.canadianchemistry.ca/responsible_care/index.php/en/responsible-care-verification-reports/year/2014

CIAC (Chemistry Industry Association of Canada). 2014b. "2014 Year-end Survey of Business Conditions." http://www.canadianchemistry.ca/library/uploads/year_end_report_2014.pdf

CIAC (Chemistry Industry Association of Canada). 2015. "Statistical Review of the Canadian Chemical Manufacturing Sector: 2015 Executive Summary." http://www.canadianchemistry.ca/library/magazine/CIAC_SummaryStats2015_eng_web.pdf

CIAC (Chemistry Industry Association of Canada). 2016. "2015 Statistical Review." http://www.canadianchemistry.ca/library/uploads/Statistical_Review_2015_ENG.pdf

Clark, T., and G. Salaman. 1996. "The Management Guru as Organizational Witchdoctor." *Organization* 3(1): 85–107.

Clarke, L. 2005. *Worst Cases: Terror and Catastrophe in the Popular Imagination*. Chicago: University of Chicago Press.

Clarke, M.C., and R.L. Payne. 1997. "The Nature and Structure of Workers' Trust in Management." *Journal of Organisational Behaviour* 18(3): 205–24.

Clarke, R. 2012. "Cyber Attacks Can Spark Real Wars." *Wall Street Journal*, 16 February. http://www.wsj.com/articles/SB10001424052970204883304577219543897943980

Clarke, R.A., and R.K. Knake. 2010. *Cyber War: The Next Threat to National Security and What to Do About It.* Toronto: Harper Collins Canada.

Cobb, R.W., and D.M. Primo. 2003. *The Plane Truth.* Washington, DC: Brookings Institution Press.

Cohen, S. 1972. *Folk Devils and Moral Panics.* London: MacGibbon and Kee.

Cohen, T. 2012. "Stakeholders Cry Foul as Feds Cut Funding for Emergency Preparedness." *Canada.com.* http://www.canada.com/news/Stakeh olders+foul+feds+funding+emergency+preparedness/6814690/story.html

Colarik, A., and L. Janczewski. 2012. "Establishing Cyber Warfare Doctrine." *Journal of Strategic Security* 5(1): 31–48.

Combs, B., and P. Slovic. 1979. "Causes of Death: Biased Newspaper Coverage and Biased Judgements." *Journalism Quarterly* 56: 837–43.

Comfort, L. 2002. "Rethinking Security: Organizational Fragility in Extreme Events." *Public Administration Review* 62(1): 98–107.

Comfort, L.K., B. McAdoo, P. Sweeney, S. Stebbins, M.D. Siciliano, L.J. Huggins, T. Serrant, et al. 2011. "Transition from Response to Recovery: A Knowledge Commons to Support Decision Making Following the 12 January 2010 Haiti Earthquake." *Earthquake Spectra* 27(S1): S411–S430.

Comfort, L.K., and A. Okada. 2013. "Emergent Leadership in Extreme Events: A Knowledge Commons for Sustainable Communities." *International Review of Public Administration* 18(1): 61–77.

Conabree, D. 2011. "Intellectual Capital and E-Collaboration: The Hidden Cost of the Status Quo." *FMI Journal* 23(1): 11–12.

Conference Board of Canada. 2013. *Canada's Chemical Industry: Canadian Industrial Profile: Winter 2013.* Ottawa: Conference Board of Canada.

Congleton, R.D., and F. Bose. 2010. "The Rise of the Modern Welfare State, Ideology, Institutions and Income Security: Analysis and Evidence." *Public Choice* 144(3-4): 535-55.

Conway, B.A., K. Kenski, and D. Wang. 2013. "Twitter Use by Presidential Primary Candidates during the 2012 Campaign." *American Behavioral Scientist* 57(11): 1596–610.

Conzelmann, T. 2012. "A Procedural Approach to the Design of Voluntary Clubs: Negotiating the Responsible Care Global Charter." *Socio-Economic Review* 10(1), 193–214. doi:10.1093/ser/mwr031

Coombs, W.T., and J.S. Holladay. 2012. "The Paracrisis: The Challenges Created by Publicly Managing Crisis Prevention." *Public Relations Review* 38(3): 408–15.

Coughlin, C. 2010. "Cyber Guards or Soldiers: Which Do We Need Most?" *Daily Telegraph*, 14 October. http://www.telegraph.co.uk/comment/columnists/concoughlin/8063120/Cyber-guards-or-soldiers-which-do-we-need-most.html

Cox, S., and T. Cox. 1991. "The Structure of Employee Attitudes to Safety: A European Example." *Work & Stress* 5(2): 93–106.

Craft, J., M. Howlett, M. Crawford, and K. McNut. 2013. "Assessing Policy Capacity for Climate Change Adaptation." *Review of Policy Research* 30(1): 42–65.

Creedy, G.D., J.S. Shrives, and G. Phillips. 2005. "Major Hazard Control in Canada: A Change in the Regulatory Landscape." In *Emergency Planning: Preparedness, Prevention & Response*, edited by the Center for Chemical Process Safety, 373–83. Hoboken, NJ: John Wiley & Sons.

Crooks, A., A. Croitoru, A. Stefanidis, and J. Radzikowski. 2013. "# Earthquake: Twitter as a Distributed Sensor System." *Transactions in GIS* 17(1): 124–47.

CSChE (Canadian Society for Chemical Engineering). 2012. "Guidelines for Site Risk Communication." Ottawa: Chemical Institute of Canada. http://www.cheminst.ca/sites/default/files/pdfs/Connect/PMS/Guidelines%20for%20Site%20Risk%20Communication.pdf

Cullen, C. 2014. "Anti-radicalization Program being Developed by the RCMP. *CBC News*, 29 August. http://www.cbc.ca/news/politics/anti-radicalization-program-being-developed-by-rcmp-1.2750854

Cummins, J.D. 2006. "Should the Government Provide Insurance for Catastrophes?" *Federal Reserve Bank of St. Louis Review* 88(4): 337–79.

Curry, B. 2009. "Inuit Fear Impact of Flu Pandemic." *Globe and Mail*, 18 August.

Dake, K. 1991. "Orienting Dispositions in the Perception of Risk: An analysis of Contemporary Worldviews and Cultural Biases." *Journal of Cross-cultural Psychology* 22(1): 61–82.

Davis, T.R. 2001. "The Regulation of Canada's Commercial Air Industry." *LawNow* 26: 51.

Dawes, S.S. 1996. "Interagency Information Sharing: Expected Benefits, Manageable Risks." *Journal of Policy Analysis & Management* 15(3): 377–94.

De Bruijne, M., and M. Van Eeten. 2007. "Systems that Should Have Failed: Critical Infrastructure Protection in an Institutionally Fragmented Environment." *Journal of Contingencies and Crisis Management* 15(1): 18–29.

De Villiers, M. 2003. *Water: The Fate of Our Most Precious Resource.* Toronto: McClelland & Stewart.

De Vries, M.S. 2000. "The Rise and Fall of Decentralization: A Comparative Analysis of Arguments and Practices in European Countries." *European Journal of Political Research* 38(2): 193–224.

Deber, R.B. 2014. "Concepts for the Policy Analyst." In *Case Studies in Canadian Health Policy and Management*, edited by R. Deber and C. Mah, 1–93. Toronto: University of Toronto Press.

Department of Defense. 1998. *Critical Infrastructure Plan.* https://fas.org/irp/offdocs/pdd/DOD-CIP-Plan.htm

Department of Homeland Security. 2008. *One Team, One Mission, Securing Our Homeland: U.S. Department of Homeland Security Strategic Plan, Fiscal Years 2009–2013.* Washington, DC: GPO.

Department of Homeland Security. 2013a. "NIPP 2013: Partnering for Critical Infrastructure Security and Resilience." http://www.dhs.gov/sites/default/files/publications/National-Infrastructure-Protection-Plan-2013-508.pdf

Department of Homeland Security. 2013b. "The National Infrastructure Protection Plan (NIPP) 2013: Partnering for Critical Infrastructure Security and Resilience." http://www.dhs.gov/publication/nipp-2013-partnering-critical-infrastructure-security-and-resilience

Department of Homeland Security and Public Safety Canada. 2010. "Canada–United States Action Plan for Critical Infrastructure." http://www.publicsafety.gc.ca/cnt/rsrcs/pblctns/cnd-ntdstts-ctnpln/index-eng.aspx

Department of Justice. 2015. "The *Anti-terrorism Act* and Security Measures in Canada: Public Views, Impacts and Travel Experiences." http://www.justice.gc.ca/eng/rp-pr/cj-jp/antiter/rro5_11/po.html

Diebel, L. 2016. "Olive Branch Could End Detroit-Windsor Bridge Wars." *Toronto Star*, 13 February. https://www.thestar.com/news/canada/2016/02/13/olive-branch-could-end-detroit-windsor-bridge-wars.html

Dietz, T., and P. C. Stern. 1995. "Toward a Theory of Choice: Socially Embedded Preference Construction." *Journal of Socio-Economics* 24(2): 261–79.

Dimock, M., C. Doherty, and D. Gewurz. 2013. *Trust in Government Nears Record Low, but Most Federal Agencies are Viewed Favourably.* Washington: The Pew Research Center for the People & the Press. http://www.people-press.org/files/legacy-pdf/10-18-13%20Trust%20in%20Govt%20Update.pdf

Donohue, G.A., P.J. Tichenor, and C.N. Olien. 1995. "A Guard Dog Perspective on the Role of Media." *Journal of Communication* 45(2): 115–32.

Douglas, M. 1982. *Essays in the Sociology of Perception*. London: Routledge & Kegan Paul.

Douglas, M. 1992. *Risk and Blame: Essays in Cultural Theory*. London: Routledge.

Douglas, M. 2001. "Dealing with Uncertainty." *Ethical Perspectives*, 8(3): 145–55.

Douglas, M., and Wildavsky, A.B. 1982. *Risk and Culture: An Essay on the Selection of Technical and Environmental Dangers*. Berkeley: University of California Press.

Downs, A. 1967. *Inside Bureaucracy*. Boston: Little, Brown.

DRDC (Defence Research and Development Canada). 2013. "Canadian Safety and Security Program." http://www.drdc-rddc.gc.ca/en/sciencetech/safety-security.page

Dryzek, J., and P. Dunleavy. 2009. *Theories of the Democratic State*. Basingstoke, UK: Palgrave Macmillan.

Dunleavy, P. 1991. *Democracy, Bureaucracy and Public Choice: Economic Explanations in Political Science*. New York: Harvester.

Dunn-Cavelty, M., and M. Suter. 2009. "Public-private Partnerships are No Silver Bullet: An Expanded Governance Model for Critical Infrastructure Protection." *International Journal of Critical Infrastructure Protection* 2(4): 179–87.

Dunsire, A. 1993. "Manipulating Social Tensions: Collibration as an Alternative Mode of Government Intervention." Discussion Paper 93/7. Kohn, Germany: Max-Planck-Institut für Gesellschaftforschung.

Eco-Efficiency Centre. 2008. "Eco-efficiency and Chemical Management: Government Regulations and Programs." http://eco-efficiency.management.dal.ca/Files/Business_Fact_Sheets/chemicals_govt_fs.pdf

Ecojustice. 2011. "Getting Tough on Environmental Crime? Holding the Government of Canada to Account on Environmental Enforcement." http://www.ecojustice.ca/publications/reports/getting-tough-on-environmentalcrime/attachment

Edelman. 2016. "Edelman Trust Barometer Archive." http://www.edelman.com/insights/intellectual-property/edelman-trust-barometer-archive/

Edelman. n.d. "Edelman – Who We Are – Media Cloverleaf." http://www.edelman.com/who-we-are/about-edelman/the-details/cloverleaf/

Edge, S.A. 2012. "The Socio-Spatial Construction and Negotiation of Knowledge, Power and Influence in the Governance of Environmental

Health Risks from Toxic Chemicals in Canada." Doctoral diss., McMaster University.

Egan, M. 2007. "Anticipating Future Vulnerability: Defining Characteristics of Increasingly Critical Infrastructure-Like Systems." *Journal of Contingencies and Crisis Management* 15(1): 4–17.

Eisenman, D.P., K.M. Cordasco, S.M. Asch, J.F. Golden, and D.C. Glik. 2007. "Disaster Planning and Risk Communication with Vulnerable Communities: Lessons from Hurricane Katrina." *American Journal of Public Health* 97(Supplement 1): S109–S115.

Eiser, J.R., and M.P. White. 2006. "A Psychological Approach to Understanding How Trust is Built and Lost in the Context of Risk." Working Paper No. 12-.2006. Canterbury, UK: School of Social Policy, Sociology and Social Research, University of Kent.

EKOS. 2007. "Wave 1: Five Years After 9/11 – Canadians Rethinking Security?" www.ekospolitics.com/articles/SM2006W1.pdf

Elliott, M.A. 2011. "The Institutional Expansion of Human Rights, 1863–2003: A Comprehensive Dataset of International Instruments." *Journal of Peace Research* 48(4): 537–46.

Eltantawy, N., and J.B. Wiest. 2011. "The Arab Spring. Social Media in the Egyptian Revolution: Reconsidering Resource Mobilization Theory." *International Journal of Communication* 5: 18.

Engdahl, E., and R. Lidskog. 2012. "Risk, Communication and Trust: Towards an Emotional Understanding of Trust." *Public Understanding of Science* 23(6): 703–17.

Engelhardt, S., and S. Maurer. 2012. *Industry Self-Governance and National Security: On the Private Control of Dual Use Technologies.* UC Berkeley Public Law Research Paper No. GSPP12-005.

Enoch, S., and C. Stadnichuk. 2015. "Following Failure: Saskatchewan Government Seems Doomed to Repeat the P3 Mistakes of Other Provinces." Regina, SK: Canadian Centre for Policy Alternatives. https://www.policyalternatives.ca/sites/default/files/uploads/publications/Saskatchewan%20Office/2015/06/SKNotes_Following_Failure_P3.pdf

Environment Canada. 2002. *CEPA Annual Report for Period April 2001 to March 2002.* Ottawa: Environment Canada. http://www.ec.gc.ca/lcpe-cepa/default.asp?lang=En&n=6DEE3880-1&offset=9

Environment Canada. 2003. *Canadian Environmental Protection Act, 1999: Annual Report, April 2001 to March 2002.* Ottawa: Environment Canada. http://www.ec.gc.ca/lcpe-cepa/documents/rpts_ann-ann_rpts/01_02/aro1_02-eng.pdf

Environment Canada. 2014a. *Amending the Environmental Emergency Regulations.* Ottawa: Environment Canada. http://www.crhnet.ca/sites/default/files/library/P01-02_Canada-E_CRHNet_2014-10-23.pdf

Environment Canada. 2014b. *Canadian Environmental Protection Act, 1999: Annual Report for April 2013 to March 2014.* Ottawa: Environment Canada. http://www.ec.gc.ca/lcpe-cepa/default. asp?lang=En&n=5CDD0D24-1&offset=3&toc=hide#_Toc400625478

Environmental Protection Agency. n.d. "Sector Programs: Chemical Manufacturing." http://www.epa.gov/regulatory-information-sector/chemical-manufacturing-sector-naics-325

Evans, P.B., H.K. Jacobson, and R.D. Putnam, eds. 1993. *Double-Edged Diplomacy: International Bargaining and Domestic Politics.* Oakland: University of California Press.

Evidence Network of Canadian Health Policy. n.d.. "About the Evidence Network." http://umanitoba.ca/outreach/evidencenetwork/about

Expert Panel on SARS and Infectious Disease Control (Ont.), and D.M.C. Walker. 2003. *For the Public's Health: Initial Report of the Ontario Expert Panel on SARS and Infectious Disease Control.* Toronto: Ontario Ministry of Health and Long-Term Care.

Faisal, M.N., D.K. Banwet, and R. Shankar. 2006. "Supply Chain Risk Mitigation: Modeling the Enablers." *Business Process Management Journal* 12(4): 535–52.

Federation of Canadian Municipalities. n.d. "Infrastructure." http://www.fcm.ca/home/issues/infrastructure.htm

Feinberg, L.E. 2002. "Homeland Security: Implications for Information Policy and Practice – First Appraisal." *Government Information Quarterly* 19: 265–88.

Fineberg, H.V. 2013. "The Paradox of Disease Prevention: Celebrated in Principle, Resisted in Practice." *JAMA* 310(1): 85–90.

Fineberg, H.V. 2014. "Pandemic Preparedness and Response – Lessons from the H1N1 Influenza of 2009." *New England Journal of Medicine* 370(14): 1335–42.

Finger, S.R., and S. Gamper-Rabindran. 2013. "Testing the Effects of Self-Regulation on Industrial Accidents." *Journal of Regulatory Economics* 43(2): 115–46.

Fink, S. 2013. *Five Days at Memorial.* New York: Crown Publishers.

Finucane, M., P. Slovic, C.K. Mertz, J. Flynn, and T. Satterfield. 2000. "Gender, Race, and Perceived Risk: The 'White Male' Effect." *Health, Risk & Society* 2(2): 159–72.

Firth-Cozens, J. 2004. "Sharing Workload in Group Practices: Unfairness and Early Experience Colour Perception of Inequality." *BMJ* 329(7467): 685.

Fischbacher-Smith, D. 2011. "Destructive Landscapes – (Re)framing Elements of Risk?" *Risk Management* 13(1): 1–15.

Fischhoff, B. 1985. "Cognitive and Institutional Barriers to 'Informed Consent.'" In *To Breathe Freely: Risk, Consent, and Air*, edited by M. Gibson, 169–85. Totowa, NJ: Rowman & Allanheld.

Fischhoff, B. 1995. "Risk Perception and Communication Unplugged: Twenty Years of Process." *Risk Analysis* 15: 137–45.

Fleming, M.H., and E. Goldstein. 2012. *Metrics for Measuring the Efficacy of Critical-Infrastructure-Centric Cybersecurity Information Sharing Efforts*. Arlington, VA: Homeland Security Studies and Analysis Institute.

Folkes, V.S. 1988. "Recent Attribution Research in Consumer Behavior: A Review and New Directions." *Journal of Consumer Research* 14(4): 548–65.

Forsyth, P. 2007. "The Impacts of Emerging Aviation Trends on Airport Infrastructure." *Journal of Air Transport Management* 13(1): 45–52.

Fowler, T., and K. Quigley. 2014. "Information, Innovation and the Boogeyman: Contextual Factors that Influence the Canadian Government's Response to Cyberspace Risk." *International Journal of Public Administration in the Digital Age* 1(2): 97–115.

Frederickson, H., and T. La Porte. 2002 "Airport Security, High Reliability, and the Problem of Rationality." *Public Administration Review* 62(S1): 33–43.

Freed, G.L., S.J. Clark, A.T. Butchart, D.C. Singer, and M.M. Davis. 2011. "Sources and Perceived Credibility of Vaccine-Safety Information for Parents." *Pediatrics* 127(S1): S107–S112.

Freeze, C. 2010. "Mounties to Recruit Women and Minorities." *Globe and Mail*, 24 September. http://www.theglobeandmail.com/news/politics/mounties-to-recruit-for-women-and-minorities/article1380277/

Frith, J. 2012. "History of Plague – Part 1. The Three Great Pandemics." *Journal of Military and Veterans' Health* 20(2). http://jmvh.org/article/the-history-of-plague-part-1-the-three-great-pandemics/

Fyfe, T., and P. Crookall. 2010. *Social Media and Public Sector Policy Dilemmas*. Toronto: Institute of Public Administration of Canada.

Gallup. 2014. "Confidence in Institutions. Gallup Historical Trends." http://www.gallup.com/poll/1597/confidence-institutions.aspx

Gamper-Rabindran, S., and S.R. Finger. 2013. "Does Industry Self-Regulation Reduce Pollution? Responsible Care in the Chemical Industry." *Journal of Regulatory Economics* 43(1), 1–30.

Gierlach, E., B.E. Belsher, and L.E. Beutler. 2010. "Cross-Cultural Differences in Risk Perceptions of Disasters." *Risk Analysis* 30(10): 1539–49.

Gil de Zúñiga, H., N. Jung, and S. Valenzuela. 2012. "Social Media Use for News and Individuals' Social Capital, Civic Engagement and Political Participation." *Journal of Computer-Mediated Communication* 17(3): 319–36.

Gillespie, N., and G. Dietz. 2009. "Trust Repair after an Organization-level Failure." *Academy of Management Review* 34(1): 127–45.

Gillum, J., and R. Plushnick-Masti. 2013. "Fertilizer Plants Go Under the Radar." *Portland Press Herald*, 20 April. http://www.pressherald. com/2013/04/20/safety-rules-limited-for-small-fertilizer-plants/

Girard, A.L., S. Day, and L. Snider. 2010. "Tracking Environmental Crime through CEPA: Canada's Environment Cops or Industry's Best Friend?" *Canadian Journal of Sociology* 35(2): 219–41.

Glenny, M. 2011a. "Canada's Weakling Web Defenses." *Globe & Mail*, 18 May. http://www.theglobeandmail.com/globe-debate/canadas-weaklingweb-defences/article580145/

Glenny, M. 2011b. "Hire the Hackers." TED Talks. http://www.ted.com/talks/misha_glenny_hire_the_hackers

Globe and Mail. "The Children Still Wait." 2009. *Globe and Mail*, 11 November. http://www.theglobeandmail.com/news/national/the-children-still-wait/article1204606/

Globe and Mail. Canada's Top Companies by Industry. 2013. *Globe and Mail*, 3 July. http://www.theglobeandmail.com/report-on-business/rob-magazine/top-1000/rankings-by-industry/article 12870820/

Gohier, P. 2011. "Montreal Is Falling Down." *Maclean's*, 23 August. http://www.macleans.ca/news/canada/montreal-is- falling-down/

González-Herrero, A., and S. Smith. 2008. "Crisis Communications Management on the Web: How Internet-Based Technologies are Changing the Way Public Relations Professionals Handle Business Crises." *Journal of Contingencies and Crisis Management* 16: 143–53.

Goode, E., and N. Ben-Yehuda. 1999. *Moral Panics: The Social Construction of Deviance*. Oxford: Blackwell.

Goodspeed, T.J., and A.F. Haughwout. 2012. "On the Optimal Design of Disaster Insurance in a Federation." *Economics of Governance* 13(1): 1–27.

Government Accountability Office. 2004. *Homeland Security: Federal Action Needed to Address Security Challenges at Chemical Facilities.* GAO-04-482T. Washington, DC: Government Accountability Office.

Government Accountability Office. 2013. *Flood Insurance: More Information Needed on Subsidized Properties.* GAO-13-607. Washington, DC: Government Accountability Office. http://www.gao.gov/assets/660/655734.pdf.

Government Accountability Office. 2014. *Maritime Security: Progress and Challenges with Selected Port Security Programs.* GAO-14-636T. Washington, DC: Government Accountability Office. http://www.gao.gov/assets/670/663784.pdf

Government of Canada. 2010a. *Canada's Cyber Security Strategy: For a Stronger and More Prosperous Canada.* Ottawa: Public Safety Canada. https://www.publicsafety.gc.ca/cnt/rsrcs/pblctns/cbr-scrt-strtgy/cbr-scrt-strtgy-eng.pdf

Government of Canada. 2010b. *The Government of Canada Response to the Commission of Inquiry into the Investigation of the Bombing of Air India Flight 182.* Ottawa: Public Safety Canada. https://www.publicsafety.gc.ca/cnt/rsrcs/pblctns/rspns-cmmssn/index-en.aspx

Government of Canada. 2010c. *Commission of Inquiry into the Investigation of the Bombing of Air India Flight 182.* Ottawa: Minister of Public Works and Government Services. p. 116. http://publications.gc.ca/collections/collection_2010/bcp-pco/CP32-89-4-2010-eng.pdf

Government of Canada. 2012. *Building Resilience against Terrorism: Canada's Counter-Terrorism Strategy.* Ottawa: Public Safety Canada. http://www.publicsafety.gc.ca/cnt/rsrcs/pblctns/rslnc-gnst-trrrsm/index-eng.aspx

Government of Canada. 2013. "Industry Profile." http://www.ic.gc.ca/eic/site/dsib-logi.nsf/eng/h_pj00541.html

Government of Canada. 2016a. *A Transformational Infrastructure Plan.* http://www.budget.gc.ca/fes-eea/2016/docs/themes/infrastructure-en.html

Government of Canada. 2016b. *Fall Economic Statement: Chapter 2 – Investing in the New Economy.* Ottawa: Finance Canada. http://www.budget.gc.ca/fes-eea/2016/docs/statement-enonce/chap02-en.html

Government of Ontario. n.d. "Critical Infrastructure: Modelling Program." https://www.emergencymanagementontario.ca/english/emcommunity/ProvincialPrograms/ci/ci.html

Graham, J. 2012. "Only 2% of Canadians Don't Believe in Climate Change. *Globe and Mail*, 15 August. http://www.theglobeandmail.com/news/politics/only-2-per-cent-of-canadians-dont-believe-in-climate-change-poll/article4482183/

Green, A., and Hrab, R. 2003. "Self-Regulation and the Protection of the Public Interest." Panel on the Role of Government, Canada. http://www.ontla.on.ca/library/repository/mon/8000/244109.pdf

Greenspon, E. 2017. *The Shattered Mirror: News, Democracy and Trust in the Digital Age.* Ottawa: Public Policy Forum. https://shatteredmirror.ca/wp-content/uploads/theShatteredMirror.pdf

Grenier, E. 2013. "Why Telephone Polling Used to Be the Best and Why It's Dying Out." *Globe and Mail*, 25 July. http://www.theglobeandmail.com/news/politics/why-telephone-polling-used-to-be-the-best-and-why-its-dying-out/article13417520/

Grigg, N.S. 2003. "Surviving Disasters: Learning from Experience." *Journal of the American Water Works Association* 95(9): 64–75.

Grube, D. 2013. "Public Voices from Anonymous Corridors: The Public Face of the Public Service in a Westminster System." *Canadian Public Administration* 56(1): 3–25.

Gunningham, N. 1995. "Environment, Self-Regulation, and the Chemical Industry: Assessing Responsible Care." *Law and Policy* 17(1): 57–109.

Ha, L., and L. Fang. 2012. "Internet Experience and Time Displacement of Traditional News Media Use: An Application of the Theory of the Niche." *Telematics and Informatics* 29(2): 177–86.

Haig, T. 2015. "Lac-Mégantic Compensation is Set at Last." *CBC News*, 14 October. http://www.rcinet.ca/en/2015/10/14/lac-megantic-compensation-is-set-at-last/

Hall, J.W., J.J. Henriques, A.J. Hickford, R.J. Nicholls, P. Baruah, M. Birkin, M. Chaudry, et al. 2014. "Assessing the Long-Term Performance of Cross-Sectoral Strategies for National Infrastructure." *Journal of Infrastructure Systems* 20(3). doi:10.1061/(ASCE)IS.1943-555X.0000196

Hamilton, G. 2014. "For Many in Lac-Mégantic the Latest Charges Over Train Disaster Miss the Mark." *National Post*, 13 May. http://news.nationalpost.com/news/canada/for-many-in-lac-megantic-the-latest-charges-over-train-disaster-miss-the-mark

Hammad, A., J. Yan, and B. Mostofi. 2007. "Recent Development of Bridge Management Systems in Canada" (presentation, Bridges – Economic and Social Linkàges (B) Session Annual Conference of the Transportation Association of Canada, Saskatoon, SK). conf.tac-atc.ca/english/resourcecentre/readingroom/conference/conf2007/docs/s7/hammad.pdf

Hammerschmid, G., and K. Wegrich. 2016. "Infrastructure Governance and Government Decision-making". In *The Governance Report 2016*, edited by Hertie School of Governance (31–54). Oxford: Oxford University Press.

Hancioglu, B. 2008. *The Market Power of Airports, Regulatory Issues and Competition Between Airports: German Airport Performance.* http://userpage.fuberlin.de/~jmueller/gapprojekt/downloads/gap_papers/Hancioglu_Market_power_of_Airports_Regulatory_jul_08.pdf

Hannah, M. 2009. "In Hudson River Landing, PR Pros Were Not First Responders." *Media Shift*, 5 February. http://mediashift.org/2009/02/in-hudson-river-landing-pr-pros-were-not-first-responders036/

Hannay, C. 2015. "Canadians Divided along Partisan Lines over Support for Refugees in Europe." *Globe and Mail*, 4 September.

Hansen, L., and H. Nissenbaum. 2009. "Digital Disaster, Cyber Security, and the Copenhagen School." *International Studies Quarterly* 53(4): 1155–75.

Hardin, R. 2006. *Trust*. Cambridge: Polity Press.

Hashim, D., P. Boffetta, C. La Vecchia, M. Rota, P. Bertuccio, M. Malvezzi, and E. Negri. 2016. "The Global Decrease in Cancer Mortality: Trends and Disparities." *Annals of Oncology* 27(5): 926–33.

Hassard, H.A., J.K.Y. Swee, M. Ghanem, and H. Unesaki. 2013. "Assessing the Impact of the Fukushima Nuclear Disaster on Policy Dynamics and the Public Sphere." *Procedia Environmental Sciences* 17: 566–75.

Haveman, J.D., H.J. Shatz, and E.A. Vilchis. 2005. "US Port Security Policy after 9/11: Overview and Evaluation." *Journal of Homeland Security and Emergency Management* 2(4).

Hay, J.B. 2006. *Who Does What? Critical Energy Infrastructure Protection in the Canadian Government*. Ottawa: Defence R&D Canada, Centre for Operational Research & Analysis.

Hayek, F. 2007. *The Road to Serfdom*. Chicago: University of Chicago Press.

Health Canada. 2009a. *About Tobacco Control*. http://www.hc-sc.gc.ca/hc-ps/tobac-tabac/about-apropos/index-eng.php

Health Canada. 2009b. *Guidelines for Canadian Drinking Water Quality – Chlorine Guideline Technical Document.* Ottawa: Health Canada. http://healthycanadians.gc.ca/publications/healthy-living-vie-saine/water-chlorine-chlore-eau/index-eng.php?page=text

Heath, R.L., and D.D. Abel. 1996. "Proactive Response to Citizen Risk Concerns: Increasing Citizens' Knowledge of Emergency Response Practices." *Journal of Public Relations Research* 8(3): 151–71.

Helmick, J.S. 2008. "Port and Maritime Security: A Research Perspective." *Journal of Transportation Security* 1(1): 15–28.

Hennink-Kaminski, H.J., and E.K. Dougall. 2009. "Myths, Mysteries, and Monsters: When Shaken Babies Make the News." *Social Marketing Quarterly* 15(4): 25-48.

Henstra, D. 2011. "The Dynamics of Policy Change: A Longitudinal Analysis of Emergency Management in Ontario, 1950–2010." *Journal of Policy History* 23(3): 399–428.

Henstra, D., and G. McBean. 2005. "Canadian Disaster Management Policy: Moving Toward a Paradigm Shift?" *Canadian Public Policy* 31(3): 303–18.

Hernandez, M.A., and M. Torero. 2011. *Fertilizer Market Situation: Market Structure, Consumption and Trade Patterns, and Pricing Behaviour.* International Food Policy Research Institute Discussion Paper No. 01058. Washington, DC: International Food Policy Research Institute.

Hess, C., and E. Ostrom. 2011. *Understanding Knowledge as a Commons: From Theory to Practice.* Cambridge: MIT Press.

Hilton, S., and E. Smith. 2010. "Public Views of the UK Media and Government Reaction to the 2009 Swine Flu Pandemic." *BMC Public Health* 2010(10): 697.

Hood, C. 1991. "A Public Management for All Seasons?" *Public Administration* 69(1): 3–19.

Hood, C. 1998. *The Art of the State: Culture, Rhetoric and Public Management.* Oxford: Oxford University Press.

Hood, C., and M.W. Jackson. 1991. *Administrative Argument.* Aldershot, UK: Dartmouth Publishing.

Hood, C., H. Rothstein, and R. Baldwin. 2001. *The Government of Risk: Understanding Risk Regulation Regimes.* Oxford: Oxford University Press.

Hosty, J. 2008. "Explosion! What Went Wrong at Sunrise Propane?" *HazMat* 20(4). http://www.hazmatmag.com/news/explosion-about bleves/1000224295/

Howlett, M., J. Craft, and L. Zibrik. 2010. "Government Communication and Democratic Governance: Electoral and Policy-Related Information Campaigns in Canada." *Policy and Society* 29(1): 13–22.

Huang, C.M., E. Chan., and A.A. Hyder. 2010. "Web 2.0 and Internet Social Networking: A New Tool for Disaster Management? Lessons from Taiwan." *BMC Medical Informatics and Decision Making* 10(1): 57.

Huberman, B.A., D.M. Romero, and F. Wu. 2008. "Social Networks that Matter: Twitter under the Microscope." https://arxiv.org/pdf/0812.1045.pdf

Huczynski, A. 2006. *Management Gurus*. New York: Routledge.

Hunter, J. 2009. "First in Line, Native Communities Still Wait for Shots; In Northern British Columbia, Band Leaders Criticize Slow Rollout of Vaccinations." *Globe and Mail*, 4 November.

IATA (International Air Transport Association). 2013. *Airport Competition*. Geneva: IATA. https://www.iata.org/whatwedo/Documents/economics/airport-competition.pdf

Ibáñez, E., K. Gkritza, J. McCalley, D. Aliprantis, R. Brown, A. Somani, and L. Wang. 2010. "Interdependencies between Energy and Transportation Systems for National Long Term Planning." In *Sustainable and Resilient Critical Infrastructure Systems*, edited by K. Gopalakrishnan and S. Peeta, 53–75. Berlin: Springer-Verlag.

ICAO (International Civil Aviation Organization). 2016. *Convention on International Civil Aviation*. Montreal: ICAO. http://www.icao.int/publications/pages/doc7300.aspx

ICP (Independent Commission on Policing). 1999. *A New Beginning: Policing in Northern Ireland, The Report of the Independent Commission on Policing for Northern Ireland*. cain.ulst.ac.uk/issues/police/patten/patten99.pdf

Imtihani, N., and Y. Mariko. 2013. "Media Coverage of Fukushima Nuclear Power Station Accident 2011 (a Case Study of NHK and BBC WORLD TV Stations)." *Procedia Environmental Sciences* 17: 938–46.

Independent Task Force Sponsored by the Council on Foreign Relations. 2003. *Emergency Responders: Drastically Underfunded, Dangerously Unprepared*. New York: Council on Foreign Relations.

Industry Canada. 2011. *Chemicals and Chemical Products (Total)*. http://www.ic.gc.ca/eic/site/chemicals-chimiques.nsf/eng/bt01270.html/

Industry Canada. 2015. *Chemical Manufacturing (NAICS 325): Establishments*. https://www.ic.gc.ca/app/scr/sbms/sbb/cis/establishments.html?code=325&lang=eng

Innovation, Science and Economic Development Canada. 2013. *Canada's Pharmaceutical Industry and Prospects.* https://www.ic.gc.ca/eic/site/lsg-pdsv.nsf/eng/hn01768.html

Insights West. 2013. *Alberta Flood Release (July 23).* Vancouver: Insights West. http://www.insightswest.com/wp-content/uploads/2013/07/NewData_ABFloodPR_23July2013_FINAL.pdf

Insurance Information Institute. 2016. *Catastrophes: Global.* New York: Insurance Information Institute. www.iii.org/fact-statistic/catastrophes-global

International Bridges and Tunnels Act, Statutes of Canada. 2007. Chapter 1. http://laws-lois.justice.gc.ca/eng/acts/I-17.05/

International Maritime Organization. n.d. "Piracy Reports." London, UK: International Maritime Organization. http://www.imo.org/en/OurWork/Security/PiracyArmedRobbery/Reports/Pages/Default.aspx

IPSOS. 2015. *In Wake of Paris Attacks, Six in Ten (60%) of Canadians Oppose Government's Plan to Settle 25,000 Refugees by Year's End* [press release]. http://www.ipsos-na.com/news-polls/pressrelease.aspx?id=7064

Ircha, M.C. 2001. "Port Strategic Planning: Canadian Port Reform." *Maritime Policy & Management* 28(2): 125–40.

Jaeger, C., O. Renn, E.A. Rosa, and T. Webler. 2001. *Risk, Uncertainty, and Rational Action.* London: Earthscan.

Jeffcott, S., N. Pidgeon, A. Weyman, and J. Walls. 2006. "Risk, Trust, and Safety Culture in U.K. Train Operating Companies." *Risk Analysis* 26(5): 1105–21.

Jenkins, B.M. 1998. "Aviation Security in the United States." *Terrorism and Political Violence* 10(3): 101–11.

Johnson, B.B., and V.T. Covello. 1987. *The Social and Cultural Construction of Risk.* Dordrecht: Reidel.

Johnson, N., and J. Mueller. 2002. "Updating the Accounts: Global Mortality of the 1918–1920 'Spanish' Influenza Pandemic." *Bulletin of the History of Medicine* 76(1). https://muse.jhu.edu/article/4826

Jones, J., and M. Salathé. 2009. "Early Assessment of Anxiety and Behavioral Response to Novel Swine-Origin Influenza A (H1N1)." *PLoS One* 4(12).

Juillet, L., and J. Koji. 2013. "Policy Change and Constitutional Order: Municipalities, Intergovernmental Relations, and the Recent Evolution of Canadian Emergency Management Policy." In *Multilevel Governance and Emergency Management in Canadian Municipalities,* edited by D. Henstra, 25–61. Montreal: McGill-Queen's University Press.

Kahai, S.K., and J.M. Ford. 1997. "Economics of Intrastate Trucking Regulation: Some Empirical Evidence." *Transportation Research Part E: Logistics and Transportation Review* 33(2): 139–45.

Kahn, M.E. 2007. "Environmental Disasters as Risk Regulation Catalysts? The Role of Bhopal, Chernobyl, Exxon Valdez, Love Canal, and Three Mile Island in Shaping U.S. Environmental Law." *Journal of Risk and Uncertainty* 35: 17–43.

Kahneman, D., and A. Tversky. 1982. "Rational Choice and the Framing of Decisions." *Journal of Business* 59(4): 251–8.

Kaplan F. 2016. *Dark Territory: The Secret History of Cyber War.* Toronto: Simon and Schuster.

Karruthers, B., and N. Hild. 2004. "Danger Zone: Update on Chemical Industry and Security in North America." *HazMat* 16(3): 32–3.

Keevil, G. 2012. "Food Scarce in Yukon Towns Cut Off by Flooding." *Globe and Mail*, 11 June. http://www.theglobeandmail.com/news/national/food-scarce-in-yukon-towns-cut-off-by-flooding/article4249680/

Kelly, J. 2005. *The Great Mortality: An Intimate History of the Black Death, the Most Devastating Plague of All Time.* Toronto: Harper.

Kemp, J. 2014. "Insurers Weigh Risks of an Oil-Train Catastrophe." *Financial Post*, 17 January. http://business.financialpost.com/news/energy/insurers-weigh-risks-of-an-oil-train-catastrophe?__lsa=7c83-718e

Kenny, C. 2007. "Security at Canada's Ports: What Makes Sense?" *New Brunswick Telegraph Journal*, 28 March. http://colinkenny.ca/en/Security-at-Canadas-Ports-What-Makes-Sense

Keohane, R.O., and L.L. Martin. 1995. "The Promise of Institutionalist Theory." *International Security* 20(1): 39–51.

Keohane, R.O., and D.G. Victor. 2011. "The Regime Complex for Climate Change." *Perspectives on Politics* 9(1): 7–23.

Keulen, S., and R. Kroeze. 2012. "Understanding Management Gurus and Historical Narratives: The Benefits of a Historic Turn in Management and Organization Studies." *Management and Organizational History* 7(2): 171–89.

Kheifets, L.I., G.L. Hester, and G.L. Banerjee. 2001. "The Precautionary Principle and EMF: Implementation and Evaluation." *Journal of Risk Research* 4(2): 113–25.

Kieser, A. 1997. "Rhetoric and Myth in Management Fashion." *Organization* 4(1): 49–74.

Kietzmann, J.H., K. Hermkens, I.P. McCarthy, and B.S. Silvestre. 2011. "Social Media? Get Serious! Understanding the Functional Building Blocks of Social Media." *Business Horizons* 54(3): 241–51.

King, A.A., and M.J. Lenox. 2000. "Industry Self-Regulation without Sanctions: The Chemical Industry's Responsible Care Program." *Academy of Management Journal* 43(4): 698–716.

Kirschenbaum, A. 2012. *Taken For a Ride: Does Airport Security Really Work?* (presentation, Canadian Risk and Hazards Network 9th Annual Symposium, Vancouver, BC, 23–26 October).

Kitzinger, J., and J. Reilly. 1997. "The Rise and Fall of Risk Reporting: Media Coverage of Human Genetics Research, 'False Memory Syndrome' and 'Mad Cow Disease.'" *European Journal of Communication* 12(3): 319.

Kline, E. 2014. *1177 B.C.: The Year Civilization Collapsed*. Princeton, NJ: Princeton University Press.

Koliba, C.J., R.M. Mills, and A. Zia. 2011. "Accountability in Governance Networks: An Assessment of Public, Private, and Nonprofit Emergency Management Practices Following Hurricane Katrina." *Public Administration Review* 71(2): 210–20.

Kolluru, R., and P.H. Meredith. 2001. "Security and trust Management in Supply Chains." *Information Management & Computer Security* 9(5): 233–6.

Koski, C. 2011. "Committed to Protection? Partnerships in Critical Infrastructure Protection." *Journal of Homeland Security and Emergency Management* 8(1).

Kosowan, R. 2016. "Theft, Fraud, and the Trucking Industry." Manitoba Trucking Association. https://www.trucking.mb.ca/blog/post/96/theft-fraud-and-trucking-industry

Kozolanka, K. 2006. "The Sponsorship Scandal as Communication: The Rise of Politicized and Strategic Communications in the Federal Government." *Canadian Journal of Communication* 31(2). http://www.cjc-online.ca/index.php/journal/article/view/1745/1858

KPMG. 2012. *Lesser Slave Lake Regional Urban Interface Wildfire – Lessons Learned: Final Report*. http://www.aema.alberta.ca/documents/0426-Lessons-Learned-Final-Report.pdf

Krajnc, A. 2000. Whither Ontario's Environment? Neo-Conservatism and the Decline of the Environment Ministry. *Canadian Public Policy* 26(1), 111–27.

Kramer, R. 1999. "Trust and Distrust in Organizations: Emerging Perspectives, Enduring Questions." *Annual Review of Psychology* 50(11): 569–98.

Krasner, S.D. 1983. *International Regimes*. Ithaca: Cornell University Press.

Krugel, L. 2014. "Railways and Crude Shippers Weigh in on Changes to Liability Rules." *Montreal Gazette*, 19 May. http://www.montrealgazette.com/business/Railways+crude+shippers+weigh+changes+liability+-rules/9854665/story.html

Kushin, M.J., and M. Yamamoto. 2010. "Did Social Media Really Matter? College Students' Use of Online Media and Political Decision Making in the 2008 Election." *Mass Communication and Society* 13(5): 608–30.

La Porte, T. 1996. "High Reliability Organizations: Unlikely, Demanding and at Risk." *Journal of Contingencies and Crisis Management* 4(2): 60–71.

La Porte, T.R., and P. Consolini. 1991. "Working in Practice but Not in Theory: Theoretical Challenges of High Reliability Organizations." *Journal of Public Administration Research and Theory* 1: 19–47.

Lachlan, K., and P.R. Spence. 2010. "Communicating Risks: Examining Hazard and Outrage in Multiple Contexts." *Risk Analysis* 30(12): 1872–86.

Lacoursiere, J.P. 2006. A Risk Management Initiative Implemented in Canada. *Journal of Hazardous Materials* 130, 311–20.

Lacoursiere, J.P. 2005. "Bhopal and Its Effects on the Canadian Regulatory Framework." *Journal of Loss Prevention in the Process Industries* 18: 353–9.

Landen, X. 2014. "Doctors a 'Death Sentence'? Patient Mistrust Aggravates Ebola Treatment." *PBS Newshour*, 13 July. http://www.pbs.org/news hour/rundown/mistrust-doctors-west-africa-makes-harder-fight-ebola/

Langer, E.J. 1975. "The Illusion of Control." *Journal of Personality and Social Psychology* 32(2): 311–28.

Lawrence, F., and Davies, H. 2015. "Revealed: BP's Close Ties with the UK Government." *The Guardian*, 21 May. https://www.theguardian.com/environment/2015/may/20/revealed-BPs-close-ties-with-the-uk-government

Lay, C. 2009. "Race, Retrospective Voting, and Disasters: The Reelection of C. Ray Nagin after Hurricane Katrina." *Urban Affairs Review* 44: 645–62.

Layne, K., and J. Lee. 2001. "Developing Fully Functional E-government: A Four Stage Model." *Government Information Quarterly* 18(2): 122–36.

Lenz, A.J., and J. Lafrance. 1996. *Meeting the Challenge: U.S. Industry Faces the 21st Century. The Chemical Industry*. Washington: US Department of Commerce, Office of Technology Policy.

Lewis, J. 2003. "Cyber Terror: Missing in Action." *Knowledge, Technology, and Policy* 16(2): 34–41.

Liang, A. 2011. "The H1N1 crises: Roles Played by Government Communicators, the Public and the Media." *Journal of Professional Communication* 1(1): 123–49.

Lieberman, J. 2012. "The Threat is Real and Must be Stopped." *New York Times*, 17 October. http://www.nytimes.com/roomfordebate/2012/10/17/should-industry-face-more-cybersecurity-mandates/the-cyber-threat-is-real-and-must-be-stopped-by-business-and-government

Lieberman, M.B. 1987. "Postentry Investment and Market Structure in the Chemical Processing Industries." *RAND Journal of Economics* 18(4): 533–49.

Lindøe, P.H., O.A. Engen, and O.E. Olsen. 2011. "Responses to Accidents in Different Industrial Sectors." *Safety Science* 49(1): 90–97.

Lipton, E., D.E. Sanger, and S. Shane. 2016. "The Perfect Weapon: How Russian Cyberpower Invaded the U.S." *New York Times*, 13 December.

Loader, B.D., and D. Mercea. 2011. "Networking Democracy? Social Media Innovations and Participatory Politics." *Information, Communication & Society* 14(6): 757–69.

Lofstedt, R. 2013. "The Substitution Principle in Chemical Regulation: A Constructive Critique." *Journal of Risk Research* 17(5): 543–564.

Loriggio, P. 2016. "Sunrise Propane, Directors Fined $5.3M for Deadly Explosion." *CBC News*, 25 January. http://www.cbc.ca/news/canada/toronto/sunrise-propane-fined-1.3419010

Lowrance, W. 1976. *Of Acceptable Risk: Science and the Determination of Safety*. Los Altos, CA: William Kaufman.

Macdonald, A. 2014. "Edmonton Pipe Bomb Incident: How Much Power Does Airport Security Have?" *CBC News*, 16 January. http://www.cbc.ca/news/canada/edmonton-pipe-bomb-incident-how-much-power-does-airport-security-have-1.2498105

Macdougall, C.W., D. Kirsch, B. Schwartz, and R.B. Deber. 2014. "Looking for Trouble: Developing and Implementing a National Network for Infectious Disease Surveillance in Canada." In *Case Studies in Canadian Health Policy and Management*, edited by R. Deber and C. Mah, 179–205. Toronto: University of Toronto Press.

Macza, M.A. 2008. "Canadian Perspective of the History of Process Safety Management" (presentation, 8th International Symposium on Programmable Electronic Systems in Safety-Related Applications, Cologne, Germany, 2–3 September).

Madden, T.F. 2012. *Venice: A New History*. London: Penguin.

Mahdi, S., P. Nightingale, and F. Berkhout. 2002. *A Review of the Impact of Regulation on the Chemical Industry: Final Report to the Royal Commission on Environmental Pollution*. Brighton, UK: SPRU Science and Technology Policy Research, University of Sussex. www.rcep.org.uk/reports/24-chemicals/documents/chin-txt.pdf

Maldonato, M., and S. Dell'Orco. 2011. "How to Make Decisions in an Uncertain World: Heuristics, Biases, and Risk Perception." *World Futures* 67(8): 569–77.

Maloney, R. 2014. "Canadians Split on Michael Zehaf-Bibeau's Motives for Ottawa Attack, Poll Suggests." *Huffington Post*, 25 November. http://www.huffingtonpost.ca/2014/11/25/michael-zehaf-bibeau-canadians-poll_n_6220488.html

Manguvo A., and B. Mafuvadze. 2015. "The Impact of Traditional and Religious Practices on the Spread of Ebola in West Africa: Time for a Strategic Shift." *Pan African Medicine Journal* 22(9): 1–4. https://www.ncbi.nlm.nih.gov/pmc/articles/PMC4709130/pdf/PAMJ-SUPP-22-1-09.pdf

Manitoba Health. 2010. *H1N1 Flu in Manitoba: Manitoba's Response Lessons Learned*. http://www.gov.mb.ca/health/documents/h1n1.pdf

Marine Transportation Security Act, Statutes of Canada. 1994. Chapter 40. http://laws-lois.justice.gc.ca/eng/acts/M-0.8/

Marowits, R. 2014. "Judges in Quebec and U.S. Approve Sale of Insolvent Railway MM&A." *Global News*, 23 January. http://globalnews.ca/news/1103508/judges-in-quebec-and-u-s-approve-sale-of-insolvent-railway-mma/

Masozera, M., M. Bailey, and C. Kerchner. 2007. "Distribution of Impacts of Natural Disasters across Income Groups: A Case Study of New Orleans." *Ecological Economics* 63(2): 299–306.

Masten, A.S. 2009. "Ordinary Magic: Lessons from Research on Resilience in Human Development." *Education Canada* 49(3).

Mather, L. 2011. "Cybersecurity Requires a Multi-Layered Approach." *Info Security Magazine* 21 April. http://www.infosecurity-magazine.com/opinions/comment-cybersecurity-requires-a-multi-layered/

Mazur, A. 1984. "Media Influences on Public Attitudes toward Nuclear Power." In *Public Reactions to Nuclear Power: Are There Critical Masses?* edited by W.R. Freudenburg and E.A. Rosa, 97–114. Boulder, CO: American Association for the Advancement of Science.

McEntire, D.A., and Dawson, G. 2007. "The Intergovernmental Context." In *Emergency Management: Principles and Practice for Local*

Government, edited by W.L. Waugh and K. Tierney. Washington, DC: ICMA.

McGregor, K. 2011, October 3. "Lawrence Martin Admits He Is Biased" [Web log message]. http://www.bluelikeyou.com/2010/10/03/lawrence-martin-admits-he-is-biased/

Meek, M.E., and V.C. Armstrong. 2007. "The Assessment and Management of Industrial Chemicals in Canada." In *Risk Assessment of Chemicals*, edited by K. Van Leeuwen and T. Vermeire, 591–621. Dordrecht, Netherlands: Kluwer Academic Publishers.

Mei, J.S.A., N. Bansal, and A. Pang. 2010. "New Media: A New Medium in Escalating Crises?" *Corporate Communications: An International Journal* 15(2): 143–55.

Meyer, E. 2004 "Case Studies in Developing Regions: Use of Dry Chlorine for Low Tech Sanitation." *Plenary Lectures and Perspectives from the International Conference on Chemistry for Water, Paris, France 2004*: 91–9.

Meyer, P. 2009. *The Vanishing Newspaper: Saving Journalism in the Information Age*. Columbia: University of Missouri Press.

Michel-Kerjan, E., and H. Kunreuther. 2011. "Redesigning Flood Insurance." *Science* 333(6041): 408–9.

Miller, J. 2006. "Who's Telling the News: Racial Representation among News Gatherers in Canada's Daily Newsrooms." *International Journal of Diversity in Organizations, Communities and Nations* 4: 133–42.

Miller, J. and C. Sack. 2010. "The Toronto-18 Terror Case: Trial by Media? How Newspaper Opinion Framed Canada's Biggest Terrorism Case." *International Journal of Diversity in Organizations, Communities and Nations* 10(1): 279–96.

Mills, A.J. 2012. "Virality in Social Media: The SPIN Framework." *Journal of Public Affairs* 12(2): 162–9.

Millward, H. 2006. "Urban Containment Strategies: A Case-Study Appraisal of Plans and Policies in Japanese, British, and Canadian Cities." *Land Use Policy* 23(4): 473–85.

Ministry of Community Safety and Correctional Services. 2010. *Sunrise Propane Explosion*. http://www.mcscs.jus.gov.on.ca/english/FireMarshal/MediaRelationsandResources/News/OFM_News_08-04-10.html

Mitchell, A., and P. Hitlin. 2013. "Twitter Reactions to Events Often at Odds with Overall Public Opinion." Washington, DC: Pew Research Center. http://www.pewresearch.org/2013/03/04/twitter-reaction-to-events-often-at-odds-with-overall-public-opinion/

Mitchell, L.M., P.H. Stephenson, S. Cadell, and M.E. Macdonald. 2012. "Death and Grief On-line: Virtual Memorialization and Changing Concepts of Childhood Death and Parental Bereavement on the Internet." *Health Sociology Review* 21(4): 413–31.

Mittelstaedt, M. 2009. "Fewer Canadians Interested in Getting H1N1 Shot, Poll Shows." *Globe and Mail*, 25 October. http://www.theglobe andmail.com/life/health-and-fitness/health/conditions/fewer-canadians-interested-in-getting-h1n1-shot-poll-shows/article4291273/

MNP LLP. 2015. *Review and Analysis of the Government of Alberta's Response to and Recovery from 2013 Floods.* Toronto: MNP LLP.

Moeller, S.D. 2006. "'Regarding the Pain of Others': Media, Bias and the Coverage of International Disasters." *Journal of International Affairs* 59(2): 173–96.

Moffet, J., F. Bregha, and M.J. Middelkoop. 2004. "Responsible Care: A Case Study of a Voluntary Environmental Initiative." In *Voluntary Codes: Private Governance, the Public Interest and Innovation*, edited by K. Webb, 177–208. Ottawa: Carleton Research Unit for Innovation, Science and Environment, Carleton University.

Molina, O., and M. Rhodes. 2002. "Corporatism: The Past, Present, and Future of a Concept." *Annual Review of Political Science* 5(1): 305–31.

Monteiro, J. 2014. *Do Airports Compete?* http://ctrf.ca/wp-content/upload s/2014/07/35MonteiroDoAirportsCompete.pdf

Monti, A. 2009. "Climate Change and Weather-Related Disasters: What Role for Insurance, Reinsurance and Financial Sectors." *West-Northwest Journal of Environmental Law and Policy* 15: 151.

Moore, M. 1995. *Creating Public Value.* Cambridge, MA: Harvard University Press.

Morano, N.H. 2010. "Framing Security Policy: Media Interference in the Case of the "Toronto 18" Terrorists Arrests" (presentation, Meeting of the Canadian Political Science Association, Montreal). http://www.cpsa-acsp.ca/papers-2010/morano.pdf

Muise, M. 2014. "Lac-Mégantic Victims Died Violent, Avoidable Deaths: Coroner." *Montreal Gazette*, 8 October. http://www.montrealgazette. com/m%C3%A9gantic+victims+died+violent+avoidable+deaths+coro ner/10273106/story.html

National Advisory Committee on SARS and Public Health. 2003. *Learning from SARS: Renewal of public health in Canada: a report of the National Advisory Committee on SARS and Public Health.* Ottawa: Health Canada.

National Commission on Terrorist Acts. 2004. *The 9/11 Commission Report: Final Report of the National Commission on Terrorist Attacks upon the United States.* http://www.npr.org/documents/2004/9-11/911reportexec.pdf

National Institute on Aging. 2011. *Global Health and Aging.* Geneva: World Health Organization. https://www.nia.nih.gov/research/publication/global-health-and-aging/preface

Negrine, R. 2007. "The Professionalisation of Political Communication in Europe." In *Professionalisation of Political Communication,* edited by R. Negrine, C. Holtz-Bacha, P. Mancini, and S. Papatha, 27–45. Chicago: University of Chicago Press.

Neptune Technologies and Bioressources. 2014. *Annual Report 2014.* http://neptunekrilloil.com/pdf/NEPT_Annual_Report.pdf

Neptune Technologies and Bioressources. 2015. *Management's Discussion and Analysis and Consolidated Financial Statements.* http://neptune krilloil.com/wp-content/uploads/2014/07/COMBINED-Neptune-MDA-Financial-Statements-FY-2014-2015-EN-EC.pdf

Neustadt, R.E., and H.V. Fineberg. 1983. *The Epidemic that Never Was: Policy-Making and the Swine Flu Scare.* New York: Vintage Books.

New Zealand, Controller and Auditor General of. 2014. *Local Government: Results of the 2012/13 Audits.* Wellington: Office of the Auditor General. http://www.oag.govt.nz/2014/local-govt/docs/local-govt.pdf

New Zealand Government. 2015. *The Thirty Year New Zealand Infrastructure Plan.* Wellington: National Infrastructure Unit. http://www.infrastructure.govt.nz/plan/2015/nip-aug15.pdf

Newkirk, R.W., J.B. Bender, and C.W. Hedberg. 2012. "The Potential Capability of Social Media as a Component of Food Safety and Food Terrorism Surveillance Systems." *Foodborne Pathogens and Disease* 9(2): 120–4.

Newport, F. 2012. "In U.S., 24% of Men, 2% of Women Are Veterans." Gallup. http://www.gallup.com/poll/158729/men-women-veterans.aspx

Nicholson, A., S. Webber, S. Dyer, T. Patel, and H. Janicke. 2012. "SCADA Security In The Light OF Cyber-Warfare." *Computers & Security* 31(4): 418–36.

Niskanen, W.A. 1971. *Bureaucracy and Representative Government.* Chicago: Aldine, Atherton.

Nørreklit, H. 2003. "The Balanced Scorecard: What is the Score? A Rhetorical Analysis of the Balanced Scorecard." *Accounting, Organizations and Society* 28(6): 591–619.

Norrington, L., J. Quigley, A. Russell, and R. Van der Meer. 2008. "Modelling the Reliability of Search and Rescue Operations with Bayesian Belief Networks." *Reliability Engineering & System Safety* 93(7): 940–9.

Nova Scotia Department of Health and Wellness. 2010, December. *Nova Scotia's Response to H1N1: Summary Report*. Halifax: Government of Nova Scotia. https://www.gov.ns.ca/dhw/publications/H1N1-Summary-Report.pdf

O'Connor, J., and J.E. Costa. 2004. *The World's Largest Floods, Past and Present: Their Causes and Magnitude*. Washington, DC: United States Department of the Interior and US Geological Survey. http://pubs.usgs.gov/circ/2004/circ1254/pdf/circ1254.pdf

O'Neill, S., K. DeJong, R. Ang, N. Green, and A. Holland. 2009. "The Control of Major Accident Hazards in Canada." Kingston, ON: Technology, Engineering & Management Course, Department of Chemical Engineering, Queen's University. http://team.appsci.queensu.ca/documents/CSChE_ControlMajorAccidentHazardaCa nada_Report.v4.pdf

Obama, B. 2010. *Public Papers of the Presidents of the United States, Barack Obama*. Washington, DC: Office of the Federal Register, National Archives and Records Administration.

Obama, B. 2015. *National Security Strategy*. http://nssarchive.us/national-security-strategy-2015/

Obar, J.A., P. Zube, and C. Lampe. 2012. "Advocacy 2.0: An Analysis of How Advocacy Groups in the United States Perceive and Use Social Media as Tools for Facilitating Civic Engagement and Collective Action." *Journal of Information Policy* 2: 1–25.

OECD (Organisation for Economic Co-operation and Development). 2001. *OECD Environmental Outlook for the Chemicals Industry*. OECD Environment Directorate. http://www.oecd.org/env/ehs/2375538.pdf

OECD (Organisation for Economic Co-operation and Development). 2008. *Protection of "Critical Infrastructure" and the Role of Investment Policies Relating to National Security*. Paris: OECD. http://www.oecd.org/investment/investmentpolicy/40700392.pdf

Office of the Commissioner of Lobbying of Canada. 2016a. "Advanced Registry Search Results." https://lobbycanada.gc.ca/app/secure/ocl/lrs/do/advSrch?V_SEARCH.command=navigate&V_TOKEN=1234567890&V_SEARCH.docsStart=0

Office of the Commissioner of Lobbying of Canada. 2016b. "Listing of Organizations, Corporations, Clients and their Beneficiaries." https://lobbycanada.gc.ca/app/secure/ocl/lrs/do/clntOrgCrpLstg?lang=eng

Office of the Ombudsman. 2016. *Fit To Drink: Challenges in Providing Safe Drinking Water in British Columbia*. Victoria: Legislative Assembly of British Columbia. http://www.wsabc.ca/wp-content/uploads/2011/04/Ombudsmans-Report-on-Drinking-Water.pdf

Oh, O., M. Agrawal, and H.R. Rao. 2011. "Information Control and Terrorism: Tracking the Mumbai Terrorist Attack through Twitter." *Information Systems Frontiers* 13(1): 33–43.

Oltedal, S., and T. Rundmo. 2007. "Using Cluster Analysis to Test the Cultural Theory of Risk Perception." *Transportation Research Part F: Traffic Psychology and Behaviour* 10(3): 254–62.

Ontario Ministry of Environment. 2007. *Guidelines for Environmental Protection Measures at Chemical and Waste Storage Facilities*. Toronto: Ontario Ministry of the Environment. https://dr6j45jk9xcmk.cloudfront.net/documents/1759/196-chemical-and-waste-storage-facilities-en.pdf

Opheim, T. 1993. "Fire on the Cuyahoga." *EPA Journal* 19(2): 44.

Osborne, D., and T. Gaebler. 1992. *Reinventing Government: How the Entrepreneurial Spirit Is Transforming the Public Sector*. Reading, PA: Addison-Wesley.

Osborne, D., and P. Plastrik. 1997. *Banishing Bureaucracy: The Five Strategies for Reinventing Government*. Reading, PA: Addison-Wesley.

Ostrom, E. 2005. *Understanding Institutional Diversity*. Princeton, NJ: Princeton University Press.

Ouchi, W.G. 1979. "A Conceptual Framework for the Design of Organizational Control Mechanisms." *Management Science* 25(9): 833–48.

Ouyahia, M.A. 2006. "Public-private Partnerships for Funding Municipal Drinking Water Infrastructure: What Are the Challenges?" Policy Research Initiative Discussion Paper. http://open.canada.ca/vl/en/doc/publications-292004

Pachur, T., R. Hertwig, and F. Steinmann. 2012. "How Do People Judge Risks: Availability Heuristic, Affect Heuristic, or Both?" *Journal of Experimental Psychology: Applied* 18(3): 314–30.

Pal, L.A. 1997. *Beyond Policy Analysis: Public Issue Management in Turbulent Times*. Scarborough, ON: ITP Nelson.

Palmer, D., and M. Maher. 2010. "A Normal Accident Analysis of the Mortgage Meltdown." *Research in the Sociology of Organizations* 30: 219–56.

Pang, A., V.H.E. Chiong, and N.B.B. Abul Hassan. 2014. "Media Relations in an Evolving Media Landscape." *Journal of Communication Management* 18(3): 271–94.

Paris, M. 2014. "The New Ministerial Responsibility: Punish the Underlings." *CBC News*, 27 January. http://www.cbc.ca/news/

politics/the-new-ministerial-responsibility-punish-the-underlings-1.2510068

Parker, G. 2013. *Global Crisis: War, Climate Change and Catastrophe in the 17th Century.* New Haven, CT: Yale University Press.

Payton, L. 2015. "Federal Budget 2015: Parliament Hill, Security Agencies Getting More Money." *CBC News,* 21 April. http://www.cbc.ca/news/politics/federal-budget-2015-parliament-hill-security-agencies-getting-more-money-1.3042728

Pell, M.B., R. McNeill, and J. Roberts. 2013. "Special Report: Poor Planning Left Texas Firefighters Unprepared." *Reuters,* 22 May. http://www.reuters.com/article/2013/05/22/us-chemical-emergency-specialreportidUSBRE94L190201305 22

Pennings, J.M.E., and D.B. Grossman. 2008. "Responding to Crises and Disasters: The Role of Risk Attitudes and Risk Perceptions." *Disasters* 32(3): 434–48.

Pentland, R., and C. Wood. 2013. *Down the Drain: How We Are Failing to Protect Our Water Resources.* Vancouver: Greystone Books.

Perrow, C. 1999. *Normal Accidents: Living with High Risk Technologies,* 2nd ed. Princeton, NJ: Princeton University Press.

Perry, D. 2015. *Putting the 'Armed' Back into the Canadian Armed Forces.* Ottawa: Conference of Defence Associations Institute. http://www.macdonaldlaurier.ca/files/pdf/MLIdefenceprocurement.pdf

Peters, B. 2001. *The Politics of Bureaucracy.* 5th ed. Routledge: London.

Peters, R., V. Covello, and D. McCallum. 1997. "The Determinants of Trust and Credibility in Environmental Risk Communication: An Empirical Study." *Risk Analysis* 17(1): 43–54.

Petit, F.D., G.W. Bassett, W.A. Buehring, M.J. Collins, D.C. Dickinson, R.A. Haffenden, A.A. Huttenga, et al. 2013a. *Protective Measures Index and Vulnerability Index: Indicators of Critical Infrastructure Protection and Vulnerability.* Oak Ridge, TN: Argonne National Laboratory, Department of Energy.

Petit, F.D., G.W. Bassett, W.A. Buehring, M.J. Collins, D.C. Dickinson, R.A. Haffenden, A.A. Huttenga, et al. 2013b. *Resilience Measurement Index: An Indicator of Critical Infrastructure Resilience.* Oak Ridge, TN: Argonne National Laboratory, Department of Energy.

Petrie, K.J., and S. Wessely. 2002. "Modern Worries, New Technology, and Medicine." *British Medical Journal* 324(7339): 690–1.

Pew Research Center. 2015. *Public Trust in Government: 1958–2015.* Washington, DC: Pew Research Center. http://www.people-press.org/2014/11/13/public-trust-in-government/

Pfeifer, J.W. 2012. *Network Fusion Information and Intelligence Sharing for a Networked World*. Monterey, CA: Naval Postgraduate School.

PHAC (Public Health Agency of Canada). 2010. *Lessons Learned Review: Public Health Agency of Canada and Health Canada Response to the 2009 H1N1 Pandemic*. Ottawa: PHAC. http://www.phac-aspc.gc.ca/about_apropos/evaluation/reports-rapports/2010-2011/h1n1/pdf/h1n1-eng.pdf

PHAC (Public Health Agency of Canada). 2017. *FluWatch*. Ottawa: PHAC. http://publications.gc.ca/site/eng/9.507424/publication.html

Philippi, A., and D. Osberghaus. 2016. "Private Flood Mitigation in Germany: Effects of Experience, Expectations, and Information" (presentation, Society for Risk Analysis Europe Annual Conference, Bath, UK, 20–22 June). http://programme.exordo.com/sra2016/delegates/presentation/116/

Physicians for Social Responsibility. 2015. *Body Count: Casualty Figures after 10 Years of the "War on Terror."* Washington, DC: Physicians for Social Responsibility. http://www.ippnw.de/commonFiles/pdfs/Frieden/Body_Count_first_international_edition_2015_final.pdf

Picard, A. 2010. "H1N1 Patients Were Younger and Need More Care, Study Says." *Globe and Mail*, 11 February.

Pidgeon, N. 1997. "The Limits to Safety? Culture, Politics, Learning and Man-made Disasters." *Journal of Contingencies and Crisis Management* 5(1): 1–14.

Pidgeon, N., R.E. Kasperson, and P. Slovic. 2003. *The Social Amplification of Risk*. Cambridge, UK: Cambridge University Press.

Pinkleton, B.E., E.W. Austin, Y. Zhou, J.F. Willoughby, and M. Reiser. 2012. "Perceptions of News Media, External Efficacy, and Public Affairs Apathy in Political Decision Making and Disaffection." *Journalism & Mass Communication Quarterly* 89(1): 23–39.

Pitt, M. 2008. *Learning Lessons from the 2007 Floods*. http://webarchive.nationalarchives.gov.uk/20100807034701/http://archive.cabinetoffice.gov.uk/pittreview/_/media/assets/www.cabinetoffice.gov.uk/flooding_review/pitt_review_full%20pdf.pdf

Poland, G., and R. Jacobson. 2001. "Understanding Those Who Do Not Understand: a Brief Review of the Anti-vaccine Movement." *Vaccine* 2001(19): 2440–5. http://www.morrisonlucas.com/GL/vaccines/Vaccine_19_2440_anti_vaccine_movement.pdf

Pooley, E. 2001. "Mayor of the World." *Time Magazine*, 31 December. http://content.time.com/time/specials/packages/article/0,28804,2020227_2020306,00.html

Powell, C. 2016. "Did Terrorism Sway Spain's Election?" *Current History* 103(676): 376–382. http://charlespowell.eu/wp-content/uploads/2016/02/2004-Did-terrorism-sway-Spain---s-election.pdf

Prakash, A. 2000. "Responsible Care: An Assessment." *Business & Society* 39(2): 183–209.

Pratt, J.W. 1964. "Risk Aversion in the Small and in the Large." *Econometrica* 32: 122–36.

Psarros, G., R. Skjong, and M.S. Eide. 2009. "The Acceptability of Maritime Security Risk." *Journal of Transportation Security* 2(4): 149–63.

Public Broadcasting Service. 2016. *Keeping the Memory of WWI Alive with Plans for a National Memorial.* www.pbs.org/newshour/bb/keeping-the-memory-of-wwi-alive-with-plans-for-a-national-memorial/

Public Safety Canada. 2007. "Canada's New Emergency Management Act: Implications for Information Sharing." *CIP Exchange* 9–10.

Public Safety Canada. 2008. *Working towards a National Strategy and Action for Critical Infrastructure.* Ottawa: Public Safety Canada. http://publications.gc.ca/site/archivee-archived.html?url=http://publications.gc.ca/collections/collection_2008/ps-sp/PS4-54-2008E.pdf

Public Safety Canada. 2009a. *Action Plan for Critical Infrastructure.* Ottawa: Public Safety Canada. http://www.publicsafety.gc.ca/cnt/rsrcs/pblctns/pln-crtcl-nfrstrctr/pln-crtcl-nfrstrctr-eng.pdf

Public Safety Canada. 2009b. *National Strategy for Critical Infrastructure.* Ottawa: Public Safety Canada. http://www.publicsafety.gc.ca/cnt/rsrcs/pblctns/srtg-crtcl-nfrstrctr/index-eng.aspx

Public Safety Canada. 2013. *Public Report on the Terrorist Threat to Canada.* Ottawa: Public Safety Canada. https://www.publicsafety.gc.ca/cnt/rsrcs/pblctns/trrrst-thrt-cnd/index-en.aspx

Public Safety Canada. 2014a. *Action Plan for Critical Infrastructure: 2014–2017.* Ottawa: Public Safety Canada. http://www.publicsafety.gc.ca/cnt/rsrcs/pblctns/pln-crtcl-nfrstrctr-2014-17/index-eng.aspx

Public Safety Canada. 2014b. *Forging a Common Understanding for Critical Infrastructure. Shared Narrative.* Ottawa: Public Safety Canada. https://www.publicsafety.gc.ca/cnt/rsrcs/pblctns/2016-frgng-cmmn-ndrstndng-crtcalnfrstrctr/index-en.aspx

Public Safety Canada. 2015. *Security of Canada Information Sharing Act: Public Framework.* Ottawa: Public Safety Canada. https://www.publicsafety.gc.ca/cnt/ntnl-scrt/cntr-trrrsm/shrng-frmwrk-eng.aspx

Public Safety Canada. 2016. *Emergency Preparedness Week Toolkit.* Ottawa: Public Safety Canada. http://www.getprepared.gc.ca/cnt/rsrcs/ep-wk/tlkt-en.aspx

Public Works and Government Services Canada. 2009. *Public Opinion Research in the Government of Canada: Annual Report 2009–2010*. Ottawa: Public Works and Government Services Canada. http://publications.gc.ca/collections/collection_2011/tpsgc-pwgsc/P100-1-2010-eng.pdf

Quebec Commission of Inquiry. 2008. *Commission of Inquiry into the Collapse of a Portion of the de la Concorde Overpass, Oct 3, 2006 – October 15, 2007*. Saint-Lazare, QC: Gibson Library Connections.

Quigley, J., T. Bedford, and L. Walls. 2007. "Estimating Rate of Occurrence of Rare Events with Empirical Bayes: A Railway Application." *Reliability Engineering and System Safety* 92(5): 619–27.

Quigley, J., and M. Revie. 2011. "Estimating the Probability of Rare Events: Addressing Zero Failure Data." *Risk Analysis* 31(7): 1120–32.

Quigley, K. 2008. *Responding to Crises in the Modern Infrastructure: Policy Lessons from Y2K*. Houndmills, Basingtoke: Palgrave MacMillan.

Quigley, K. 2013. "Man Plans, God Laughs: Canada's National Strategy for Protecting Critical Infrastructure." *Canadian Public Administration* 56(1): 142–64.

Quigley, K., and B. Bisset. 2014. "Analysis of the Risk Regulation Regime in Canada for Controlling Major Incidents Involving Dangerous Chemicals." Halifax: Dalhousie University.

Quigley, K., C. Burns, and K. Stallard. 2013. "Communicating Effectively about Cyber-security Risks: Probabilities, Peer Networks and a Longer Term Education Program." Public Safety Canada Contract: No. 7181309 - Identifying and Effectively Communicating Cybersecurity Risks. http://cip.management.dal.ca/wp-content/uploads/2013/04/Quigley-Burns-Stallard-Cyber-Security-Paper-Final-1.pdf

Quigley, K., C. Burns, and K. Stallard. 2015. "'Cyber Gurus': A Rhetorical Analysis of the Language of Cybersecurity Specialists and the Implications for Security Policy and Critical Infrastructure Protection." *Government Information Quarterly* 32(2): 108–17.

Quigley, K., C. Macdonald, and J. Quigley. 2016. "Pre-existing Condition: Taking Media Coverage into Account when Preparing for H1N1." *Canadian Public Administration* 59(2): 267–88.

Quigley, K., and B. Mills. 2014. "An Analysis of Transportation Security Risk Regulation Regimes: Canadian Airports, Seaports, Rail, Trucking and Bridges." Halifax: Dalhousie University.

Quigley, K. and B. Mills. 2016. "'Set Adrift': Fatalism as Organizational Culture at Canadian Seaports." *Journal of Homeland Security and Emergency Management* 13(1): 191–218.

Quigley, K., and J. Quigley. 2013. "Of Gods and Men: Selected Print Media Coverage of Natural Disasters and Industrial Failures in Three Westminster Countries." *Journal of Homeland Security and Emergency Management* 10(1).

Quigley, K., J. Quigley, B. Mills, and K. Stallard. 2013. "Analysis of Selected Print Media Coverage of Two Cases of Failed Terrorist Plots: *The Australian*'s coverage of the 'Sydney Five' (2005) and *The Globe and Mail*'s coverage of the 'Toronto 18' (2006)." Halifax: Dalhousie University.

Railway Safety Act Review Secretariat. 2007. *Stronger Ties: A Shared Commitment to Railway Safety.* Ottawa: Transport Canada. https://www.tc.gc.ca/media/documents/railsafety/TRANSPORT_Stronger_Ties_Report_FINAL_e.pdf

Railway Safety Act, Revised Statutes of Canada. 1985. Chapter 32, 4th supplement. http://www.tc.gc.ca/eng/acts-regulations/acts-1985s4-32.htm

Rajabiun, R., and C.A. Middleton. 2013. Multilevel Governance and Broadband Infrastructure Development: Evidence from Canada. *Telecommunications Policy* 37(9): 702–14.

Rakobowchuk, P. 2014. "No More Charges Coming in Case of Lac-Megantic Rail Disaster, Crown Says." *Globe and Mail,* 11 September.

Raschky, P.A., and H. Weck-Hannemann. 2007. "Charity Hazard – A Real Hazard to Natural Disaster Insurance?" *Environmental Hazards* 7(4): 321–9.

Raynauld, V., and J. Greenberg. 2014. "Tweet, Click, Vote: Twitter and the 2010 Ottawa Municipal Election." *Journal of Information Technology & Politics* 11(4): 412–34.

Reid, R. 1998. "Status of Water Disinfection in Latin America and the Caribbean." In *Proceedings of the Symposium PAHO/WHO, Water Quality: Effective Disinfection,* Peru, 27, 29.

Reniers, G., and Y. Pavlova. 2013. *Using Game Theory to Improve Safety within Chemical Industrial Parks.* London, UK: Springer.

Renn, O. 2008. "White Paper on Risk Governance: Toward an Integrative Framework." In *Global Risk Governance: Concept and Practice using the IRGC Framework*, edited by O. Renn and K. Walker. Dordrecht: Springer.

Renn, O., W.J. Burns, J.X. Kasperson, R.E. Kasperson, and P. Slovic. 1992. "The Social Amplification of Risk: Theoretical Foundations and Empirical Applications." *Journal of Social Issues* 48(4): 137–60.

Renn, O., and K. Walker. 2008. *Global Risk Governance: Concept and Practice Using the IRGC Framework.* Dordrecht: Springer.

Rid, T. 2013. *Cyber War Will Not Take Place*. New York: Oxford University Press.

Rinaldi, S. M., J.P. Peerenboom, and T.K. Kelly. 2001. "Identifying, Understanding, and Analyzing Critical Infrastructure Interdependencies." *IEEE Control Systems* 21(6): 11–25.

Robert, B., and L. Morabito. 2011. *Reducing Vulnerability of Critical Infrastructures – Methodological Manual*. Montreal: Presses Internationales Polytechnique.

Robertson, C., and E. Lipton. 2010. "BP Is Criticized over Oil Spill, but U.S. Missed Chances to Act." *New York Times*, 1 May. http://www.nytimes.com/2010/05/01/us/01gulf.html?pagewanted=all

Robertson, G. 2015. "New Rail Safety Rules for Canada, U.S. Reveal Disparity in Oversight." *Globe and Mail*, 29 July. http://www.theglobe-andmail.com/report-on-business/canada-us-finalize-new-rail-safety-rules-to-avoid-future-derailments/article25758051/

Roe, E., and P.R. Schulman. 2008. *High Reliability Management*. Stanford: Stanford Business Books.

Rosen, H., J. Wen, and T. Snoddon, T. 2012. *Public Finance in Canada*. 4th ed. New York: McGraw-Hill.

Rosen, S. 1999. "Most – But Not All – Regions See Food Gains." *Food Review* 22(3).

Rosen, W. 2007. *Justinian's Flea: The First Great Plague and the End of the Roman Empire*. London: Viking Penguin.

Rossi, J. 2014. "'Mal-Adaptive' Federalism: Addressing the Structural Barriers to Interstate Coordination of Sustainability Initiatives." *Case Western Reserve Law Review* 64(4): 1759–89. Vanderbilt Law and Economics Research Paper No. 14-15.

Rousseau, D., S. Sitkin, R. Burt, and C. Camerer. 1998. "Not So Different After All: A Cross-discipline View of Risk." *Academy of Management Review* 23(3): 393–404.

Roux-Dufort, C. 2007. "Is Crisis Management (Only) a Management of Exceptions?" *Journal of Contingencies and Crisis Management* 15(2): 105–14.

Røvik, K. 2011. "From Fashion to Virus: An Alternative Theory of Organizations' Handling of Management Ideas." *Organization Studies* 32(5): 631–53.

Roy, J. 2012. "Social Media's Democratic Paradox: Lessons from Canada." *European Journal of ePractice* 16: 5–15.

Royal Canadian Mounted Police. 2014. *Independent Review – Moncton Shooting – June 4, 2014*. Ottawa: Royal Canadian Mounted Police.

http://www.rcmp-grc.gc.ca/en/independent-review-moncton-shooting-june-4-2014

Royal College of Physicians. 2009. *Trust in Doctors: Annual Survey of Trust in Professions*. London, UK: Royal College of Physicians. http://www.ipsos-mori.com/DownloadPublication/1305_sri-trust-in-professions-2009.pdf

Royal Society. 1992. *Risk Analysis, Perception and Management*. London, UK: Royal Society.

Rubim de Pinho Accioli Doria, M. 2010. "Innovation and Regulation in the Chemical Industry: The Case of the European Union, 1976–2003." PhD diss., University of Trento.

Rubin, A. 2011. "All Your Devices Can Be Hacked." TED Talks. http://www.ted.com/talks/avi_rubin_all_your_devices_can_be_hacked.html

Rudner, M. 2009. "Protecting Canada's Critical National Infrastructure from Terrorism: Mapping a Proactive Strategy for Energy Security." *International Journal* 64(3): 775–97.

Rusnell, C., and J. Russell. 2004. "Skylar Murphy Didn't Plan to Use Pipe Bomb on Plane, RCMP Say." *CBC News*, 16 January. http://www.cbc.ca/news/canada/edmonton/skylar-murphy-didn-t-plan-to-use-pipe-bomb-on-plane-rcmp-say-1.2499162

Russell, D., and J. Simpson. 2010. "Emergency Planning and Preparedness for the Deliberate Release of Toxic Industrial Chemicals." *Chemical Toxicology* 48: 171–6.

Rutsaert, P., Á. Regan, Z. Pieniak, Á. McConnon, A. Moss, P. Wall, and W. Verbeke. 2013. "The Use of Social Media in Food Risk and Benefit Communication." *Trends in Food Science & Technology* 30(1): 84–91.

Sagan, S. 1993. *The Limits of Safety: Organizations, Accidents, and Nuclear Weapons*. Princeton, NJ: Princeton University Press.

Samenow, J. 2013. "Weather Service Updates Criteria for Hurricane Warnings, after Sandy Criticism." *Washington Post*, 4 April. https://www.washingtonpost.com/news/capital-weather-gang/wp/2013/04/04/weather-service-changes-criteria-for-hurricane-warnings-after-sandy-criticism/

Sanchez, R. 2013. "Boston Marathon Bombings: How Social Media Identified Wrong Suspects." *The Telegraph*, 19 April. http://www.telegraph.co.uk/news/worldnews/northamerica/usa/10006028/Boston-marathon-bombings-how-social-media-identified-wrong-suspects.html

Sandman, P. 2012. *Responding to Community Outrage: Strategies for Effective Risk Communication*. Falls Church, VA: American Industrial

Hygiene Association. http://petersandman.com/media/Respondingto
CommunityOutrage.pdf

Sato, K. 1988. "Trust and Group Size in a Social Dilemma." *Japanese Psychological Research* 30(2): 88–93.

Savoie, D. 2003. *Breaking the Bargain: Public Servants, Ministers, and Parliament.* Toronto: University of Toronto Press.

Savoie, D.J. 2015. *What Is Government Good At? A Canadian Answer.* Montreal: McGill-Queen's University Press.

Schabas, R., and N. Rau. 2009. "Flu Vaccine May Come Too Late." *Globe and Mail,* 27 October.

Schein, R., K. Wilson, and J.E. Keelan. 2010. *Literature Review on Effectiveness of the Use of Social Media: A Report for Peel Public Health.* Mississauga, ON: Peel Public Health.

Schierow, L.J. 2005. *Chemical Plant Security.* CRS Report for Congress. Washington, DC: Congressional Research Service, Library of Congress.

Schneier, B. 2003. *Beyond Fear: Thinking Sensibly About Security in an Uncertain World.* Gottingen: Copernicus.

Schultz, F., S. Utz, and A. Göritz. 2011. "Is the Medium the Message? Perceptions of and Reactions to Crisis Communication via Twitter, Blogs and Traditional Media." *Public Relations Review* 37(1): 20–7.

Schultz, F., and S. Wehmeier. 2010. "Institutionalization of Corporate Social Responsibility within Corporate Communications. Combining Institutional, Sensemaking and Communication Perspectives." *Corporate Communications* 15(1): 9–29.

Schwartz, N. 2016. "Vowing to Squeeze Businesses, Trump Has Tactics Challenged." *New York Times,* 4 December. https://www.nytimes.com/2016/12/04/us/politics/trump-takes-twitter-aim-at-companies-looking-to-move-jobs-abroad.html?_r=0

Science Media Centre of Canada. 2013. *The SMCC Story.* Ottawa: Science Media Centre of Canada. http://sciencemediacentre.ca/site/?page_id=24

Seglins, D. 2015. "Lac-Mégantic Disaster Led to Transport Canada Shakeup, Says Minister Lisa Raitt." *CBC News,* 1 July. http://www.cbc.ca/news/canada/lac-m%C3%A9gantic-disaster-led-to-transport-canada-shakeup-says-minister-lisa-raitt-1.3134120

Seib, G. 2008. "In Crisis, Opportunity for Obama." *Wall Street Journal,* 21 November. http://www.wsj.com/articles/SB122721278056345271

Seidenstat, P. 2004. "Terrorism, Airport Security, and the Private Sector." *Public Administration Review* 2(1): 275–91.

Sencer, D., and D. Millar. 2006. "Reflections on the 1976 Swine Flu Vaccination Program." *Emerging Infectious Diseases* 12(1): 29–33. https://wwwnc.cdc.gov/eid/article/12/1/05-1007_article

Sharif, A.M. 2008. "Transformational Government: What Is the Shape of Things to Come?" *Transforming Government: People, Process and Policy* 2(1): 71–75.

Sheppard, K. 2014. "McCain Calls Sony Hack an 'Act Of War.'" *Huffington Post*, 21 December. http://www.huffingtonpost.com/2014/12/21/sony-north-korea-war_n_6362454.html

Sheps, S.B., and K. Cardiff. 2011. "Patient Safety: A Wake-up Call." *Clinical Governance* 16(2): 148–58.

Shirky, C. 2008. *Here Comes Everybody*. London: Allen Lane.

Shirley, M., and P. Walsh. 2000. "Public versus Private Ownership: The State of the Debate." Policy Research Working Paper 2420. Washington, DC: The World Bank, Development Research Group.

Shore, J.J.M. 2008. *The Legal Imperative to Protect Critical Energy Infrastructure*. Ottawa: Canadian Centre of Intelligence and Security Studies.

Shore, J.J.M., and C. Schafer. 2015. *Review of Commissions of Inquiry with Respect to Findings of Major, O'Connor, Iacobucci Concerning Information Sharing that Affects Critical Infrastructure Protection*. Critical Infrastructure Protection – Information Sharing Protocol Project, CSSP-2013-CP-1026. Ottawa: National Defence.

Shrives, J. 2004. "Environment Canada's New Environmental Emergency Regulations." *Canadian Chemical News* 56(2): 17–21.

Shrubsole, D. 2000. "Flood Management in Canada at the Crossroads." *Global Environmental Change Part B: Environmental Hazards* 2(2): 63–75.

Signorini, A., A.M. Segre, and P.M. Polgreen. 2011. "The Use of Twitter to Track Levels of Disease Activity and Public Concern in the US During the Influenza A H1N1 Pandemic." *PloS One* 6(5): e19467.

Singh, P., P. Singh, I. Park, J. Lee, and H.R. Rao. 2009. "Information Sharing: A Study of Information Attributes and their Relative Significance during Catastrophic Events." In *Cyber-Security and Global Information Assurance: Threat Analysis and Response Solutions*, edited by K.J. Knapp. Hershey, PA: Information Science Reference.

Sjöberg, L. 1998. "Risk Perception: Experts and the Public." *European Psychologist* 3(1): 1–12.

Sjöberg, L. 2000. "Factors in Risk Perception." *Risk Analysis* 20(1): 1–12.

Sloan, E. 2012. "Homeland Security and Defence in the Post 9/11 Era." In *Canada's National Security in the Post 9/11 World: Strategy, Interests and Threats*, edited by D. McDonough. Toronto: University of Toronto Press.

Slovic, P. 1987. "Perception of Risk." *Science* 236(4799): 280–5.

Slovic, P., M.L. Finucane, E. Peters, and D.G. MacGregor. 2004. "Risk as Analysis and Risk as Feelings: Some Thoughts about Affect, Reason, Risk, and Rationality." *Risk Analysis* 24(2): 31122.

Slovic, P., B. Fischhoff, and S. Lichtenstein. 1979. "Rating the Risks." *Environment* 21(3): 14–20.

Slovic, P., B. Fischhoff, and S. Lichtenstein. 1982. "Why Study Risk Perception?" *Risk Analysis* 2(2): 83–93.

Slovic, P., E. Peters, M.L. Finucane, and D.G. Macgregor. 2005. "Affect, Risk, and Decision Making." *Health Psychology* 24(4): 35-40.

Smith, J. 2014. "Ottawa Shooting Not Terrorism, Says Thomas Mulcair." *Toronto Star,* 29 October. https://www.thestar.com/news/canada/2014/10/29/ottawa_shooting_not_terrorism_says_thomas_mulcair.html

Smith, L.C., and S.R. Stephenson. 2013. "New Trans-Arctic Shipping Routes Navigable by Midcentury." *Proceedings of the National Academy of Sciences* 110(13): E1191–E1195.

Smith, P.K., and G. Steffgen. 2013. *Cyberbullying through the New Media: Findings from an International Network*. London, UK: Psychology Press.

Smithson, J., and S. Venette, S. 2013. "Stonewalling as an Image-Defense Strategy: A Critical Examination of BP's Response to the Deepwater Horizon Explosion." *Communication Studies* 64(4): 395–410.

Smolash, W.N. 2009. "Mark of Cain (ada): Racialized Security Discourse in Canada's National Newspapers." *University of Toronto Quarterly* 78(2): 745–63.

Société Mutuelle de Prévention inc. 2015. *Définition.* http://www.mutuelledeprevention.com/mutuelle.aspx

Society of Actuaries. 2014. *Emerging Risks Survey.* Schaumburg, IL: Society of Actuaries. https://www.soa.org/Research/Research-Projects/Risk-Management/2014-emerging-risks-survey.aspx

Soumerai, S.B., D. Ross-Degnan, and J.S. Kahn. 1992. "Effects of Professional and Media Warnings about the Association between Aspirin Use in Children and Reye's Syndrome." *Millbank Quarterly* 70: 155–82.

Spellman, F., and R. Bieber. 2009. *Chemical Infrastructure Protection and Homeland Security*. Toronto: Scarecrow Press.

Standing Senate Committee on National Security and Defence. 2007. *Canadian Security Guide Book. An Update of Security Problems in Search of Solutions. Seaports.* Ottawa: Standing Senate on National Security and Defence. 39th Parliament – 1st Session. March.

Standing Senate Committee on National Security and Defence. 2008. *Emergency Preparedness in Canada.* Ottawa: Standing Senate on National Security and Defence. http://www.parl.gc.ca/content/sen/committee/392/defe/rep/rep13aug08vol1-e.pdf

Standing Senate Committee on Social Affairs, Science and Technology. 2010. *Canada's Response to the 2009 H1N1 Influenza Pandemic.* Ottawa: Standing Senate Committee on Social Affairs, Science and Technology http://www.parl.gc.ca/content/sen/committee/403/soci/rep/rep15dec10-e.pdf

Star Staff. 2013. "Climate Change Caused Calgary, Ontario Flooding, Majority Believe." *Toronto Star*, 24 July. http://www.thestar.com/news/gta/2013/07/24/climate_change_caused_calgary_ontario_flooding_poll.html

Starr, C. 1969. "Social Benefit Versus Technological Risk." *Science (New York)* 165(3899): 1232–8.

Statistics Canada. 2003. *The Future for Canada–US Container Port Rivalries.* Ottawa: Statistics Canada. http://publications.gc.ca/Collection/Statcan/54F0001X/54F0001XIE2001.pdf

Statistics Canada. 2009. *Drinking Water Plants and Sewage Treatment Plants in Canada, by Population Served, 2009.* Ottawa: Statistics Canada. http://www.statcan.gc.ca/pub/16-201-x/2010000/t236-eng.htm

Statistics Canada. 2012. *Leading Causes of Death in Canada, 2009.* Ottawa: Statistics Canada. http://www.statcan.gc.ca/pub/84-215-x/84-215-x2012001-eng.htm

Statistics Canada. 2015. "Passengers Enplaned and Deplaned on Selected Services – Top 50 Airports. Air Carrier Traffic at Canadian Airports." Ottawa: Statistics Canada. http://www.statcan.gc.ca/pub/51-203-x/2015000/t002-eng.htm

Steinberg, T. 2000. *Acts of God: The Unnatural History of Natural Disaster in America.* Oxford: Oxford University Press.

Stern, J., and J. Berger. 2015. *ISIS: The State of Terror.* New York: Harper Collins.

Stewart, M.G., and J. Mueller. 2011. "Cost-benefit Analysis of Advanced Imaging Technology Full Body Scanners for Airline Passenger Security Screening." *Journal of Homeland Security and Emergency Management* 8(1).

Stiglitz, J. 2008. "Government Failure vs. Market Failure: Principles of Regulation" (presentation, Tobin Project's Conference on Government and Markets: Toward a New Theory of Regulation, Yulee, FL, 1–3 February). http://policydialogue.org/files/events/Stiglitz_Principles_of_Regulation.pdf

Stohl, M. 2007. "Cyber Terrorism: A Clear and Present Danger, the Sum of All Fears, Breaking Point or Patriot Games?" *Crime, Law and Social Change* 46: 223–38.

Strolovitch, D., D. Warren, and P. Frymer. 2006. *Katrina's Political Roots and Divisions: Race, Class, and Federalism in American Politics. Understanding Katrina: Perspectives from the Social Sciences.* Brooklyn, NY: Social Science Research Council. http://understandingkatrina.ssrc.org/FrymerStrolovitchWarren/

Strunsky, S. 2013. "Port Authority Puts Sandy Damage at $2.2 Billion, Authorizes $50 Million to Power Wash PATH Tunnels." *NJ.com,* 13 October. http://www.nj.com/news/index.ssf/2013/10/port_authority_sandy_22billion_outlines_recovery_measures.html

Sunstein, C. 2005. *Laws of Fear: Beyond the Precautionary Principle.* New York: Cambridge University Press.

Sunstein, C.R. 2003. "Terrorism and Probability Neglect." *Journal of Risk and Uncertainty* 26(2–3): 121–36.

Surminski, S., and J. Eldridge. 2015. "Flood Insurance in England: An Assessment of the Current and Newly Proposed Insurance Scheme in the Context of Rising Flood Risk." *Journal of Flood Risk Management.* doi: 10.1111/jfr3.12127

Tait, J. 2008. "Risk Governance of Genetically Modified Crops – European and American Perspectives." In *Global Risk Governance: Concept and Practice Using the IRGG Framework,* edited by G. Renn and K. Walker, 133–53. Dordrecht: Springer.

Taleb, N.N. 2007. *The Black Swan: The Impact of the Highly Improbable.* New York: Random House.

Tamtik, M. 2016. "Policy Coordination Challenges in Governments' Innovation Policy – The Case of Ontario, Canada." *Science and Public Policy* 43(4): 1–11.

Tausczik, Y., K. Faasse, J.W. Pennebaker, and K.J. Petrie. 2011. "Public Anxiety and Information Seeking Following the H1N1 Outbreak: Blogs, Newspaper Articles, and Wikipedia Visits." *Health Communication* 27(2): 179–85.

Taylor-Gooby, P. 2006. "The Efficiency/Trust Dilemma in Public Policy Reform." Working Paper 9-2006. Canterbury, UK: School of Social Policy, Sociology and Social Research, University of Kent.

Thielman, S. 2016. "Trump's Tweet about Lockheed-Martin Cuts $4bn in Value as Share Prices Fall." *The Guardian*, 12 December. https://www. theguardian.com/business/2016/dec/12/lockheed-martin-share-prices-donald-trump-tweet

Thompson, M., R. Ellis, and A. Wildavsky. 1990. *Cultural Theory.* Boulder, CO: Westview Press.

Toro, F. 2014. "Keep Calm and Nenshi On: How Floods Turned the Calgary mayor into a Folk Hero." *The Guardian*, 13 December. Accessed 19 July 2016. https://www.theguardian.com/public-leaders-network/2014/dec/30/nenshi-calgary-mayor-alberta-floods

Toronto Star. 2010. "Sunrise Propane Blast Report to be Made Public." *Toronto Star,* 5 August. https://www.thestar.com/news/gta/2010/08/05/sunrise_propane_blast_report_to_be_made_public.html

TransForce. 2016. *New Horizons, 2016 Annual Report.* https://adobeindd.com/view/publications/48013a13-66e8-467a-b3bd-f859cb4b65e0/1/publication-web-resources/pdf/TFI_AR2016_digital_EN.pdf

Transport Canada. 2011a. *Transportation in Canada 2011.* Ottawa: Transport Canada. http://www.tc.gc.ca/media/documents/policy/Transportation_in_Canada_2011.pdf

Transport Canada. 2011b. *Transportation in Canada 2011: Statistical Addendum.* Ottawa: Transport Canada. https://www.tc.gc.ca/media/documents/policy/Stats-Addend-2011-eng.pdf

Transport Canada. 2012a. *Road Transportation.* Ottawa: Transport Canada. http://www.tc.gc.ca/eng/road-menu.htm

Transport Canada. 2012b. *Rail Transportation.* Ottawa: Transport Canada. https://www.tc.gc.ca/eng/policy/anre-menu-3020.htm

Transport Canada. 2013a. *National Civil Aviation Security Program (CARAC).* Ottawa: Transport Canada. http://www.tc.gc.ca/media/documents/security/NCASP_FINAL_ENGLISH_%282%29.pdf

Transport Canada. 2013b. *Program Activity Architecture 2011–2012.* Ottawa: Transport Canada. http://www.tc.gc.ca/eng/corporate-services/planning-paa-32.htm#s1

Transport Canada. 2013c. *Transport Canada Announces Emergency Directive to Increase Rail Safety.* Ottawa: Transport Canada. http://news.gc.ca/web/article-en.do?nid=831429

Transport Canada. 2013d. *National Safety Code 1987.* Ottawa: Transport Canada. http://www.tc.gc.ca/eng/motorvehiclesafety/safevehicles-motorcarriers-safetycode-index-290.htm

Transport Canada. 2013e. *Canadian Port Authorities.* Ottawa: Transport Canada. http://www.tc.gc.ca/eng/policy/acf-acfi-menu-2963.htm

Transport Canada. 2013f. "Harper Government Introduces Administrative Monetary Penalties Regulations to Support the *International Bridges and Tunnels Act*." http://www.tc.gc.ca/eng/mediaroom/releases-2012-h084e-6815.htm

Transport Canada. 2014. *2014 TSB Recommendations & TC Responses*. Ottawa: Transport Canada. https://www.tc.gc.ca/eng/railsafety/tsb-2014-962.html

Transport Canada. 2015a. *Transport Canada 2015-16 Report on Plans and Priorities*. Ottawa: Transport Canada. https://www.tc.gc.ca/eng/corporate-services/planning-1216.html

Transport Canada. 2015b. *Follow-up Audit of Rail Safety*. Ottawa: Transport Canada. https://www.tc.gc.ca/eng/corporate-services/aas-audit-1269.html#print_version.

Transport Canada. 2016. *Canadian Motor Vehicle Traffic Collision Statistics: 2014*. Ottawa: Transport Canada. https://www.tc.gc.ca/media/documents/roadsafety/cmvtcs2014_eng.pdf

Transportation of Dangerous Goods Act, Statutes of Canada. 1985. Chapter 34. http://www.tc.gc.ca/eng/acts-regulations/acts-1992c34.htm

Treasury Board of Canada Secretariat. 2007. *Canadian Cost-Benefit Analysis Guide*. Ottawa: Treasury Board of Canada Secretariat. https://www.tbs-sct.gc.ca/rtrap-parfa/analys/analys-eng.pdf

Tremayne, M., ed. 2012. *Blogging, Citizenship and the Future of Media*. London: Routledge.

Trivedi, B. 2012. "Celebrate Chemistry, Realistically." *Chemical & Engineering News* 90(5): 4.

TSB (Transportation Safety Board of Canada). 2014. *Lac-Megantic Runaway Train and Derailment Investigation Report*. Gatineau, QC: Transportation Safety Board of Canada. http://www.tsb.gc.ca/eng/rapports-reports/rail/2013/r13d0054/r13d0054-r-es.asp

Tversky, A., and D. Kahneman. 1973. "Availability: A Heuristic for Judging Frequency and Probability." *Cognitive Psychology* 5(1): 207–33.

UK Office of Cyber Security. 2011. *The UK Cyber Security Strategy*. London, UK: Cabinet Office. https://www.gov.uk/government/uploads/system/uploads/attachment_data/file/60961/uk-cyber-security-strategy-final.pdf

United States Senate Permanent Subcommittee on Investigations. 2012. *Federal Support for and Involvement in State Fusion Centers*. http://www.hsgac.senate.gov/download/?id=49139e81-1dd7-4788-a3bb-d6e7d97ddeo4

Utz, S., F. Schultz, and S. Glocka, S. 2013. "Crisis Communication Online: How Medium, Crisis Type and Emotions Affected Public Relations in the Fukushima Daiichi Nuclear Disaster." *Public Relations Review* 39: 40–6.

Vaccari, C. 2008. "Surfing to the Elysee: The Internet in the 2007 French Elections." *French Politics* 6(1): 1–22.

van Asselt, M., S. van 't Klooster, P. van Notten, and L.A. Smits. 2010. *Foresight in Action: Developing Policy-Oriented Scenarios.* Abingdon: Earthscan.

van Courtland Moon, J.E. 1984. "Chemical Weapons and Deterrence: The World War II Experience." *International Security* 8(4): 3–35.

Van der Heijden, K. 2005. *Scenarios: The Art of Strategic Conversation* 2nd ed. Hoboken, NJ: John Wiley & Sons.

Van Praet, N. 2013. "Railway in Lac Mégantic Disaster Files for Bankruptcy, Setting Stage for Massive Legal Battle." *Financial Post* 7 August. http://business.financialpost.com/2013/08/07/mma-railway-files-for-bankruptcy-lac-megantic/

Vaughan, D. 1996. *The Challenger Launch Decision: Risky Technology, Culture and Deviance at NASA.* Chicago: Chicago University Press.

Veil, S.R., T. Buehner, and M.J. Palenchar. 2011. "A Work-in-Process Literature Review: Incorporating Social Media in Rsk and Crisis Communication." *Journal of Contingencies and Crisis Management* 19(2): 110–22.

Vescio, S. 2012. "An Introduction to Cargo Theft in Canada." McCague Borlack LLP. http://mccagueborlack.com/emails/articles/cargo-theft.html

Veterans Affairs n.d. *General Statistics: War Participation.* Ottawa: Veterans Affairs. http://www.veterans.gc.ca/eng/news/general-statistics

Vince, G. 2013. "Global Transformers: What if a Pandemic Strikes?" BBC, 11 July. http://www.bbc.com/future/story/20130711-what-if-a-pandemic-strikes

Vincent, D. 2015. "24% of Canadians Like Tory Plan on Syrian Refugees, Poll Shows." *Toronto Star*, 11 September.

Vithoontien, V. 2004. "Identifying Linkages between the Chemical Conventions for Possible Future Activities" (presentation, World Bank 8th Annual Financial Agents Workshop, Washington, DC).

Vogel, D. 1986. *National Styles of Regulation: Environmental Policy in Great Britain and the United States.* Ithaca, NY: Cornell University Press.

Volchek, K., M. Fingas, M. Hornof, L. Boudreau, and N. Yanofsky. 2006. "Decontamination in the Event of a Chemical or Radiological Terrorist

Attack." In *Protection of Civilian Infrastructure from Acts of Terrorism*, edited by K.V. Frolov and G.B. Baecher, 125–45. Houten, Netherlands: Springer.

Von Solms, R., and J. Van Niekerk. 2013. "From Information Security to Cyber Security." *Computers and Security* 38: 97–102.

Wahba, P., and J. Gordon. 2013. "Rail at Center of Quebec Town Tragedy and Heart of Its Recovery." *Reuters*, 15 July. http://in.reuters.com/article/canada-train-idINDEE96E02H20130715

Wahlberg, A., and L. Sjoberg. 2000. "Risk Perception and the Media." *Journal of Risk Research* 3(1): 31–50.

Walkerton Commission of Inquiry. 2002a. *Chapter 1: Introduction. Part One of the Walkerton Commission of Inquiry.* Toronto: Ministry of the Attorney General. http://www.archives.gov.on.ca/en/e_records/walkerton/

Walkerton Commission of Inquiry. 2002b. *Chapter 11: The Management of Municipal Water Systems. Part Two of the Walkerton Commission of Inquiry.* Toronto: Ministry of the Attorney General. http://www.archives.gov.on.ca/en/e_records/walkerton/

Walsh, V., and G. Lodorfos. 2002. "Technological and Organizational Innovation in Chemicals and Related Products." *Technology Analysis and Strategic Management* 14(3): 273–98.

Walter, T., J. Littlewood, and M. Pickering. 1995. "Death in the News: The Public Invigilation of Private Emotion." *Sociology* 29(4): 579–96.

Walton, D.N. 1996. *Argumentation Schemes for Presumptive Reasoning.* Mahwah, NJ: L. Erlbaum Associates.

Wason, P.C. 1960. "On the Failure to Eliminate Hypotheses in a Conceptual Task." *Quarterly Journal of Experimental Psychology* 12(3): 129–40.

Water Security Agency. 2015. *Annual Report for 2014-2015.* Regina: Government of Saskatchewan. https://www.wsask.ca/Global/About%20WSA/Annual%20Reports%20and%20Plans/Water%20Security%20Agency%20Annual%20Reports/WSA-AR- Report-14- 15.pdf

Waterer, G.W., D.S. Hui, and C.R. Jenkins. 2010. "Public Health Management of Pandemic (H1N1) 2009 Infection in Australia: A Failure!" *Respirology* 15(1): 51–6.

Weaver, R., and D. Jackson. 2012. "Tragic Heroes, Moral Guides and Activists: Representations of Maternal Grief, Child Death and Tragedy in Australian Newspapers." *Health Sociology Review* 21(4): 432–40.

Weick, K.E., and K.H. Roberts. 1993. "Collective Mind in Organizations: Heedful Interrelating on Flight Decks." *Administrative Science Quarterly* 38(3): 357–81.

Weick, K.E., and K.M. Sutcliffe. 2001. *Managing the Unexpected: Assuring High Performance in an Age of Complexity*. San Francisco: Jossey-Bass.

Weinhold, B. 2011. "Alberta's Oil Sands: Hard Evidence, Missing Data, New Promises." *Environmental Health Perspectives* 119(3): 126–31.

Wengelin, M. 2006. "The Swedish Port Security Network – An Illusion or r Fact?" *Journal of Homeland Security and Emergency Management* 3(1).

Wente, M. 2009. "Swine Flu Snafus: How Many Bureaucrats Does It Take to Give Your Kid a Shot in the Arm?" *Globe and Mail*, 7 November.

Westfall, P.H., and J.M. Hilbe. 2007. "'The Black Swan': Praise and Criticism." *American Statistician* 61(3): 193–4.

Weston, G. 2011. "Foreign Hackers Attack Canadian government." *CBC News*, 16 February. http://www.cbc.ca/news/politics/foreign-hackers-attack-canadian-government-1.982618

Whelan, E., W. Golden, and B. Donnellan. 2013. "Digitising the R&D Social Network: Revisiting the Technological Gatekeeper." *Information Systems Journal* 23(3): 197–218.

White, C., L. Plotnick, J. Kushma, S. Hiltz, and M. Turoff. 2009. "An Online Social Network For Emergency Management." *International Journal of Emergency Management* 6(3).

White, P., and D. Bascaramurty. 2009. "Four More Die Of Swine Flu: Deaths in Manitoba and Quebec Push National Toll to 11." *Globe and Mail*, 17 June.

Whittington, L., L. Casey, J. McDiarmid, and B. Campion-Smith. 2013. "Lac Megantic Explosion: Ottawa Approved Having Only One Engineer on Ill-Fated Train." *Toronto Star*, 9 July. https://www.thestar.com/news/canada/2013/07/09/ottawa_okayed_having_only_one_engineer_on_illfated_train.html

Willis, H., G. Lester, and G. Treverton. 2009. "Information Sharing for Infrastructure Risk Management: Barriers and Solutions." *Intelligence and National Security* 24(3): 339–65.

Wilson, J.Q. 1980. *The Politics of Regulation*. New York: Basic Books.

Winfield, M. 2014. "Opinion: One Year After Lac-Mégantic, Changes to Railway Safety Appear Mostly Cosmetic." *Montreal Gazette*, 19 August.

Winseck, D. 2008. "The State of Media Ownership and Media Markets: Competition or Concentration and Why Should We Care?" *Sociology Compass* 2(1): 34–47.

Wise, D. 1994. *Process Engineering for Pollution Control and Waste Minimization*. Boca Raton, FL: CRC Press.

Wood, J. 2013. "Little Support for Flood Policies in Poll." *Edmonton Journal*, 17 October. http://www.pressreader.com/canada/edmonton-journal/20130924/281496453982389/TextView

Woods, A. 2013. "Lac Megantic: MMA Railway Gets Permission to Operate until Oct. 1." *Toronto Star*, 16 August. https://www.thestar.com/news/canada/2013/08/16/mma_railway_will_likely_challenge_order_to_cease_operations.html

Wordsworth, A., J. Jackson, J. Ginsburg, and R. Lindgren. 2006. *Creating Community Right-To-Know Opportunities in the City Of Toronto*. Canadian Environmental Law Association. http://s.cela.ca/files/uploads/538_rttknow.pdf_

World Health Organization. 2000. *Canada: Rapport analytique. Evaluation des services d'eau potable et assainissement 2000 dans les Amériques*. Geneva: World Health Organization. http://www.bvsde.ops-oms.org/frwww/eva2000/Canada/informe/inf-01.htm

World Health Organization. 2015. *WHO Report on the Global Tobacco Epidemic, 2015*. Geneva: World Health Organization. http://www.who.int/tobacco/global_report/2015/report/en/

World Meteorological Organization. 2007. *Summary For Policy Makers. Climate Change 2007: Impacts, Adaption and Vulnerability*. Brussels: United Nations Environmental Programme. http://www.meteotrentino.it/clima/pdf/rapporti_meteo/IPCC_Impacts_Adaptation_and_Vulnerability.pdf

Wriggins, J. 2014. "Flood Money: The Challenge of U.S. Flood Insurance Reform in a Warming World." *Penn State Law Review* 119(2): 361–437.

Wyden, R., T. Harkin, and S. Whitehouse. 2014. *Health Prevention: Cost-effective Services in Recent Peer-Reviewed Health Care Literature*. GAO-14-789R. Washington, DC: US Government Accountability Office. http://www.gao.gov/products/GAO-14-789R

Yates, D., and S. Paquette. 2011. "Emergency Knowledge Management and Social Media Technologies: A Case Study of the 2010 Haitian Earthquake." *International Journal of Information Management* 31(1): 6–13.

Young, L. 2004. "Regulating Campaign Finance in Canada: Strengths and Weaknesses." *Election Law Journal* 3(3): 444–62.

Young, O.R. 1989. "The Politics of International Regime Formation: Managing Natural Resources and the Environment." *International Organization* 43(03): 349–75.

Young, O.R. 1996. "Institutional Linkages in International Society: Polar Perspectives." *Global Governance* 2: 1.

Zhang, W., T.J. Johnson, T. Seltzer, and S.L. Bichard. 2009. "The Revolution Will Be Networked: The Influence of Social Networking Sites on Political Attitudes and Behavior." *Social Science Computer Review* 28(1): 75–92.

Zinn, J. 2004. "Literature Review: Sociology and Risk." Working paper. Canterbury, UK: Social Contexts and Responses to Risk Network, University of Kent. http://www.kent.ac.uk/scarr/papers/papers.htm

Zukin, C. 2015. "What's the Matter with Polling?" *New York Times*, 20 June. http://www.nytimes.com/2015/06/21/opinion/sunday/whats-the-matter-with-polling.html?_r=0

Index